# JUNIOR CYCLE HISTORY

# ARTEFACT

## A FORWARD-THINKING APPROACH TO LOOKING BACK

Gregg O'Neill
Eimear Jenkinson

educate.ie

PUBLISHED BY:
**Educate.ie**
Walsh Educational Books Ltd
Castleisland, Co. Kerry, Ireland
**www.educate.ie**

*EDITOR:* Anna Kealy

*DESIGN:* Kieran O'Donoghue

*LAYOUT:* Jen Patton, Liz White Designs

© Gregg O'Neill and Eimear Jenkinson, 2018

**ISBN: 978-1- 912239-38-2**

For permission to reproduce artwork, the author and publisher acknowledge the following copyright holders:

Advertising Archives • AKG Images • Alamy Ltd • An Post • Australian War Memorial Research Centre • Barrow Coakley Aerial Photography (barrowcoakley.ie) • Boyne Valley Tours (newgrange. com) • Bridgeman Images • ceidefields.com • Claire Rourke • Crown Copyright HES • Communautés européennes 2000 • Dublin City Library and Archive • GAA Museum • Getty Images • *Good Housekeeping* magazine • Hachette Book Group Ireland • Irish Archaeological Consultancy • Irish Election Literature • Irish Photo Archive / Lensmen Photographic Archive • McCord Museum (M965.199.9804) • National Library of Ireland • National Museum of Ireland • National Museum of Northern Ireland • National Museum of Wales / Amgueddfa Genedlaethol Cymru • Noel Meehan Copter View Ireland • Louise Nugent (http://pilgrimagemedievalireland.com) • Pacemaker Press • Victor Patterson • *Punch* magazine • Royal Irish Academy • Royal Society of Antiquaries of Ireland • RTÉ Archives • Shutterstock Inc. • Solo Syndication • Ed Stein • *The Irish Times* • Top Foto / Topham Partners LLP • United States Holocaust Memorial Museum, courtesy of National Archives and Records Administration, College Park • The Viking Ship Museum, Roskilde, Denmark / Werner Karrasch • Wikicommons (National Archive (UK), SnapperQ)

The author and publisher have made every effort to trace all copyright owners, but if any material has inadvertently been reproduced without permission, they would be happy to make the necessary arrangement at the earliest opportunity, and encourage owners of copyright material not acknowledged to make contact.

## Acknowledgements

I would like to thank Sinéad Keogh and everyone at Educate.ie for having the confidence in me to ask me to work on this book. Thank you to my fantastic co-author Eimear Jenkinson. You have been an absolute pleasure to work with. Many thanks to our editor Anna, who has been a rock of support through this whole process and whose advice and enthusiasm have made this a better book. Thank you to the design team who have created such an appealing and accessible book for teachers and students alike. To the whole community of staff and students in CBC Monkstown: this book has benefited from all the things I have learned from you over the years. And finally, thanks to all my family and friends, especially my mother Adrienne, whose advice, support and encouragement have got me through this project.

Gregg O'Neill

I would like to sincerely thank our publisher, Sinéad, and everyone at Educate.ie for giving me the chance to be involved with this book. Thank you to Gregg for all of your help and support along the way. I have really enjoyed working with you and look forward to continuing to do so in the future. Thank you to our editor, Anna, for your keen eye, enthusiasm, advice and judgement along the way. Thank you to Claire for all of your help with the images and visuals that have made *Artefact* so appealing. Thank you to all of my colleagues and friends in Ardgillan CC and also the Dublin branch of the HTAI for their support. Thank you to all of my friends, near and far, for their messages of encouragement and constant interest in the development of this book. Finally, thank you to my family, in particular my mam, dad, Niamh, Eoin and Damien for their encouragement, love and support always.

Eimear Jenkinson

# Welcome to *Artefact*

Welcome to *Artefact* – Common Level History for Junior Cycle.

Throughout this book you will learn about, and develop your own opinions on, the events of the past. From your study of notable people, exciting inventions, devastating wars, fascinating voyages of discovery and many testing and thrilling events in between, you will discover how what happened in times gone by has impacted on our lives today and shaped our world.

This book, together with its accompanying *Sources and Skills Book* and *Research Portfolio*, is designed to help you do your very best in your Junior Cycle History course and assessments. By the time you complete third year, you will know all about the skills of historians and archaeologists and will have many of these skills yourself.

You will learn how to understand time and timelines and make some timelines of your own. You will work with evidence to find out about the past and decide whether what you have discovered is reliable fact or biased opinion. You will do research, debate and discuss ideas with classmates and become a confident, critical thinker, coming to your own conclusions about many issues and events. You will gain understanding of causes and consequences – why things happened and what the results were. You will learn about Irish, European and world history from ancient times right up to recent events. Through your study, you may see the world, Ireland and even your own local area in a new light as you discover how they are linked to the past!

We hope that the topics, tasks and ideas in *Artefact* allow you to enjoy looking back on the past, help you to understand the present and, looking forward, equip and inspire you to study history on into the future.

*Gregg O'Neill and Eimear Jenkinson*

*May 2018*

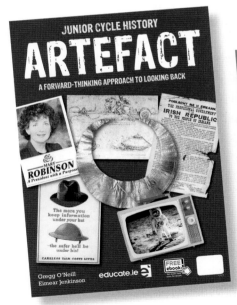

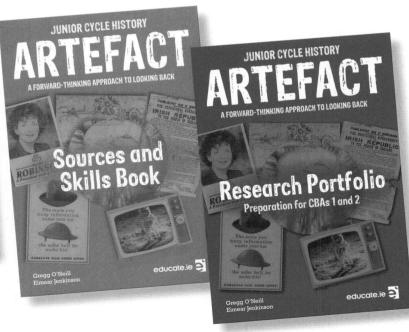

# Key Features

- *Artefact* follows a chronological approach, with topics presented in sequence spanning Irish, European and world history and meeting all of the learning outcomes of the Junior Cycle History specification.

- **Introductory chapters** on The Historian and The Archaeologist introduce the key skills and concepts involved in studying the past. These are reinforced throughout chapters with **evidence tasks** for every topic and regular questions and discussions on concepts such as commemoration, reinterpretation, cause and consequence, identity and more.

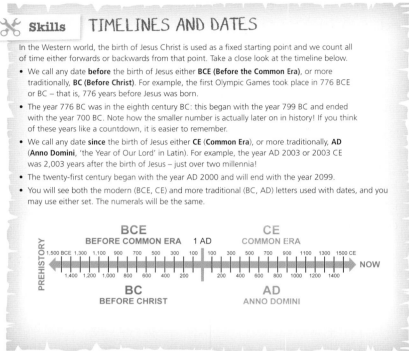

### ✂ Skills   TIMELINES AND DATES

In the Western world, the birth of Jesus Christ is used as a fixed starting point and we count all of time either forwards or backwards from that point. Take a close look at the timeline below.

- We call any date **before** the birth of Jesus either **BCE (Before the Common Era)**, or more traditionally, **BC (Before Christ)**. For example, the first Olympic Games took place in 776 BCE or BC – that is, 776 years before Jesus was born.
- The year 776 BC was in the eighth century BC: this began with the year 799 BC and ended with the year 700 BC. Note how the smaller number is actually later on in history! If you think of these years like a countdown, it is easier to remember.
- We call any date **since** the birth of Jesus either **CE (Common Era)**, or more traditionally, **AD (Anno Domini**, 'the Year of Our Lord' in Latin). For example, the year AD 2003 or 2003 CE was 2,003 years after the birth of Jesus – just over two millennia!
- The twenty-first century began with the year AD 2000 and will end with the year 2099.
- You will see both the modern (BCE, CE) and more traditional (BC, AD) letters used with dates, and you may use either set. The numerals will be the same.

- At the start of each chapter you will see a **timeline** to help you understand when events occurred. It shows three points – what came just before, the current event and what happens next.

**Early Christian Ireland** c. 400–800   **The Middle Ages in Ireland** c. 800–1500   **The Plantations** c. 1500–1700

- **Illustrated characters** at the start of each chapter give a sense of fashion and appearance in the time period.

- **Working with the Evidence** tasks feature in every chapter and offer a wide variety of key documents, photographs, speeches, maps, paintings and other artefacts to interrogate and explore each new topic.

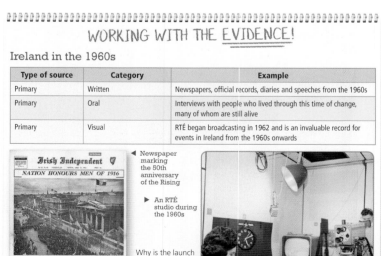

## WORKING WITH THE EVIDENCE!

### Ireland in the 1960s

| Type of source | Category | Example |
|---|---|---|
| Primary | Written | Newspapers, official records, diaries and speeches from the 1960s |
| Primary | Oral | Interviews with people who lived through this time of change, many of whom are still alive |
| Primary | Visual | RTÉ began broadcasting in 1962 and is an invaluable record for events in Ireland from the 1960s onwards |

◄ Newspaper marking the 50th anniversary of the Rising

► An RTÉ studio during the 1960s

Why is the launch of RTÉ such an important event for historians? How did television change how we view the past?

- Chapters are broken down into into sub-topics to make it easier to work through detailed issues and events. Each sub-topic opens with a small number of **learning intentions** and contains **Checkpoint** questions to assess knowledge before moving on.

- **Literacy** and **skills** are integrated throughout, denoted by icons for ease of use.

- **Life in Time** features showcase key historical figures with biographical information and details on their contribution to history.

In this topic, you will learn about:

❯ The Laois-Offaly Plantation and its results
❯ The Munster Plantation and its results

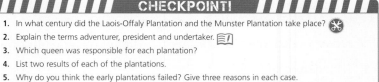

## CHECKPOINT!

1. In what century did the Laois-Offaly Plantation and the Munster Plantation take place?
2. Explain the terms adventurer, president and undertaker.
3. Which queen was responsible for each plantation?
4. List two results of each of the plantations.
5. Why do you think the early plantations failed? Give three reasons in each case.

✔ I know the main events and results of the Laois-Offaly and Munster Plantations.

← TIME TO GO BACK ◀ I CAN MOVE FORWARD →

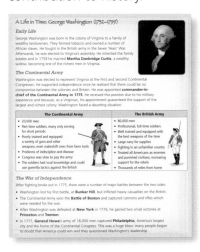

- **Collaborate tasks** throughout allow students to work together to research and discuss topics and ideas.

 COLLABORATE:
With your group, research the design and construction of an important Renaissance building. For example, you could look at St Peter's Basilica in Rome or the Duomo in Florence. Present a visual report to your class.

- **Did You Know?** features throughout each chapter offer additional interesting and fun facts to complement the topic.

**DID YOU KNOW?**

Christendom was also home to many non-Christians. Most towns across medieval Europe had small Jewish communities, while for centuries the Muslim territory of Al-Andalus (now Andalusia in southern Spain) was a beacon of culture and learning.

▲ The Alhambra, Andalusia

- Regular **weblinks** offer opportunites to explore topics further and investigate historical repositories!

https://educateplus.ie/go/book-kells 🔗

- Chapters end with: a useful **summary**; comprehension-style **Understanding History** and overarching **Exploring History questions** that are useful for summative assessment; and a bank of **key terms with definitions** for ease of revision.

- The *Sources and Skills Book* contains revision exercises and additional evidence questions for every chapter and the *Research Portfolio* contains a Life in Time or Past in My Place task for every chapter.

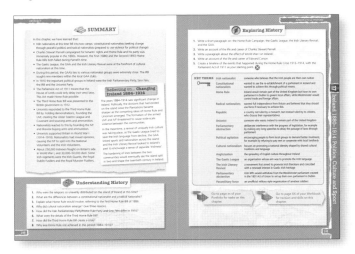

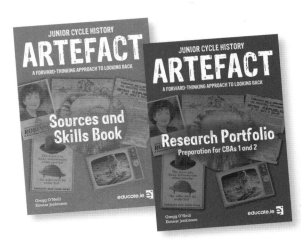

**Welcome to Artefact**

# Information for Teachers

## The Three Strands

The Junior Cycle History specification is common level and contains three strands:

1. The nature of history
2. The history of Ireland
3. The history of Europe and the wider world

The nature of history is an overarching strand concerning the skills and attitudes students will develop in their study of history. *Artefact* introduces these concepts with chapters on The Historian and The Archaeologist and reinforces them throughout with tasks, questions and discussions. Through these tasks, students will develop their historical consciousness, work with evidence and acquire the big picture.

The history of Ireland and the history of Europe and the wider world are contextual strands through which students can continue to develop their historical skills as they explore and gain knowledge of key events of the past. They will recognise key changes; explore people, culture and ideas; and apply historical thinking to the topics they encounter.

On the contents page, you will see the chapters of *Artefact* coloured according to the strand that they relate to.

**Key**

1 The nature of history

2 The history of Ireland

3 The history of Europe and the wider world

You will also see the number of the relevant learning outcome(s) that it relates to listed beside each chapter. This is to assist you in navigating the new course and choosing the sequence of topics you will cover. It is recommended that you tackle the course chronologically, in the order topics are presented, so that students can consider events in the context of what was happening in the rest of the world and so that they can tackle simpler topics in first year before moving on to more difficult material later on.

## A Comprehensive Approach

Throughout *Artefact*, you will see that popular and familiar topics have been used to fulfil learning outcomes. Where useful, a narrative has been knitted together for students that will help them overcome any gaps in understanding as they move through topics and time periods. *Sources and Skills Book* and *Research Portfolio* tasks move beyond the basics of Q&A and matching to offer interesting, innovative assessments such as 'Choose Your Own Gladiator'. We hope that this comprehensive approach will foster in your students a love of history that will encourage them to continue their study into Leaving Certificate and equip them with the skills and knowledge to do so.

## A Note on Choice

The Junior Cycle History specification allows a degree of flexibility for teachers in how they choose to meet the learning outcomes in each strand. Some outcomes are quite specific in their intention, but others can be tackled in a number of different ways. To cater to this flexibility, we have offered as much choice as possible in the space available for you to choose your route through the course. Therefore, some learning outcomes will show up beside a few different topics, in particular:

- **LO 2.1** requires students to study 'one example of settlement, such as the growth of towns, and one plantation'. You could achieve the study of settlement through studying either Chapter 3 Ancient Ireland or Chapter 7 Medieval Ireland *and* Chapter 11 The Plantations.

- **LO 3.3** requires students to study one revolution in Europe or the wider world. You could choose between Chapter 12 The American Revolution or Chapter 13 The French Revolution to achieve this outcome.

It is perfectly acceptable to tackle a learning outcome more than once as you travel through the course, and indeed for many of them you will. But, where choice is provided and you would like to narrow down the material to be covered, here are some questions you might ask yourself:

1. Does it suit the ability of the class and will it interest them?
2. Does it fit chronologically with other topics I am teaching/draw good links with the rest of the course?
3. Is there a local history link or a CBA possibility within this topic for your class?
4. Is it historically important?
5. Would it provide a useful base of knowledge for further study at Leaving Certificate?
6. Do I have the knowledge and resources to teach this topic?

These questions should help you to pick and choose topics you might like to teach within *Artefact*. The *Artefact* Teacher's Resource Book also offers plenty of guidance and planning material for each strand and outcome of the course to support you.

## Assessment

The new Junior Cycle History course will be assessed via:

- Two Classroom-Based Assessments:
  - **CBA 1** The Past in My Place, in Second Year
  - **CBA 2** A Life in Time, in Third Year
- An Assessment Task based on the second CBA and marked by the SEC
- A final, common level written exam at the end of Third Year

While the assessment guidelines for the two CBAs are not yet available, each chapter of *Artefact* contains a Research Portfolio task to give your students plenty of practice on the skills they will need to complete their CBAs. For every chapter, they are provided with a list of potential people or a place/event to investigate, sample research questions and space to write up their work, providing invaluable preparation for their assessments.

*Gregg O'Neill and Eimear Jenkinson*
*April 2018*

# Contents

Contents

# The Nature of History: The Historian

Before we begin to learn about different events and people in the past, it is important to learn about what history is and why we study history.

Historians and archaeologists are some of the people involved in the study of history. They often work together and both are essential to our understanding of the past.

In this chapter, we will learn about the historian.

# WORKING WITH THE <u>EVIDENCE</u>!

## How do we know about the past?

| Type of source | Category | Example |
|---|---|---|
| Primary | Tactile | The Tara Brooch |
| Secondary | Written | *The Making of Europe* (Educate.ie) |

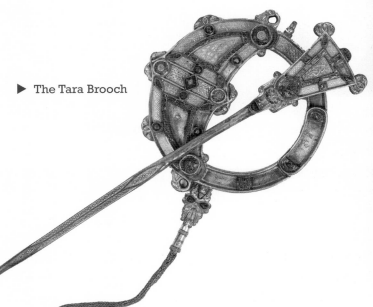

▶ The Tara Brooch

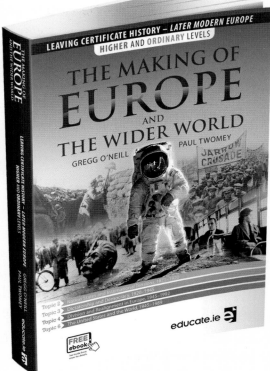

▲ History textbook

How can we use these sources to help us learn about the past?

# 1.1: What is History?

In this topic, you will learn about:
- What history means
- The difference between history and prehistory

## History

**History** is <u>the study of the past</u>. It comes from the Greek word *historia*, which means 'knowledge from investigation'. History is based on evidence and the study of sources. A **source** <u>is something that gives us information or evidence about a person, place or thing in the past</u>.

History concerns itself with the story of human activity. That story continues right up to today – in fact, this morning's news is already part of history! When we study history, we don't just look at the lives of important people, we look at the everyday lives of ordinary people throughout time. We learn about their jobs, their clothing, where they lived and what they did for entertainment. We also learn about major events from the past. When studying history, we investigate not only *what* happened but *why* it happened.

## The difference between history and prehistory

We use the word **prehistory** to speak about <u>the period of time before writing was used</u>. We rely on archaeology for evidence from this period of time. **Archaeology** <u>is the study of the remains left by people in the past</u>. An example of a prehistoric source might be a weapon made by people to hunt for food. You will learn about archaeology in chapter 2.

We use the word **history** when we are speaking about everything that has happened since people began to use writing. We can therefore use written sources and documents as evidence. An example of written evidence might be the *Annals of the Four Masters*, an account of Irish history written by Irish monks.

▼ Written source: a manuscript

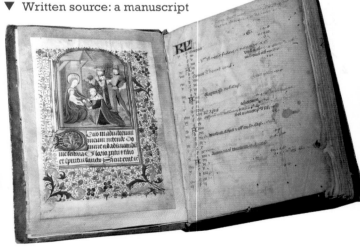

▲ Tactile sources: tools and weapons

## CHECKPOINT!

1. Define the terms history and prehistory in your own words.
2. Where does the word history come from?
3. Define the term source in your own words. 
4. Give two examples of a source.
5. Define the term archaeology in your own words. 

 I can explain what history is and the difference between history and prehistory.

 TIME TO GO BACK  I CAN MOVE FORWARD

# 1.2: The Study of History

In this topic, you will learn about:
- ❷ Reasons why we study history
- ❷ Who studies history

## Why we study history

Through history, we learn **how people lived before us**. We gain an understanding of **how past events unfolded** and what their causes and consequences were. Studying history helps us to understand **how human experience has shaped our society and the world** of today. We can learn **to recognise patterns of change**. All of this has an impact on us in the present day.

Examining history helps us see **how to avoid the mistakes** that our ancestors made. We also want to know **how to flourish** – how many civilisations prospered and became powerful. We can **be inspired** by people in the past. We can **develop an appreciation of the cultural achievements** of previous generations. It develops our **historical consciousness**, which means being able to place ourselves in past human experience, linking the past, the present and the future.

▲ Poster to recruit Irish soldiers for World War I

▲ The French Revolution represented in *Liberty on the Barricades* by Delacroix

▼ Early sixteenth-century Aztec carving

## Who studies history?

Anybody can study history. As a student taking History, **you** are a historian!

A **historian** is someone who is an expert in, or a student of, history. Historians gather evidence from a variety of sources to piece together information about the past. They are interested in the reasons why things happened and also in what the results were. An **archaeologist** investigates places and objects left by people in the past, including the time before written records were kept. Much of what we know about early history comes from archaeology.

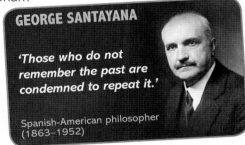

**GEORGE SANTAYANA**

'Those who do not remember the past are condemned to repeat it.'

Spanish-American philosopher (1863–1952)

---

## CHECKPOINT!

1. Define the term historian in your own words.
2. Name three groups of people who study history.
3. List three reasons why we study history.
4. Define the term historical consciousness in your own words.

✔ I understand why it is important to study history.

◀ TIME TO GO BACK ▶ I CAN MOVE FORWARD ➤

**1 The Nature of History: The Historian**

# 1.3: The Job of the Historian

In this topic, you will learn about:
- How historians find evidence
- The difference between primary and secondary sources

## Finding evidence

The job of the historian involves gathering as much evidence as possible from different sources. This is so that they can cross-check their work. **Cross-checking** is when more than one source is used to make sure the information is correct.

A historian may go to libraries, archives and museums for many of these sources. An **archive** is a place that catalogues and stores a collection of written and other sources. A good example is the National Archives of Ireland in Dublin. Here, the records of the Irish State are held. A **museum** is a place that collects and displays objects for public education and appreciation. The **National Museum in Dublin** is a good example. Among the things you can see there are beautiful Bronze Age Irish metalwork, Viking artefacts and treasures from ancient Egypt.

The internet can also be used to gather evidence. Many sources are available online in digital form. If used correctly, the internet can be an excellent information source (see more on page 11).

▲ An archivist at work

COLLABORATE: Have you ever heard the term 'vox pop'? This is when a journalist asks questions of people out in public and notes their answers and opinions. It comes from the Latin term *vox populi,* or 'voice of the people'. Work in small groups to complete a vox pop on the job of the historian. Talk to at least four people and find out why they believe studying history is important.

Visit **www.educateplus. ie/resources/artefact** for a video and a worksheet on the role of the historian

▶ National Museum of Ireland – Archaeology

# Sources used by historians

Historians use many types of source for information or evidence. Sources can be split into two categories: primary and secondary. A **primary source** is a source from the time of the event; a first-hand account of what happened. A **secondary source** is a source from a later date, after the time of the event.

| Examples of Primary Sources | |
|---|---|
| Artefacts | Photographs |
| Diaries | Cartoons and drawings |
| Letters | Government records, e.g. a census |
| Emails | Newspapers |
| Interviews | Magazines |
| Speeches | Autobiographies |
| Posters | Maps |

| Examples of Secondary Sources |
|---|
| TV/film and radio documentaries |
| Podcasts |
| Websites |
| History books and textbooks |
| Biographies |
| Handling boxes |
| Movies |

Some of these words might be new to you. An **artefact** is any human-made object, e.g. pottery, a tool or a weapon, such as a spear. An **autobiography** is an account of a person's life written by the person themselves. A **biography** is an account of a person's life written by someone else. A **census** is an official survey of a population. In Ireland, a census is held every five years. A **handling box** contains replicas (copies) of artefacts, so that anyone can examine them without damaging an original.

**DID YOU KNOW?**

The most recent census in Ireland was held in 2016 and the results can be found online.

https://educateplus.ie/go/cso

▲ Primary source: Bronze Age funerary urn

▼ Secondary source: a handling box

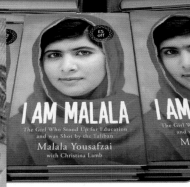

▲ Primary source: an autobiography

## CHECKPOINT!

1. List four places a historian can find evidence.
2. Define the terms cross-checking and artefact in your own words.
3. List three examples of primary sources and three examples of secondary sources.
4. We must be cautious about accepting secondary sources as fact. Discuss the list of secondary sources above with your group and decide which source you think is the least reliable.

 I know the variety of sources that a historian might use.

 TIME TO GO BACK ◀ ▶ I CAN MOVE FORWARD ➡

**1 The Nature of History: The Historian**

# 1.4: Working with Sources

## Reliability of sources

Historians must be careful of a number of things when using sources. They must find out how reliable a source is. Historians have to examine the point of view of the person behind the source. To do this, they need to be aware of the issues of accuracy, bias, exaggeration and propaganda.

In this topic, you will learn about:

❯ Judging how reliable sources are and the usefulness and limitations of sources

❯ Different types and categories of sources

- **Accuracy** involves judging how accurate/correct the information you are using is.
- **Bias** is when an account is not balanced, but unfairly favours one side. Sometimes a person may be unaware that their interpretation is not a fair one; sometimes it is deliberate, to influence others. Think of how newspapers sometimes report the same event very differently. Historians must watch out for bias in their sources – and in themselves!
- **Exaggeration** is when something is represented as better or worse than it actually was.
- **Propaganda** is information that has been designed to influence the attitudes of the general public. It is generally biased, often appeals to the emotions (fear, anger, loyalty) and may even be made up! Propaganda is common during wartime, for example to convince the public that war is justified.

## Types of source

Sources can also be categorised into different types, such as written, visual, aural, oral and tactile. A **tactile source** is one that can be touched – a physical object, like an artefact. All sources are useful, but they may each also have limitations or problems. Generally, primary sources tell us more clearly what life was like at the time, whereas secondary sources give us background information that helps us to understand primary sources.

| Source Type | | How are these sources useful? | How can they be limiting or have problems? |
|---|---|---|---|
| **Written Sources** e.g. diaries, letters, emails, autobiographies, biographies and government records | **Primary** | • We can see which language someone used then, and how. <br> • They can tell us what people at the time were thinking. <br> • They may tell the story of a life or provide rich detail. <br> • They can provide us with information about local or world events at the time. <br> • Official records can provide information about the state and its population at the time. | • They may contain bias. <br> • They may be exaggerated. <br> • They may provide only some of the facts from the time. <br> • They may be written in a different language, e.g. Latin. |
| | **Secondary** | • They can give us information gathered about the time. <br> • They can be well-rounded, if they have been properly researched. | • They may contain bias. <br> • They may be exaggerated. |

| Source Type | | How are these sources useful? | How can they be limiting or have problems? |
|---|---|---|---|
| **Visual Sources** e.g. photographs, posters, art, cartoon drawings, maps, documentary films | Primary | • Photographs capture a moment in time. <br>• They can give us faces for the names we learn about in history. | • Images could have been edited or changed for reasons of propaganda. <br>• They may even have been created for the sole purpose of propaganda. |
| | Secondary | • They can be well-rounded and useful, if they have been properly researched and stick to the facts. | • The director or artist may be biased. |
| **Aural Sources** e.g. recorded interviews, podcasts and speeches | Primary | • Recordings can tell us what someone then was thinking. <br>• Speeches and interviews can tell us a lot about the issues of the time. <br>• How someone truly feels about something is clearer when you listen to them speak about it. | • They may contain bias. <br>• They may be exaggerated. <br>• If they are being interviewed a long time after the event, the person may have forgotten details. |
| | Secondary | • They can be well-rounded and useful, if they have been properly researched and stick to the facts. | • The interviewer or sound editor may be biased. |
| **Oral Sources** e.g. interviews carried out by the researcher | Primary | • In an interview we can learn what someone thinks or once experienced. <br>• We might hear stories or details from a person's life. <br>• Someone's attitude is clearer, from their voice or expression, when you are speaking with them in person. | • They may contain bias. <br>• They may be exaggerated. <br>• If they are being interviewed a long time after the event, the person may have forgotten details. <br>• The person might not be prepared to speak openly with you. |
| | Secondary | • A story from someone else could be passed down through generations | • Details may be left out, as it is not information from the original person. <br>• They may contain bias. <br>• They may be exaggerated. |
| **Tactile Sources** e.g. artefacts and handling boxes | Primary | • Objects can give us information about how life was lived then. <br>• We can see how objects have changed over time. <br>• They can show us what materials people used then. | • They may be damaged when found, or missing pieces, and so they may not give a complete picture. |
| | Secondary | • They can provide us with examples of recreated items that may be too far away in museums for us to study. | • They may not be made with the same materials as the original items. |

## CHECKPOINT!

1. Define the terms primary source and secondary source in your own words. 📖✎

2. Explain bias and propaganda in your own words. 📖✎

3. List three examples of written sources.

4. List three examples of tactile sources.

5. Name three things historians need to consider when studying sources.

✓ I understand how different sources can be useful, but I know that they can also have limitations or problems.

TIME TO GO BACK   I CAN MOVE FORWARD

1 The Nature of History: The Historian

Go to page 6 of your *Sources and Skills Book* for an evidence task.

COLLABORATE: Work together in small groups to see if you can think of other ways that any of the sources on pages 6–7 can be useful. How might they be limiting or problematic?

# WORKING WITH THE EVIDENCE!

## Propaganda posters

Study these two propaganda posters. For each, ask yourself: what period of history is it from? Why was it made and who made it?

(Source A)

▲ British World War II propaganda poster

(Source B)

▲ German World War II propaganda poster: 'Hard times; hard duties; hard hearts'

1. What type of source are A and B?

2. What does Source A encourage people to do? Why do you think Britain wanted people to do this?

3. What does Source B encourage people to do? Why do you think Germany made this poster?

4. What problems could a historian encounter when using propaganda posters as a source?

5. What are the benefits to historians of using propaganda posters as a source?

6. Name other ways propaganda could be used, other than in posters.

# 1.5: Time and Timelines

The timing of events is important to the historian. When historians find out information about the past, they must put events into the sequence in which they happened. This is called **chronology** and makes it easier for people to follow the story of what happened.

To help with this, historians:

- divide time into hours, days, weeks, months and years.
- group years into **decades** (10 years), **centuries** (100 years) and **millennia** (1,000 years).
- organise events using a common feature from a period of history. For example, the era when tools were made of stone is called 'the Stone Age' and it was followed by the Bronze and Iron Ages.
- use timelines to show the order in which events happened. Your book has timelines for you to practice putting events into sequence.

**DID YOU KNOW?**

Some cultures use different calendar systems. For example, 2018 is the Islamic year 1439 (it uses a different starting point) and the Chinese Year of the Earth Dog (it counts in cycles rather than in a straight line).

 **Skills** ## TIMELINES AND DATES

**DID YOU KNOW?**

Some historians now believe that Jesus the man was born roughly four years earlier than previously thought, making his date of birth 4 BC – before himself! While this is an example of reinterpretation, it does not affect how we use dates.

In the Western world, the birth of Jesus Christ is used as a fixed starting point and we count all of time either forwards or backwards from that point. Take a close look at the timeline below.

- We call any date **before** the birth of Jesus either **BCE (Before the Common Era)**, or more traditionally, **BC (Before Christ)**. For example, the first Olympic Games took place in 776 BCE or BC – that is, 776 years before Jesus was born.
- The year 776 BC was in the eighth century BC: this began with the year 799 BC and ended with the year 700 BC. Note how the smaller number is actually later on in history! If you think of these years like a countdown, it is easier to remember.
- We call any date **since** the birth of Jesus either **CE (Common Era)**, or more traditionally, **AD (Anno Domini**, 'the Year of Our Lord' in Latin). For example, the year AD 2003 or 2003 CE was 2,003 years after the birth of Jesus – just over two millennia!
- The twenty-first century began with the year AD 2000 and will end with the year 2099.
- You will see both the modern (BCE, CE) and more traditional (BC, AD) letters used with dates, and you may use either set. The numerals will be the same.

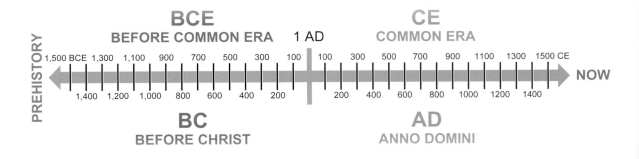

# 1.6: Reinterpreting History

Over time a new piece of evidence may emerge. This new piece of evidence may lead to an event or time in history being reinterpreted. **Reinterpretation** means to see something in a new or different light. New evidence sometimes creates doubt about what we believe happened during some events, and therefore it needs to be studied carefully.

One example of this is **the sinking of the Titanic** in 1912 following its collision with an iceberg. New evidence has recently come to light on what caused the supposedly unsinkable ship to sink. It states that the hull of the ship was weakened due to a major fire there, making it easier for the iceberg to breach the hull. Historians and scientists are studying the evidence to establish whether this theory is correct.

COLLABORATE: You have learned about the possibility of history having to be reinterpreted when new evidence is discovered. Work in small groups to find an example of something else that had to be re-examined and reinterpreted due to new evidence being found.

▶ Front page of *The New York Times* newspaper the day after the sinking of the *Titanic*

https://educateplus.ie/go/titanic-video

# CHECKPOINT!

1. Define the term chronology in your own words. 📖
2. List three ways historians put events in order.
3. What centuries do these years belong to: (a) AD 1066; (b) 514 BC? ✂
4. Which is earlier: 30 BC or 41 BC? ✂
5. Define the term reinterpretation in your own words. 📖

✓ I understand how events are put into chronological order and that some events may need to be reinterpreted later.

◀ TIME TO GO BACK   ❯ I CAN MOVE FORWARD ➡

**Skills** HOW TO RESEARCH ONLINE

**In this topic, you will learn about:**
❯ Steps to help you research online
❯ Citing
❯ Plagiarism

Researching involves finding information to help you write about a person, event or topic. As you know, you can gather research from many different sources. These sources can be primary or secondary. We will look at researching information online because this is a method most of you are likely to use. You can do this in your school's computer room or at home.

The following steps will help you to research information online by yourself:

- **Organise your search**: Decide on the question(s) you want to answer and write them down. This will help you to identify the general key words that are relevant to your topic. Search them on Google. If the results aren't what you want, change the keywords to make your search more specific.

- **Search further**: Look beyond the first few results on Google. Flick through a few pages if you need to, to find a relevant source.

- **Is it a reliable source?** Look at the actual URL address to see where you're going before you click on a search engine result. Use your instinct to decide whether it seems reliable. Is it from a well-known site? Is it from an educational or government institution? These would be more reliable. Is it a forum or opinion site? These would be less reliable.

- **Is it accurate?** You cannot believe everything you read. Make your own judgement by checking more than one source if you're not sure whether it is true.

- **What is the purpose of the website?** Be wary of websites that are cluttered with advertisements or are trying to sell you something. Their purpose is not to give you accurate information, it is to make money.

- **What is the background of the source?** When reading articles, look for the author's name and when the article was written. Is it recent or outdated? Is there an author's name? If there is not, then it is probably not a good source.

- **Write notes:** Write down notes from the information you have read into your class copy. Make sure to stick to one source at a time and write a heading with the source's name in it. That way you will know later that your information came from that source specifically.

- **How do I cite?** To **cite** means <u>to refer to evidence you have gathered or read</u>. Use quotation marks and cite sources when you are writing up your information. If you are taking information word for word from an online source, you must always give the URL and the date you accessed the website. If there is an author's name and a date the page was created, include those too.

- **Avoid plagiarism: Plagiarism** means <u>passing someone else's work or ideas off</u> <u>as your own, without citing the real source</u>. Plagiarism is not acceptable. You cannot just copy and paste information and say it is your own; you must give the original author credit for their work.

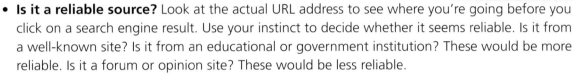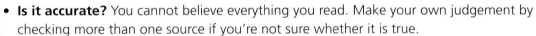

 You learned how to cite from a website just above. Citing from a book is not that different! You must identify: the author, book title, year, publisher and page number. Pick a favourite line to quote from a book you like, write a citation for it and ask your teacher to check that you got it right.

 **SUMMARY**

In this chapter, we have learned that:

- History is the study of the past.
- Sources give us evidence about the past.
- Sources can be primary or secondary, and can be further categorised into written, visual, oral, aural and tactile sources.
- The time before writing was in use is called prehistory. We depend on archaeology for evidence about the prehistoric era.
- Historians use museums, libraries and archives to find evidence. They cross-check their sources.
- Historians must judge how reliable or accurate a source is by being aware of the possibility of bias, exaggeration and propaganda.
- History must sometimes be reinterpreted when new evidence is discovered.
- Historians put events into chronological order using hours, days, weeks, months and years. Years are often counted in decades (ten years), centuries (100 years) or millennia (1,000 years).
- Historians make timelines and use BCE/BC and CE/AD when specifying years.
- When researching online: organise your search; delve further; ask 'is it a reliable source?'; ask 'is it accurate?'; ask 'what is the purpose of the website?'; look for the background of the source; take notes; cite carefully; and avoid plagiarism.

### Reflecting on... **the Work of the Historian**

The historian's work shows us the importance of enquiry, research and discovery in gathering information about the past. We recognise the important role of reliable evidence in enabling us to understand the past.

## Understanding History

1. History is the study of the _____. History is based on _____ and the study of _____. A source is something that gives us _____ about a person, place or thing in the past. We use the word _____ when we are speaking about the period of time before writing was used. We rely on _____ for evidence from this period of time. Archaeology is the study of the remains left by _____ in the past.

2. List the most important reasons why you feel we should study history.

3. What is the difference between a historian and an archaeologist?

4. Which years mark the beginning and end of: (a) the fourteenth century; (b) the third century BC; (c) the twenty-first century? ✂

 ## Exploring History

1. A census is a good way to learn about the past in a country. Use the link

   https://educateplus.ie/go/census1911 🔗

   to go to the 1911 census records. Find your county and then your local area. Pick any person (or a family) and write down six pieces of information about them from the evidence.

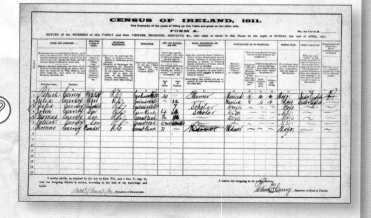

CENSUS OF IRELAND, 1911.

**2.** Why do you think the Italian dictator Benito Mussolini had the horse handler removed from the original photograph? Is the edited photograph a primary or a secondary source? Why?

| **KEY TERMS** | | |
|---|---|---|
| | **History** | the study of the past |
| | **Source** | anything that gives us information or evidence about a person, place or thing in the past |
| | **Prehistory** | the period of time before writing was in use |
| | **Archaeology** | the study of the remains left by people in the past |
| | **Historical consciousness** | being able to place ourselves in past human experience, linking the past, the present and the future |
| | **Historian** | someone who is an expert in, or a student of, history |
| | **Archaeologist** | someone who investigates places and objects left by people in the past, including the time before records were written |
| | **Cross-checking** | when more than one source is used to make sure the information is correct |
| | **Archive** | a place that catalogues and stores a collection of sources |
| | **Museum** | a place that collects and displays objects for public education and appreciation |
| | **Primary source** | a source from the time of the event; a first-hand account of what happened |
| | **Secondary source** | a source from a later date; from after the time of the event |
| | **Artefact** | any human-made object, e.g. pottery, a tool or a weapon such as a spear |
| | **Autobiography** | an account of a person's life written by the person themselves |
| | **Biography** | an account of a person's life written by someone else |
| | **Census** | an official survey of a population |
| | **Handling box** | contains replicas (copies) of artefacts, so that anyone can examine them without damaging an original |
| | **Accuracy** | judging how accurate/correct the information you are using is |
| | **Bias** | when an account is not balanced, but unfairly favours one side. Sometimes it is unconscious; sometimes it is deliberate, to influence others |
| | **Exaggeration** | when something is represented as better or worse than it actually was |
| | **Propaganda** | information that has been designed to influence the attitudes of the general public. It is generally biased, often appeals to the emotions (fear, anger, loyalty) and may even be made up |
| | **Tactile source** | a source that can be touched; a physical item or object such as an artefact |
| | **Chronology** | putting events into the sequence in which they happened |
| | **Reinterpretation** | to see something in a new or different light |
| | **Cite** | to refer to evidence you have gathered or read |
| | **Plagiarism** | passing off someone else's work or ideas as your own, without citing their real source |

 Go to page 1 of your *Sources and Skills Book* for more exercises.

 Go to page 1 of your *Research Portfolio* for a task based on this chapter.

**1 The Nature of History: The Historian**

Archaeology is essential to our understanding of history. As we know, history uses many types of source to learn about the past, including written, visual, aural and oral. However, only part of history can be told using these sources. We also need evidence for the early history of people – our prehistory, or the time before writing – and this comes from material and tactile things such as artefacts and bodies.

In this chapter, we will learn about the important job of the archaeologist.

# WORKING WITH THE EVIDENCE!

## How do we know about the past?

| Type of source | Category | Example |
|---|---|---|
| Primary | Tactile | A gold lunula artefact from the Bronze Age |
| Primary | Tactile | The Brockagh Axe artefact from the Bronze Age |

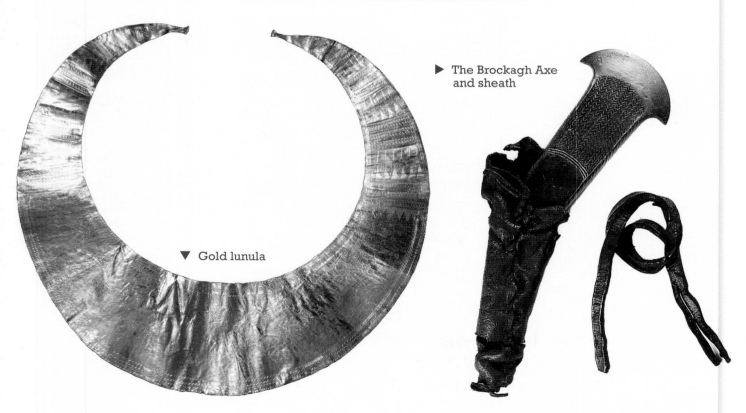

► The Brockagh Axe and sheath

▼ Gold lunula

The period when people made tools and weapons using bronze is known as the **Bronze Age** (2,000–500 BC). What can each of these sources tell us about the people who lived then?

# 2.1: What is Archaeology?

> **In this topic, you will learn about:**
> ❯ What archaeology is
> ❯ How archaeologists find sites
> ❯ How evidence is preserved

▲ The 2012 excavation of the Leicester car park where the body of King Richard III was found. He had died in battle in 1485.

## Archaeology

Archaeology is the study of the remains left by people in the past. When archaeologists dig up the ground to find evidence left by people in the past, this is known as an **excavation**. Like detectives, they study this evidence carefully so that we can learn from it.

Archaeology is our only source of information about **prehistoric times**, so a lot of archaeology focuses on that era. However, archaeologists also investigate remains from more recent times and work alongside historians to build a complete picture of what life was like for people.

▲ Bective Abbey

▲ Aerial photograph of the Hill of Tara

## How archaeologists find sites

There are many ways for an object to end up in the ground. It may have been dropped by someone, been buried or hidden, become covered by soil over time or had something built over it.

Archaeologists excavate sites for many different reasons:

- Sometimes the **ruins of an old building** or structure are still visible above the ground and it is decided that they might be worth a closer look. Bective Abbey in Co. Meath is an example.

- An **aerial photograph** is taken of the ground from an elevated position, for example from a helicopter or drone. Shapes that are not obvious to us at ground level are sometimes revealed to be the lines of ancient structures, like the Hill of Tara in Co. Meath.

- An **old document, map or other records** might reveal that a building or structure once existed on the site, and archaeologists might decide to investigate. This is called **research archaeology**.

- Before you can get planning permission for a road or new building, you must make sure there is no evidence on the site that will be lost forever. This is called **rescue archaeology**. Before the M3 motorway was built in Co. Meath, a total of 126 sites between Clonee and Kells were excavated.

- Sometimes archaeological sites are discovered purely **by accident**. For example, a farmer ploughing a field might find something and report it, leading to a full investigation of the site. That is exactly how the Ardagh Chalice (see page 41) was found!

▲ Rescue archaeology in Co. Meath ahead of the construction of the M3 motorway

## How evidence is preserved

Evidence such as bodies and artefacts can be preserved for thousands of years if the conditions are right. As a general rule: when both air and moisture are present, things decay rapidly.

However, the **extreme heat** of deserts, for instance, dries out objects quickly and this can prevent decay, preserving them. When bodies are buried in airtight coffins or sealed tombs – or completely covered in volcanic ash, as occurred in Pompeii (see chapter 5) – the **airless conditions** can slow decay and preserve objects. European **peat bogs** preserve bodies extremely well, due to the combination of cold, acidic water and airlessness below the water level.

### CHECKPOINT!

1. Define the term excavate in your own words. 📖
2. Define the term aerial photograph in your own words. 📖
3. List five ways that archaeologists find sites to excavate.
4. List three ways that evidence can be preserved.

 I can explain how archaeologists find sites to excavate and how evidence is preserved.

 ⬅ TIME TO GO BACK ◆ I CAN MOVE FORWARD ➡

# 2.2: The Job of the Archaeologist

## Excavating a site

When they find a site to excavate, archaeologists:

**In this topic, you will learn about:**

❯ How sites are excavated
❯ The skills and methods archaeologists use
❯ Some Irish archaeological sites
❯ What it means to conserve the past

- carry out a **survey** to see if the site is worth excavating.

- dig test trenches. A **test trench** is a <u>sample hole dug to see if there is anything of interest present and judge whether it is worth excavating the whole site</u>. Trenches are measured and marked in grids so that the exact position of anything found there can be recorded.

- remove the topsoil using a digger or a pick axe. **Topsoil** is <u>the topmost, most recent layer of soil</u>.

- dig very carefully to make sure they do not damage anything. Archaeologists use **trowels** and **shovels** for this, to remove smaller amounts of soil.

▼ An excavation taking place. Can you identify what each archaeologist is doing?

- use **brushes** to remove soil delicately from any objects found.

- use **sieves** to ensure nothing is thrown away in the soil. A sieve catches even the smallest pieces of artefacts.

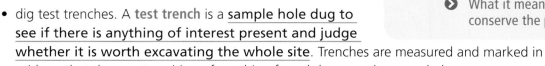

- **record** the position of every artefact found. Everything is carefully drawn and photographed.

- catalogue the details of each artefact on **computers** and in the excavation's **site book**.

- put artefacts into separate, labelled bags and then boxes, which are numbered and sent to the **laboratory** for tests.

Go to page 10 of your *Sources and Skills Book* for an exercise on a dig.

Once the tests are finished, artefacts are usually brought to **museums** where they can be displayed for people to learn from.

## CHECKPOINT!

1. Define the terms test trench and topsoil in your own words. 📖
2. Name three tools used by archaeologists.
3. List all the steps involved in excavating a site.
4. Why do archaeologists have to be careful when excavating?

✔ I can explain how archaeologists excavate a site.
◀ TIME TO GO BACK ◀ ▶ I CAN MOVE FORWARD ▶

Visit **www. educateplus.ie/ resources/artefact** for a video and a worksheet on the role of the archaeologist

**2 The Nature of History: The Archaeologist**

## 2.3: Skills and Methods Used in Archaeology

Archaeologists use various skills and methods when carrying out their work. These include skills used to locate information within sites, as well as many different methods of dating artefacts or any remains that are found. When examining bodies, archaeologists also have ways of learning how the person died and sometimes even what they looked like. All the skills and methods you will learn about next have been used on important Irish archaeological sites and have helped us to learn a lot about early Ireland.

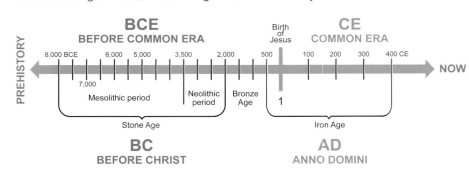

PREHISTORY

**BCE** BEFORE COMMON ERA

Birth of Jesus

**CE** COMMON ERA

8,000 BCE   6,000   5,000   3,500   2,000   500   1   100   200   300   400 CE   → NOW

7,000

Mesolithic period   Neolithic period   Bronze Age

Stone Age   Iron Age

**BC** BEFORE CHRIST   **AD** ANNO DOMINI

 **Skills**

## 1. RADIO-CARBON DATING (ALSO CALLED CARBON-14 DATING)

All living things – humans, animals and plants – contain a substance called **carbon-14** when they are alive. After death, the level of carbon-14 in the once-living tissue begins to drop at a steady rate. This means that **the older the tissue, the less carbon-14 it contains – and *how little* can tell us *how old***. Measuring age by this method is called **radio-carbon dating**.

**Example | Mount Sandel** *(Mesolithic period: 8,000–3,500 BC)*

In the 1970s, archaeologists found Mesolithic evidence at Mount Sandel in Co. Derry. **Mesolithic** means '**of the Middle Stone Age**'. The first people came to Ireland during the Mesolithic period, probably from Scotland across to Northern Ireland on wooden boats. Most of Ireland was then covered in dense forest, so the earliest settlements were near the coast or rivers. At this time, people were **hunter-gatherers**: they hunted animals and gathered berries and nuts, but had not yet learned how to farm. The archaeologists excavating the site found animal and bird bones and also the shells of hazelnuts. Using radio-carbon dating, these shells were tested to establish a date for the site. They date from 7,000 BC – so Mount Sandel is between 9,000 and 10,000 years old!

Learn more about Mount Sandel here:

https://educateplus.ie/go/mount-sandel

▼ Mesolithic campsite

► Map of prehistoric sites near the coast in Northern Ireland

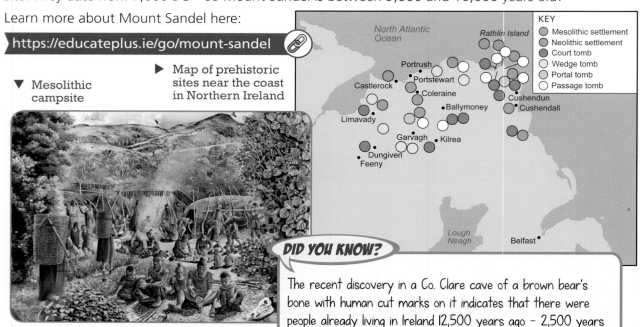

KEY
- Mesolithic settlement
- Neolithic settlement
- Court tomb
- Wedge tomb
- Portal tomb
- Passage tomb

North Atlantic Ocean

Rathlin Island

Portrush
Portstewart
Castlerock
Coleraine
Cushendun
Cushendall
Limavady
Ballymoney
Garvagh   Kilrea
Dungiven
Feeny

Lough Neagh

Belfast

**DID YOU KNOW?**

The recent discovery in a Co. Clare cave of a brown bear's bone with human cut marks on it indicates that there were people already living in Ireland 12,500 years ago – 2,500 years before Mount Sandel suggests! This is a good example of reinterpretation and is being studied closely now.

# 2. GEOPHYSICAL SURVEYING

A **geophysical survey** is __like an x-ray of the ground__: maps and images of any archaeological evidence underground are made without an excavation. Geophysical surveys can locate artefacts, as well as ruined buildings and structures. This method was used in recent years to investigate Newgrange, Ireland's most famous passage tomb, at Brú na Bóinne, Co. Meath.

**Example | Newgrange passage tomb** *(Neolithic period, 3,500–2,000 BC)*

A **passage tomb** is __a narrow passage with one or more burial chambers, made of large stones and covered in earth or stone__. Other Neolithic passage tombs at Brú na Bóinne include Knowth and Dowth. **Neolithic** means '__of the new Stone Age__' and it is when the first farmers came to Ireland. Until 1962, Newgrange had not been excavated properly. Inside is a passage 20 metres long, which leads into a 6-metre high central chamber with three sections. The aim of the geophysical survey was to see whether there were any hidden passageways or chambers, but none were discovered. The central chamber has a **corbelled roof** – __a domed roof built by overlapping stones until they meet at the top__. A capstone was placed over this. To this day, no water leaks into the chamber, so it was a good technique!

▲ Aerial photograph of Newgrange passage tomb

**DID YOU KNOW?**

Newgrange is older than the Pyramids in Egypt! Newgrange is estimated to date from between 3,000 and 2,500 BC. The Pyramids are estimated to date from between 2,600 and 2,500 BC.

Outside, a series of stones surrounds the passage tomb in a circle. Each stone was decorated with carvings, including diamond and spiral shapes. A large decorated stone sits directly in front of the entrance to the passage tomb. Above the passage entrance is a gap known as a roof box. Every 21 December – the winter solstice and shortest day of the year – the rising sun shines through the roof box and right along the passage, all the way into the chamber!

You can go on a virtual 3D tour of Newgrange, including the passage and corbelled roof, using this link:

▲ Entrance to Newgrange, showing the decorated stone and roof box

**DID YOU KNOW?**

In 2016, there were 32,682 entries for the lottery to be present in the chamber at Newgrange at sunrise on the winter solstice! Only twenty people can fit inside at a time.

https://educateplus.ie/go/newgrange-360

**2 The Nature of History: The Archaeologist**

# 3. POLLEN ANALYSIS

**Pollen analysis** is <u>the study of pollen remains to find out what was growing at a site during a particular time period</u>. Archaeologists have records of when certain pollens were common, so if they find that pollen when excavating, they can match it to the correct period. Pollen analysis can be used to date objects and can also tell us when forests were cleared and farming began in an area. This method was used at the important Neolithic site of the Céide Fields in Co. Mayo.

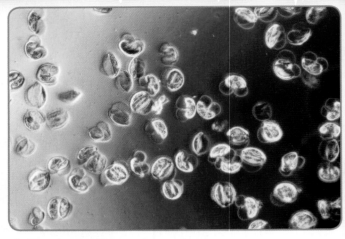

▲ Pine tree pollen under a microscope

**Example | The Céide Fields** *(Neolithic period, 3,500–2,000 BC)*

The Céide Fields were discovered by accident in the 1930s by a teacher who, while cutting turf in the bog, noticed a pile of stones. Buried underneath the bog, archaeologists found stone walls stretching for several kilometres. People lived here between 4,000 and 3,000 BC. These Neolithic people were mainly dairy farmers. That they built walls shows that they were organised, protected their animals from wild animals and that they divided up the land amongst them. The pollen analysis showed a dramatic drop in tree pollens, proving that pine forest areas were cleared to create fields for farming. Among the interesting objects found were a stone cutting of a primitive plough, a quern used for grinding corn, some arrowheads and pieces of pottery. The blanket bog which grew over the fields preserved the site, leaving it in excellent condition for archaeologists to study it.

▲ Aerial photograph of the Céide Fields

COLLABORATE: You have learned about the possibility of history having to be reinterpreted when new evidence is discovered. Work in small groups to find out why some archaeologists think that the date we have for the Céide Fields may be wrong!

# 4. STRATIGRAPHY

The method of **stratigraphy** is used <u>to date artefacts and evidence by how deep in the ground they were when found</u>: the deeper they are, the older they will be.

If you were to drop something today, it would lie on the surface, but over thousands of years it would become covered by soil, leaves and other matter and eventually it would end up buried many metres deep. This method is used in most archaeological excavations.

**Stratigraphic Profile**

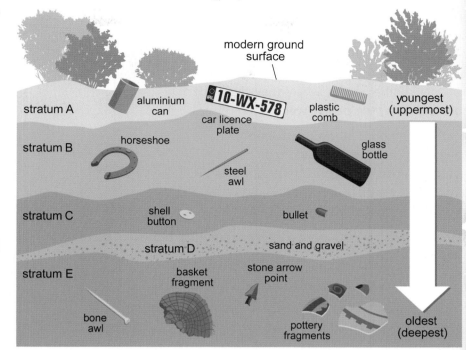

▲ The deeper in the ground something lies, the older it is

# 5. DENDROCHRONOLOGY

**Dendrochronology**, also called tree-ring dating, is <u>a method of dating that uses the unique growth patterns of tree rings as a guide</u>. If you cut through a tree trunk, you will see rings spreading from the centre outwards: each one is a year of growth. The rings are wider when the tree grew fast, for example when the summer was good.

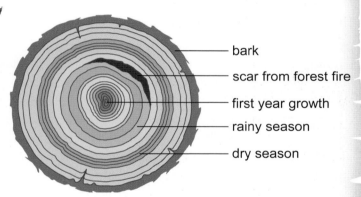

- bark
- scar from forest fire
- first year growth
- rainy season
- dry season

Archaeologists have created a continuous record of tree ring patterns dating back to 5,300 BC, which makes it possible to figure out when a tree was cut down to make an artefact or structure. It can also be used to date wooden objects. Well-preserved wood is needed for this, however, and that is not present on most sites. This is therefore not a widely used method.

## CHECKPOINT!

1. Define the term radio-carbon dating in your own words. 📖
2. In what period of history did the first people come to Ireland?
3. What was a hunter-gatherer?
4. Define the terms geophysical surveying and pollen analysis in your own words. 📖
5. When was the middle Stone Age? Name one archaeological site from that time.
6. Define the terms stratigraphy and dendrochronology in your own words. 📖

 I understand how archaeologists learn about the past from excavations.

2 The Nature of History: The Archaeologist

# 6. DNA TESTING, 3D RECONSTRUCTION AND BONES

Archaeologists sometimes find bodies when they excavate sites. Modern methods reveal a lot about these bodies. **DNA testing** can tell us about the origins and ethnicity of the person – in other words, where they came from and who their people were.

Another method is **3D reconstruction**, or using computer modelling and then clay to reconstruct part of a body. If most of a skull is found, for example, a person's face can be reconstructed based on their skull structure.

Archaeologists can also learn a lot by **examining bones**:

- The pelvis shows whether the person was male or female.
- Teeth can give us a rough idea of a person's age.
- Bones can show signs of disease or bad nutrition, or if they are damaged it could be that the person's death was violent.
- The thigh bone is a good indicator of overall height.
- Skin or hair can be analysed for information about typical diet.

These methods were all used on Clonycavan Man.

Skin/Hair:
What was this person's typical diet?

Skull:
What might their face have looked like?

Teeth:
How old was this person?

Pelvis:
Were they male or female?

Thigh bone:
How tall were they?

▲ Archaeologists get information from various parts of a skeleton

---

**Example | Clonycavan Man** *(Iron Age, 500 BC– AD 400)*

Clonycavan Man's body is believed to be 2,300 years old: it dates from the **Iron Age**, the period <u>when people made tools and weapons from iron</u>. He was found in a Co. Meath peat bog in 2003. Only his head and upper body were preserved. He had crooked teeth and a thin beard and pores are visible on his squashed nose. We know that his diet consisted mostly of fruit and vegetables. His hair style was very distinctive and he used an ancient hair gel made of plant oil and pine resin. Its ingredients came from France and Spain, which shows that he was wealthy. Archaeologists think he may once have been a king and was ritually sacrificed. His skull was split by a sharp object, and there was a large cut across his nose and under his right eye. It is estimated that he was aged 24–40 when he died.

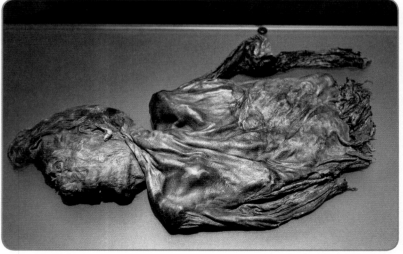

▲ Clonycavan Man's head and torso

▶ A facial reconstruction of Clonycavan Man in the National Museum of Ireland

## Conservation

**Conservation** is <u>when historic objects are protected and preserved so that they do not decay</u>. Objects found by archaeologists can be displayed under the correct conditions in museums and heritage sites. Documents, maps, photographs and so forth can be safely stored in places such as archives and libraries. Historic buildings are also looked after and restored when necessary, so that they will stay in good condition. Conserving the past benefits us, as we can continue to learn about and engage with our history.

## CHECKPOINT!

1. Draw a timeline to represent the following periods in Irish history in chronological order: the Iron Age; the Neolithic era; the Mesolithic era; the Bronze Age.

2. Name three things archaeologists can learn from studying the bones of a skeleton.

3. Define the term conservation in your own words.

4. Give three examples of things that might undergo conservation.

✓ I know the main skills and methods used by archaeologists and what it means to conserve the past.

← TIME TO GO BACK ◆ I CAN MOVE FORWARD →

# WORKING WITH THE <u>EVIDENCE</u>!

## Finding evidence on a dig

Study these photographs of an archaeologist working on an excavation and their tools, then answer the following questions.

1. What type of source is a photograph?

2. What steps can you see being carried out?

3. What tools can you identify in the picture below?

4. Name one possible problem when excavating a site.

5. If this archaeologist finds artefacts, what should they do with them?

6. Name two methods of dating that this archaeologist might use and explain why you've chosen them.

COLLABORATE: Work together in small groups to make a list of facts about each of the archaeological sites and examples discussed in topic 2.3.

# SUMMARY

In this chapter, we have learned that:

- Archaeology is the study of remains left by people in the past.
- An excavation is when archaeologists dig to find evidence left by people in the past.
- Archaeologists identify sites for excavation in various ways, among them research archaeology, rescue archaeology, visible ruins, aerial photography – and even by accident!
- Evidence can sometimes last a very long time, especially under airless or very dry conditions.
- Steps when carrying out an excavation include: digging test trenches; removing topsoil; using shovels, trowels and brushes; cataloguing all finds; taking photographs; and storing finds in labelled bags and boxes.
- Some skills and methods used by archaeologists are: radio-carbon dating; stratigraphy; dendrochronology; geophysical surveying; pollen analysis; 3D reconstruction; DNA testing and bone analysis.
- Fascinating archaeological discoveries in Ireland include Mount Sandel, Newgrange passage tomb, the Céide Fields and the Clonycavan Man.
- The Mesolithic period, the Neolithic period, the Bronze Age and the Iron Age are all periods of history that archaeologists have investigated in Ireland.

## Reflecting on... **the Job of the Archaeologist**

The job of the archaeologist shows the importance of enquiry and discovery in unlocking information about the past. Understanding the archaeologist's methods helps us to appreciate the contribution of new technology to historical investigation.

# Understanding History

1. Archaeology is the study of the remains left by _____ in the past. Archaeologists dig holes to find these remains: this is called _____ a site. Archaeology is our only source of information from _____ times. However, archaeologists also investigate remains from more recent times and work alongside _____ build a complete picture of what life was like for people in the past.

2. Why is the study of archaeology important?

3. Explain the terms rescue archaeology and research archaeology. 📖/

4. Work with a partner. Each choose five from the key terms below and give a definition in your own words. 👥

| Artefact | Stratigraphy | Radio-carbon dating | Mesolithic |
|----------|--------------|---------------------|------------|
| Topsoil | Dendrochronology | Geophysical survey | Neolithic |
| Passage tomb | 3D reconstruction | Aerial photograph | Iron Age |
| Test trench | Pollen analysis | Bronze Age | Excavate |

**Exploring History**

1. Write a short paragraph about each of the following methods of dating: stratigraphy, dendrochronology and radio-carbon dating.

2. What kind of source is the artefact in the image to the right? What can we, as historians and archaeologists, learn about people's lives from finds such as this plough?

© ceidefields.com

**2 The Nature of History: The Archaeologist**

**KEY TERMS**

| | |
|---|---|
| Bronze Age | the period of time when people made tools and weapons using bronze |
| Excavation | when archaeologists dig up the ground to find evidence left by people in the past |
| Aerial photograph | a photograph taken of the ground from an elevated position, for example from a helicopter |
| Test trench | a sample hole dug to judge whether it is worth excavating the whole site |
| Topsoil | the topmost, most recent layer of soil |
| Radio-carbon dating | a method of dating based on the falling levels of carbon-14 in tissue over time |
| Mesolithic | of the Middle Stone Age |
| Hunter-gatherer | someone who hunted animals for food and gathered berries and nuts |
| Geophysical survey | a survey of what's underneath the ground, like an x-ray of the ground |
| Passage tomb | a narrow passage with one or more burial chambers, made of large stones and covered in earth or stone |
| Neolithic | of the New Stone Age. This is when the first farmers came to Ireland |
| Corbelled roof | a domed roof, built by placing stones overlapping each other until they meet at the top |
| Pollen analysis | the studying of pollen remains to tell archaeologists what was growing during the time period |
| Stratigraphy | a method of dating artefacts and evidence by how deep in the ground they were when found |
| Dendrochronology | a method of dating that uses the unique growth patterns of tree rings as a guide |
| Iron Age | the period of time when people made tools and weapons using iron |
| Conservation | when historic objects are protected and preserved so that they do not decay |

Go to page 7 of your *Sources and Skills Book* for more exercises.

Go to page 2 of your *Research Portfolio* for tasks based on this chapter.

| Old Stone Age | Ancient Ireland | Early Christian Ireland |
|---|---|---|
| Before 8,000 BC | c. 8,000 BC–AD 400 | c. AD 400–800 |

In the last chapter, we learned about the work of an archaeologist. Now we will look at **Ancient Ireland**. This period covers the Stone and Bronze Ages, when people first arrived in Ireland and began to build communities. This was a time before writing was used in Ireland – the prehistoric era – so our knowledge depends completely on archaeology. Then came the Iron Age and with it the Celtic people, their more complex society, their ironworking skills and an early form of writing.

| Old Stone Age | Middle Stone Age (Mesolithic) | New Stone Age (Neolithic) | Bronze Age | Iron Age | Early Christian Ireland |
|---|---|---|---|---|---|

| No evidence of people living in Ireland | 8,000 BC | First people in Ireland | 3,500 BC | First farmers in Ireland | 2,300 BC | First use of metal | 500 BC | Year 1 Iron replaced bronze; arrival of Celts | AD 400 | Arrival of Christianity |

# WORKING WITH THE EVIDENCE!

## Prehistoric artefacts

| Type of source | Category | Example |
|---|---|---|
| Primary | Tactile | Mesolithic stone arrow head artefact |
| Primary | Tactile | Bronze Age axe head artefact |

Look at these two tools. What was each of them used for? What can we tell about how life in Ireland changed over this time period by looking at these two artefacts?

## 3.1: Mesolithic Ireland: The Hunter-Gatherers

**In this topic, you will learn about:**
- ❯ The first people who lived in Ireland
- ❯ The tools and weapons they used
- ❯ Their homes
- ❯ Their burial practices

### The first settlers in Ireland

The first people arrived in Ireland during the **Mesolithic (Middle Stone) Age** (8,000–3,500 BC). They probably travelled across from Scotland in dugout canoes made from tree trunks. As you saw in the last chapter, **Mount Sandel in Co. Derry** is our most important source of information for this period.

### Tools, weapons and work

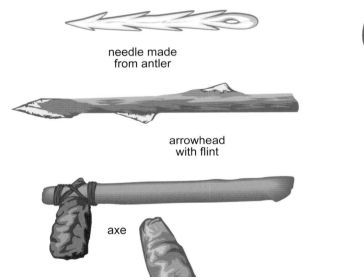

needle made from antler

arrowhead with flint

axe

flint scraper

arrowhead

◀ Mesolithic tools and weapons

This period in history is known as the Stone Age because **all tools and weapons were made from stone**. People sharpened pieces of stone (mainly **flint**) and fixed them to wooden shafts to use as arrows, axes, spears and harpoons. Mesolithic people were **hunters-gatherers**: they got all their food by hunting, fishing and gathering fruit, nuts and berries. Food was cooked over a fire on a **spit**. People clothed themselves in **animal skins** and used bones to make needles for sewing.

3

Settlement in Ireland Option One: Ancient Ireland

# Houses

The Mesolithic people were **nomadic**: <u>they regularly moved from place to place</u>, probably when food supplies in an area ran low. Archaeologists believe they lived in temporary dwellings such as tents – or basket-like houses made from saplings driven into **post holes** in a circle and tied at the top. The walls would have been covered with skins, reeds or sods of turf.

Mesolithic temporary houses

making flint-tipped arrows

preparing animal skins

a dugout canoe

fishing

cooking meat on a spit

using flint to make a fire

▲ A Mesolithic campsite and activities

# Burials

A burial site in Hermitage, Co. Limerick tells us that the Mesolithic people **cremated** (burned) the bodies of the dead and <u>buried them with axes and other valuable items</u> – called **grave goods**. These are very important for archaeologists, as the objects are well preserved and also suggest that the people believed in some form of afterlife.

## CHECKPOINT!

1. Why is this period called the Stone Age?
2. Explain the terms: hunter-gatherer; nomadic; grave goods. 📖
3. What weapons and tools did they use? What were these made from?
4. Describe a Mesolithic house.
5. Why might archaeologists think that the Mesolithic people believed in an afterlife?

✔ I can describe life in Mesolithic Ireland.

◀ TIME TO GO BACK ▶ I CAN MOVE FORWARD ➔

# 3.2: Neolithic Ireland: The First Farmers

In this topic, you will learn about:
- The first farmers in Ireland
- The tools and weapons they used
- Their homes
- Their burial practices

## The first farmers

Between 4,000 and 3,500 BC, new settlers arrived in Ireland, bringing new skills: **farming**, **bread-making**, **tomb-building** and **pottery-making**. Farming was the single most important change. They cut down trees and cleared land to plant crops and keep animals. There are several major Neolithic sites in Ireland: **the Céide Fields** in Co. Mayo (see page 20), **Lough Gur** in Co. Limerick and the **Boyne Valley** in Co. Meath.

## Tools, weapons and work

The land was ploughed with stone **mattocks** and **ploughs**. The first farmers grew crops like **wheat** and **barley** and domesticated animals like **sheep** and **pigs**. They hunted and gathered, like the Mesolithic people, but it was no longer their main source of food. To make **bread**, they ground wheat into flour on a **saddle stone**. The first **pots** were made from local clay and used to store food, tools or the ashes of the dead.

## Houses

Farming meant that the Neolithic people could settle in one place with a secure food supply from the crops and animals they cultivated. Their houses were therefore more **permanent** than those of Mesolithic people. Their houses had poles driven into the ground (leaving **post holes**) or walls of wattle and daub – wooden sticks woven together like a basket (wattle) and covered with a mixture of mud, dung, sand and straw (daub). The roof was thatched with straw or rushes.

▲ A mattock, a Neolithic tool

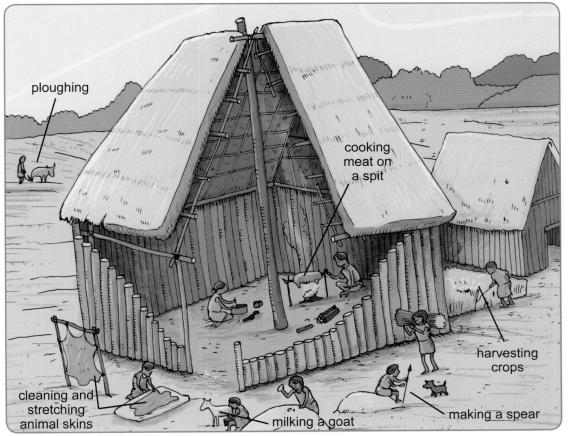

ploughing

cooking meat on a spit

harvesting crops

cleaning and stretching animal skins

milking a goat

making a spear

▲ A Neolithic settlement and activities

## Burials

A significant change in Neolithic Ireland was a new emphasis on building tombs for cremated remains and grave goods. There were three main types of **megalithic** (**huge stone**) tombs:

- **Passage graves**: As we saw in chapter 2, these were huge mounds built over a central passage, which led to a chamber for the dead.

- **Court cairns**: These had an open space (**court**) at the front and a chamber originally covered by a mound of stones **(cairn)** for the dead behind.

- **Portal dolmens**: Two or more standing stones and a huge **capstone** resting across the top with the remains placed inside.

▲ A court cairn

The megaliths for these tombs would have been floated along rivers on rafts or rolled for miles on logs. Building these tombs would have taken hundreds of people. The Neolithic people clearly had **knowledge of the stars** and were **skilled engineers**.

▼ A portal dolmen

Go to page 14 of your *Sources and Skills Book* for an evidence task.

 **CHECKPOINT!**

1. What important change took in place in Ireland during the Neolithic period?
2. What foods were produced by Neolithic farmers?
3. Describe Neolithic houses and how these were different from Mesolithic houses.
4. Describe (a) a passage tomb; (b) a court cairn; (c) a portal dolmen.
5. Explain the following terms: wattle and daub; megaliths. 📖

✓ I can describe life in Neolithic Ireland.

← TIME TO GO BACK ◆ I CAN MOVE FORWARD →

## 3.3: The Bronze Age

In this topic, you will learn about:

- ❯ The first metal workers in Ireland
- ❯ The tools and weapons they used
- ❯ Their homes
- ❯ Their burial practices

## Metal comes to Ireland

Archaeologists believe the first use of metal in Ireland was around 2,000 BC: this was the Bronze Age. Bronze was **stronger** than stone but was also much **easier to shape**, so people had greater control over the tools and weapons they could make. Bronze is an **alloy** (combination) of copper and tin. Copper was mined at Mount Gabriel in Co. Cork, but tin had to be imported, probably from Cornwall in Britain. Bronze was made by the process of **smelting** copper and tin – melting metal at a high temperature to separate it from the ore – combining them and pouring them into moulds to set.

▲ The smelting process

## Tools, weapons and work

Metalworkers (**smiths**) made tools such as sickles (to cut crops), axes and ploughs and weapons such as knives, swords, shields and spears. Farming remained the main source of food for Bronze Age people. They grew wheat and barley, kept animals such as pigs, sheep and cattle and hunted wild animals, especially birds and fish. Clothes were woven from sheep's wool, dyed with berries and stitched with bronze needles.

As skills developed, smiths made bronze pots and cauldrons for cooking, horns for music and **jewellery** in gold and bronze like bracelets, armlets, earrings, necklaces, **torcs and lunulae** like that on page 14.

**Querns** were used to grind corn into flour for bread. Bronze was used to make pots for cooking. Meat was cooked in a **fulacht fiadh**. This was a stone-lined pit which was filled with water. Stones were then heated in a fire and lowered into the water to make it boil. The meat was wrapped in straw and left boiling until ready to eat.

◀ Heating the water in a fulacht fiadh

## Houses

While most houses in the Bronze Age were very similar to Neolithic houses (wattle-and-daub walls, thatched roofs), there were a couple of changes. Firstly, they were **bigger** (usually about 6 metres across) and **circular**. Secondly, houses and other smaller buildings were **enclosed behind timber fences, earth embankments and ditches**. These may have been to defend the people from attacks, keep their animals safe at night, or both.

## Burials

Some Bronze Age burials were similar to those of Neolithic period. **Wedge tombs** were smaller versions of portal dolmens.

As the population of the island grew during the Bronze Age, **cist graves** became more common. These were less difficult to build; just stone-lined graves in the ground. The body was buried in a crouched or **foetal position** with its grave goods.

▲ An archaeologist excavating a cist grave

Go to page 15 of your *Sources and Skills Book* for an evidence task.

# CHECKPOINT!

1. Which two metals were used to make bronze?
2. Why was the use of metal important?
3. What was a fulacht fiadh and how was it used?
4. What types of jewellery were made in the Bronze Age?
5. How were houses in the Bronze Age (a) similar to and (b) different from those of the Neolithic period?
6. Describe a cist grave.

 I can describe life in Bronze Age Ireland.

 TIME TO GO BACK ◀ ▶ I CAN MOVE FORWARD ➡

# 3.4: The Iron Age: Celtic Ireland

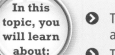

**In this topic, you will learn about:**

- The coming of the Celts and iron to Ireland
- The homes of the Celts
- Celtic art
- Celtic burials

## The arrival of the Celts

Archaeologists have evidence that iron was in use in Ireland from **as early as 500–300 BC**. The Celts are thought to have arrived in Ireland from central Europe (around modern Austria and Switzerland) at this time, bringing with them their **culture**, **language**, **religion** and the **knowledge of ironworking**. Iron was a far stronger metal than bronze and it became the main metal used for tools and weapons. Celtic culture quickly became dominant in Ireland.

The Celts were a highly organised society. The country was divided into many **tuath** (kingdoms), each ruled by a **rí** (king). Under him were the **warriors and nobles** (called **aos dána**), then the **farmers,** and at the bottom of society, the **labourers and slaves**. The aos dána were people with special skills:

- **judges** (brehons, who knew the complex laws);
- **druids** (pagan priests);
- **filí** (poets, who preserved the history and stories in their poetry);
- **doctors** or healers;
- **musicians** and bards;
- **craftspeople** (skilled metalworkers, masons and so forth).

▲ Social structure of the Celts

## Celtic houses

The discovery of weapons and the remains of fortified homes show that conflict and warfare were common in Iron Age Ireland. We see two main types of settlement from this time:

- **Crannógs**: Man-made islands. Tree trunks were driven down into the bed of a lake and a platform was built on top. They were designed for defence and could only be reached by bridge or boat. Over 1,200 crannóg sites have been found in Ireland.

- **Ring-forts** (**raths**): Circular enclosures surrounded by a ditch, earth bank and wooden fence. Some also had an

▲ Reconstruction of a crannóg

underground passage (**souterrain**) for food storage or an escape route during an attack. Aided by aerial photography, archaeologists have found over 40,000 raths (see page 15).

The houses inside were similar to Bronze Age houses: wattle-and-daub walls and thatched roofs.

## Celtic art

The Celts brought their unique style of art to Ireland. Known as the **La Tène style** (after the hoard found in La Tène, Switzerland), it featured spirals, florals, fantasy animals and curved lines. The Celts also crafted intricate golden jewellery. This style continued to evolve and has had a huge influence on later generations of Irish art.

▶ The Broighter Collar

## Celtic burials

Celtic burials were very similar to those of the Bronze Age: they cremated bodies and buried the remains in pits or cist graves, along with grave goods. One important difference was that the Celts often marked graves with **ogham stones**. These standing stones, which were also used to mark boundaries, feature the earliest form of writing in Ireland. Ogham was a series of horizontal and diagonal lines along a central vertical line.

# CHECKPOINT!

1. When did the Celts arrive in Ireland?
2. How was Celtic society organised?
3. Describe (a) a crannóg and (b) a ring-fort.
4. What was the La Tène style?
5. What did the Celts do with their dead?
6. What was ogham? Why is it important?

 I can describe the Celts and life in Iron Age Ireland.

◀ TIME TO GO BACK ◀ ▶ I CAN MOVE FORWARD ➡

▲ Ogham stone

 **SUMMARY**

In this chapter, we have learned that:

- The Stone (Mesolithic, Neolithic) and Bronze Ages are the prehistoric era in Ireland: no written records exist from these eras. The Iron Age brought ogham, Ireland's earliest form of writing.
- The first people arrived in Ireland during the Mesolithic era. They were hunter-gatherers who used stone weapons and tools, lived nomadic lives and cremated their dead.
- During the Neolithic period, farming was introduced to Ireland. People now lived in permanent houses, farmed crops and reared animals for food. They built large tombs to house their dead, such as passage tombs, portal dolmens and court cairns.
- In the Bronze Age, metal tools and weapons became common in Ireland. The people continued to farm and lived in larger houses protected by wooden defences. Graves became smaller.
- The Iron Age brought a new people to Ireland: the Celts. They were a more organised society, and their culture and social structure dominated Ireland until the arrival of Christianity.

## Reflecting on... Ancient Ireland

In this short chapter, we have covered over 8,000 years of Irish history! The little we know about ancient Ireland is thanks to archaeology. The key turning point in human history was the invention of farming. This allowed the creation of non-nomadic communities, which would in time grow into towns and cities with sophisticated social structures.

**Understanding History**

1. Describe the lives of people who lived in Mesolithic Ireland.
2. Why were these people nomadic?
3. How were people's lives affected by the introduction of farming?
4. What evidence is there that the Neolithic people were (a) highly organised; (b) skilled engineers; (c) religious?
5. Is there any evidence of conflict in Bronze Age Ireland?
6. Why do you think graves became smaller in the Bronze Age?
7. Why was the arrival of the Celts so important for Irish history?
8. What evidence is there of conflict in Celtic Ireland?

 **Exploring History**

1. Write a paragraph on how the following changed across the eras of ancient Ireland:
   • Food       • Tools and weapons       • Burials       • Houses       • Work
2. How have the archaeologists' skills you learned about helped us to understand the lives of people in ancient Ireland? Give three examples.

| KEY TERMS | Nomadic | people who regularly move from place to place |
|---|---|---|
| | Grave goods | valuable items buried with a body |
| | Wattle and daub | wooden sticks woven together like a basket (wattle) and covered with a mud paste (daub), used to make walls of houses |
| | Megalith | 'huge stone' |
| | Smelting | melting metal at a high temperature to separate it from the ore |

 Go to page 12 of your *Sources and Skills Book* for more exercises.

 Go to page 4 of your *Research Portfolio* for a task based on this chapter.

**3 Settlement in Ireland Option One: Ancient Ireland**

| The Iron Age | Early Christian Ireland | The Middle Ages |
|---|---|---|
| c. 500 BC– AD 400 | c. 400– AD 800 | c. 500– AD 1500 |

In Ireland, **the Iron Age** – when iron was used to make tools and weapons – took place between 500 BC and AD 400. Towards the end of the Iron Age, by the early fifth century AD, Christianity had arrived in Ireland.

This development had an enormous impact on culture and society in Ireland. Many fascinating archaeological sites and a wealth of artefacts date from this time.

# WORKING WITH THE <u>EVIDENCE</u>!

## Early Christian Ireland

| Type of source | Category | Example |
|---|---|---|
| Secondary | Written | Manuscript: a reproduction of the *Book of Durrow* |
| Primary | Tactile | Building: round tower in Monasterboice, Co. Louth |

▼ Round tower in Monasterboice

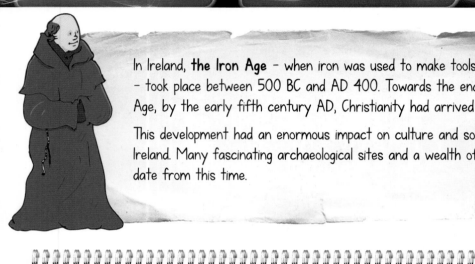

▲ Reproduction of the *Book of Durrow*

How does each of these sources show us that monks in Early Christian Ireland were highly skilled?

# 4.1: Early Christian Ireland

In this topic, you will learn about:
- How Christianity came to Ireland
- Early Irish monasteries
- How monasteries looked

## The arrival of Christianity in Ireland

Early Christian Ireland is the period when Christianity first came to Ireland. At that time, the people of Ireland were **the Celts**, farmers and warriors who had come from Central Europe and whose religious beliefs were pagan. A **pagan** is someone who worships various gods, often with a focus on nature or the earth. **Druids** were spiritual figures similar to priests in pre-Christian Celtic Ireland.

By the third century AD, the Roman Empire had spread as far as England and was mainly Christian, so some Christians were probably also in Ireland by then. For historians, the first official source about Christianity in Ireland is dated AD 431, when a bishop named **Palladius** was sent to the 'Irish who believe in Christ'.

Of course, the most famous bishop to travel to Ireland was **St Patrick**. He was brought to Ireland from Wales as a slave when he was 16 years old. After six years he escaped to Britain, but later returned as a bishop to spread Christianity. Between AD 432 and 461, St Patrick worked, mainly in the north, and founded many churches and missions. We know all of this from his book, '**St Patrick's Confessio**'. In it he says that he 'baptised thousands' and 'ordained clerics everywhere'.

https://educateplus.ie/go/st-patricks-confessio

St Patrick began to convert the pagan Celts to Christianity. **Pagan festivals** continued, but gradually became absorbed into Christianity: for example, Samhain became Hallowe'en. St Patrick is said to be buried at Down Cathedral, Co. Down.

▲ This rock marks where St Patrick is thought to be buried, at Down Cathedral

▲ St Patrick represented in stained glass

# Early Irish monasteries

Some Christians chose to live apart from the rest of society **in a closed religious community**, or **monastery**, to devote their lives to God. The **first Irish monastery**, called Inis Mór, was founded by St Enda on the Aran Islands around **AD 500**. Many followed his example, such as St Ciarán in Clonmacnoise, St Colmcille in Derry and St Brendan in Clonfert.

**Monks** are <u>men who dedicate themselves to a religious order and to life in a monastery</u>. The monks lived very **strict, simple lives** and spent their days **praying** and **working.** They prayed six to eight times every day. Farm work included ploughing, milking, harvesting and grinding corn. The monks were often **self-sufficient** – they produced all the food they needed. Monasteries became **centres of learning** and Irish monasteries were famous as the best in the world for the teaching of poetry, literature, arts and the Gospel. Ireland became known as **'the Land of Saints and Scholars'**, a saying that is still popular to this day.

Large monasteries such as Clonard, Kells, Clonmacnoise, Glendalough and Clonfert were built along important routes and had regular contact with nearby towns. But small monasteries were also built in far more remote spots, such as **Sceilg Mhicíl** in Co. Kerry. Here, about a dozen monks lived on a steep rocky island with a small stone church.

A **beehive hut** <u>was a small stone hut, shaped like a beehive, where a monk slept</u>. To plant and grow food, soil had to be brought from the mainland! The extreme isolation meant that monks could better focus on God and work.

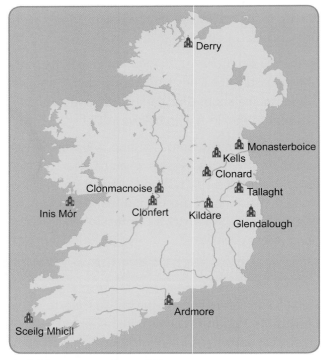

▲ Irish monasteries *c.*650

The beehive huts at the monastery on Sceilg Mhicíl

▼ Monastery at Clonmacnoise

▲ The beehive huts at the monastery on Sceilg Mhicíl

# The layout of an early Irish monastery

▼ An early Irish monastery

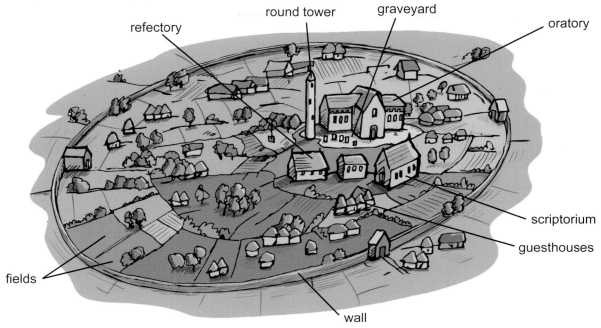

- The **oratory** or church, made of wood or stone, was <u>where the monks attended Mass or prayed</u>.
- The **scriptorium** was <u>where manuscripts were copied by hand and illustrated</u>.
- A **manuscript** <u>is a book written by hand</u>. The monks who did this work were called **scribes**.
- The **refectory** <u>was where the monks ate their meals</u>.
- The **round tower** <u>was a bell tower and a safe place for people (and treasures) if the monastery came under attack</u>. A round tower's door was many metres above ground and could not be reached without a ladder. Its few windows were very high up, so that a lookout could spot attackers and access would be difficult. Many round towers are still visible in Ireland, including **Glendalough** in Co. Wicklow, **Kells** in Co. Meath and **Ardmore** in Co. Waterford.
- Large monasteries had a **guesthouse** for travellers or visiting tradesmen.
- All monasteries had **fields** to grow crops and graze animals.
- There was a **cemetery** (graveyard) for the monks' simple graves.
- Large monasteries had a **circular wall** or bank for protection.

▲ Round tower in Clonmacnoise

## CHECKPOINT!

1. How did Christianity arrive in Ireland and when?
2. Explain the terms monastery and beehive hut.
3. Name three examples of Early Christian Ireland monasteries.
4. Explain the terms scriptorium, refectory, oratory, round tower and manuscript.

 I can explain how Christianity came to Ireland and what monasteries were like in Early Christian Ireland.

 ← TIME TO GO BACK ◆ I CAN MOVE FORWARD →

# 4.2: The Art of Early Christian Ireland

**In this topic, you will learn about:**

➤ The art produced by Irish monks

Early Christian Ireland monasteries were famous for their great works of art, which were made **to honour God** and show **the monastery's importance**. These works of art included manuscripts, metalwork and high crosses.

## Manuscripts

Christianity helped to spread reading and writing in Ireland. Manuscripts contained the Gospels and the Psalms from the Bible, accounts of the lives of saints and also Celtic myths and sagas. They were written **in Latin**, on **parchment** made from sheepskin or **vellum** made from calfskin. They were decorated with **Celtic patterns** in vivid colours made from berries, crushed acorns, powdered rocks, metals and beetles. For pens, monks used **quills** – goose feathers sharpened and dipped in ink.

- The **Cathach of St Columba** is the oldest Irish manuscript. It dates from the late sixth century AD.
- The **Book of Durrow** was probably created between AD 650 and 700 and is kept in the Trinity College Library.
- The most famous is the **Book of Kells**, also kept at Trinity College Dublin. It dates from around AD 800 and is a beautifully decorated copy of the four Gospels.

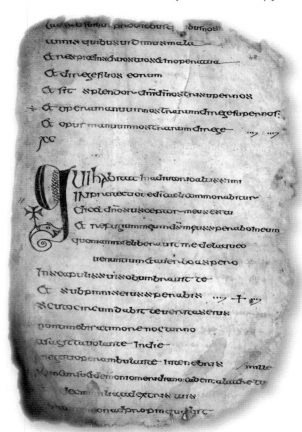

▲ The *Cathach* of St Columba

▲ The *Book of Kells*

**DID YOU KNOW?**

The Book of Kells attracts over 500,000 visitors to Trinity College each year! Every day a librarian very, very carefully turns to a new page. After all, it is now over 1,200 years old. Luckily, since 2013 anyone can admire any page right up close at this link:

➤ https://educateplus.ie/go/book-kells

# Metalwork

Irish monks were very skilled craftsmen and created beautiful metalwork pieces. These included **chalices, brooches, bells, cups and belts**. The monks decorated **silver** with **gold, amber, enamel** and **coloured glass**. They also made intricate gold writing, called filigree. **Celtic designs** can be seen in their work, which shows the overlap between Christian beliefs and pagan traditions.

- The **Ardagh Chalice** (eighth century) and the **Derrynaflan Chalice** (early ninth century) are examples of chalices made using these skills.
- The **Bell of St Patrick and its Shrine** (cover) is another fine example. The bell dates from the eighth to the ninth century, while the shrine is from a later date.
- The **Cross of Cong** is a later example of detailed metalwork. It dates from the early twelfth century.

All of these are on display in the National Museum in Dublin.

▼ The Derrynaflan Chalice

▲ The Ardagh Chalice

▶ The Cross of Cong

▼ The Bell and Shrine of St Patrick

▲ Detail from the Cross of Cong

**4 Culture and Society in Early Christian Ireland**

## Stone crosses

Stonemasonry was very important in Early Christian Ireland. Gifted stonemason monks carved what we call high crosses. A **high cross** is a free-standing stone cross, usually with elaborate carvings showing biblical scenes, for example of Adam and Eve or the Crucifixion. Most people at the time could not read or write, so these scenes helped to teach Bible stories. Complex Celtic patterns surrounded these.

- Two of the most beautiful high crosses in Ireland are the **Cross of the Scriptures** in Clonmacnoise, Co. Offaly (late tenth century), and **Muiredach's Cross** in Monasterboice, Co. Louth (mid-ninth to early tenth century).

 COLLABORATE: Work together to come up with any examples of metalwork, manuscripts or high crosses from your local area.

▲ Muiredach's cross in Monasterboice

## CHECKPOINT!

1. Name three types of art produced by Irish monks.
2. What materials were used in the scriptorium?
3. Name two examples of metalwork from Early Christian Ireland.
4. Describe the kinds of decoration used on metalwork pieces.
5. Explain the term high cross.
6. Why did monks carve scenes from the Bible on high crosses?

✓ I can describe the different types of art produced by monks in Early Christian Ireland.

⬅ TIME TO GO BACK ◀▶ I CAN MOVE FORWARD ➡

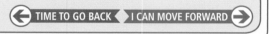

# WORKING WITH THE EVIDENCE!

## Early Christian Irish art

Study this photograph of the Cathach of St Columba's Shrine (the cover that protects the Cathach manuscript). It was used as a protector by the O'Donnell clan when going into battle – 'an Cathach' means 'the battler'.

1. What type of source is this shrine?
2. When is the Cathach believed to date from? Can you remember without checking?
3. Describe what you can see on the shrine.
4. The manuscript has been damaged and is incomplete. Name a disadvantage/limitation of this for a historian.
5. Why did monks produce decorated manuscripts and metalwork such as this shrine?

42

# 4.3: The Impact of Irish Monks Abroad

**In this topic, you will learn about:**

➤ Irish monks spreading Christianity abroad

▶ The valley in Glendalough

After the fall of the Western Roman Empire, much of Europe went through a period of unrest and war known as **the Dark Ages** (from about AD 500 to 1000). These hard and savage times in Europe – and later, the new threat of Viking attacks at home – led to many monks travelling abroad to found monasteries throughout Europe. The Irish monks abroad produced manuscripts in the Irish style and worked to convert Europe to Christianity. This time is now known as **the 'Golden Age'** of Irish monasteries.

**St Columbanus** left a monastery in Bangor, Co. Down and went to Europe with a dozen companions, where he founded several monasteries, including **Luxeuil** in France and **Bobbio** in Italy. More examples of monasteries set up by Irish monks can be seen to the right. Another example is **St Colmcille**. He founded monasteries in Durrow and Derry in Ireland, and on Iona, an island off the Scottish coast. Iona is actually where **the Book of Kells** was made – it was simply found in Kells much later.

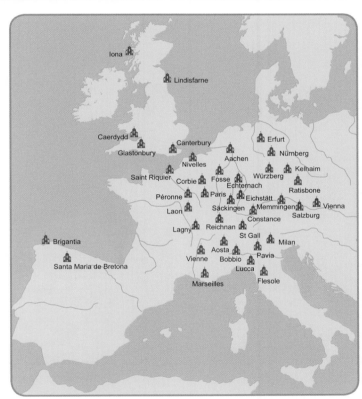

▲ Monasteries in Britain and Western Europe founded by Irish monks

## CHECKPOINT!

1.  Why do you think war followed the fall of the Roman Empire?
2.  Explain what is meant by the Dark Ages. 📖!
3.  What work did Irish monks do when they went abroad?
4.  Name three modern European countries where Irish monks founded monasteries.

 I understand how the Irish monks had an impact abroad.

◀ TIME TO GO BACK ❯ I CAN MOVE FORWARD ➤

**4** Culture and Society in Early Christian Ireland

# 4.4: The Arrival of the Vikings

## The Vikings

In eighth-century Scandinavia (modern-day Denmark, Sweden and Norway), the people we now know as Vikings were farmers and fishermen with superb shipbuilding and navigational skills. This allowed them to voyage to many countries, including Ireland. The Vikings' boats were called **longships** and were <u>capable of crossing stormy seas but still shallow enough to sail up rivers</u>.

**In this topic, you will learn about:**
- Viking raids
- Viking settlements

**DID YOU KNOW?**

This is a full-size reconstruction of a sunken Viking longship found in the Danish harbour of Roskilde. Using dendrochronology, it was found that the original was built in Dublin, using Glendalough oak trees felled in 1042! In 2007, a crew of 67 sailed the *Sea Stallion from Glendalough* 'home' to Dublin via Scotland. The voyage took almost seven weeks!

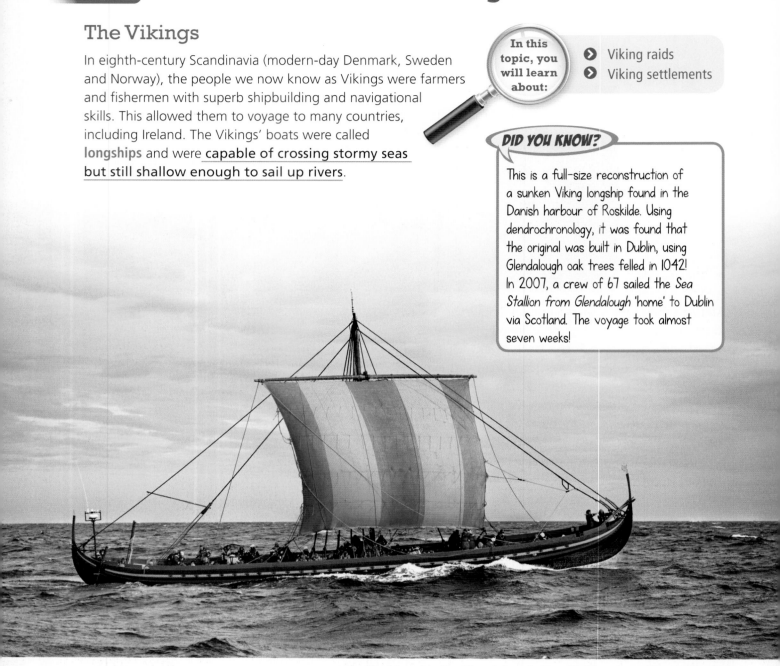

▲ *Havhingsten fra Glendalough (Sea Stallion from Glendalough)*

## Viking raids in Ireland

The first recorded Viking attacks on Ireland took place in AD 795 and focused on rich monasteries. Those on Lambay Island, Co. Dublin and Rathlin Island, Co. Antrim were both pillaged and burned that year. By the mid-ninth century, the Vikings were establishing **longphorts**, <u>camps by the water used as a base for raids</u>. Many longphorts were temporary, while others grew into important trading posts and eventually large towns. Wexford, Waterford, Limerick and Dublin were all once longphorts.

Early Christian Irish monasteries were easy targets for raiders. To the pagan Vikings, Christian monasteries were not sacred in any way – they were isolated places, full of treasures and with no warriors to defend them. In addition, the Vikings took captives to sell as slaves, as well as cattle and any food stores. As you know, round towers were very useful in Irish monasteries for warning and protection in times of attack – but not just by Vikings. At this time, monasteries were often attacked by the native Irish as well!

## A Viking settlement in Ireland

Very important Viking remains and examples of beautiful craftsmanship were found in Dublin at Wood Quay, Christ Church and in the Temple Bar area. At Wood Quay, the remains of about 200 houses from the tenth and eleventh centuries were uncovered, giving us a wealth of information about Viking life.

The houses were rectangular and their **thatched roofs** (of barley straw) were supported by posts inside the house. The walls were **wattle and daub**, a woven mesh plastered with a mixture of mud, dung, sand and straw. Once dry, it was quite strong and helped to insulate a house. Inside, **hearths** (for a fire) and benches were found, and also evidence of **workshops**. Streets and **pathways** were surfaced with gravel, stones, wattle mats or split logs. Back yards were divided by posts and wattle **fences**. Even toilet areas and **rubbish pits** were identified! Some amazing artefacts such as glass beads, necklaces and brooches were found there.

Underneath Dublin's streets lay the archaeological footprint of many generations who lived in the bustling international port known to the Vikings as **Dyfflin**.

Go to page 24 of your *Sources and Skills Book* for more on Wood Quay.

**DID YOU KNOW?**

The Wood Quay Viking site was discovered when Dublin City Council was starting to build its new offices. Many people were outraged that the building was going ahead when the site was not fully excavated. This led to 20,000 people taking to Dublin's streets on 23 September 1978 in the famous 'Save Wood Quay' protest march.

## CHECKPOINT!

1. Explain the terms longphort and longship.
2. When did the Vikings arrive in Ireland?
3. List two examples of Viking sites in Dublin.
4. Name three things found in Wood Quay by archaeologists.
5. What does the archaeological evidence tell us about how the Vikings impacted on Ireland?

✓ I understand the impact that the arrival of the Vikings had on Ireland.

TIME TO GO BACK ◀ ▶ I CAN MOVE FORWARD ➡

**4 Culture and Society in Early Christian Ireland**

 **SUMMARY**

In this chapter, we have learned that:

- Early Christian Ireland is the period when Christianity first came to Ireland.
- A bishop named Palladius was sent to Ireland in AD 431 to spread Christianity.
- The most famous bishop to travel to Ireland was St Patrick. He is believed to have been in Ireland between 432 and 461.
- From the sixth century on, many monasteries were built in Ireland. The first monastery, named Inis Mór, was founded by St Enda. The first convent was founded by St Brigid at Kildare.
- Other examples of monasteries include Clonard, Kells, Clonmacnoise, Glendalough, Clonfert and Sceilg Mhicíl.
- Some monastery buildings were: beehive huts, an oratory, a refectory, a scriptorium and a round tower.
- Art created by the monks included manuscripts, metalwork and stone high crosses.
- The Vikings began to raid and settle in Ireland in the eighth century.
- Amazing evidence giving insight into their lives in Dublin was found at Wood Quay.
- Many Irish monks went abroad to save or spread Christianity.

### Reflecting on... Early Christian Ireland

The arrival of Christianity to the island of Ireland is historically significant. Irish monasteries became centres of learning. Christianity helped to spread reading and writing in Ireland. Great works of art were also created by Irish monks. Christianity therefore contributed to the culture and society of Early Christian Ireland.

 **Understanding History**

1. How did Christianity arrive in Ireland?
2. What was life in a monastery like? Give five pieces of information.
3. Give two examples of each of the following: manuscripts, metalwork and stone crosses.
4. What was the impact of the arrival of the Vikings?
5. What was the effect of Irish monks travelling abroad?
6. With a partner, take turns to explain at least five terms each from the box below.

| Pagan | Monastery | Round tower | Chalice | Longship |
|-------|-----------|-------------|---------|----------|
| Druid | Beehive hut | Oratory | Manuscript | Longphort |
| Monk | Refectory | Scriptorium | High cross | Wattle and daub |

 **Exploring History**

1. Write a short paragraph about each of the following types of art produced by Irish monks: manuscripts, metalwork, stone crosses.

**2.** Look at the following source, an extract from St Columbanus's writing 'The Rule of the Monks':

*The food of the monks should be poor and confined to the evening; let it be such as to avoid gorging, and their drink such as to avoid drunkenness, so that it may sustain them but do them no harm: vegetables, beans, flour mixed with water, along with a small loaf of bread, lest the stomach be strained and the mind stifled. For those who seek eternal rewards should only take account of a thing's usefulness and use. Use of life must be kept under control, just as work must be kept under control. This is true discretion, so that the possibility of spiritual progress may be maintained with an abstinence that scourges the flesh. For if abstinence goes too far, it will be a vice, not a virtue. A virtue tolerates and embraces many material things. Therefore we must fast daily, just as we must feed daily. While we must eat daily, we must regale the body rather poorly and sparingly. The reason we must eat daily is because we must advance daily, pray daily, toil daily, and read daily.*

(a) What kind of source is this?

(b) What can we learn about the lives of monks from this source? List three pieces of information.

(c) List one useful thing about this source, and one limitation/negative thing about this source.

(d) What is St Columbanus famous for?

| **KEY TERMS** | | |
|---|---|---|
| | **Pagan** | someone who worships various gods, often with a focus on nature or the earth |
| | **Druid** | a spiritual figure similar to a priest in pre-Christian Celtic Ireland |
| | **Monastery** | a closed religious community living by the rules of an order |
| | **Monk** | a man dedicated to a religious order and to life in a monastery |
| | **Beehive hut** | an early Christian stone hut, shaped like a beehive, where monks slept |
| | **Oratory** | where the monks attended Mass or prayed |
| | **Scriptorium** | a room where manuscripts were copied by hand and illustrated |
| | **Manuscript** | a book written by hand, often in Latin, on sheepskin parchment or vellum (calfskin) |
| | **Refectory** | the hall where the monks ate their meals |
| | **Round tower** | a bell tower and safe place for people (and treasures) if the monastery came under attack |
| | **High cross** | a free-standing stone cross, usually with elaborate carvings showing biblical scenes |
| | **Longship** | a Viking boat, capable of crossing stormy seas but still shallow enough to sail up rivers |
| | **Longphort** | a Viking camp by the water, used as a base for raids |

 Go to page 17 of your *Sources and Skills Book* for more exercises.

 Go to page 6 of your *Research Portfolio* for a task based on this chapter.

4 Culture and Society in Early Christian Ireland

| Iron Age Europe | Ancient Rome | Early Christian Ireland |
|---|---|---|
| c. 1,200–1 BC | 753 BC–AD 476 | c. AD 400–800 |

Rome was one of the greatest powers in the Ancient World. It grew from a collection of small villages on the river Tiber in Italy to control an empire that included Italy, Spain, France, North Africa, Greece, the Middle East, most of Britain and parts of Germany.

The Roman Empire lasted for nearly a thousand years and it has had a huge and enduring influence on the world we live in today.

# WORKING WITH THE EVIDENCE!

## Remnants of Ancient Rome

| Type of source | Category | Example | |
|---|---|---|---|
| Primary | Written | Histories, plays and stories by Romans such as Julius Caesar, Pliny and Virgil | |
| Visual | Visual | Remains of Roman art: statues, wall paintings and mosaics | |
| Physical | Tactile | The ruins of many buildings and everyday artefacts (such as coins, weapons, tools and toys) have survived | |
| | | The Roman town of Pompeii was buried by the eruption of Mount Vesuvius in AD 79. The volcanic ash preserved the city just as it was and archaeologists have been excavating it since 1748 | |

▲ Pompeii's streets today

▲ An intact mosaic uncovered in Pompeii. It reads: 'Beware of the dog'.

# 5.1: Rome's History

In this topic, you will learn about:
- The history of the Roman Empire
- Roman towns

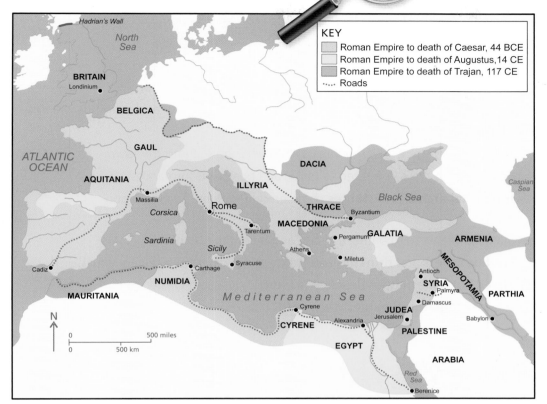

**KEY**
- Roman Empire to death of Caesar, 44 BCE
- Roman Empire to death of Augustus, 14 CE
- Roman Empire to death of Trajan, 117 CE
- ······ Roads

▲ The Roman Empire in the second century AD, showing its growth over time

## The history of the Roman Empire

The Ancient Romans believed that the Trojan prince **Aeneas** escaped his city's destruction by the Greeks at the end of the mythical **Trojan War**. He then came to Italy and Rome was founded by his descendants, the twin brothers **Romulus and Remus**, in 753 BC. Until 509 BC, the city was ruled by kings. They were expelled and the city declared a **republic** (when the wealthy elite in the Senate ruled in the name of the people). The Roman Republic managed to conquer all of Italy by the 270s BC and then expanded to control North Africa, Greece and Spain by 140 BC.

The republic collapsed in the 40s BC and was replaced by the empire, under the first emperor, **Augustus**. By AD 100, Rome controlled all of Europe around the Mediterranean Sea, along the Rhine and Danube rivers and up to **Hadrian's Wall** in northern Britain. Rome became rich from its conquests and founded towns and cities all over its empire. From the second century AD onwards, Germanic tribes from across the Rhine began attacking the empire and eventually, the last emperor was forced from the throne in 476 and the empire fell.

**DID YOU KNOW?**

The Romans never invaded Ireland, but Roman coins have been found at sites on the east coast, suggesting that there was trade with parts of the empire.

## CHECKPOINT!

1. Name three sources of evidence on Ancient Rome.
2. Who did the Romans believe founded their city?
3. Look at the map above and name five modern countries which were once ruled by Rome.
4. Why do you think the Romans never settled in Ireland?

 I can briefly describe the history of Rome.

 TIME TO GO BACK ◀ ▶ I CAN MOVE FORWARD ➡

**5 An Ancient Civilisation: Rome**

# Roman towns

As their empire expanded into Europe, the Romans controlled each local area from towns they founded. Romans lived here with the native peoples, many of whom became **citizens** (people who had rights under Roman law) of the empire. Most Roman towns were designed in a similar way and shared many of the same features.

- Towns had **walls** for defence.
- Streets were laid out in a **grid system**; they met at right angles to form rectangular blocks.
- The **forum**, a large town square, was the centre of business, political activity and religious worship.
- The gods were worshipped in **temples**.
- **Aqueducts** brought fresh water from nearby mountains and rivers straight into the town.
- People went to the **theatre** to see plays and listen to music and poetry performances.
- Monuments such as **triumphal arches** and **statues** commemorated Rome's victories and history.
- **Public baths** were where people went to bathe, exercise and meet their friends.
- Many towns also had **public toilets** and **drinking fountains** using water from the aqueduct.
- Roman **streets** were paved but quite dirty, as people threw their household waste there.
- The **amphitheatre** is where gladiatorial games were held.

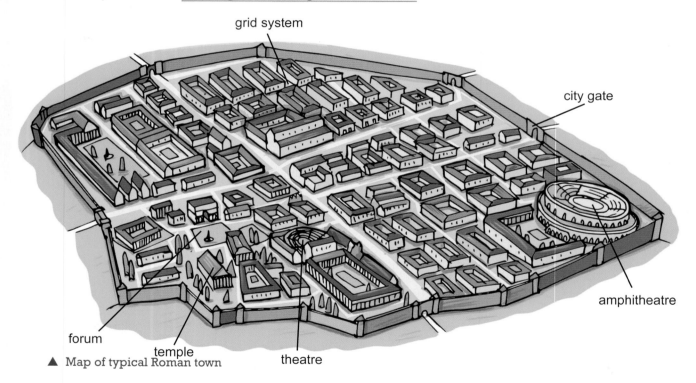

grid system

city gate

amphitheatre

forum

temple

theatre

▲ Map of typical Roman town

## CHECKPOINT!

1. What system was used to lay out Roman towns?
2. What was the role of the forum in a Roman town?
3. Name three buildings that were used for leisure activities.
4. How was life in a Roman town (a) similar and (b) different to our lives today?

 I understand the layout and features of a typical Roman town.  ← TIME TO GO BACK  ▸ I CAN MOVE FORWARD →

# 5.2: Daily Life in Rome

In this topic, you will learn about:

- ❯ The people of Ancient Rome
- ❯ Roman homes
- ❯ Slaves in Rome
- ❯ Roman education
- ❯ Marriage in Ancient Rome

## The people of Ancient Rome

| Patricians | Plebeians |
|---|---|
|  |  |
| The **patricians** were the wealthy noble families who ruled Rome. They had huge estates and hundreds of slaves. They controlled the Roman government and army. | The **plebeians** were the poor, who made up the vast majority of the population. They farmed, worked in trades and served in the army. |
| Patricians served in the Senate, were military generals or governors of Rome's provinces. | They were given a **dole** payment of free grain so that they would support the rule of the patricians. |
| Men wore a **toga** (a long white robe draped over the shoulder and down to the feet), and women wore a **stola** (a long dress). | Plebeian men wore a **tunic** to their knees and women wore a plain stola. |
| | Some plebeians became quite wealthy through trade and business and were known as **equites**. They had money but no political power. |
| A patrician house in a town was called a **domus** and in the countryside was a **villa**. | Most plebeians lived in apartment blocks called **insulae**. |
| *Women, both patrician and plebeian, were citizens but unable to vote or take part in public life.* | |

**5** An Ancient Civilisation: Rome

# A patrician domus

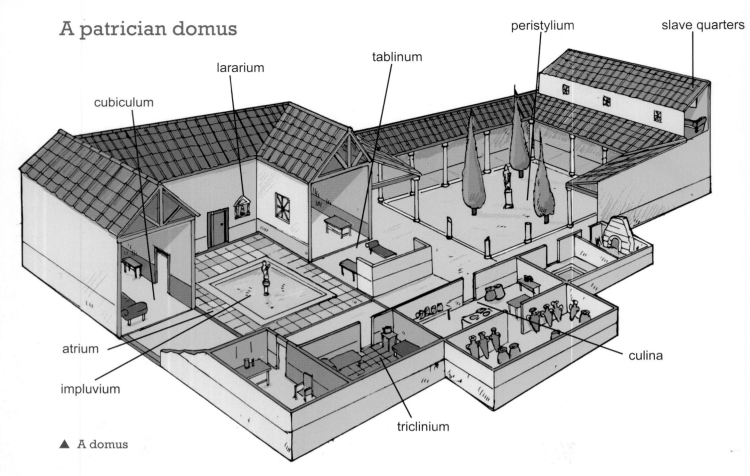

cubiculum

lararium

tablinum

peristylium

slave quarters

atrium

impluvium

culina

triclinium

▲ A domus

A patrician family lived in a large detached house called a domus. It had a central courtyard called the **atrium** where guests were met and which had a pool called an **impluvium** to collect rainwater and a shrine to the family gods (the **lararium**). Other rooms led off this: the bedrooms (**cubiculum**), the kitchen (**culina**), the study (**tablinum**) and the dining-room (**triclinium**). Upstairs were the **slave quarters** and outside was a walled garden (**peristylium**). The walls were decorated with paintings and the floors with **mosaics**, pictures made from small pieces of stone, glass or tile. The houses of the richest patricians also had running water and underfloor heating. A domus had small windows and was usually quite dark inside, with the atrium and oil lamps providing light.

▼ An insulae

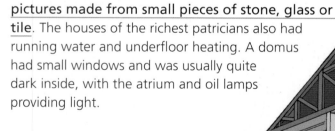

# A plebeian insulae

The plebeians lived in apartment blocks called insulae. In Rome, these were usually five storeys high. The ground floor had **shops** or workshops that opened to the street. Above them were apartments. The higher you went, the smaller the apartments became. Those at the top were made of wood and often entire families had to share a single room. The poorest

Romans lived on these higher floors. There was **no running water** and rubbish was thrown into the streets below. There was a constant **danger of fire** from wood-burning stoves for cooking. Fire could spread quickly through the wooden structures.

## CHECKPOINT!

1. Explain the following terms: patrician; plebeian; toga; stola; domus; insulae.
2. What are the most important differences between a domus and an insulae?
3. Describe a domus house.
4. Describe an insulae apartment block.
5. Why was there a risk of fire in the insulae?

✔ I understand the differences between patricians and plebeians and can describe Roman homes. ← TIME TO GO BACK ◆ I CAN MOVE FORWARD →

## Slaves

Slavery was an everyday feature of Roman life. By law, slaves were the property of their masters. In Rome itself there were over **300,000** slaves, who came from a number of different sources:

- Any **prisoners of war** became slaves.
- The **children of slaves** were automatically slaves themselves.
- People captured by pirates or bandits while travelling were often sold as slaves.
- Parents in debt sometimes sold their own children into slavery.

Thousands of slaves worked on Rome's **public building projects** such as aqueducts. Most patricians would have owned several dozen. In a domus, the slaves did the **cooking**, **cleaning** and other manual labour. Others worked on huge farms or in mines, where they were treated harshly and often **worked to death**. A runaway slave was branded with his master's initials. These cruel conditions led to some rebellions – the most famous was led by the gladiator **Spartacus** in 71 BC.

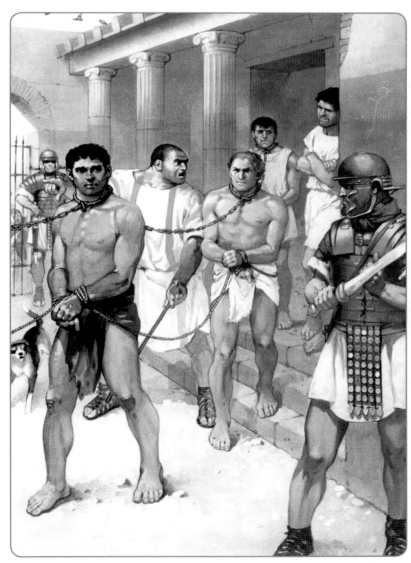

▲ Slaves being sold

**Well-educated slaves**, often Greeks, were highly valued and were treated well. They were usually employed as **teachers**, **secretaries** and **doctors** and were sometimes given their freedom after many years of service to their master. This was called **manumission**.

## Women and marriage

Roman girls usually married by the age of 14 or 15. Marriages were to benefit the families involved, and the girl had little or no say in the man her father chose; however, divorce was legal. The <u>wedding ceremony</u> (**conferratio**) was held at the bride's house. A wife was expected to run her husband's home, make his clothes, supervise slaves, bear a son and oversee the rearing of children. Many women died in childbirth, so men often married several times and a girl could easily end up marrying a man her father's age.

## Education in Ancient Rome

Plebeian children received a basic education at home and then began working with their parents. A wealthy Roman's education had three different stages:

▼ An abacus and a wax tablet with stylus

1.  Boys (and some girls) from the age of seven to twelve attended a **ludus**, where they learned reading, writing and arithmetic.

2.  At 12, boys could attend a **grammaticus**, where they learned history, grammar and geometry and studied literature by Greek and Roman writers such as Homer and Virgil. Girls of the same age were at home being taught by their mothers how to spin, weave and run a household.

3.  At 16, a patrician boy was taught **oratory** (<u>the art of public speaking</u>) by a **rhetor** to prepare him for a career in public life.

Discipline was very strict in Roman schools and students would be beaten for making mistakes. They wrote with a pointed wooden **stylus** on a **wax tablet** which could later be melted down and reused. They used an **abacus** to learn arithmetic.

**DID YOU KNOW?**

Roman schoolboys were accompanied to school by a slave whose job it was to sit at the back of the class and beat him if he made mistakes or was not paying attention!

 Go to page 30 of your *Sources and Skills Book* for an exercise on a Roman school day.

## CHECKPOINT!

1.  What were the Romans' main sources of slaves?
2.  What sorts of work did slaves do?
3.  What did Roman children learn at (a) a ludus; (b) a grammaticus and (c) with a rhetor?
4.  How was education different for boys and girls?
5.  Why were marriages arranged in Ancient Rome?
6.  Explain the following terms: manumission; conferratio; rhetor; stylus. 📖❗

✔ I can talk about slavery, marriage and education in Ancient Rome.  ⬅ TIME TO GO BACK ❯ I CAN MOVE FORWARD ➡

# 5.3: Entertainment in Rome

Public entertainment was very important in Rome. Along with the grain dole, public entertainment was the main way that ambitious politicians and emperors ensured they had the support of the people.

**In this topic, you will learn about:**

❯ The public baths
❯ Chariot racing in the Circus Maximus
❯ Roman theatre
❯ Gladiatorial games in the amphitheatres

## The public baths

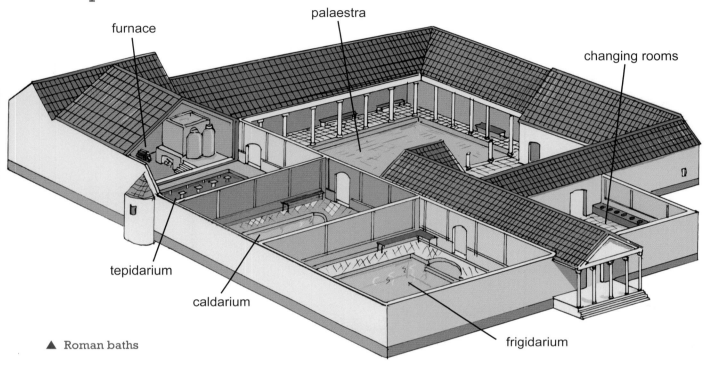

▲ Roman baths

Labels: furnace · palaestra · changing rooms · tepidarium · caldarium · frigidarium

Every Roman town had public baths. Bathing was very important to the Romans. Most homes did not have running water, so it was the easiest way to stay clean. The baths were also a social place where people **met friends, did business and exchanged news**. The largest baths in every town were free to use for citizens.

A typical visit to the baths would involve each of the three main rooms: the **tepidarium** (the medium heat room); the **caldarium** (the hot room, much like a sauna); and the **frigidarium** (the cold water bath). Visitors rubbed **oil** into their skin, worked up a sweat in the caldarium and then used a wooden **strigil** to scrape their skin, removing dry skin and dirt along with the oil. There was also an exercise yard (the **palaestra**) and rooms where a massage or food was available. Most baths had separate areas for men and women, though smaller ones just had separate bathing times.

▶ An oil flask and strigil

## Chariot racing at the Circus Maximus

Rome's chariot racing arena, the Circus Maximus, was 500 m long and could hold up to 250,000 people. There was no seating division based on social status or gender. Four teams (red, white, blue and green) would race in **chariots** pulled by teams of two, four or six horses. They raced around the track seven times at incredibly **high speeds**. It was a very dangerous sport and there were often crashes that killed men and horses. **Gambling** on the races was a popular activity.

▲ Painting of a chariot race

▶ The Circus Maximus today

## Roman theatre

Most Roman towns also had a theatre. These were large **semi-circular** buildings with stone seats for the audience, who were not separated by gender or social status. **Tragedy** and **comedy** plays were both very popular with the Romans, with subjects ranging from stories about the gods and heroes to everyday life events. The actors were all male and wore **masks** while performing.

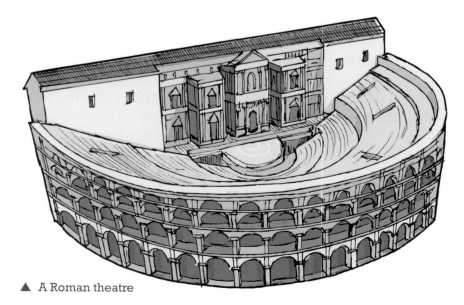

▲ A Roman theatre

## Amphitheatres and gladiators

The most popular entertainers were **gladiators**. They <u>fought in oval arenas called **amphitheatres** in nearly every major Roman city</u>. The most famous amphitheatre was **the Colosseum** in Rome, which could hold over 50,000 spectators in tiered seating. It even had a canopy to protect people from the sun. Seating was strictly arranged by social status: closest to the action were male patricians, behind them male plebeians, then male foreigners, then at the very back women and slaves.

Gladiators were mostly former soldiers who were captured in battle and sold as slaves. Gladiators were often dressed in very different styles. They trained in special schools and were treated like modern sports stars by ordinary Romans. Each gladiator would be proficient in using one set of weapons. For example, a **retiarius** would use a trident and a net or a **murmillo** would use a soldier's shield and sword. Gladiators **rarely fought to the death** because they were so expensive to buy, train and feed that their owners wanted a longer return on their investment. Instead, most fights ended when one of the fighters was too badly injured to continue.

Amphitheatres also featured fights between people and exotic **wild animals** (such as lions), the **executions** of criminals and myths acted out for the crowd. The Colosseum in Rome could even be flooded for mock sea battles.

▲ A painting of a victorious gladiator in the arena

▲ The ruins of the Colosseum today

## CHECKPOINT!

1. Why was public entertainment so important in Rome?
2. Why did people use public baths in Rome?
3. Explain the following terms: tepidarium; caldarium; frigidarium; strigil; palaestra. 📖
4. Look at the illustration of the Circus Maximus on page 56. Describe it.
5. Why was chariot racing so dangerous?
6. Describe a Roman theatre.
7. Why do you think actors wore masks in Roman plays?
8. Describe the Colosseum in Rome.
9. Where did most gladiators come from?
10. Why was it rare for gladiators to fight to the death?
11. Other than gladiatorial contests, what events were held in amphitheatres?

 I can describe the main types of public entertainment in Ancient Rome. ⬅ TIME TO GO BACK ◆ I CAN MOVE FORWARD ➡

**5**

**An Ancient Civilisation: Rome**

# 5.4: The Roman Army

❯ The training and life of a soldier
❯ Roman weapons and equipment

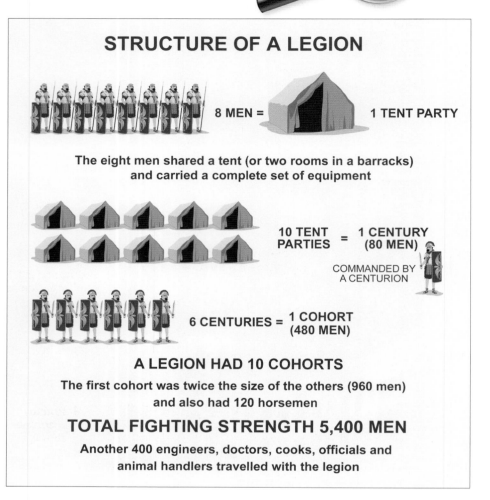

**STRUCTURE OF A LEGION**

8 MEN = 1 TENT PARTY

The eight men shared a tent (or two rooms in a barracks) and carried a complete set of equipment

10 TENT PARTIES = 1 CENTURY (80 MEN)

COMMANDED BY A CENTURION

6 CENTURIES = 1 COHORT (480 MEN)

**A LEGION HAD 10 COHORTS**

The first cohort was twice the size of the others (960 men) and also had 120 horsemen

**TOTAL FIGHTING STRENGTH 5,400 MEN**

Another 400 engineers, doctors, cooks, officials and animal handlers travelled with the legion

The army was central to Roman life – it allowed Rome to conquer and keep control over its vast empire. Ambitious generals could also use the army to gain political power. For ordinary Romans, being a soldier was a really good profession to have. Individual Roman foot soldiers were called **legionaries**, as together they made up a **legion**.

## The life of a Roman soldier

A soldier enlisted at the age of 20 and served for **25 years**. At the end of his service he received a final payment and a plot of **land to farm** somewhere in the empire. This allowed Rome to settle loyal soldiers throughout the empire.

Soldiers were trained to fight with various weapons, on foot and on horseback. They trained with wooden weapons twice the weight of ordinary weapons. Soldiers marched up to 30 km every day, carrying over 35 kg of weapons and equipment. At their destination, they then had to build a camp. There, soldiers practised all the time to ensure they were always battle-ready. When not on campaign, soldiers were often employed to build public works such as aqueducts, bridges, defensive walls and roads.

Soldiers could serve in the **infantry** (foot soldiers), the **cavalry** (on horseback) or the **artillery** (projectile weapons). Roman engineers developed catapults, ballistas and other machines of war to throw boulders, urns of burning pitch or huge crossbow bolts over great distances at an enemy army or city.

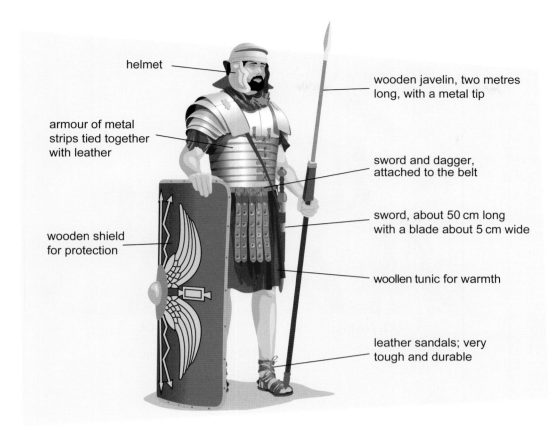

helmet

armour of metal strips tied together with leather

wooden shield for protection

wooden javelin, two metres long, with a metal tip

sword and dagger, attached to the belt

sword, about 50 cm long with a blade about 5 cm wide

woollen tunic for warmth

leather sandals; very tough and durable

◀ Legionary in full battle readiness

**5**

**An Ancient Civilisation: Rome**

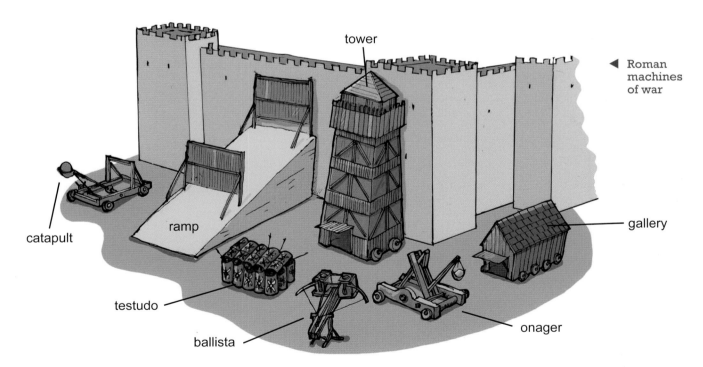

tower

ramp

catapult

testudo

ballista

gallery

onager

◀ Roman machines of war

## CHECKPOINT!

1. Why did Rome need a large professional army?

2. For how long did a soldier serve?

3. What weapons did a Roman soldier use?

4. Why do you think they trained with weapons twice the weight of normal weapons?

5. Describe the structure of a legion.

6. Write a paragraph on the daily life of a soldier.

 I can describe the life of a Roman soldier and Roman weapons and equipment.

 ← TIME TO GO BACK ◆ I CAN MOVE FORWARD →

# 5.5: Religion in Rome

## The Roman gods and goddesses

In this topic, you will learn about:
- Roman gods and goddesses
- Roman funerals
- The growth of Christianity

Religion was very important to the Ancient Romans. They were **polytheists**, which means they believed in many different gods. Most of the Roman gods and goddesses had come from Greek beliefs; their names were often different but their myths, functions and personalities stayed the same.

| ROMAN NAME | GREEK NAME | GOD OF... |
|---|---|---|
| Jupiter (King of the Gods) | Zeus | The sky, thunder and lightning |
| Juno (Queen of the Gods) | Hera | Marriage |
| Neptune | Poseidon | The sea |
| Pluto | Hades | The underworld |
| Vesta | Hestia | Hearth and home |
| Minerva | Athena | Wisdom |
| Diana | Artemis | The moon and hunting |
| Apollo | Apollo | The sun, music, prophecy and healing |
| Venus | Aphrodite | Love |
| Vulcan | Hephaestus | Metalwork |
| Mars | Ares | War |
| Ceres | Demeter | The harvest and farming |
| Bacchus | Dionysus | Wine and drama |
| Mercury | Hermes | Messenger of the gods |

**COLLABORATE:** Work together to answer the following questions:

1. Why do you think the Romans had so many different gods?
2. What can we learn about the Romans from this list of their gods?
3. Make a list of who you think would have prayed to each of these gods.

The Romans believed that the gods controlled what happened to them in their daily lives. When a Roman wanted the help or protection of a particular god or goddess, they would make offerings to them. Every morning, they would pray at the family shrine, the **lararium**. They would also make **offerings** of money, food or animals for sacrifice at temples. The **Pantheon** in Rome is the best surviving example of a Roman temple.

▲ The Pantheon

## Funerals

Many children died young, women often died in childbirth and people could die unexpectedly from illness or injury, so Roman funerals were frequent and important ceremonies. Romans believed that when a person died, they had to cross the **River Styx** into the **Underworld**. A coin was placed in the mouth of the deceased to pay **Charon**, the ferryman of the dead.

◀ A patrician funeral

A patrician's body was dressed finely and carried through the city on a litter. The family hired musicians and professional mourners to walk behind the dead person, crying loudly and reciting the person's achievements. A very rich or powerful family might even organise funeral games. A plebeian's body was also carried in procession outside the town walls, where all burials took place.

There, the body was **cremated** and the ashes placed in an urn. A patrician's urn was placed in the family vault and a plebeian's urn was buried in a simple grave with a headstone. To ensure they were remembered, patricians often had sculptures made of themselves for display in the family domus.

## The growth of Christianity

After the death of Jesus around AD 33, Christianity spread through the Roman Empire. Christian communities were always small groups within cities in the empire. The Christians believed in only one god (this made them **monotheists**) and they rejected the state gods of Rome. While the Romans were generally very tolerant of other religions, Christians refused to participate in any ceremonies to do with the gods of Rome. This led to their persecution (sometimes even execution) by the Roman authorities.

In AD 313, the **Emperor Constantine** lifted the ban on Christianity in the empire, and he himself became a Christian on his death bed. Christianity then grew rapidly in popularity and at the end of the fourth century it became the official religion of the Roman Empire.

## CHECKPOINT!

1. Where did the Roman gods and goddesses come from?
2. Where and how did the Romans worship the gods?
3. Describe the funeral of a Roman patrician.
4. Why were Christians seen as a threat by the Roman empire?
5. Why is Constantine so important a figure in both Christian and Roman history?

 I understand the role of religion in Roman life.

 TIME TO GO BACK ◀ ▶ I CAN MOVE FORWARD ➡

**5 An Ancient Civilisation: Rome**

# 5.6: The Legacy of Rome

## Architecture

The Romans were great **engineers** and builders. Many of their innovations and techniques have been used in building ever since. They invented **concrete** to make their buildings more durable. They used rounded **arches and pillars** to hold up large ceilings and built huge domes on their temples. Many Roman buildings were so well built that they are still standing today, like the Pantheon in Rome. These techniques were copied in the Renaissance and still influence modern architecture.

## Christianity

The fact that the Roman Empire became Christian meant that the Catholic Church became the world's **most powerful religion** in the following centuries.

## Language

**Latin** was the language of the Roman Empire. It is not spoken today, but many modern European languages (French, Spanish, Italian and Romanian) are based on it. English is not related to Latin (it is a Germanic language) but almost a quarter of English words are directly influenced by Latin.

## Calendar

In 45 BC, Julius Caesar introduced a new calendar to replace the old Roman one, which was too inaccurate. His new **Julian calendar** had 365 days divided into 12 months and an extra day every four years. It was changed slightly by Pope Gregory XIII in 1582 and called the **Gregorian calendar**, but remains the basis for the calendar we use today.

 **COLLABORATE:** Work in groups to find out which names of the months come from Roman times and what they mean.

 **CHECKPOINT!**

1. What Roman inventions helped the development of architecture?
2. How did the Romans help the spread of Christianity?
3. What modern languages are descended from Latin?
4. What changes did Julius Caesar make to the calendar?

✓ I understand how the legacy of Rome has influenced our world today.

 ← TIME TO GO BACK ❬ ❭ I CAN MOVE FORWARD →

Go to page 27 of your *Sources and Skills Book* for an exercise on Roman architecture.

# SUMMARY

In this chapter, we have learned that:

- Rome rose from a cluster of small villages on the Tiber to control the entire Mediterranean world and most of Western Europe. It was the most powerful empire in the ancient world.

- Roman society was divided into patricians and plebeians. The patricians were the wealthy elite who ran the empire, lived in a domus and had many slaves. Their sons were well educated and their daughters married into other patrician families.

- Plebeians were the vast majority of the population. They were poorer, lived in insulae apartment blocks and worked for a living as craftsmen and soldiers.

- All Romans enjoyed a vast selection of public entertainments: public baths, chariot racing, theatre and gladiator fights. Gladiators were slaves who fought in amphitheatres.

- The Roman army was the most successful fighting force in the ancient world. Men signed up for 25 years of service and were highly trained. They fought with a vast array of weapons and could march long distances in a short time.

- The Romans worshipped many different gods and goddesses. Their religion dominated every aspect of their lives. They offered sacrifices to the gods and held elaborate funerals. Christianity was initially persecuted by the Roman Empire but became the official religion of the empire in the late fourth century.

- Rome's legacy has lived on in European civilisation and beyond through architecture, Christianity, language, the calendar and more.

## Reflecting on... Ancient Rome

A foundation stone of Western society, Rome's achievements in engineering, warfare and culture are impressive to this day. The story of the growth and ultimate fall of Rome is often used to examine problems in modern society. However, we must remember that its success was built on conquest and slavery – it is an excellent example of the importance of seeing history 'warts and all'.

# Understanding History

1. How was Rome governed under (a) the republic and (b) the empire?
2. Describe a typical Roman town. What are the main buildings you would find there?
3. Describe the differences between the homes of a patrician and a plebeian.
4. What jobs did slaves do in Rome?
5. Describe (with the aid of a diagram or drawing) a venue for entertainment in Rome.
6. In what ways was entertainment in Rome (a) similar to and (b) different from public entertainment today?
7. How were Roman soldiers trained?
8. Why was the Roman army so successful?
9. What evidence is there that religion was important in the lives of Romans?
10. What change did Constantine introduce to the Roman Empire?

5 An Ancient Civilisation: Rome

**11.** Look at this picture of a Roman domus.

(a) Name the features listed A to H.

(b) Imagine you are trying to sell this domus in Ancient Rome. Write an ad for it. Describe the house, its features and why someone would want to buy it.

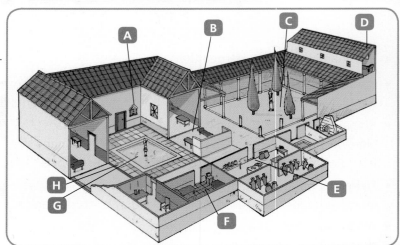

 **Exploring History**

**1.** Write about the life of a young person living in Rome under the following headings:

- Home
- Education
- The baths
- Entertainment

**2.** Write about three ways Ancient Rome has influenced the world we live in.

**3.** Write an account of religion and funeral practices in Rome.

| KEY TERMS | | |
|---|---|---|
| | **Republic** | when the wealthy elite in the Senate ruled in the name of the people |
| | **Citizens** | people who had rights under Roman law |
| | **Forum** | large town square that was the centre of business, political administration and religious worship |
| | **Amphitheatre** | where gladiatorial games were held |
| | **Patricians** | the wealthy noble families who ruled Rome |
| | **Toga** | a long white robe draped over the shoulder and down to the feet |
| | **Stola** | a long dress |
| | **Domus** | the large house of a patrician |
| | **Plebeians** | the poor, who made up the vast majority of the Roman population |
| | **Dole** | a payment of free grain given to the plebeians |
| | **Insulae** | the apartment blocks lived in by plebeians |
| | **Mosaic** | picture made from small pieces of stone, glass or tile |
| | **Manumission** | the freeing of a slave by their master after many years of service |
| | **Conferratio** | Roman wedding ceremony |
| | **Oratory** | the art of public speaking |
| | **Gladiators** | slaves who fought in amphitheatres for the entertainment of the crowd |
| | **Legionaries** | Roman foot soldiers |
| | **Polytheists** | people who believed in many different gods |
| | **Monotheists** | people who believed in only one god |

 Go to page 25 of your *Sources and Skills Book* for more exercises.

 Go to page 7 of your *Research Portfolio* for a task based on this chapter.

# Life and Death in Medieval Times

**LO: 3.6**

| Early Christian Ireland | The Middle Ages | The Renaissance |
|---|---|---|
| c. 400–800 | c. 500–1500 | c. 1350–1650 |

The Middle Ages was the period of European history from about AD 500 to around 1500. It is called the 'middle' ages because it refers to the period between the end of the Roman Empire in the fifth century and the start of the Renaissance in the fifteenth century (see chapter 8). It is also called the **medieval** period. It was a time when there was widespread war and violence. Life was difficult, especially for people at the lower levels of society.

## WORKING WITH THE EVIDENCE!

### The Middle Ages

| Type of source | Category | Example |
|---|---|---|
| Primary | Tactile | Ruins of castles, churches and monasteries |
| Primary or secondary | Written | Books and letters |
| Secondary | Visual | Works of art, such as the Bayeux Tapestry |

▲ Conwy Castle

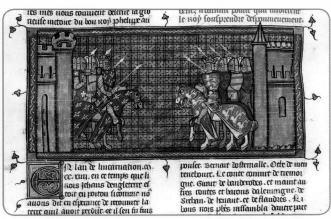

▲ Grandes Chroniques de France, an illustrated history from the fourteenth century

# 6.1: The Feudal System

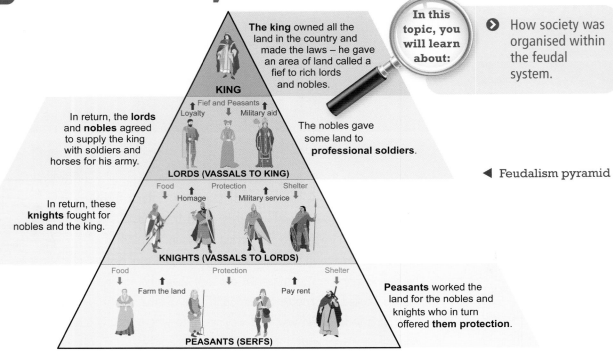

The king owned all the land in the country and made the laws – he gave an area of land called a fief to rich lords and nobles.

**KING**

Fief and Peasants
Loyalty ↑ ↓ Military aid

In return, the **lords** and **nobles** agreed to supply the king with soldiers and horses for his army.

The nobles gave some land to **professional soldiers.**

**LORDS (VASSALS TO KING)**

◀ Feudalism pyramid

Food ↓ | Protection ↑ | Shelter ↓
Homage ↑ | Military service ↓

In return, these **knights** fought for nobles and the king.

**KNIGHTS (VASSALS TO LORDS)**

Food ↓ | Protection ↓ | Shelter ↓
Farm the land ↑ | Pay rent ↑

**Peasants** worked the land for the nobles and knights who in turn offered **them protection**.

**PEASANTS (SERFS)**

In this topic, you will learn about:

❯ How society was organised within the feudal system.

After the fall of Rome, there was no single strong ruler in Europe. Warfare was constant and people looked to local leaders for protection. The stronger rulers came to control more and more territory and became kings. They organised society under the feudal system.

**Feudalism** was the system of land ownership where <u>rulers divided land among their followers in return for loyalty and taxes</u>. These followers were called nobles or **vassals** and were given land (called a **fief**). They swore an **oath of fealty** to the king, promising to fight for him, provide him with troops and pay him taxes. Those nobles then gave some of their land to knights, who swore to be loyal and fight for them. Knights then looked after the peasants (**serfs** and **freemen**) on this land.

## CHECKPOINT!

1. Explain the following terms: vassals; fief; oath of fealty. 📖

2. Explain, with the aid of a diagram, the feudal system.

✔ I can explain the feudal system.  ◀ TIME TO GO BACK ◆ I CAN MOVE FORWARD ➤

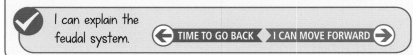

# WORKING WITH THE EVIDENCE!

## The Bayeux Tapestry

Look at the image of Norman soldiers on horseback and English soldiers on foot. List the different types of weapons and armour you can see. Which group do you think won the battle? Explain why.

## 6.2: Life in the Medieval Countryside

In this topic, you will learn about:
- ❯ Life in a medieval manor village
- ❯ Farming in the Middle Ages
- ❯ Peasants in the Middle Ages

### A medieval manor

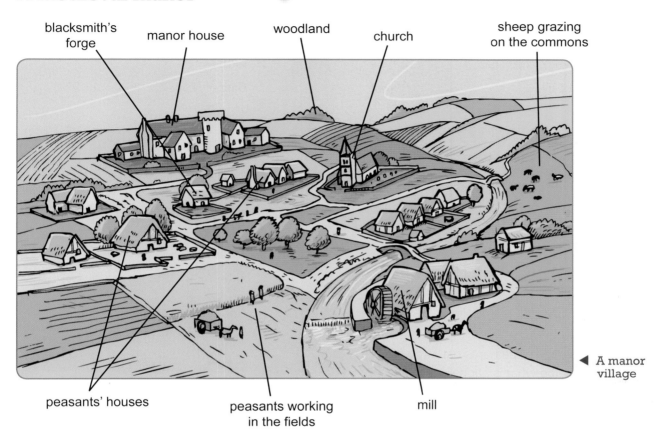

blacksmith's forge    manor house    woodland    church    sheep grazing on the commons

peasants' houses    peasants working in the fields    mill

◀ A manor village

The vast majority of people in the Middle Ages lived in the countryside. Most were **peasants** (people who worked on a lord's land) and lived in villages called **manors** that were owned by a lord or knight. Each manor was quite small, usually made up of about fifty houses for the peasants, as well as the **manor house** of the lord or knight and the **church** of the local priest.

A manor usually had a **mill** for grinding the wheat to make bread, a blacksmith's **forge** to make tools and weapons and a house for the **bailiff**, the man who ran the manor in the lord's absence. He was responsible for collecting taxes and keeping law and order in the village.

Most manors had **woodland** around them. The peasants could collect wood here to build their homes and make fires. However, they were strictly forbidden to hunt the animals in the forest and they would face very harsh punishments – such as losing a hand – if they were caught! Only the lord was allowed to hunt in the forests.

### Farming on the manor

Farming was the main occupation of the peasants on a medieval manor. They used the **open field system** of farming:

- The land for crops was divided into **three huge fields**. Each field was divided into long strips of land and tended by different families. Each family had strips in each of the three fields.

- They practised **crop rotation** – in other words, the crop planted in each field changed each year.

- In one field they planted wheat (to make bread), in the second they planted oats (for porridge) and barley (for beer) and the third field was left **fallow** – empty – for one year so that the soil could recover its nutrients and be fertile again the next year.

- A fourth large field called **the commons** was used for grazing the animals that belonged to the peasants.

|  | **Field 1** | **Field 2** | **Field 3** |
|---|---|---|---|
| **Year 1** | Wheat | Oats and barley | Fallow |
| **Year 2** | Oats and barley | Fallow | Wheat |
| **Year 3** | Fallow | Wheat | Oats and barley |

# WORKING WITH THE EVIDENCE!

## Working in the fields

This illustrated psalter was created for a Lord Luttrell about 1330. It was found again in 1794 and is a fascinating visual source on medieval manor life.

Look at these pictures of peasants hard at work in the fields. Describe what is happening in each picture.

In a small group, discuss the work they are doing, the tools being used and the clothes they are wearing. What do you think the person on the left in the bottom panel is doing?

▶ Luttrell Psalter triptych

# Peasants

## Freemen and serfs

There were two kinds of peasant in the Middle Ages: freemen and serfs. Freemen had to pay rent to the lord and pay a **tithe** (a tenth of their income to the local priest) but did not have to work the land for free. They could marry and leave the manor as they wished.

**DID YOU KNOW?**

The average life expectancy for a male child born in England in 1300 was 31 years. In 2000, it was 77. Why do you think it has changed so much?

Serfs, on the other hand, essentially belonged to their lord. They worked six days a week farming the lord's lands. In return they received a small plot of land to farm and build a house on. They could not leave the manor or marry without the lord's permission. They paid taxes to the lord and a tithe to the priest. If a serf escaped and stayed free for a year and a day, he became a freeman.

## How serfs lived

A serf's home was tiny – a single room with **wattle and daub walls**, an earthen floor and a thatched roof. Outside they grew vegetables and kept a few animals. Inside was cramped, dark and smoky from the fire. At night, the animals were kept inside for warmth and safety. Men wore tunics and leggings, while women wore long dresses with a head scarf. Their shoes were made from leather. All clothing was handmade, of wool or linen, and dyed using berry juice.

◀ An agricultural calendar from *c.*1306, showing the work done by serfs at various times of year

For food, a serf family had only what they could produce from their small plot. Their main diet consisted of **bread**, **cheese** and a vegetable and oat soup called **pottage**. They drank **ale** (a weak beer made from barley) because it was safer to drink than water. They ate meat very rarely, possibly only at Christmas and Easter.

A female serf looked after the home, cooked, made clothes and reared the children until they were old enough to work in the fields with their father. The only leisure time was on Sundays and the various saints' days. On these days, after Mass, there was singing and dancing, drinking and village games.

## CHECKPOINT

1. What crops were grown in the manor's fields and what was made from them?
2. The church and the manor house were usually the only stone buildings. Why do you think this was?
3. Explain the following terms: tithe; open field system; fallow; commons; bailiff. 📖
4. Name two differences between a serf and a freeman.
5. Describe a serf's house.
6. What were a peasant's clothes made from?
7. What different types of work were done by male and female serfs?
8. Describe leisure time for a serf.

 I can describe a medieval manor, how it was farmed and the life of a serf.

 ← TIME TO GO BACK ◀ ▶ I CAN MOVE FORWARD →

**6** Life and Death in Medieval Times

# 6.3: Life in a Medieval Castle

## Building castles

Nobles and lords lived in castles to protect themselves from attacks and as a base to run their lands from. When a lord was first given land by his king, or when he conquered new land, he had to build a castle very quickly, so he built a temporary castle called a **motte and bailey**. A motte was a small artificial hill with a wooden tower or **keep** at the top. Below this hill was a large enclosed area where the soldiers lived (the bailey), surrounded by high wooden fences and a **ditch or moat**. Once his control of an area was secured, a lord would build a permanent stone castle.

In this topic, you will learn about:
❯ Why castles were built
❯ Kinds of castles
❯ Castles and war
❯ The lord and lady of a castle

▼ Motte and bailey

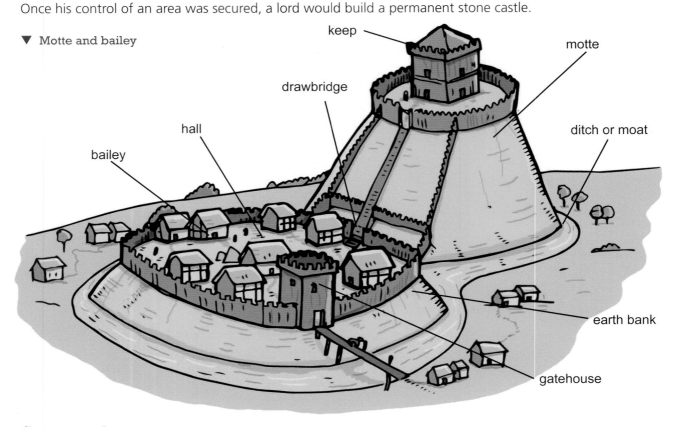

## *Stone castles*

Stone castles in the Middle Ages were huge fortifications. It took several hundred men working for several years to complete one. A typical castle had the following key parts:

- The **curtain walls** enclosed the castle and protected those inside.

- The **keep** was the main building inside the walls. It held the **lord's apartments**, the **great hall** and a **chapel**. The windows were narrow to keep in the heat and to make defence easier.

- Below the keep were the **dungeons**, used to keep stored food cool and to hold prisoners.

- **Battlements** ran along the top of the keep and the walls. Soldiers would patrol along them day and night. **Towers/turrets** were built into the walls at regular intervals, especially at corners.

- The enclosed area around the keep was called the **bailey**. Here the stables, workshops, kitchen, well for water and soldiers' lodgings were situated. If the castle was under attack, animals and people from the surrounding area could be brought inside for their protection.

- In the **gatehouse**, the **drawbridge** and the **portcullis** were found. The drawbridge could be raised and lowered to control entry to the castle. It was raised at night and if the castle was under attack. The portcullis was a metal grid which could be lowered over the gate if necessary.

- The castle was surrounded by a deep ditch filled with water called the **moat**.

▼ Stone castle

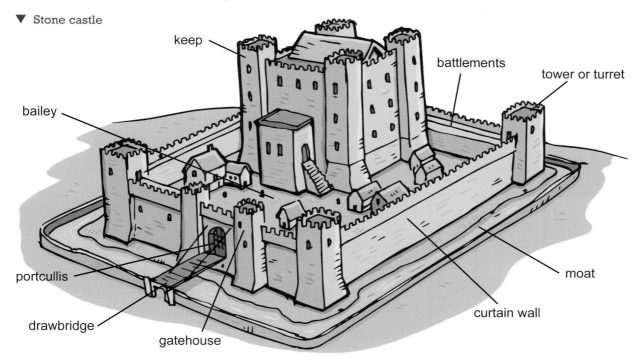

## Castles and war

Warfare was widespread during the Middle Ages. Castles were key to the defence of a lord's lands and a kingdom generally. Their high walls and well-armed soldiers and knights made them a difficult target. Even if an attacking army surrounded the castle and waited for surrender (a **siege**), the castle could hold out for a long time once it had enough **food stores** and a **well**. Defenders could fire arrows down from the walls, or pour boiling water or oil down on the attackers. Castles were often built on hills or beside rivers to add to their defences.

Laying siege to a castle could be difficult and time-consuming, so the attacking army used various means to try to breach the castle's walls, such as **catapults** and **siege towers**. Gunpowder was brought to Europe from China in the 1400s and the **cannon** was invented. This meant that a castle's walls could be easily and quickly destroyed and they were no longer key to warfare.

Go to page 37 of your *Sources and Skills Book* for an evidence task on medieval castles.

## CHECKPOINT!

1. Why were castles built in the Middle Ages?
2. Describe a motte and bailey castle.
3. What were the main defensive features of a castle?
4. Why were castles so difficult to capture?

 I can describe a medieval castle.

 ◀ TIME TO GO BACK ◀ ▶ I CAN MOVE FORWARD ▶

**6** Life and Death in Medieval Times

# Lords and ladies

A medieval lord was very powerful; he owned huge amounts of land and commanded many knights and soldiers. The lady of the castle usually married at a young age. Marriages were arranged by the two families, often to seal an alliance. A **dowry** (sum of money or land) was paid to the groom.

The lady's main duty was to bear children as **heirs**. The family lived upstairs in the keep, near the chapel and a warm sunny room called a **solar**. Here, the lady would weave, teach the children or play music. She also ran the household, instructing the servants, supervising the storage and preparation of food and acting for her husband when he was away. The lord's duties were to maintain order in his lands, act as a judge and train soldiers. In his leisure time, he went hunting or hawking and held **tournaments** (events for knights) featuring mock battles and jousting contests.

◀ A medieval lord and lady at feast

Feasts were held in the **great hall**, which had big fireplaces and tapestries on the walls. Beef, pork, mutton, duck, deer, pheasant or rabbit were served – either farm animals or what the lord caught while hunting. Without refrigeration, meat could not be kept fresh for long. People **salted, smoked or dried meat and fish** and used herbs and spices to vary the strong flavour. Spices were very expensive as they had to be transported from Asia. Forks were not yet used in Europe and instead of plates people often ate from large pieces of hard bread called trenchers. Musicians (**minstrels**) and comic performers (**jesters**) provided entertainment.

Men wore long tunics and trousers of fine wool or linen and women wore full-length dresses. Clothing that was embroidered or dyed in vivid colours showed off the wearer's wealth. The richest nobles wore silk brought from Asia.

## CHECKPOINT!

1. How were marriages arranged between nobles?
2. What was a solar?
3. What was the role of the lady of the castle?
4. How did the lord spend his time?
5. Describe a medieval feast.
6. Wealth and status were very important. Name two ways that a lord could display his wealth.

✔ I can describe the life of a lord or lady of a castle.

 ← TIME TO GO BACK ◆ I CAN MOVE FORWARD →

## 6.4: Soldiers in the Middle Ages

There were three main types of soldier in the Middle Ages:

- **Foot soldiers** made up the largest part of any medieval army. They fought with swords, daggers and spears and had shields and leather padded jackets for protection. They were peasants, who returned to the fields when the battle or war was over.

- **Archers** fought with a bow and arrow, or sometimes a longbow or crossbow. They wore little protective clothing.

- **Knights** were <u>minor nobles who fought on horseback and swore an oath of chivalry</u>. They wore full body armour (plate armour), chainmail, a shield and a helmet for protection and used lances, swords and maces in battle. There were only a few hundred knights in a medieval army.

  COLLABORATE:

Imagine you have a medieval army made up of 5,000 foot soldiers, 500 archers and 50 knights. In small groups, discuss how you would arrange them in battle to give you the best chance of victory against an army of the same size.

**6 Life and Death in Medieval Times**

73

## Becoming a knight

There were two ways for a man to become a knight. If a foot soldier showed exceptional bravery on the battlefield, he could be knighted by a lord. However, this was very rare and the main way was a three-stage process followed by the sons of nobles:

*Stage 1: Page*

At the age of seven, a boy would be sent to live with the family of another lord; this was known as fostering. He would learn to ride a horse, use a sword, sing and dance. He was taught manners, helped the lady of the castle and served the lord and lady at table.

*Stage 2: Squire*

Aged 14, the boy began to learn to fight on horseback. He would accompany the lord into battle, look after his horse and weapons and help the lord dress for battle and tournaments.

*Stage 3: Knight*

At the age of 21, he was eligible to become a knight. He spent the night before the ceremony in prayer in the chapel. Then, dressed in a white robe and full armour, he took part in the ceremony of dubbing. He swore the **oath of chivalry** (to stay loyal to his lord, protect the poor and weak and be brave in battle) and the lord touched him on the shoulders with a sword and told him 'Arise, sir knight'.

The lord would give a manor to the knight to run. When he was not fighting in real wars and battles, he would often take part in tournaments. These featured mock battles, where knights fought with wooden weapons, and jousting matches, where two knights on horseback rode straight at each other and each tried to knock his rival off his horse using a lance.

◀ Jousting

## CHECKPOINT!

1. Name three differences between a foot soldier and a knight.
2. Why do you think that foot soldiers and archers had very little protection?
3. Explain what happened at the page and squire stages of becoming a knight.
4. Explain the following terms: fostering; dubbing; oath of chivalry. 📖
5. Why do you think knights engaged in tournaments?

 I know about medieval soldiers and the training and life of a knight.

# 6.5: Life in a Medieval Town

## Medieval towns

Towns in the Middle Ages were much smaller than towns today. Most had only about 1,000 people and the largest had only about 5,000 people. Most were built on rivers or on the coast so that the people could make money from trade. Sometimes they were built near castles for protection and to cater to the needs of the castle. A town needed a **charter** from the king. This was <u>a contract where the town was granted freedom to run its own affairs but had to pay taxes</u> to the king.

In this topic, you will learn about:

❯ The parts of a medieval town
❯ Craftsmen and guilds

A corporation and a mayor ran a town. They kept the walls in good repair, tried to deal with dirt and sewage, paid town guards and enforced the curfew and the other laws of the town.

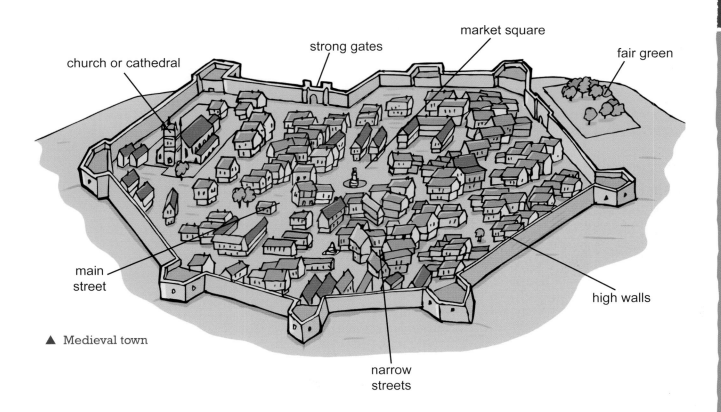

church or cathedral · strong gates · market square · fair green · main street · high walls · narrow streets

▲ Medieval town

Every town was different, but they all shared common features:

* Towns had **high walls** to protect them against attack
* Strong **gates** were the only way in and out of the town. The gates were opened at dawn and closed at sundown. Anyone who wanted to come into the town to conduct business (especially to sell goods) had to pay a **toll** (a tax for entry) at the gates.
* The main or **high street** ran from the main gates to the **market square** in the middle of the town. This was the only street that was wide and paved with stones or wooden planks and was where the richest people had their houses.
* **Narrow streets** ran off the main street and these contained houses and shops for the townspeople.

- The **church** was located near the centre of the town. Larger towns had several churches and even a cathedral, if a bishop was based there.
- Outside the walls was the **fair green** for the annual fair. This was a huge market where traders from all over the country sold exotic things like silks and spices, as well as tools and weapons.

## Houses

The average person's house in a town was made of **wood**. They were usually several storeys high. The higher floors usually stuck out over the street, which blocked the sun and made the streets very dark. Only important buildings – the church or town hall and richer people's homes – were made of stone. Craftsmen had their shops or **workshops on the ground floor**, with their family living on the floor above and the bedrooms on the floor above that.

Many houses had back gardens where people grew vegetables and kept animals such as pigs, hens and cows. People kept **dung heaps** in their gardens where they threw some of their waste, especially food waste. Fire was a constant danger, due to all the wooden buildings. Towns imposed **curfews**, which meant people had to extinguish their fires at sundown.

▲ A wooden house in a medieval town

## Streets

The streets were little more than mud tracks with an open drain down the middle. They were **incredibly dirty**, as people emptied the contents of their chamber pots outside each morning. Animals often roamed the streets. Life generally was very cramped and people lived very close together. This meant that disease could spread very easily; you will learn more about this in topic 6.7.

## CHECKPOINT!

1. Where were towns built in the Middle Ages and why were they built there?
2. How did towns protect themselves?
3. Describe a house in a medieval town.
4. Explain the following terms: charter; fair green; curfew. 📖
5. Why did disease spread so easily in towns?

✓ I can describe life in a medieval town.

 ← TIME TO GO BACK ▶ I CAN MOVE FORWARD →

## Craftsmen

Craftsmen produced the everyday goods that the town needed, from food to tools to clothes – for example, butchers, bakers, blacksmiths, carpenters, stonemasons, coopers (barrel-makers), weavers and tanners (leather-makers). A craftsman would open a shop on the ground floor of his house. As most people could not read, his shop sign was a picture, not words (a fishmonger might use a fish as a symbol). Shops of the same trade were often found in the same street.

## Guilds

The craftsmen of each town formed **guilds**, <u>organisations of people who worked in the same trade</u>. Guilds charged a fee for membership. A guild set standards for the quality of members' work (you could be fined for substandard work), set prices and wages, decided who could trade in the town and cared for old and sick members and the families of dead members.

### *Becoming a master craftsman*

Girls were taught by their mothers to cook, clean, make clothes and look after a household. They were often married around the age of twelve to a man their father had chosen.

However, boys usually took up their father's trade. Having begun in his father's workshop, a boy became an **apprentice** at around twelve: he lived with a master craftsman, slept in the workshop, received no pay and was often treated harshly.

▲ Medieval bakers at work

After seven years, he became a **journeyman**. Now he could be paid for his work and could travel to different workshops and towns for work and experience. Eventually, he applied to become a **master craftsman**. He created a **masterpiece** (<u>the best example of his work</u>). If the guild decided it was good enough, he was accepted and could open his own workshop, train apprentices and sell his work.

 COLLABORATE: Many surnames come from the jobs that people had in the Middle Ages. For example, 'Smith' refers to someone who worked with metal, like a blacksmith. Use the internet to find as many examples of these names as you can.

### ///////// CHECKPOINT! /////////

1. Why did craftsmen use pictures on their signs?

2. What were guilds and what did they do?

3. Explain the following terms: apprentice; journeyman; master craftsman; masterpiece.

 I can describe the life and training of a craftsman.     TIME TO GO BACK ◆ I CAN MOVE FORWARD ➔

# 6.6: Religion in the Middle Ages

**In this topic, you will learn about:**
- The power of the Catholic Church
- The role of religious belief in people's lives

◄ Christendom

## Christendom

Medieval Europe was almost entirely Catholic. Religious belief was very strong and had a huge influence on people's daily lives. Many people lived in constant fear of going to hell if they did not obey the Church's teachings. So important was religion and so powerful was the Catholic Church that Europe was often called **Christendom**, which means the 'kingdom of Christ'.

▲ A medieval monk, bishop and priest

**DID YOU KNOW?**

Christendom was also home to many non-Christians. Most towns across medieval Europe had small Jewish communities, while for centuries the Muslim territory of Al-Andalus (now Andalusia in southern Spain) was a beacon of culture and learning.

▲ The Alhambra in Andalusia

The Pope in Rome was the head of the Catholic Church and was the most powerful ruler in Europe. Europe was divided into **dioceses**, run by archbishops and bishops, and then into smaller **parishes**, run by priests. Kings often gave land and money to bishops and this made the Church very wealthy. Bishops would build huge churches called **cathedrals** in their dioceses to symbolise their power.

# Cathedrals in the Middle Ages

There were two different styles of cathedrals built in the Middle Ages: the older style was based on Roman architecture and was called **Romanesque** and the second type was called **Gothic**.

| Romanesque features | Gothic features |
|---|---|
| Rounded doorways, arches and windows | Pointed doorways, arches and windows |
| Fewer, smaller windows | More, larger windows |
| Low ceilings | High ceilings |
| Large pillars | Narrow pillars |
| Weight of the roof supported by the walls and pillars inside | Weight of the roof partially supported by **flying buttresses** on the outside, allowing for fewer pillars, higher ceilings and more windows |

# Priests in the Middle Ages

The manor village and town often made up a parish. The local church was one of the few buildings to be made of stone. The local priest was rare in being **able to read and write**, and so he was often asked to help with **letters**, or to advise people on **legal problems**. Priests were often appointed as secretaries to lords and knights.

In some places, priests taught children a very **basic education** focused on the Bible. They said **Mass in Latin** every Sunday and ensured the local religious holidays were observed. They tended to the sick and presided at marriages and baptisms. As each peasant had to pay the priest a tithe every year, most priests were **quite wealthy**. They passed some of their earnings to their bishops, further increasing the wealth of the Church. They helped maintain order by encouraging the people to accept their hard lives and to look forward to getting their reward in heaven.

## CHECKPOINT!

1. What was Christendom?
2. Explain the structure of the Catholic Church.
3. Why was the Church so wealthy in the Middle Ages?
4. Why was the priest an important person in manors and towns?

 I can talk about Christianity in the Middle Ages.

 TIME TO GO BACK | I CAN MOVE FORWARD

**6** Life and Death in Medieval Times

# Monasteries

Some people wanted to withdraw completely from the world so that they could focus on prayer and being closer to God. They set up monasteries (for men, who became monks) and convents (for women, who became nuns). These were **closed communities**, separated from the world around them. They lived their lives according to **strict rules** and spent most of their time **praying, fasting** and **working**. An abbot was head of a monastery – or an abbess, of a convent.

Monasteries were very important in medieval life. They were the first places to offer **education** to children based on ability, regardless of the wealth of their parents. They provided **help to the poor and the sick** and offered **shelter to travellers**. They also copied books in their scriptoriums.

The **church** where the monks prayed was looked after by the sacristan. The monks ate in the **refectory**. The **dormitory** was a large room where the monks slept. The **cloisters** were covered walkways for prayer. The monks gathered in the **chapter house** for readings. In the **almonry**, the almoner gave aid to the poor. The **infirmary** was where the infirmarian looked after the ill of the monastery and nearby community. Guests and travellers could stay in the **hostel**, which was managed by the hosteller.

**DID YOU KNOW?**

Before printing, the only way to share knowledge was to copy books by hand! Monks did most of this 'scribing' and often illustrated the manuscripts too, leaving us beautiful works of art as well as precious historical sources! But it was slow and often frustrating work. Here are some scribbles left by various monks in their manuscripts' margins:

I am very cold.

That's a hard page and a weary work to read it.

Thank God, it will soon be dark.

Oh, my hand.

While I wrote I froze, and what I could not write by the beams of the sun I finished by candlelight.

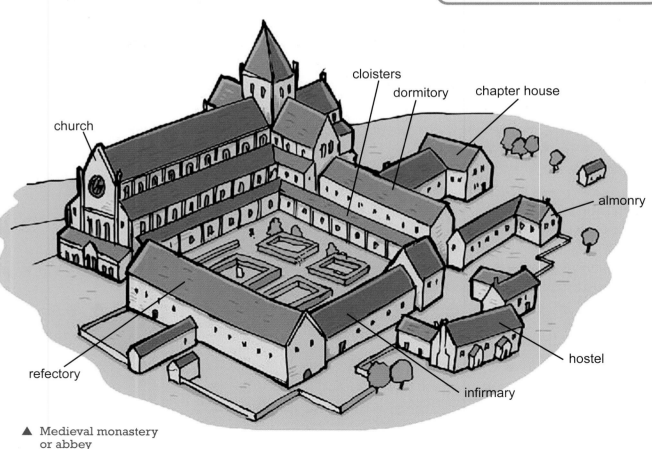

▲ Medieval monastery or abbey

## Becoming a monk

A boy who wanted to become a monk would join a monastery as a **novice** around the age of 15 (though much younger children could be sent). There he was taught to live his life according to the **Rule of St Benedict**, the strict set of rules that monks had to live by. He learned to read and write in Latin (the language of the Church) and would study church teachings and history.

After a number of years, if the abbot decided that he was suited to become a monk, he swore his solemn vows of **poverty** (he could not own anything), **chastity** (he could not get married) and **obedience** (he must do what the abbot told him). The crown of his head was then shaved – this was called a **tonsure** and symbolised the crown of thorns worn by Jesus during the crucifixion. He would also receive his **habit**, or monks' garments. He was now a member of a monastic order.

There were various monastic orders that monks could join: two major orders were the **Benedictines** and the **Cistercians**.

## Friars

Some monks preferred to live **amongst the people** so that they could better help them. These monks, called **friars**, travelled around the countryside or set up friaries in towns. They spent their time tending to the poor and the sick. They saw this as following the example of Jesus' life as told in the Bible. Friar orders such as the **Franciscans**, the **Augustinians** and the **Dominicans** became very popular from about 1200 onwards.

---

## CHECKPOINT!

1. Why did people join monasteries and convents?
2. Describe the role of the following monks in a monastery: abbot; sacristan; infirmarian; almoner; hosteller.
3. Explain the following parts of a monastery: cloisters; dormitory; scriptorium; refectory.
4. Why were monasteries so important in medieval life?
5. Explain the following terms: tonsure; the rule of St Benedict; habit.
6. What was the difference between friars and monks?

 I can talk about medieval friars, monks and monasteries.     ⬅ TIME TO GO BACK ⟩ I CAN MOVE FORWARD ➡

---

 Go to page 38 of your *Sources and Skills Book* for an activity on the life of a monk.

**6 Life and Death in Medieval Times**

# 6.7: Health and Medicine in the Middle Ages

In this topic, you will learn about:
- Medieval medicine
- Illness in the Middle Ages
- The Black Death

## Medicine in the Middle Ages

Medieval medicine was based on the writings of the Ancient Greeks. Their beliefs about the body were very far from modern medicine. For example, Hippocrates, the 'Father of Medicine', believed that the body was made up of four **humours**: blood, black bile, yellow bile and phlegm. If a person was sick, it was due to an imbalance between these humours. This could be treated by:

▲ Doctor bleeding a patient

- **Bleeding:** cutting the patient so that they bled
- **Cupping:** placing heated metal cups on the skin to draw fluids to the surface
- **Leeching:** using leeches to draw the blood or other fluids out of the body
- **Amputation:** cutting off a limb

Herbal medicine was common, with mixtures of **herbs** given to the sick. Monasteries specialised in the care of the sick and functioned as the first hospitals.

## Illness in the Middle Ages

Medieval conditions were cramped and filthy and people lacked the basics of good sanitation or hygiene. Even minor wounds often became infected and the person might lose a limb or even die. People who were poor and did not have a good diet were less able to fight off **infections**. Among the diseases widespread in the Middles Ages were: typhoid, leprosy, smallpox, puerperal fever, dysentery and influenza.

COLLABORATE: Pick one of the diseases mentioned above. Find out about its symptoms, the mortality rate, how people caught it and whether a treatment exists for it today. Use at least two sources.

Women faced the added danger of **childbirth**. Midwives would help, but usually had no training beyond their experience at previous births. Women could lose a lot of blood – and if there was a problem, mother and child might both die. Death from infection soon after the birth was common.

# The Black Death

The worst disease to affect Europe in the Middle Ages was the **bubonic plague**, also known as 'the Black Death'. This peaked between 1347 and 1350 and is estimated to have killed at least **a third of Europe's population**. The plague was carried by **fleas**, which are thought to have first arrived via ships' rats from the Black Sea area and to have spread with the trade network throughout Europe.

The symptoms included oozing swellings all over the body, darkly discoloured skin and the filling of the lungs with phlegm. It was **extremely contagious** and could be contracted by sneezing, spitting or touching dead bodies. It spread quickly in towns and as it worsened, bodies were simply left in the street to be collected. This only spread it even faster. Once infected, people had a 70–80% chance of dying within a week.

People at the time had no idea what caused the plague or how to avoid catching it. Many believed it was a result of God's anger at human sin and sought to cure it through prayer, fasting or even beating themselves with whips. Others blamed groups who were outsiders – especially Jews, who were accused of deliberately infecting towns with the plague.

**DID YOU KNOW?**

This alarming costume was worn by doctors trying to fight the plague! Every inch of skin was covered by boots, breeches, gloves, a mask with glass eyes, their doctor's hat and a long overcoat smeared in fat or wax, all in the hope of repelling infection. The beak of the mask was filled with dried flowers and herbs, vinegar or scented oils to mask the stench of the dead and dying.

▼ Art showing the dead dancing or inviting the living to dance, called a danse macabre or Totentanz, was common at this time

## The impact of the Black Death

So many people died within such a short period that Europe was greatly changed by the Black Death:

- The feudal system, especially serfdom, declined as many serfs left manors and moved to the towns to replace those who had died.
- The peasants who remained on the land were able to demand better treatment from their lords, a reduction in the taxes they paid and more land because there were fewer of them to do the work.
- The failure to find a cure for the Black Death meant that doctors began to question their practices. This would lead to big changes in medicine during the Renaissance, as we will see in the next chapter.

## CHECKPOINT!

1. What were medieval medical practices based on?
2. What did people believe caused illnesses?
3. What were the main treatments for illness in the Middle Ages?
4. Why did diseases spread so easily?
5. Why was childbirth so dangerous for women?
6. What was the Black Death?
7. How was it spread?
8. What were the symptoms?
9. How did people respond to the plague?
10. Why did the Black Death lead to better conditions for peasants?

 I can describe medicine in the Middle Ages and understand the Black Death and its lasting impact.

 TIME TO GO BACK ◀ ▶ I CAN MOVE FORWARD ➡

  Go to page 39 of your *Sources and Skills Book* for an activity on the Black Death.

 **SUMMARY**

In this chapter, we have learned that:

- Life in the Middle Ages was very tough. The society built on the feudal system meant that the large majority of the population were kept as peasants.

- People lived in towns, monasteries, castles and manors in the countryside.

- War was a constant presence in people's lives in the Middle Ages.

- Young noblemen were brought up to be knights.

- Religion was central in people's lives. The Pope was Europe's most powerful ruler, and bishops and monasteries were very wealthy.

- Death and illness were encouraged by the dirty conditions that most people lived in. There was little understanding of how the body worked or how disease was spread.

### Reflecting on... the Middle Ages

The Middle Ages came to an end as people began questioning many accepted beliefs of their time. This, together with the rediscovery of ancient Greek and Roman knowledge, led to the revolutions in art and science that mark the Renaissance.

 **Understanding History**

1. What was the feudal system?
2. How was the land on a manor divided up?
3. How did noble families create good relationships between them?
4. What were the main duties of (a) the lord and (b) the lady of a castle?
5. What were the advantages of living in a town?
6. What was the function of a craft guild?
7. Why did people become monks and nuns in the Middle Ages?
8. Why was illness so common and so dangerous in the Middle Ages?
9. What impact did the Black Death have on Europe?

 **Exploring History**

1. Write about the life of either a knight, a craftsman or a monk using the following headings:
   - Training
   - Place where he lived
   - Food and clothes
   - Work and daily life

2. Imagine you are travelling back in time to the Middle Ages and you have to choose where to live. Write out the advantages and disadvantages of living in a town, a manor, a castle and a monastery.

3. Compare the life of child who was the son or daughter of a lord with the life of a peasant's child.

4. Write a short account of medicine in the Middle Ages.

5. One writer has described life in the Middle Ages as 'nasty, brutish and short'. Do you agree with this assessment? Give reasons for your answer.

**6 Life and Death in Medieval Times**

**KEY TERMS**

| | |
|---|---|
| Feudalism | the system of land ownership where rulers (kings, lords) divided land among their followers in return for loyalty and taxes |
| Peasants | the people who worked on a lord's land. Serfs were the property of the lord and had very few rights. Freemen had more freedom, but still had to pay rent, taxes and tithes |
| Bailiff | the official on the manor who was in charge of collecting taxes and maintaining order when the lord was away |
| Open field system | the system of farming where peasants were each given strips of land to farm in large fields |
| Fallow | the one field left empty every year to let it regain its nutrients |
| The commons | a large field on the manor where the peasants' animals grazed |
| Tithe | the payment of one-tenth of a peasant's annual income to the Church |
| Knights | warriors of noble birth who fought on horseback and swore an oath of chivalry |
| Oath of chivalry | sworn by a knight to be loyal to a lord and protect the weak |
| Charter | a contract whereby a town was granted freedom to run its own affairs but paid taxes to the king |
| Curfew | a rule that required people in towns to put out their fires at night |
| Guild | an organisation of people who worked in the same trade |
| Masterpiece | a piece of work presented to the guild to judge if someone was good enough to become a master craftsman |
| Christendom | the 'kingdom of Christ', referring to Europe |
| Rule of St Benedict | the strict set of rules that monks lived by |
| Friars | monks who travelled around the country tending to the poor and the sick |

Go to page 32 of your *Sources and Skills Book* for more exercises.

Go to page 10 of your *Research Portfolio* for a task based on this chapter.

| Early Christian Ireland c. 400–800 | The Middle Ages in Ireland c. 800–1500 | The Plantations c. 1500–1700 |
|---|---|---|

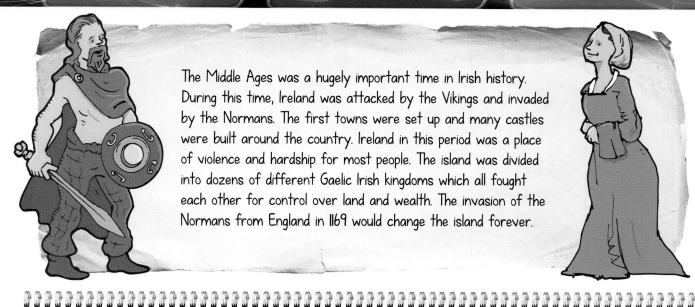

The Middle Ages was a hugely important time in Irish history. During this time, Ireland was attacked by the Vikings and invaded by the Normans. The first towns were set up and many castles were built around the country. Ireland in this period was a place of violence and hardship for most people. The island was divided into dozens of different Gaelic Irish kingdoms which all fought each other for control over land and wealth. The invasion of the Normans from England in 1169 would change the island forever.

# WORKING WITH THE <u>EVIDENCE</u>!

## Medieval Ireland

| Type of source | Category | Example |
|---|---|---|
| Primary | Tactile | Artefacts and physical remains from the Wood Quay excavations (see chapter 4)<br>Trim Castle |
| Primary | Written | The *Annals of the Four Masters*: an account of Irish history written by Irish monks<br>The *Topographia Hibernica*: written by a Norman priest, Gerald of Wales, who travelled in Ireland after the Norman Conquest |

▲ Trim Castle

▲ *Topographica Hibernica*

# WORKING WITH THE EVIDENCE!

## The Wood Quay excavations

1. In this photo of an excavation at Wood Quay, can you identify what is circled in red at A, B and C?
2. What can we learn about Viking Dublin from the excavations in the photograph? List three things.

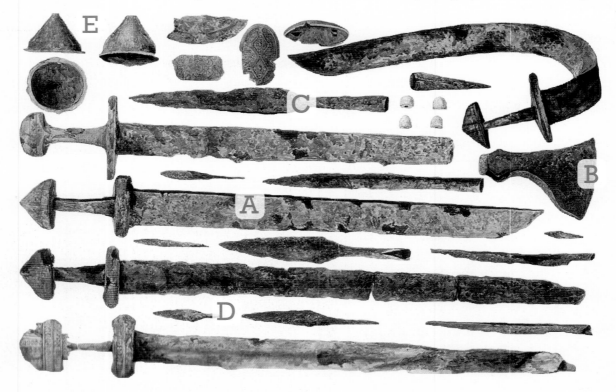

3. Identify the items marked A to E.
4. What can we learn about Viking Dublin from the artefacts in the photograph? List two things.

# 7.1: The Vikings in Ireland

In chapter 4, you learned about the Vikings and their origins in Scandinavia. They came to Ireland in their **longships** and raided the Irish monasteries from AD 795. By the mid-800s, they had established settlements in Ireland. These **longphorts** were originally built as bases for attacking the native Gaelic Irish, but they soon developed into centres for trade and commerce.

**In this topic, you will learn about:**
- The Viking settlements in Ireland
- Viking Dublin

## WORKING WITH THE EVIDENCE!

### Viking settlements in Ireland

Look at the map to the right. What do the locations of the Viking settlements have in common? Why do you think they were built in those locations?

> **DID YOU KNOW?**
>
> The Vikings' impact can be seen in some Irish placenames: Longford is almost unchanged from 'longphort', while the 'ford' in Waterford, Wexford and Carlingford is from 'fjord', Skerries comes from 'sker', meaning 'sea rock' and Leixlip was once 'lax hlaup' or 'salmon leap'.

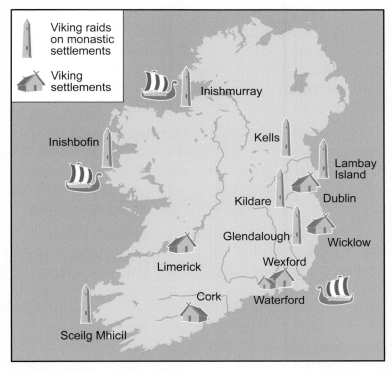

▲ Known Viking settlements

The first Viking settlement was founded in 841 on the south bank of the river **Liffey**. It was situated beside the deep pool of the river **Poddle**, the **dubh linn** (dark pool) that Dublin was named after. Other Viking settlements were founded all over the country, for example in **Cork**, **Waterford**, **Wexford**, **Limerick** and **Lough Foyle**. They were all built on the coast and many of them were beside large rivers. Both of these things would help the Vikings raid the rest of the country and trade with the outside world. Regular Viking raids died out by the mid-tenth century, but the settlements remained. They were now part of Irish life. The Vikings traded with the Gaelic Irish and became wealthy. They were often attacked by Irish tribes.

> **DID YOU KNOW?**
>
> Many Norse words found their way into the Irish language, especially words about the sea or trade. Bád, scod, stiúir, pingin, margadh, bróg and cnaipe are just some you might recognise!

▶ A model of how Viking Dublin is likely to have looked

# Viking Dublin

The Viking town at Dublin was protected by a ditch and an earthen mound with a high wooden fence on top. In the late eleventh century, stone walls were built around Dublin. New, larger walls had to be built as the town expanded.

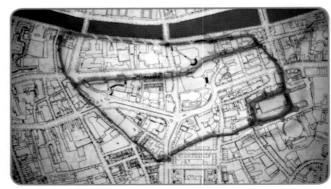

▲ Can you see where the original stone walls had to be expanded?

As you saw in chapter 4, life in Viking Dublin was tough. The houses were of **wattle and daub** with thatched roofs. **Evidence was found at Wood Quay of craftsmen** such as blacksmiths, carpenters, jewellers and leather-workers. For example, some craftsmen made things like combs from bone or the antlers of deer hunted in the mountains around the town. There is also evidence of wool-weaving workshops producing **cloth for export** – and there was a **slave trade**. Coins found at Wood Quay prove that Dublin traded with the English towns of Chester and Bristol.

The Vikings were **converted to Christianity** by Irish monks and the first Bishop of Dublin was appointed in 1028. In his time, the first church on the site of **Christ Church Cathedral** was built. Dublin soon grew to be the largest and most important town in Ireland, with a population of about 4,000 by the eleventh century. A sign of the town's growth was that there was a suburb north of the Liffey built in the late eleventh century.

Throughout this period, there was constant warfare in Ireland between alliances of different Irish kings. Dublin was often involved in these conflicts. As the largest and wealthiest town on the island, it had a large army to fight for it and was often attacked for its wealth. The most famous battle fought near Dublin was at **Clontarf in 1014**, when an alliance of Gaelic clans under the High King of Ireland, **Brian Boru**, fought a Gaelic Irish and Viking army under the control of **Sitric Silkenbeard**, the Viking King of Dublin. Brian's wife, **Gormlaith**, had been married to the previous Viking King of Dublin. Her son from this marriage, Sitric, was encouraged by her to fight Brian. Brian's army won the battle but he was killed in his tent by the retreating Viking warriors. You can learn more about Viking Dublin at the link below:

www.dublinia.ie

**DID YOU KNOW?**

Sitric also minted Ireland's very first coins, around 995. In 2015, some turned up in Wales as part of a treasure hoard. Imagine what they might have bought and the people who carried them!

## CHECKPOINT!

1. Where were the first Viking settlements built and why were they built there?
2. Describe Viking Dublin.
3. What evidence is there that the town expanded over time?
4. What crafts were practised in Dublin?
5. Why was Dublin involved in conflict with the Gaelic Irish?
6. What happened at the Battle of Clontarf in 1014?

I can describe Viking Dublin.

◀ TIME TO GO BACK ◀ ▶ I CAN MOVE FORWARD ▶

Go to page 43 of your *Sources and Skills Book* for an activity on the Wood Quay protests.

## 7.2: The Norman Invasion

### The Normans

In this topic, you will learn about:
- The Normans
- The Norman conquest of Ireland

While the Vikings were settling in Ireland, they were settling elsewhere in Europe too. One of these areas was in north-west France. As they were also called **Norsemen**, this area became known as **Normandy** and the people who lived there were the Normans. Normandy was ruled by dukes and it became one of the most powerful regions in France in the Middle Ages.

In 1066, the King of England, **Edward the Confessor**, died without leaving a son to succeed him. **William, the Duke of Normandy**, laid claim to the English crown but this was rejected by the English nobles led by **Harold, the Earl of Hereford**. William invaded the country and defeated Harold and his army at the **Battle of Hastings**. William became King of England and was known as **William the Conqueror**. He and his successors spent the next hundred years establishing their control over England and Wales. The story of the Norman Conquest is told in the **Bayeux Tapestry**.

▲ The Bayeux Tapestry

### The Normans conquer Ireland

In 1167 the King of Leinster, **Dermot MacMurrough**, was stripped of his kingdom by **Rory O'Connor**, the High King of Ireland. MacMurrough travelled to England where he asked the king, **Henry II**, for help in regaining his lands. MacMurrough offered to become Henry's vassal in return for this help. Henry did not provide him with help directly but did allow him to recruit soldiers from amongst his own Norman lords. MacMurrough made a deal with **Richard de Clare** (nicknamed **Strongbow**) for a Norman army: Strongbow would marry MacMurrough's daughter, Aoife, and he would become King of Leinster upon MacMurrough's death.

In 1169, MacMurrough invaded Ireland with a force of 40 knights, 500 foot soldiers and 360 archers. They easily defeated the Vikings of Wexford. The Normans were successful in their military campaign because of their use of horses and archers and their better armour and swords. Their battle tactics were also more coordinated than those of the Viking and Irish armies they faced. In 1170, Strongbow arrived with an army of 200 knights and 1,000 foot soldiers. He and MacMurrough combined their armies and marched on Dublin. While talks were ongoing with the bishop of Dublin about a surrender, Norman knights stormed the walls and took the town by surprise. The Viking king and his men fled.

▲ *The Marriage of Strongbow and Aoife*, National Gallery of Ireland

In 1171, MacMurrough died and Strongbow became King of Leinster. Henry II, fearing that Strongbow could become too powerful, landed in September 1171 with a force of 500 knights and 4,000 soldiers. He wanted to establish himself as the ruler of Ireland and ensure that he controlled both the Normans and Gaelic Irish. The Normans had begun to conquer large parts of the island and many of the Irish kings submitted to Henry and swore allegiance to him as they thought this might stop the Norman expansion into their territory. Henry gave himself the title of '**Lord of Ireland**'.

## CHECKPOINT!

1. Where in France did the Vikings settle?
2. Why did the Normans invade England in 1066?
3. Why did Dermot MacMurrough seek help from Henry II? What was the king's answer?
4. What did MacMurrough promise to Strongbow in return for his help?
5. What advantages did the Normans have over the Gaelic Irish in battle?
6. Why did Henry II come to Ireland in 1171?
7. What was the result of his visit?

 I understand how the Normans came to Ireland.

 TIME TO GO BACK ◆ I CAN MOVE FORWARD

# 7.3: Life in Medieval Dublin

**In this topic, you will learn about:**

❯ Important buildings in medieval Dublin

❯ Daily life inside and outside the town walls

❯ Key events in the history of medieval Dublin

**DID YOU KNOW?**

Here, 'pale' came from the Latin for fence or stake (**pale**isade, **impale**), so the phrase 'beyond the Pale' came to mean past a boundary, outside a 'safe area' – and of a person, that their behaviour is strange, unreasonable or uncivilised!

Dublin became the centre of Norman rule in Ireland. The area surrounding the city, roughly the land between modern Dundalk and Dalkey, was known as '**the Pale**'. This was the area of the island directly under the control of the English king. Outside the Pale, the Normans conquered large areas of land in Leinster, Munster, Connacht and the midlands. These areas were ruled by Norman lords under the feudal system. They soon adopted many Irish customs (including the language), intermarried with the leading Gaelic families and became known as the **Anglo-Irish**. The rest of the island, especially the western coast and Ulster, remained under the control of Gaelic Irish kings.

## Medieval Dublin

Dublin was similar to other towns of the Middle Ages. It had many of the same buildings and features.

▲ Medieval Tower, Dublin Castle

- The **walls** surrounded the city. Entry and exit was controlled through a series of **gates** and those wishing to come in had to a pay a **toll**. The first **prisons** in Dublin were located in the towers in the gates, such as **Newgate Prison** near the Cornmarket. A large section of the original wall still exists in **Cook Street** today. The people needed the walls to protect them from raids by the Gaelic Irish chieftains in the mountains around Dublin.

- **Dublin Castle** was the seat of English rule in the country from the 1200s until 1922. In the early thirteenth century, the Normans replaced an earlier fortress on the site with a stone castle. The castle was rebuilt many times over the centuries and only one of the original towers still stands today, the Record Tower or Medieval Tower.

- **Christ Church Cathedral** was rebuilt between 1172 and 1191. It was originally home to an Augustinian monastery. In 1213 the parish Church of St Patrick was also made a cathedral.

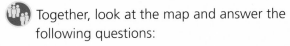

# WORKING WITH THE EVIDENCE!

## The streets of medieval Dublin

Together, look at the map and answer the following questions:

1. How do you think the following streets got their names: Fishamble St; Winetavern St; Cook St?

2. What you think happened at the Cornmarket?

3. What was the Fair Green used for?

4. Looking at the map and your answers so far, what can you tell about life in Dublin?

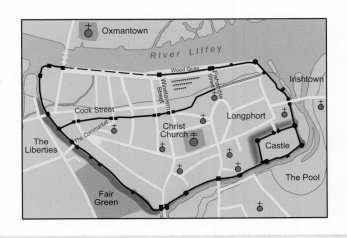

## Inside the walls

Like all medieval cities, Dublin was very **unsanitary**. The streets were narrow and dark and people threw their rubbish into the street. To deal with the problem, the council passed a law that every householder had to clean the street in front of their house and fined them if they did not. Animals were banned from wandering the streets. In 1305, three watchmen were appointed to patrol the streets at night to try and deal with the waste. In 1224, a conduit was built to bring **fresh water** into Dublin from the mountains and in the fourteenth century the main streets were paved, both of which helped a little.

Many of the people who lived within the city walls worked at a trade or a craft, often to serve the needs of the castle. Evidence of a **wide variety of craftsmen** has been found: goldsmiths, carpenters, smiths, butchers, fishmongers, tanners, weavers, coopers, shoemakers, tailors and bakers. As Dublin was a port, **foreign trade** was very important. Artefacts from Wood Quay tell us that wine from France and iron and pottery from Britain were imported into Dublin. Exports included hides, grain and pulses.

## Outside the walls

After the Vikings were expelled from Dublin, they moved to the north bank of the Liffey. This area became known as **Ostmantown** (Ostman is an old word for Viking) or **Oxmantown** (which is the modern area of Stoneybatter in Dublin 7). Also outside the walls were **the Liberties** (where people did not have to pay taxes but lived without the protection of the walls) and **Irishtown**, which was where the Gaelic Irish were supposed to live. They were not officially allowed to live in the city and the Irish language was banned in Dublin, but neither of these measures was effective at keeping the populations separate. By the 1500s, the Irish language was used as much as English in everyday life and official city documents were written in both languages.

## Key events in medieval Dublin

**1152**   The Bishop of Dublin was made an Archbishop.

**1190**   Dublin was devastated by fire.

**1204**   The first fair was held on **Fair Green**.

**1320**   A university was established at **St Patrick's Cathedral**.

**1317**   Dublin was besieged by an invading Scottish army. The bridge over the Liffey was destroyed and the areas outside the walls were set on fire.

**1348**   The **Black Death** ravaged the city. Anyone who wanted to enter the city had to wait outside the walls for three days to prove they did not have the plague. There were mass burials in the **Blackpitts** area.

## CHECKPOINT!

1.  Why did Dublin need walls?
2.  How did the Vikings and Gaelic Irish come to live outside the walls of Dublin?
3.  What were the Liberties?
4.  How did the city council try to deal with Dublin's dirt?
5.  What goods were (a) imported into and (b) exported from Dublin?

 I can describe life in medieval Dublin.     TIME TO GO BACK    I CAN MOVE FORWARD

## 7.4: The Impact of the Normans on Ireland

In this topic, you will learn about:
❯ How the Norman Conquest affected Ireland

The Normans had a huge impact on Ireland after their conquest:

- They introduced the **feudal system** to Ireland.
- They built big castles, such as Trim, Carrickfergus and Kilkenny. Smaller castles and tower houses were also built. Towns, manors and villages grew up around these bases of Norman power.
- Farming practices shifted from the Gaelic focus on keeping herds of cattle to growing crops on manors.
- English **Common Law** replaced the old Gaelic **Brehon Law** system.
- Norman names became very common in Ireland. Names that include 'Fitz' (which means 'son of') are Norman names, as are Burke, Butler, Browne and Barry.
- The Normans introduced English rule to Ireland. It would last for nearly 800 years.

 **COLLABORATE:** In pairs, research the origin of your surname(s) and report back to the rest of the class. What does it mean? Where did it originate?

 **SUMMARY**

In this chapter, we have learned that:

- The Middle Ages in Ireland were a time of conflict which saw the coming of two groups of outsiders who would have a huge impact on Ireland.
- The Vikings started raiding Irish monasteries in the 790s. From the 840s they were building settlements along the coasts and rivers. Their largest settlement was at Dublin.
- Dublin grew wealthy from trade and developed into the main town in medieval Ireland.
- In 1169, the Normans invaded Ireland to restore the former King of Leinster, Dermot MacMurrough, to his kingdom.
- They defeated the Vikings and Gaelic Irish and captured Dublin. The city became the base of English rule in Ireland, as the Normans tried to conquer the rest of the country.
- Medieval Dublin was cramped and dirty. Dublin Castle was the centre of the city's life.
- The Normans changed much of Irish life: they built castles and towns, introduced new legal and farming practices and brought new families and names into the country.

### Reflecting on... Medieval Ireland

The Middle Ages was a key turning point in Irish history. The Norman invasion in 1169 would begin the troubled history of English rule in Ireland and set the stage for nearly 800 years of conflict. We can also see how first the Vikings and then the Normans played an important role in the formation of Irish identity. Neither people remained completely separate from the native Irish and contributed distinct traits which influenced the development of Ireland in the centuries that followed.

7 Settlement in Ireland Option Two: Medieval Ireland

**Understanding History**

1. Name two sources of information on medieval Ireland.
2. What kinds of site did the Vikings choose for their settlements? Give two examples.
3. How did the Vikings become wealthy? What evidence do we have for this?
4. Why did the Normans conquer Ireland relatively easily?
5. Which parts of the island were left under Gaelic control after the conquest?
6. What was the role of Dublin Castle in the Middle Ages? Why did it need high walls?
7. What areas were built outside the walls of medieval Dublin and who lived there?
8. Name two streets in medieval Dublin and what went on there.
9. What impact did the Normans have on Ireland? Give two examples.
10. Find out the correct year the following events took place and then place them in order on a timeline in your copy, starting with the earliest.

   - Dermot MacMurrough is expelled from his kingdom in Leinster
   - The founding of a university at St Patrick's Cathedral
   - The arrival of the Black Death in Dublin
   - Dublin is founded by the Vikings

   - The Battle of Hastings
   - The Battle of Clontarf
   - The Normans invade Ireland
   - The first Viking raid on Ireland
   - A great fire destroys Dublin
   - A Scottish army lays siege to Dublin

 **Exploring History**

1. Imagine you lived in medieval Dublin after the Norman Conquest. Write an account of what life is like in the city. In your account, write about the following:
   - The main buildings in the city
   - The jobs people do in the city
   - Life on the streets
   - The areas around the city
2. Write an account of how Dublin changed and developed from the Viking settlement to the Middle Ages.
3. Write an account describing how the Normans came to Ireland and the impact they had on the island.

| **KEY TERMS** | Normans | descendants of the Vikings who settled in Normandy in France and conquered England and Ireland |
|---|---|---|
| | The Pale | the area around Dublin directly under the control of the English king |
| | Anglo-Irish | descendants of the Norman conquerors who adopted many Irish customs and intermarried with the leading Gaelic families |

 Go to page 40 of your *Sources and Skills Book* for more exercises.

 Go to page 12 of your *Research Portfolio* for a task based on this chapter.

| The Middle Ages | The Renaissance | The Age of Exploration |
|---|---|---|
| c. 500–1500 | c. 1350–1650 | c. 1400–1750 |

The Renaissance was a hugely important period in European history. 'Renaissance' (or 'rebirth') refers to the rebirth of European interest in the civilisations of Ancient Greece and Rome. During the Renaissance, people began to look at the world around them in new ways. They questioned old ideas from the Middle Ages and developed new ideas about art, architecture, science, literature and medicine.

At first, these ideas were based on what they learned from the ancient world – but in time, people began to come up with their own ideas about the world.

Humanism is the idea that human beings should be at the centre of everything and we should think about the world in terms of the lives people live. This led to artists focusing on recreating the real world, nature and real people in their work. This was a different approach to the Middle Ages, when everything was seen in the context of what the Church taught.

# WORKING WITH THE EVIDENCE!

## The Renaissance

| Type of source | Category | Examples |
|---|---|---|
| Primary | Written | Letters, diaries and official documents, like *The Notebooks of Leonardo da Vinci* |
| Primary | Visual | Paintings and sculptures by artists like da Vinci, Michelangelo, Botticelli, Dürer and Raphael |

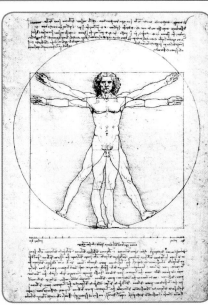

◄ *Vitruvian Man* from da Vinci's personal notebooks

► Raphael's *Sistine Madonna*

Look at the image of Raphael's *Sistine Madonna*. Describe it, addressing the colours, the bodies and the background of the painting.

# 8.1: The Causes of the Renaissance

In this topic, you will learn about:

❯ Why the Renaissance started in Italy
❯ The role of money and patrons in creating the Renaissance
❯ The city of Florence as a centre of the Renaissance

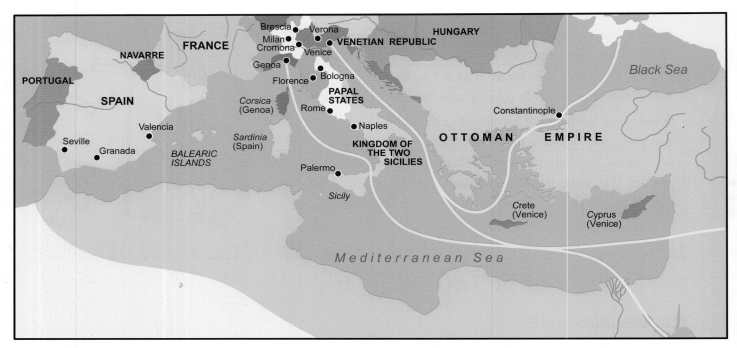

▲ From this map, why do you think Italy became the centre of the Renaissance?

While the Renaissance would affect all of Europe, it began in Italy. There are several reasons for this:

1. **The ruins of the Roman Empire:** Italy was the centre of the ancient Roman Empire. This meant that the remains of Roman buildings and art were everywhere. As Italian towns and cities expanded, they dug up Roman statues. The Italian language was based on Latin, which made it easier for people to read ancient works when they became available. All these things inspired Italians and many of them wanted to copy the achievements of their ancestors.

2. **The fall of Constantinople in 1453:** Constantinople was the capital of the Eastern Roman (Byzantine) Empire. It was captured by the Ottoman Turks in 1453. Many Greek scholars fled to Italy. They brought priceless ancient Greek and Roman manuscripts with them. These books were full of ideas from the ancient world which Italians had never seen.

3. **Wealth from trade:** Italy's position in the middle of the Mediterranean meant that it had grown rich on trade in goods coming overland from the East, such as silks and spices. These merchants had money to spend on works of art and architecture to demonstrate their wealth and power.

4. **New ideas from trade:** Traders brought back more than goods from the East. These merchants travelled to China, India and Arabia and returned with ideas from these advanced civilisations. For example, they learned about mathematics from the Arabs and introduced the Arabic number system to Europe, which we still use today.

5. **Competition between Italian city states:** Italy was not a single country ruled by one king; it was made up of many independent city states, all in competition with each other over territory, trade, wealth and power. To show who was richest and most powerful, they all hired artists to build great buildings and produce works of art. Many of these works of art were to show their city in a very positive light. Florence was one of the most important Italian cities.

6. **Patrons:** A **patron** was a wealthy person who commissioned (hired) an artist to produce a work of art for them. There were many different types of patrons in the Renaissance. The Catholic Church (especially popes like **Julius II**) spent huge sums of money to beautify their churches and cathedrals. Kings and governments wanted artworks that would glorify their countries and cities. Private individuals used art to demonstrate their wealth. The **de Medici of Florence** were among the most important families of art patrons.

▼ The de Medici family

**8 The Renaissance**

## Florence: A Renaissance city

By 1400, Florence was the wealthiest city in Italy, with a population of over 100,000. Its wealth came initially from the wool trade and later from banking. Florentines were very proud of their city and were willing to spend lavishly on works of art to decorate their city.

Florence was a republic, but most of the power in the city lay in the hands of the **de Medici** family. They owned the largest bank in the city and used their money to ensure that the men who ran the city did what they wanted. They tried to ensure that Florence remained at peace with its neighbours, as peace was good for trade and business. They were very important patrons, especially **Cosimo de Medici (1389–1464)** and his grandson **Lorenzo (1449–1492)**. They sponsored artists and architects, opened schools for the study of Roman and Greek manuscripts and established an academy for sculptors in their own palace.

**DID YOU KNOW?**

Lorenzo de Medici spent so much on sponsoring artists that he nearly bankrupted the family bank!

▲ A Renaissance painting of Florence

 PATRON'S DEN! Imagine your group has to get a patron's support for a work of art or project. Make a presentation to the class (or another group) and explain why the patron should support your application. Include items like your experience, examples of your previous work, how you will go about the work and why it is in the patron's best interests to give you their money.

## CHECKPOINT!

1. What does Renaissance mean?
2. Explain the term humanism. 📖
3. List the reasons why the Renaissance began in Italy.
4. What was a patron? Give an example of one from the Renaissance.
5. Look at the list of reasons why the Renaissance originated in Italy. Which of them do you think was the most important? Give reasons for your answer.

 I can explain the causes of the Renaissance.

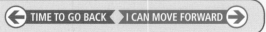 ⬅ TIME TO GO BACK ◆ I CAN MOVE FORWARD ➡

## 8.2: Changes in Art

**In this topic, you will learn about:**
- The differences between medieval art and Renaissance art
- The life of Leonardo da Vinci
- The life of Michelangelo Buonarroti

# WORKING WITH THE EVIDENCE!

## Medieval vs. Renaissance painting

With a partner, look at the two pictures below and list all the differences between them.

◀ Medieval painting: *Santa Trinita Maestà* by Cimabue

▼ Renaissance painting: *Birth of Venus* by Botticelli

8

The Renaissance

## Differences between medieval and Renaissance art

| Medieval Painting | Renaissance Painting |
|---|---|
| **Themes** ||
| Medieval artists mainly painted religious images. They painted scenes from the Bible, especially the life of Jesus. These were intended to encourage people to follow the teachings of the Catholic Church. | In the Renaissance, many artists still painted religious images (especially when the Church was their patron!) – but they also produced works showing ancient Greek and Roman mythological scenes, portraits of people, landscapes, nature themes and scenes from everyday life. |
| **Materials and colours** ||
| In the Middle Ages, paintings were either done on wooden panels (which cracked easily) or **onto walls while the plaster was wet**, which was called **fresco** (meaning 'fresh').<br><br>Powdered pigments were mixed with egg yolk to produce **egg tempera** paint. This dried very quickly and meant that artists could not use a wide variety of colours or fix mistakes. | Renaissance artists painted on **canvas** (a thick woven sheet of flax) or onto wet plaster on walls.<br><br>The paint was mixed with oil, so it dried much more slowly. This allowed artists to be much more precise in their work, to vary the colours used and add shading.<br><br>They developed a technique called **sfumato**, meaning 'smoky'. It involved **blurring or smudging lines and colours to soften textures and create a 'smoky' effect**. |

| Medieval Painting | Renaissance Painting |
|---|---|
| **Perspective** ||
| Medieval art was flat with no real depth to the images, which appeared **two-dimensional**. | Renaissance artists used **perspective** to **create depth and distance in a painting**. They made objects and people appear smaller in the background and larger in the foreground, creating a **three-dimensional** effect. |
| **People** ||
| In medieval art, people did not look 'real'. Their bodies were not to scale. Their limbs were often the wrong size or one person was out of proportion to the others. Many of the faces were the same and had lifeless expressions. | Many Renaissance artists studied **anatomy** (**the study of the structure of the human body**). This helped them make people look 'real'. They painted wrinkles, muscles, tendons, folds in clothes and how light and shadows fell. They used real-life people as models for their work. |
| The key difference between the art of the Middle Ages and the art of the Renaissance was **realism**. When people looked at the works created by the Renaissance masters, they saw images that were recognisably of real people, in real settings. ||

Look again at the paintings above. Can you identify any of these differences between them?

# CHECKPOINT!

1. How did subject matter differ between medieval and Renaissance paintings?
2. How was paint made in (a) the Middle Ages and (b) the Renaissance?
3. Explain the following terms: fresco; sfumato; perspective; anatomy.
4. How did Renaissance artists make their paintings more realistic?

✔ I know the differences between medieval and Renaissance art. ◀ TIME TO GO BACK ◆ ▶ I CAN MOVE FORWARD ➔

Go to page 49 of your *Sources and Skills Book* for an activity on a Renaissance portrait.

## A Life in Time: A Renaissance Artist: Leonardo da Vinci (1452–1519)

Leonardo da Vinci was one of the greatest geniuses of the Renaissance and all of history. He was an incredibly skilled painter and a visionary inventor. He is considered the ideal **'Renaissance man'** because his interests and skills ranged over so many different areas.

### Early life

Da Vinci was born in 1452 in Vinci, near Florence. Despite his father's desire that he train as a lawyer, he was determined to become an artist. At 14, he became an apprentice to **Andrea del Verrocchio** in Florence.

▶ Leonardo da Vinci

There he was trained to prepare paints, learned to sketch and so on. Often the master would paint the main figures in a painting and allow his apprentices to fill in the smaller figures. When Leonardo completed the face of an angel on one of Verrocchio's works, his master realised what a talent the boy had.

## Leonardo in Milan

Work was difficult to get in Florence, especially when the city became involved in a war with its neighbours. In 1482, Leonardo went to work for the Duke of Milan, Ludovico Sforza. He was initially hired as a military engineer, but none of his proposed inventions could be made to work. While in Milan, he painted **The Virgin of the Rocks**, which showed his love of nature.

He also completed **The Last Supper** on the wall of a monastery. It shows the moment when Jesus tells the disciples that one of them will betray him. The painting shows his excellent use of **perspective**. As well as creating depth in the room, da Vinci also made Jesus the focus of attention. Instead of painting on wet plaster, da Vinci decided to experiment with using oil and tempera directly onto the dry wall. This was a disaster, as the paint soon began peeling off the wall.

▲ *The Virgin of the Rocks*

▼ *The Last Supper*, which has undergone many attempts at conservation over the centuries

8

The Renaissance

## The Mona Lisa

In 1499, da Vinci returned to Florence, where he painted his most famous work, the **Mona Lisa**. It was a portrait of the wife of a wealthy Florentine merchant and took over two years to complete. In it, he made use of the **sfumato** technique to make the skin appear soft. Leonardo used tiny brush strokes to blend the colours from one area into the next, leaving no hard lines. He also used light and shadow to focus attention on her smile and eyes.

## Leonardo's notebooks

Over 5,000 pages from Leonardo's notebooks have survived. He wrote them in **mirror writing** and from right to left so that no-one else could read them. He made sketches of people, animals and ideas for machines. To more accurately recreate the human body in his art, he drew detailed drawings of human anatomy, many of them coming from his dissections of corpses. His notebooks also contain drawings for machines that could be tanks, submarines, cannons and aeroplanes – centuries before any of these would be invented.

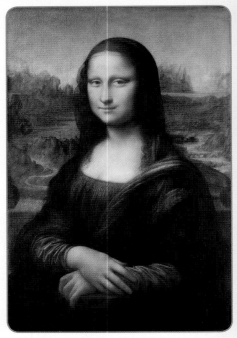

▲ The *Mona Lisa*

## Later life

Leonardo found it hard to complete tasks. He left many sketches and half-completed works, but only fifteen of his works were fully finished. He went to live in France in 1516 at the invitation of King Francis I and died there in 1519.

**DID YOU KNOW?**

Da Vinci was the first person to explain why the sky is blue. He worked out that molecules in the air scatter blue light from the sun!

▲ A page from da Vinci's personal notebooks

## CHECKPOINT!

1. Why is Leonardo da Vinci considered the ideal 'Renaissance man'?
2. Describe his training as an artist.
3. Why can *The Last Supper* be considered both a success and failure?
4. What technique is shown in The *Mona Lisa*?
5. Why did Leonardo dissect corpses?
6. Name some of the machines that he imagined and drew in his notebooks.

✓ I understand Leonardo da Vinci's role in the Renaissance and can describe his life and major works.

 ← TIME TO GO BACK ◆ I CAN MOVE FORWARD →

## A Life in Time: A Renaissance Artist: Michelangelo Buonarroti (1475-1564)

### Early life

Michelangelo was born near Florence in 1475, the son of a local noble, and was apprenticed to the sculptor Domenico Ghirlandaio. He showed great interest in sculpture and closely studied the work of the great Florentine artist **Donatello**. He produced an excellent copy of an ancient Roman statue and this brought him to the attention of **Lorenzo de Medici**. Lorenzo invited him to live with him and study in his sculpture academy.

### Michelangelo's sculptures

Michelangelo left Florence for Rome in 1496, after Lorenzo's death. Soon a cardinal commissioned him to sculpt the *Pietà*, which means 'sorrow'. The *Pietà* is a white marble statue showing Mary holding the body of Jesus after he has been taken down from the cross. It is very detailed and realistic, especially in the folds of Mary's dress and the body of Jesus. It is housed in **St Peter's Basilica** in Rome.

In 1501 Michelangelo returned to Florence, where he won a competition (defeating even da Vinci) to carve a single huge block of white marble. He created the statue of *David*, from the biblical story of David and Goliath, to celebrate Florence defeating France in war. At five metres high, it was the largest free-standing statue since Ancient Rome. David is naked, with a slingshot resting on his shoulder and is very detailed (veins, ligaments, muscles, etc.). The statue represents the ideal human body and is evidence that Michelangelo made a close study of anatomy.

▲ Michelangelo Buonarroti

▲ The *Pietà*

### The Sistine Chapel

In 1508, Michelangelo began to paint the ceiling of the **Sistine Chapel**, commissioned by **Pope Julius II**. It took him four years to paint this **fresco**, lying on his back high up on scaffolding. The finished ceiling shows scenes from the Old Testament, especially the book of Genesis, from the creation of Adam to Noah's flood. It contains over 300 different figures. Some years later, he painted *The Last Judgement* on the wall behind the altar in the Chapel.

▼ Ceiling of the Sistine Chapel

8

The Renaissance

### Later life

Michelangelo spent the rest of his life in Rome. He wrote poetry and designed buildings as an architect. Near the end of his life, he was the chief architect for **St Peter's Basilica**. He designed the dome based on ancient Roman ideas, but died aged 89 in 1564, before it was completed. His body was smuggled back to Florence, where he was placed in a tomb under the epitaph 'il Divino Michelangelo' ('the divine Michelangelo').

▲ St Peter's Basilica

 **COLLABORATE:**

With your group, research the design and construction of an important Renaissance building. For example, you could look at St Peter's Basilica in Rome or the Duomo in Florence. Present a visual report to your class.

# WORKING WITH THE EVIDENCE!

## Medieval vs. Renaissance sculpture

| Medieval Sculpture | Renaissance Sculpture |
|---|---|
|  ◀ Medieval sculpture: Chartres Cathedral sculptures | ◀ Renaissance sculpture: Michelangelo's *David* |

Look at the images above and list all the differences you can see between the statues.

## CHECKPOINT!

1. Describe Michelangelo's training as an artist.
2. Why did he travel to Rome in 1496?
3. Name and describe one of Michelangelo's sculptures.
4. Do you think Michelangelo would have found working on the Sistine Chapel difficult? Give a reason for your answer.
5. Why do you think that 'il Divino Michelangelo' was written on his tomb?

 I can describe the life and major works of Michelangelo Buonarroti.

 ◀ TIME TO GO BACK ◀ ▶ I CAN MOVE FORWARD ➡

Go to page 50 of your *Sources and Skills Book* for an exercise on an apprentice who worked with Michelangelo painting the Sistine Chapel.

# 8.3: Technological Change: The Printing Press

**In this topic, you will learn about:**

❯ The spread of the Renaissance outside of Italy
❯ The invention of the printing press and its impact
❯ The life of William Shakespeare

## The spread of the Renaissance

The Renaissance spread from Italy into the rest of Europe. France, England, Germany, Scandinavia and other parts of Europe were eager to follow the example set by Italy and they embraced the ideas of the Renaissance. This was helped by:

- artists visiting Italy and learning directly from Italian masters
- outside trade with Italy, which spread the ideas around Europe
- northern European rulers and merchants becoming patrons to artists in their own countries
- the invention of the movable type printing press – the single most important cause of the spread of the Renaissance.

## The printing press

Before the 1400s, all books in Europe had to be copied by hand. Because of this, very few books were in circulation, they were very precious, and very few people learned to read and write.

Johannes Gutenberg (1398–1468) was a German goldsmith. In 1450, he is believed to have invented the **movable type printing press**. He placed individual metal letters into a frame to form words, coated them with ink and pressed the frame onto paper. The process could be repeated as many times as copies of the page were needed. He then moved the letters around in the frame to make the next page, and so on. The first book he printed was the **Gutenberg Bible**.

▶ A page from the Gutenberg Bible

◀ An early printworks using the Gutenberg press

COLLABORATE: Look at this engraving of an early print shop where the Gutenberg press is in use. Can you identify the following aspects of the printing process in the picture?

- Metal letters being placed on a frame
- Ink being spread onto a page
- Sheets drying
- The letter frame being pressed onto a page
- The pages being bound together into a book

## The effects of the printing press

Gutenberg's invention spread quickly. Printing presses were operating in every major European city by 1500. This growth in printing had very important consequences for European history:

- Printed books were much cheaper than handwritten manuscripts, allowing more people to buy them.
- More people learned to read and write.
- People read more and were introduced to new ideas.
- Fiction became more popular as people began to read for entertainment.
- The control that the Catholic Church had over learning and ideas declined. It was now possible for people to challenge the Church and spread their ideas to a wide audience very quickly. This would be key to the Reformation (as we will see in chapter 10).
- The use of Latin declined as writers wrote in the **vernacular** (language as spoken by people in their native country).

**CHECKPOINT!**

1. Before the printing press, how were books produced in Europe?
2. Describe how printers used Gutenberg's printing press.
3. Name and explain two effects of the invention of the printing press.
4. What is the vernacular?

 I understand why the invention of the printing press was such an influential event. ◀ TIME TO GO BACK ◆ I CAN MOVE FORWARD ➡

COLLABORATE: Can you think of any inventions from the last 100 years that had a huge effect on society, like the printing press did in the Renaissance?

## A Life in Time: A Renaissance Writer: William Shakespeare (1564–1616)

### Early life

William Shakespeare is considered one of the greatest writers ever in the English language. He was born in Stratford-on-Avon, England in 1564. Little is known about his life before he got married, at 18 years of age, to Anne Hathaway, the daughter of a wealthy landlord. After the births of their three children, Shakespeare moved to London to become an actor and write plays and poetry.

### Life in the theatre

There, Shakespeare joined a company of actors called **The King's Men**. Actors both acted and wrote their own plays and he wrote his first, **The Comedy of Errors**, in 1594. He quickly became the most popular and famous playwright in England. His work was even performed at the Royal Court. In 1599, the company opened a theatre called The Globe. It was a round building with an open roof and could hold 2,000 people, who stood during performances.

### Shakespeare's works

Shakespeare wrote 38 plays, all of which were performed at the Globe. These include:

- Comedies such as *A Midsummer Night's Dream*, *Much Ado About Nothing* and *The Merchant of Venice*
- Tragedies such as *Hamlet*, *Romeo and Juliet* and *Macbeth*
- Histories: some based on English history, like *Henry V* and *Richard III*, and others set in the ancient past, like *Julius Caesar*.

As well as the plays, Shakespeare wrote 154 sonnets. A **sonnet is a fourteen-line rhyming poem form popular during the Renaissance**. Shakespeare's works made him rich and he retired to his home town, where he died in 1616. His plays and poems are still staged and studied all over the world today.

▲ William Shakespeare

▲ The Globe Theatre

▲ A modern adaptation of *Romeo and Juliet*

**DID YOU KNOW?**

In Shakespeare's time, women were not permitted to appear in plays, so all the female parts in his plays were performed by men!

8

The Renaissance

## CHECKPOINT!

1. Where and when was William Shakespeare born?
2. Where were Shakespeare's plays performed?
3. Name the three types of plays he wrote and give an example of each.
4. Why do you think his work is still performed and studied today?

✔ I can talk about the life of William Shakespeare and can name some of his most famous works.

← TIME TO GO BACK ◆ ▶ I CAN MOVE FORWARD →

# 8.4: Health, Medicine and Science in the Renaissance

**In this topic, you will learn about:**

- Advances in medicine during the Renaissance
- How science changed during the Renaissance
- The life of Galileo Galilei

## WORKING WITH THE EVIDENCE!

### Medieval vs Renaissance medicine

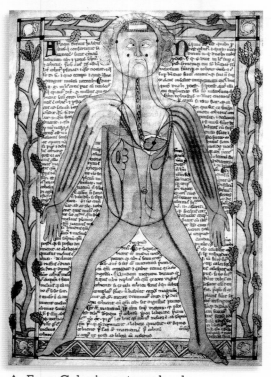

▲ From Galen's anatomy book

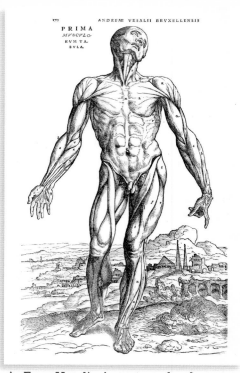

▲ From Vesalius's anatomy book

Look at these images of the human body, one medieval and one from the Renaissance. List all the differences between them that you can see.

## Medicine during the Renaissance

In chapter 6, we learned about medieval medicine and how it was based on some very strange ideas about the body. This began to change in the 1500s, when doctors such as **Andreas Vesalius (1514–1564)** began to investigate anatomy, the study of the structure of the human body. They carried out dissections to learn more. Vesalius wrote *On the Fabric of the Human Body*, which was full of correct information and had 270 accurate drawings of the human bones, muscles, veins and organs.

Other Renaissance doctors followed Vesalius's lead and made further important discoveries. For example, **William Harvey (1578–1657)** discovered that the heart pumped blood around the body. Medical treatments such as surgery improved considerably, as they were now based on correct information.

### CHECKPOINT!

1. What contribution did Andreas Vesalius make to medical knowledge?
2. What is anatomy?
3. What did William Harvey discover?
4. Reread the section on medieval medicine in chapter 6. What are the main differences between medieval and Renaissance medicine?

 I understand how the Renaissance helped to advance medical knowledge. ◀ TIME TO GO BACK ❯ I CAN MOVE FORWARD ➡

# Science during the Renaissance

The influence of **humanism** meant that people were very interested in understanding the world around them. Since ancient times, people had believed that our planet was the centre of the solar system and that the sun and the other planets rotated around it. The Catholic Church held this view, as it supported their belief that God had created the Earth and humankind and made them central. As astronomers began to examine the skies, this belief was challenged.

## A Life in Time: A Renaissance Scientist: Galileo Galilei (1564–1642)

### Early life and work

Galileo was born in Pisa in 1564 and studied mathematics at Pisa University. He developed a number of theories about space and time, including the **Law of Falling Objects**. He proved that all objects fall to ground at the same speed regardless of weight, supposedly by dropping objects from the Leaning Tower of Pisa.

▲ Galileo Galilei

### The astronomer

While Professor of Mathematics in Padua, Galileo heard of a Dutch invention called the **telescope**, and improved upon it to magnify objects many hundreds of times using increasingly small and powerful lenses. He used his telescope to study the planets and stars (**astronomy**) and made several important discoveries, which he published in *The Starry Messenger* in 1610:

- the surface of the moon has craters and mountains
- Saturn has rings
- Jupiter has four moons
- there are spots on the sun

### Galileo vs. the Catholic Church

In the 1540s a Polish priest and astronomer, **Nicolaus Copernicus**, wrote a book called *On the Revolutions of the Heavenly Spheres*, where he declared that the Earth rotates around the sun. He published it at the very end of his life for fear of the Catholic Church's reaction. Galileo read it and backed up Copernicus in *Dialogue Concerning the Two Chief World Systems* in 1632. The Church was furious. The Pope ordered that Galileo be put on trial before **the Inquisition** (a Church court). He was convicted of **heresy** (knowingly holding a view that went against the official teachings of the Catholic Church). Galileo was terrified of being burned at the stake, the usual punishment for heretics, and eventually agreed to say he was wrong. His books were banned by the Church and he was kept under house arrest until his death in 1642.

## CHECKPOINT!

1. Before the Renaissance, what did people believe about the relationship between the Earth and the sun?
2. What was Galileo's Law of Falling Objects?
3. Name two of his astronomical discoveries.
4. Why did his book *Dialogue Concerning the Two Chief World Systems* get him into trouble with the Catholic Church?
5. What does Galileo's trial by the Inquisition in the 1630s tell us about the Church at the time?

 I understand the contribution made by Galileo to science during the Renaissance.

 ← TIME TO GO BACK ◆ I CAN MOVE FORWARD →

# SUMMARY

In this chapter, we have learned about how the Renaissance changed history.

*Changes in art*

- During the Renaissance, the focus of art was on the accurate recreation of the world in painting and sculpture, and artists created new techniques to achieve this. For example, da Vinci used perspective to great effect in *The Last Supper* and sfumato in the *Mona Lisa*.

- Artists based their work on the close study of the body and nature. For example, Michelangelo captured details of muscles and limbs accurately in both his paintings (the Sistine Chapel ceiling) and his sculptures *(David)*.

*New discoveries*

- Renaissance people began to question accepted beliefs from the Middle Ages. They made many important discoveries in the fields of science and medicine. Their scientific method (observe, measure theorise and experiment) is the same basic approach used by today's scientists. Galileo proved that the Earth rotated around the sun but this brought him into conflict with the Catholic Church.

- In medicine, as more doctors performed autopsies on bodies and carried out detailed examinations of how the body worked, a completely new understanding of how to treat injuries and disease was developed.

*Spread of knowledge and ideas*

- The single most important invention of the Renaissance was the printing press. More people wrote books, more people learned to read, and ideas and new knowledge spread quickly throughout Europe. We will see in the next two chapters how new ideas led to the voyages of exploration and to a direct challenge to the Church's authority in the Reformation.

## Reflecting on... the Renaissance

The Renaissance is often described as 'the birth of the modern world'. By the 1600s, old ideas in science, medicine, religion and art were gone and new ideas were being embraced, based on looking at the real world and trying to understand it. This process was gradual and met a lot of resistance, but it changed our world forever.

# Understanding History

1. Give three reasons why Italy was the centre of the early Renaissance.
2. What was the role of money in the Renaissance?
3. Name three artistic techniques developed during the Renaissance and give an example of a work of art that features each of them.
4. Did Michelangelo deserve the title 'il Divino Michelangelo'? Explain your answer.
5. Explain why the printing press was such an important invention during the Renaissance.
6. What change during the Renaissance allowed improvements in medical knowledge?
7. How did Galileo challenge the teachings of the Catholic Church and how did the Church respond?
8. Draw a timeline in your copy. Find out the year when the events below took place. You can use the internet to help you. When you have all the right dates, enter them in your timeline.

- Shakespeare wrote *Hamlet*
- The Ottoman Turks conquered Constantinople
- The *Gutenberg Bible* was published
- Death of Michelangelo
- Leonardo painted *The Last Supper*
- Birth of Leonardo da Vinci

- Michelangelo sculpted *David*
- Martin Luther began the Reformation in Wittenberg
- Galileo published *Dialogue Concerning the Two Chief World Systems*
- Christopher Columbus sailed to the Americas

9. Look at this picture of *The Anatomy Lesson* by Rembrandt and answer the questions that follow.

(a) How can you tell that this is a Renaissance painting?

(b) Why were dissections of dead bodies not very common before the Renaissance?

(c) Name one Renaissance doctor who studied anatomy.

(d) Why did artists like Michelangelo and da Vinci study anatomy?

(e) Name two Renaissance discoveries that increased scientific knowledge.

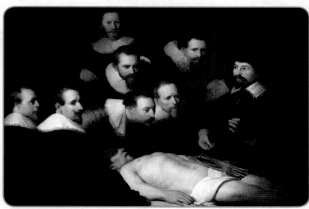

 **Exploring History**

1. Write an account of the life of a Renaissance artist under the following headings:
   - Early life and training
   - Major works and patrons
   - Artistic techniques
   - Later life

2. Write an account of the importance of anatomy study to Renaissance (a) art and (b) medicine.

3. Write about the changes that occurred in the Renaissance under the following headings:
   (a) art; (b) medicine; (c) science; (d) literature.

4. Write about the role of patrons and money in the Renaissance, using examples for the artists, writers and scientists you have studied.

| KEY TERMS | Renaissance | means 'rebirth'. Refers to the period of European history that saw huge changes in art, literature and science |
|---|---|---|
| | Humanism | the idea that human beings should be at the centre of everything and we should think about the world in terms of the lives people live |
| | Patron | a wealthy person who commissioned (hired) an artist to produce an artwork |
| | Fresco | a method of painting directly onto wet plaster |
| | Sfumato | a painting technique that blurs or smudges lines and colours to soften textures and create a 'smoky' effect |
| | Perspective | the creation of depth and distance in painting |
| | Anatomy | the study of the structure of the human body |
| | Movable type printing press | a method of printing books that placed individual metal letters into a frame to form words, coated them with ink and pressed the frame onto paper |
| | Vernacular | language as spoken by people in their native country |
| | Sonnet | a fourteen-line rhyming poem form popular during the Renaissance |
| | Astronomy | the study of the planets and stars |
| | Heresy | knowingly holding a view that went against the official teachings of the Catholic Church |

 Go to page 45 of your *Sources and Skills Book* for more exercises.

 Go to page 15 of your *Research Portfolio* for a task based on this chapter.

8 The Renaissance

# The Age of Exploration and Conquest

LO: 3.2

| The Renaissance c. 1350–1650 | The Age of Exploration and Conquest c. 1400–1750 | The Reformation c. 1500–1700 |
| --- | --- | --- |

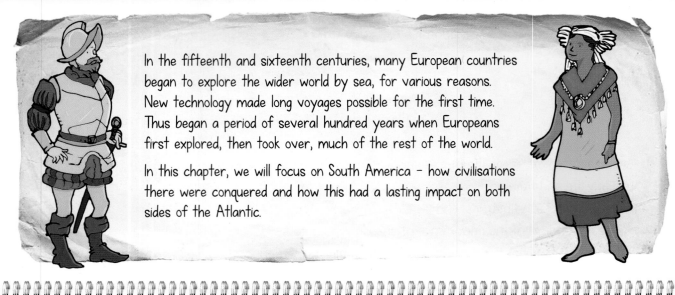

In the fifteenth and sixteenth centuries, many European countries began to explore the wider world by sea, for various reasons. New technology made long voyages possible for the first time. Thus began a period of several hundred years when Europeans first explored, then took over, much of the rest of the world.

In this chapter, we will focus on South America – how civilisations there were conquered and how this had a lasting impact on both sides of the Atlantic.

# WORKING WITH THE EVIDENCE!

## The Age of Exploration and Conquest

| Source on … | Type of source | Category | Examples |
| --- | --- | --- | --- |
| The European explorers/ conquistadores | Primary | Written | Documents such as diaries and letters, logbooks from the ships and public records such as treaties and laws related to the voyages |
| The colonised American peoples | Primary | Tactile/Visual | Their archaeological, architectural or artistic remains |
| | Secondary | Written | Accounts written by their European conquerers |

◀ Page from a captain's logbook

◀ Aztec painting from the *Codex Magliabechiano*

What problem is there in relying on accounts by Europeans for our knowledge of the cultures of South America?

# 9.1: The Reasons for European Exploration

## Problems of sea travel

Travel by sea was limited and difficult in the early 1400s.

In this topic, you will learn about:

❯ The problems faced by sailors
❯ The reasons why Europeans began to explore the world beyond Europe

- Ships could not navigate accurately, often ending up very far from where they had planned to go.
- Many sailors were afraid of the unknown. Some believed that the earth was flat and they would sail off the edge if they went too far. Others believed the seas were full of monsters.

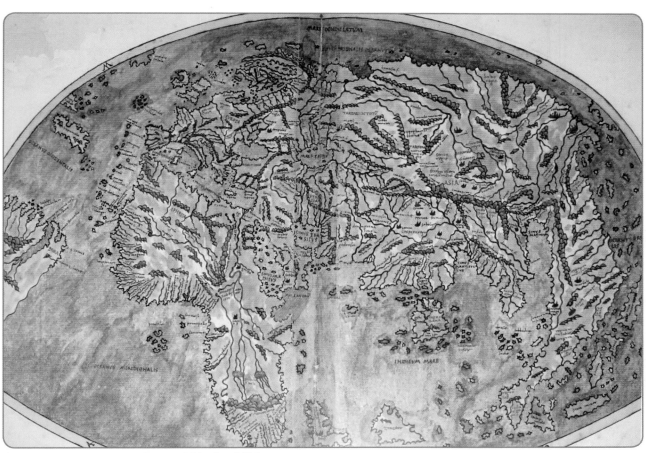

▲ How Europeans saw the world in the 1400s

## Reasons to explore

Europeans began to explore the wider world from the mid-1400s onwards for several reasons:

1. **The influence of the Renaissance:** People were eager to learn and were questioning their existing beliefs. In particular, the rediscovery of the *Geographia* by the Roman writer **Ptolemy** changed how people understood the world.

2. **The stories of Marco Polo:** Polo was a fourteenth-century Italian who had travelled to China and wrote about the great wealth and incredible things he had seen. His book made people want to see these wonders for themselves.

3. **New trade routes:** The trade in **silks and spices** (needed to help preserve and flavour food) from the East was very profitable. After the Black Death, Europe's population grew rapidly and became wealthier. Explorers and traders could grow very rich if they could find ways to get more goods to Europe more quickly.

9

The Age of Exploration and Conquest

4. **The fall of Constantinople:** The Great Silk Road was the main overland route for spices and other goods from the East to reach Europe. It was cut off in 1453, when Constantinople was conquered by the Turks. New routes between Europe and Asia were needed.

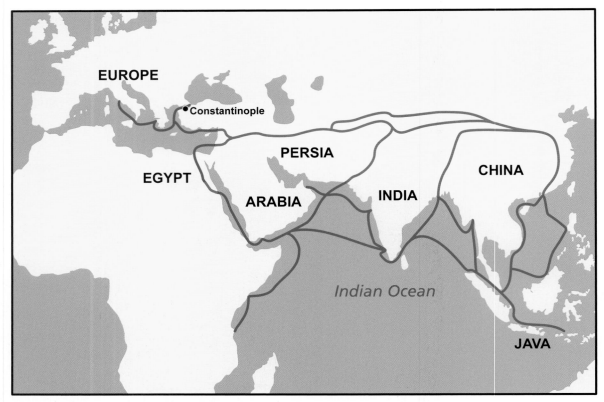

▲ Trade routes from Europe to east Asia

5. **Desire for empire:** Many European rulers sponsored voyages of exploration so that they could expand their territory to any newly discovered lands. Countries on the Atlantic coast (Portugal, Spain, France and England) especially wanted to undermine Italy's power by bypassing the Mediterranean as the centre of trade.

6. **Spreading Christianity:** The Pope encouraged Christian rulers to defeat Muslims, who had gained control of the Middle East. Christian explorers often aimed to convert the people of any new lands they discovered to Christianity.

**DID YOU KNOW?**

Legends were told in Europe of a mythical Christian kingdom in Africa or Asia ruled by a king named Prester John. If he could only be found, he would unite with Christendom to defeat the Muslims.

 COLLABORATE: Look at the map above. Imagine you were a king or a merchant living in the 1400s. With the direct route east along the Silk Road blocked, how else might you reach China or India?

## CHECKPOINT!

1. What problems did sailors face on long voyages in the 1400s?
2. What role did the following factors have in the voyages of discovery: (a) the Renaissance; (b) trade routes; (c) the desire for empire; (d) religion?
3. Which of the causes of the voyages do you think was the most important? Give a reason for your answer.

✓ I understand the causes and problems of the voyages of exploration.

 ⬅ TIME TO GO BACK ◆ I CAN MOVE FORWARD ➡

# 9.2: Technological Change: Advances in Exploration

Before this period, European sailors usually stayed quite close to coastlines. For ships to sail straight out into the vast ocean without a single landmark, and hope to return, far better navigation was needed. Several advances in technology made this possible.

In this topic, you will learn about:
❯ Maps
❯ Equipment
❯ Ships
❯ Life on board a ship

compass

astrolabe

log and line

quadrant

portolan chart

▲ Navigational instruments

## New maps

To navigate properly, new and more accurate maps were needed. **Cartographers** (people who draw maps) started using maps from Constantinople, which were far more detailed. The Portuguese developed **portolan charts**, which mapped harbours and coastlines more precisely, recording information like currents, tides and depth. As explorers returned from their voyages, the information they brought was used to update maps.

## New equipment

New inventions allowed a ship to calculate its position and speed more accurately:

- A **quadrant** and an **astrolabe** helped determine a ship's **latitude** (distance from the equator) by using the position of the stars and the sun.

- A **compass** was used to identify north, so the direction a ship was sailing in could be calculated.

- A **log and line** measured a ship's speed in knots. The line had knots in it at regular intervals and was tied around a log. A sailor would hold the line, throw the log overboard and measure the ship's speed by how many knots passed through his hand in a given time (measured by an hourglass). The speed was recorded in the ship's **logbook**.

- To measure the depth of water, especially around a coast, a **line and lead weight** was used. The line was marked with depths and dropped into the water to ensure it was not too shallow for the ship.

Together, these instruments allowed sailors to work out exactly where they were, based on how far they had travelled and how fast, their distance from the equator and the direction of travel. No longer would a ship be lost if it were blown off course in a storm.

## New ships

The fifteenth century saw a new design of ship: the **caravel**. It was <u>large and sturdy enough to make long voyages and able to sail in all winds</u>. The caravel's features combined the best of the Atlantic and Mediterranean ships.

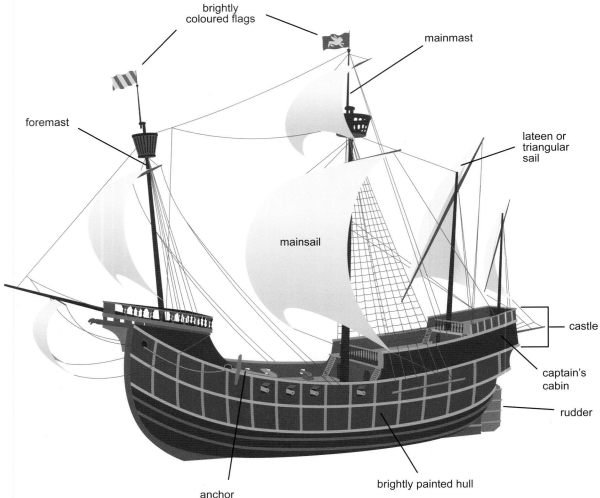

brightly coloured flags

mainmast

foremast

lateen or triangular sail

mainsail

castle

captain's cabin

rudder

anchor

brightly painted hull

▲ A caravel

- Triangular lateen sails allowed ships to sail into the wind and made them easier to manoeuvre in bays and along coasts.
- **Carvel-built hulls**, with planks fitted edge to edge (rather than overlapping planks, like Viking longships had) were far lighter, so ships could be made bigger, could have more masts and could carry more men and supplies.
- **Rudders** made the caravel easier to steer.
- A **castle** at the back of the deck provided improved crew quarters and served as a lookout point and a defensible area in case of attack.

Soon caravels were improved upon: **naos** were bigger versions, better suited to Atlantic crossings.

### Technology of Exploration

- Portolan charts
- Quadrant
- Astrolabe
- Compass
- Log and line
- Line and lead weight
- Caravels
- Lateen sails
- Carvel-built hulls
- Rudders

## Life on board ship

Life on board ship during a voyage of discovery was extremely tough.

- The captain had his own cabin, but most sailors slept on the deck in the open air or else below decks, in hammocks.

- Sailing and maintaining the ship required **constant hard work**, which included raising and managing the sails, steering and cleaning the ship, making repairs and preparing food for the crew.

- The captain and officers were usually from wealthier social classes, while sailors tended to be poor. This caused tension on the ship. **Mutiny** (sailors rebelling against their captain) was not unusual. **Harsh discipline** was used to keep order. Men were flogged (whipped) or put in chains for breaking minor rules. Execution was common.

- **Food** that would last for long voyages tended to be dry and very salty. When the crew ran out of meat and vegetables, they ate flat hard bread made from water, flour and salt called ship's biscuit.

- Ill health was common: the lack of fresh water led to **typhoid** and the lack of foods rich in vitamin C (such as citrus fruit) led to **scurvy**, which caused exhaustion, tooth loss, vomiting and eventually death.

▲ The crew of Ferdinand de Magellan swearing loyalty to him following an unsuccessful mutiny

## CHECKPOINT!

1. What information did a portolan chart give to sailors?
2. What instruments were invented to (a) calculate latitude; (b) show direction; (c) measure speed?
3. What sort of sails did a caravel have and what were they used for?
4. What was a carvel-built hull?
5. Describe life on a ship under the following headings: (a) discipline; (b) food; (c) disease.

 I can explain how advances in technology made the voyages of exploration possible and what life was like on board ship.

 ← TIME TO GO BACK ◆ ▶ I CAN MOVE FORWARD →

**9 The Age of Exploration and Conquest**

# 9.3: The Voyages of Exploration

In this topic, you will learn about:

- ❯ The beginnings of the Age of Exploration in Portugal
- ❯ The major voyages of exploration
- ❯ The life of Christopher Columbus

## The early Portuguese voyages of exploration

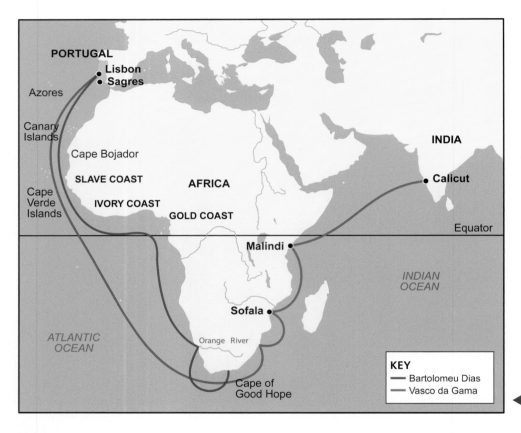

**KEY**
— Bartolomeu Dias
— Vasco da Gama

◀ Early Portuguese voyages around Africa

The first major voyages of discovery set out from **Portugal** in the 1400s. Portugal was ideally located on the edge of Europe and close to Africa. Its kings wanted to find new trade routes that could make Portugal rich enough to protect itself from its more powerful neighbours, especially Spain.

Having driven Portugal's Muslims out in the early fifteenth century, the Portuguese attacked the Muslim states in North Africa and along the African Atlantic coast. Returning soldiers told stories of fabulously wealthy states further south. In response, **Prince Henry the Navigator** set up a **school of navigation** at **Sagres**, which brought together cartographers, instrument-makers, astronomers and experienced sailors. The Portuguese focused on exploring the African coast to try to find a way around Africa to Asia.

- Over the following decades they discovered the **Azores, the Canary Islands and the Cape Verde Islands** and rounded **the Gold Coast** (modern-day **Sierra Leone**). They set up bases all along the coast to trade with the native peoples for gold and slaves.

- In 1487, **Bartolomeu Dias** rounded the southern tip of Africa, now called the **Cape of Good Hope**.

- In 1497, **Vasco da Gama** continued sailing up the eastern African coast. From modern-day Kenya, he sailed east to **Calicut** in India. The round trip took two years.

Da Gama had proven that it was possible to successfully sail around Africa and reach India (and later China). The results of this were:

- Trade made Portugal **wealthy**.

- Portugal established a large **empire in Africa and Asia** (and later, South America).

- Portugal gained **control of the spice trade** by defeating various Arab and Muslim kingdoms.

- Imports of spices into Europe increased.

- **Other European rulers** wanted to copy Portugal's success by engaging in **voyages of their own**.

## CHECKPOINT!

1. Why were the earliest voyages of exploration begun by Portugal?
2. What did Prince Henry do to support these voyages?
3. What voyages did (a) Bartolomeu Dias and (b) Vasco da Gama undertake?
4. What were the results of the Portuguese voyages of exploration?

 I can describe Portugal's role in the early voyages of exploration and the results of these voyages.

 ← TIME TO GO BACK ◇ I CAN MOVE FORWARD →

**9**

**The Age of Exploration and Conquest**

▼ Monument to Henry the Navigator, Lisbon

# The discovery of the 'New World'

As Portugal controlled the trade routes around Africa, its rival **Spain** had to look west to the Atlantic Ocean for opportunities to discover and conquer new lands. The most famous explorer of the Atlantic was **Christopher Columbus**, who reached **the Americas** in 1492.

## A Life in Time: Christopher Columbus (1451–1506)

### Early life

Christopher Columbus was born in **Genoa**, Italy in 1451. As a young man, he sailed the Mediterranean on merchant ships, and also along the African and European Atlantic coasts. He was shipwrecked off the Portuguese coast and when he came ashore he made his way to Sagres. He lived there for nine years with the map-makers and sailors of the navigation school.

### Proof of a round world

Like many, Columbus was convinced that our planet was round, not flat, and that the Far East could be reached by sailing west across the Atlantic. He read the works of Marco Polo and Ptolemy and studied a map by **Toscanelli**. This map led Columbus to believe that **Cathay** (China) and **Cipangu** (Japan) were only 4,500 km west of Europe. However, the map was wrong – by about 10,000 km – and did not show the large continent in the way.

**DID YOU KNOW?**

A young Columbus docked at Galway in 1477. He later wrote of seeing two bodies 'of extraordinary appearance' in a canoe-like boat. He took them for Chinese and it strengthened his belief that China lay to the west. However, the bodies were probably those of unlucky Inuit who had drifted south on the strong current.

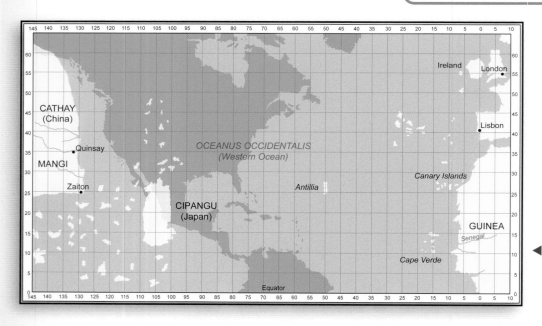

◀ The real location of the Americas (in green) overlaid on Toscanelli's map of the Atlantic Ocean

### Preparing for the voyage

Columbus approached the rulers of France, England and Portugal to sponsor his voyage west, but they all turned him down. Finally, he convinced **King Ferdinand** and **Queen Isabella** of Spain. They gave him three ships – two caravels, the **Nina** and the **Pinta**, and a nao, the **Santa Maria** – and permission to recruit a crew from the port of **Palos**. In return, Columbus would claim any lands he discovered for Spain. He recruited a crew of 80 men. All three ships were stocked with hard bread, wine, salted meat, dried fish, beans, rice and fresh water before they sailed.

## The voyage

The small fleet left Palos on **3 August 1492**. They took on fresh supplies in the Canary Islands and then set out across the Atlantic. As the weeks passed with no land in sight, the crew grew increasingly afraid that they would go too far to have food for the return journey. To reassure them, Columbus kept a fake logbook to show them that they had travelled much shorter distances than the reality. He also threatened any man who mutinied (rebelled) with hanging. After four weeks with no sign of land, he was forced to

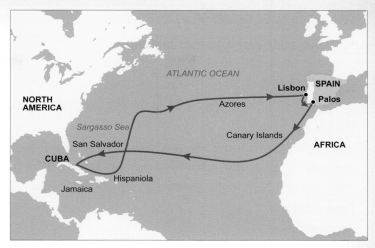

▲ Columbus's first voyage

promise them that they would turn around if they had not seen land within the next few days. At last, on **12 October 1492**, 69 days after they left Spain, land was sighted. Columbus named it **San Salvador** and the inhabitants **Indians**, as he was sure he had reached India. This is why the Caribbean is still often called 'the West Indies'. In fact, he had found what we now know as the American continent, then often called **'the New World'**.

## Return to Spain and later life

Columbus spent the next two months **exploring the islands** around San Salvador in the Bahamas. He was looking for the cities and great wealth that he had expected to find in Asia. He returned to Spain in early 1493 and was given a hero's welcome. He presented Ferdinand and Isabella with some native people as **slaves**, **exotic fruit**, **maize** (a type of corn), **parrots** and some **gold**. They believed he had found a sea route to Asia and appointed him governor of their new territory.

Columbus returned to the New World three more times and **continued his search for China**. Settlers went with him and **began to farm sugar**. Columbus mistreated the native peoples, selling them into slavery and torturing and killing many. The Spanish settlers complained to their king and queen about his **poor leadership and brutality** and he was **removed as governor** in 1499.

As more people came to the New World, it became increasingly clear that Columbus had not reached Asia at all, but an entirely different continent. Columbus died in 1506, a broken man who still insisted that he had found his way to the East.

## CHECKPOINT!

1. Where did Columbus learn to sail?
2. Why was he so sure he could reach the East by sailing across the Atlantic?
3. What agreement did he reach with the King and Queen of Spain?
4. Why did the crew become concerned during the voyage? How did Columbus respond to their concerns?
5. Where did he land? Where did he believe he had landed?
6. What he did bring back with him to Spain?
7. Why was he removed as governor in 1499?

 I know about the main voyages of exploration and how Columbus reached the Americas.

 ← TIME TO GO BACK ◆ I CAN MOVE FORWARD →

**9 The Age of Exploration and Conquest**

## The age of exploration after Columbus

After Columbus had established settlements in the New World, many others followed him. Explorers continued to explore the rest of the world over the next 200 years. Some of the most important voyages were:

- 1497: **John Cabot** landed in **Newfoundland**, Canada and claimed it for the English king **Henry VII**.
- 1519–1522: **Ferdinand Magellan** led a fleet on a voyage to finally prove that the world was round by **circumnavigating (sailing around) the globe**.
- 1642: **Abel Tasman** was the first European to find **Tasmania**, south of Australia, and **New Zealand**.

# WORKING WITH THE EVIDENCE!

## Colombus returns to the Spanish court

▲ Columbus returning to the Spanish court in 1493

1. Columbus returned to Spain with some inhabitants of the land he discovered (marked X). Why did Columbus call these people Indians?
2. Name two new products brought from the New World to Europe by explorers or traders.
3. What do you think the artist thought of the inhabitants of the Americas? Give a reason for your answer.

Go to page 56 of your *Sources and Skills Book* to read about Columbus's first impressions of the New World.

## 9.4: Conquering the New World: The Conquistadores

Rumours of the wealth of the New World spread quickly around Europe: stories of entire cities made of gold, of untold riches that were simply waiting for Europeans to come and take them from the native peoples. Unsurprisingly, these stories prompted men to travel across the sea looking for wealth and adventure. These men were known as **conquistadores** (Spanish for 'conquerers'). They would conquer major American civilisations, such as the Aztecs and the Incas.

**In this topic, you will learn about:**

- Why the Spanish set out to conquer South America
- The conquest of the Aztecs by Hernán Cortés
- The conquest of the Incas by Francisco Pizarro

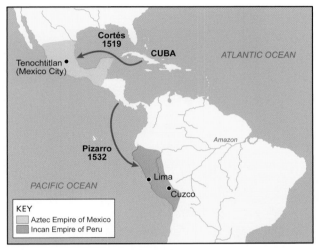

▲ Location of the Aztec and Incan Empires

**DID YOU KNOW?**

The cacao bean – from which we get chocolate – was sacred to the Aztecs, used only by the elite and in the most important rituals. The drink was very different to ours: bitter, heavily spiced and quite intoxicating! The Spanish brought the beans home, but didn't enjoy the taste: our chocolate is the result of their experiments with milk and sugar. The word 'chocolate' comes from the Aztec word 'xocoatl'.

**COLLABORATE:** Research different aspects of life in the Aztec empire, such as religion, warriors, cities, education or the lives of women. Present your findings to the rest of the class.

### Conquering the Aztecs: Hernán Cortés

The **Aztecs** came from the south of modern-day Mexico. They conquered rival tribes and by the 1420s their empire covered central Mexico. By 1519, there were around 489 cities in the Aztec empire. Its capital, **Tenochtitlan**, was a city of over 250,000 people located on an island in the middle of a lake. Mexico City stands on the same spot today.

The Aztecs had a complex society, with a king and priests at the top, but it was very different from European society. They had **no iron or steel**, so most weapons and tools were made from wood, stone or copper. Nor were there horses, cattle, sheep, pigs or goats on the continent before Europeans imported them. For meat, the Aztecs ate turkeys, dogs and guinea pigs.

The Aztecs worshipped many gods. The most important was the sun god, **Huitzilopochtli**. They believed that if he grew weak the sun would not rise and the universe would end, so he had to be nourished by human blood sacrifice.

▲ Tenochtitlan

▲ Human sacrifice

## A Life in Time: Hernán Cortés (1485–1547)

Hernán Cortés was born in Spain and trained as a soldier. He travelled to the New World and gained experience in the conquest of Cuba in 1511. He was ambitious and believed he could earn a fortune in the New World. Inspired by tales of vast amounts of gold, he decided to attack the Aztecs.

### Attacking the Aztecs

In February 1519, Cortés landed with 11 ships, 500 soldiers and 13 horses. He had the ships burned to show his men that there was no going back. He made contact with local tribes that had been conquered by the Aztecs. Many of the native peoples were terrified of the Spaniards' horses and cannons (which they had never seen before) but the Aztecs' brutal rule encouraged them to help Cortés. Cortés was given a slave girl called **Malinche**, who spoke several local languages. She quickly learned Spanish and acted as his translator. She also bore him a son.

▲ A painting of Cortés and his conquest of the Aztecs

### Meeting Montezuma

With his men and native troops Cortés marched to **Tenochtitlan**, where he was greeted by the Aztec king, **Montezuma**. The Aztecs believed that one of their gods, **Quetzalcoatl**, would one day return from over the sea. When Cortés arrived – with his pale skin and feathered helmet, riding a strange beast – the Aztecs took him for this god and worshipped him. However, the Spaniards soon began to steal gold. When there were protests, the Spaniards captured Montezuma and tried to rule through him.

### *The destruction of Tenochtitlan*

The Aztecs revolted and the Spaniards were driven out of the city, but Montezuma was killed in the violence. Cortés and his men fled to regroup amongst local allies, but later returned with 100,000 men and laid siege to Tenochtitlan for three months. Eventually they constructed a small fleet of ships that could cross the lake. The city fell and its people were massacred. When the Spanish king appointed him governor of **New Spain**, Cortés built his capital on the site of Tenochtitlan.

## CHECKPOINT!

1. Give three examples of how Aztec and European society differed.
2. Why did Cortés decide to attack the Aztecs?
3. Why did he burn his ships upon landing?
4. Who did the Aztecs believe Cortés was?
5. Why did the Aztecs revolt against the Spaniards?
6. How did Tenochtitlan eventually fall?

 I understand how the Spanish conquered the Aztecs.

 ← TIME TO GO BACK ◇ I CAN MOVE FORWARD →

## Conquering the Incas: Pizarro

▲ Machu Picchu

To the south of the Aztecs lay an even more powerful and rich civilisation. The **Incas** controlled a huge amount of territory in the Andes mountains, along the western coast of South America. The Incan empire was ruled from its capital in **Cusco** by a god-king.

The Incas were sophisticated **engineers and architects** and also very fine artists. They used no written script, but kept records using a system of knotted string. Roads ran to every corner of their empire and they collected **tribute** from their subjects.

▶ A gold artefact from Incan civilisation

9

The Age of Exploration and Conquest

# The fall of the Incas

**Francisco Pizarro** (1475–1541) was born into poverty in Spain. He received no education and found his way to the New World by serving on a ship. There he found work as a soldier on missions to explore central America. He gained a reputation for toughness and ruthless behaviour. He heard rumours of the great wealth of the Incas and was granted a commission to conquer them by **King Charles V** of Spain in 1528. He gathered a small army of 180 men and 27 horses and invaded the Incan empire in 1532.

Pizarro met the Incan king, **Atahualpa**, at the town of **Cajamarca**. To give him an excuse to attack the Incas, Pizarro had a priest approach Atahualpa with a bible. The king threw it aside. Claiming that this was an insult to the Christian faith, Pizarro ordered his men to attack. Although vastly outnumbered by the Incan warriors, the Spanish had superior weapons. They won and captured Atahualpa.

The Incas offered to fill a room with gold and silver in return for their king. Pizarro accepted the treasure, but had the king executed anyway. The death of Atahualpa threw the empire into chaos, as he had left no heir. Pizarro defeated the remaining Incan armies at Cusco. He declared their empire the Spanish province of **New Castile** and established a new capital city at **Lima**. Huge deposits of gold and silver were later found in the Andes, making Spain the wealthiest country in Europe.

▲ A painting of Pizarro encountering the Incas

## CHECKPOINT!

1. Why did Pizarro want to attack the Incas?
2. Describe what happened at Cajamarca.
3. What did the Incas offer to do for the return of their king?
4. Why was Pizarro able to defeat the Incas so easily?

 I understand how the Spanish conquered the Incas.    ◀ TIME TO GO BACK   I CAN MOVE FORWARD ▶

Go to page 57 of your *Sources and Skills Book* to read a letter about the aftermath of the conquests.

# 9.5: The Impact of Colonisation

In this topic, you will learn about:

> The effects of colonisation on both the colonised and the colonisers

**Colonisation** is <u>when a country takes over another territory and settles some of its own people there to control it</u>. After Europeans discovered lands in the Americas, Africa and Asia, they conquered these areas and set up **colonies** in each. This process of colonisation had a huge impact, both on the peoples native to those areas (the **colonised**) and on the countries who did the colonising (the **colonisers**).

## The impact of colonisation on the peoples of South America

1. **The native population was decimated:** In 1519 (the year Cortés arrived in the Aztec empire), the native population of South America was roughly 25 million. By 1605, this had fallen to about 3 million. Violence and mistreatment were partly to blame – but the main cause was disease. Europeans introduced epidemic diseases such as **smallpox**, **measles** and **influenza** to the New World. American peoples had no resistance to these, unlike many Europeans. Almost 90% of the native population died as a result.

2. **The destruction of cultures:** The decline in the native population contributed to the loss of old and advanced civilisations. As Spanish and Portuguese became the languages of the ruling classes, native languages and customs were wiped out.

3. **The spread of Christianity:** Priests, especially the **Jesuits**, set up the Catholic Church in the New World and carried out hundreds of thousands of conversions. Privately, many native people continued to worship the old gods, though without the human sacrifices. Whenever this was discovered, the local populations were severely punished.

4. **Massive growth in the slave trade:** As Catholics could not be taken as slaves, and there was a need to replace the native workforce as they died off due to disease, millions of Africans were transported across the Atlantic. The '**slavery triangle**' developed: <u>ships sailed to African slaving ports and took slaves to the Americas</u>. There they toiled on the sugar, tobacco, coffee and cotton plantations and in the gold and silver mines. Those ships <u>then sailed back to Europe, full of food and precious materials</u>.

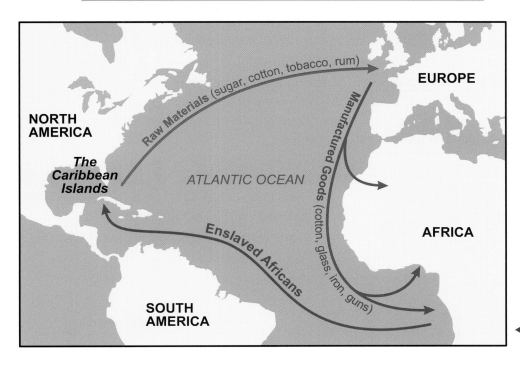

◀ The Atlantic slavery triangle

# The impact of colonisation on Europe

1. Other European states saw the wealth and power that Spain was gaining from its conquests in South America and decided to create empires of their own:

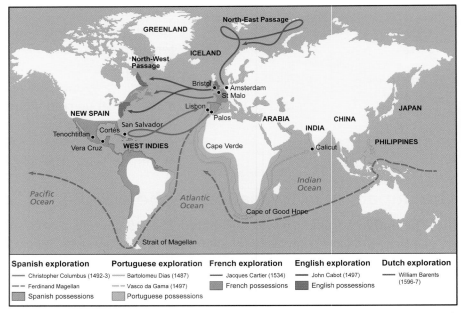

▲ European empires c.1650

   • **Portugal** explored and settled the east coast of South America, **modern-day Brazil**. Portuguese is spoken in Brazil and is Uruguay's second language, while the rest of South America speaks Spanish.

   • **England** (Britain from 1707) set up colonies in **eastern North America**. Britain later expanded its empire to cover **India, large sections of Africa, Australia and New Zealand**.

   • **France** conquered parts of North America, mainly inland areas, as well as **parts of Africa and Asia**.

   • **The Netherlands** conquered the Spice Islands in Asia (**modern-day Indonesia**).

2. So many countries were scrambling for territory that **conflict** between them was inevitable:

   • **Spain and Portugal** nearly went to war over South America. The Pope pressured them to sign the **Treaty of Tordesillas** in 1494, which divided the New World between the two countries.

   • Other conflicts included: Britain and Spain (1585–1604); France and Spain (1595–1598); and Britain and France (1756–1763).

3. Huge deposits of **gold and silver** from the Andes were shipped back to **Spain**. It became the most powerful country in Europe throughout the 1500s and 1600s. **Italy's power declined** as the focus for trade shifted away from its city states and to the Atlantic coast.

4. The 'Columbian exchange': the exchange of foods and animals between Europe and the Americas changed both continents forever. Horses, cattle, sheep, new farming methods and new technologies (like steel) were introduced to the Americas and potatoes, chillies, avocado, cocoa (chocolate), coffee, tomatoes and tobacco reached Europe.

## CHECKPOINT!

1. What is colonisation? Give an example of a coloniser and a country they colonised.

2. How were the people of South America affected by European diseases?

3. What was the 'slavery triangle'?

4. Name two European countries that established empires, and detail where.

5. Why did colonisation lead to conflict between European powers? Give an example.

6. What was the 'Columbian exchange'?

 I can explain the impact of European conquests on the New World and on Europe.

 ⬅ TIME TO GO BACK ◆ I CAN MOVE FORWARD ➡

 **SUMMARY**

In this chapter, we have learned how the voyages of exploration changed world history.

*Causes of the voyages of exploration*

- The influence of the Renaissance
- Marco Polo's stories of the wonders of the East
- A need for new trade routes
- Competing European states wanting to expand, build empires and spread Christianity.

*New technology*

- New portolan maps
- New equipment: the astrolabe, quadrant, compass, log and line
- New ships: caravels with lateen sails and new carvel-built hulls.
- These innovations allowed Portuguese explorers (like da Gama) to sail around Africa and Spanish explorers (like Columbus) to sail across the Atlantic.

*Impact of European conquest on the New World*

- South America's major native civilisations fell to Spanish conquistadores: the Aztecs to Cortés and the Incas to Pizarro.
- The native population was decimated, both by violence and by European diseases.
- Native cultures were destroyed.
- Christianity spread in the New World as the native people converted in large numbers.
- The slave trade between Africa, the Americas and Europe became established.
- New animals (horses, cattle, sheep), farming methods and technology reached the New World.

*Impact of European conquest on Europe*

- Empires were founded by Spain, Portugal, France, Britain and the Netherlands.
- Conflicts became more frequent as those empires fought over territory and wealth.
- Many new goods from the Americas reached Europe (for example, potatoes, tomatoes and tobacco).

**Reflecting on... the Age of Exploration and Conquest**

The European Age of Exploration and Conquest was an incredibly important period in world history. Until quite recently, Western historians treated it as the story of heroic explorers and the dangerous voyages they made. However, our understanding has since shifted to see the terrible and lasting effects that European colonisation had upon other peoples of the world.

**9**

**The Age of Exploration and Conquest**

# Understanding History

1. How did the Renaissance contribute to the voyages of exploration?
2. What role did the desire for wealth play in the voyages of exploration?
3. Give three examples of technological changes that allowed the voyages to happen.
4. Which technological innovation do you think was the most important? Give your reasons.
5. Describe the Portuguese voyages around Africa to Asia.
6. What were the main obstacles that Christopher Columbus faced in trying to reach Asia by sailing west?
7. How were the conquistadores able to defeat the Aztecs and Incas so easily?
8. Why did the native populations of the Americas drop so dramatically?
9. How was Africa negatively affected by the discovery of the New World?
10. Which European countries established empires after the discovery of the Americas?

# Exploring History

1. Write about the life of Christopher Columbus under the following headings:
   - His early life
   - The preparations for his first voyage
   - His voyage to America
   - His later life

2. Write about the life of a Tenochtitlan citizen during the siege by Cortés under the following headings:
   - Aztec society before the arrival of Cortés
   - The Spaniards' arrival in the city
   - The fighting between the Aztec and the Spanish forces

3. Write an account of the impact of the European conquest of the New World on (a) the native populations and (b) Europeans.

| KEY TERMS | | |
|---|---|---|
| | Quadrant, astrolabe | instruments that determined a ship's latitude (the distance from the equator) by using the position of the stars and the sun |
| | Compass | instrument used to identify north, and so calculate the direction of the ship |
| | Log and line | measured a ship's speed in knots by letting out a rope with knots tied in it at regular intervals |
| | Caravel | a type of ship large and sturdy enough to make long journeys and sail in all winds. Caravels used lateen sails and had carvel-built hulls |
| | Conquistadores | Spanish for 'conquerers': soldiers who conquered the native peoples of South America |
| | Colonisation | when a country takes over another territory and settles some of its own people there to control it |
| | Slavery triangle | the trade triangle whereby ships delivered African slaves to the Americas, American goods to Europe, then sailed back to Africa to repeat the process |
| | Columbian exchange | the introduction of European animals and foods to South America and of American animals and foods to Europe |

 Go to page 51 of your *Sources and Skills Book* for more exercises.

 Go to page 19 of your *Research Portfolio* for a task based on this chapter.

| The Age of Exploration and Conquest c. 1400–1750 | The Reformation c. 1500–1700 | The Plantations in Ireland c. 1500–1700 |
| --- | --- | --- |

The Reformation was a period in history when people began to question the teachings of the Catholic Church and to challenge the authority of the Pope. It began in Germany in 1517 as a **protest** against abuses of power in the Catholic Church and was originally about reforming the Church. **The supporters of this desire for reform were called** Protestants.

In this chapter, we will learn about the causes of the Reformation, its central figure, Martin Luther, and the response of the Catholic Church in the form of the Counter-Reformation.

# WORKING WITH THE EVIDENCE!

## Criticism of the Church

| Type of source | Category | Examples |
| --- | --- | --- |
| Primary | Written | Writings of the Reformers like Martin Luther, John Calvin, Henry VIII |
|  | Visual | Contemporary artwork (see below) |
| Primary | Written | Official documents like parliamentary debates, royal orders and papal proclamations |

This is an image used by opponents of the Catholic Church to highlight the differences between the church founded by Jesus (on the left) and the one ruled by the Pope (on the right). What differences can you see between the two?

# 10.1: The Causes of the Reformation

- ❯ The position of the Catholic Church in the early 1500s
- ❯ The problems within the Church that caused people to call for reform
- ❯ The factors outside the Church that caused change

▲ The power and wealth of the Church

## The Catholic Church in 1500

We saw in chapter 6 how important religion was in people's lives in the Middle Ages and how powerful the Catholic Church was. It was incredibly wealthy, had priests in every community and the Pope had power over the kings of Europe.

## The causes of the Reformation

### 1. The influence of the Renaissance

The Church had helped to create the Renaissance by funding artists. However, an unintended consequence was that it also encouraged people to question old beliefs.

- As more people learned to read, they could read the Bible for themselves rather than accept everything told to them by priests and bishops. Their interpretations of the meaning of the Bible often differed from those of the Church.

- The invention of the **printing press** meant that the ideas of the Reformers (like Martin Luther) could spread quickly around Europe and this encouraged people to support them and challenge the Church themselves.

▲ An early printing works

## 2. The wealth of the Church

The Church was the wealthiest organisation in Europe.

- Bishops and monasteries were huge land owners. It is estimated that one-third of all the land in Germany belonged to the Church. This wealth was resented by kings and nobles.
- Everyone had to pay their **tithe** (one-tenth of their income) to their local bishop every year. This was greatly resented by ordinary people, especially when they saw these bishops and cardinals living extravagant lifestyles.

## 3. Abuses within the Church

There were many **abuses of power** within the Catholic Church. These made people think that the popes, bishops and priests were more interested in their own wealth and power than in serving God. These abuses included:

- **Simony:** the buying or selling of positions within the Church. As priests and bishops had the chance to become very wealthy, bishops and cardinals were often willing to accept bribes to appoint a particular person to those jobs.
- **Nepotism:** the appointing of relatives to Church jobs regardless of merit. This was made even worse when many members of the clergy broke their vows of celibacy and fathered children.
- **Pluralism:** holding more than one Church job at the same time. Bishops and priests would often preside over a number of dioceses and parishes in order to increase their wealth.
- **Absenteeism:** a priest or bishop being absent from their parish or diocese for long periods of time. As **pluralism** became more widespread, many areas were left without a priest or bishop and that meant that people could not go to Mass or receive the **sacraments**.

- The **sale of indulgences**: Catholics believed that when an average person died their soul would go to **purgatory** (a place between heaven and hell) until they atoned for their sins on Earth. The Church began to sell special prayers, called indulgences, that were said to reduce the time a soul spent in purgatory. The idea that forgiveness of sins could be bought for money outraged many, especially as it seemed to target the poor and ignorant – and enrich particular churches or monasteries.

- **Misbehaviour of priests and popes**: many priests and bishops did not live very Christian lives. Many of them openly had mistresses and fathered children (breaking their vows of **celibacy**). Some parish priests could not read or write and so were unable to properly say Mass and perform their duties. At the very top, popes (such as **Julius II** or **Alexander VI**) often appeared to be more concerned with pursuing their own power and expanding the land they ruled than in running the Church.

▲ Indulgences being counted in front of the Pope

## 4. The power of kings

Kings around Europe had spent most of the Middle Ages bringing their nobles and lords under control and establishing their rule throughout their kingdoms. The Church, however, remained outside their authority as it was controlled from Rome, not locally. They resented this and looked for ways to weaken its power and gain control over its wealth.

> **DID YOU KNOW?**
>
> Among the worst popes was Alexander VI (1492–1503), a Borgia of Spain. He fathered at least four children, was accused of bribing the cardinals to elect him, made his teenage son Cesare a cardinal, gave away Church lands to other sons and later tried to take over Italy with armies led by Cesare.

## CHECKPOINT!

1. How did the Renaissance influence the start of the Reformation?
2. Why was the printing press an important factor in the Reformation?
3. Explain the following terms: simony; nepotism; pluralism; absenteeism. 📖
4. What was an indulgence and why was their sale so controversial?
5. Why did the (a) wealth and (b) power of the Catholic Church cause resentment?

✓ I understand the main causes of the Reformation.

⬅ TIME TO GO BACK ◆ I CAN MOVE FORWARD ➡

# 10.2: Martin Luther

**In this topic, you will learn about:**
❯ The life of Martin Luther
❯ Luther's ideas and beliefs
❯ The impact of Luther's actions

## A Life in Time: Martin Luther (1483–1546)

### Early life

Martin Luther was the man who started the Reformation. He was born to a wealthy family in **Saxony**, **Germany** (then part of the Holy Roman Empire) in 1483. After studying law, he decided to become an **Augustinian monk**. He studied theology and became Professor of Theology at the **University of Wittenberg**.

### Justification by faith alone

Luther spent much of his time studying the Bible in great detail to ensure he was doing all he could to go to heaven. The Catholic Church taught that to get into heaven you had to have **faith** in God and perform **good works** (prayer, fasting, pilgrimages, indulgences, giving to charity). However, Luther found no mention in the Bible of good works and came to believe that only God could forgive sins and only faith in God would help him. He called this teaching '**justification by faith alone**', which meant that only faith in God could get a person into heaven.

### The sale of indulgences and the Ninety-Five Theses

In 1517, **John Tetzel** arrived in Wittenberg selling **indulgences** to the local people. Half of the money he raised was for the rebuilding of St Peter's Basilica, with the other half going to the **Archbishop of Mainz**. Luther was furious, especially as Tetzel was telling people that they were guaranteed a place in heaven if they bought an indulgence from him. Luther wrote to the archbishop in protest, but he was ignored.

▲ An artist's impression of Luther nailing the *Ninety-Five Theses* to the church door

Luther wrote out **ninety-five theses** (arguments) in Latin. He is said to have nailed them to the door of a church in Wittenberg, though some historians doubt that this actually happened. His initial aim seems to have been to encourage debate amongst scholars at the university. However, the Ninety-Five Theses were quickly **translated into German**. Thanks to **the printing press**, they spread all over Germany and turned into a full-scale public attack on the authority of the Pope.

Some of the main ideas within Luther's ninety-five theses included:

- The Pope had no power to forgive sins
- Indulgences do not save people from punishment for their sins
- As one of the richest men in Europe, the Pope should rebuild St Peter's himself, instead of taking money from the poor

# WORKING WITH THE EVIDENCE!

## Excerpts from the Ninety-Five Theses

Read the document below and, with your group, answer the questions below:

32. Those who believe that they can be certain of their salvation because they have indulgence letters will be eternally damned, together with their teachers.

36. Any truly repentant Christian has a right to full remission of penalty and guilt, even without indulgence letters.

47. Christians are to be taught that the buying of indulgences is a matter of free choice, not commanded.

50. Christians are to be taught that if the Pope knew the exactions of the indulgence preachers, he would rather that the Basilica of St Peter were burned to ashes than built up with the skin, flesh, and bones of his sheep.

54. Injury is done to the Word of God when, in the same sermon, an equal or larger amount of time is devoted to indulgences than to the Word.

62. The true treasure of the Church is the most holy gospel of the glory and grace of God.

1. Rewrite each of the theses above in your own words. 📖
2. What dangers are caused by the sale of indulgences, according to Luther?
3. From the theses shown above, is Luther totally against the sale of indulgences? Explain your answer.
4. Why do you think that the Pope became alarmed by the theses? Give reasons for your answer.

Go to page 62 of your *Sources and Skills Book* for a question on paintings of Luther's actions.

### The response of the Catholic Church

At first, **Pope Leo X** did not consider Luther to be a real problem. It was only in 1519, after the theses had spread, that he sent the theologian **John Eck** to debate Luther in public. In that debate, Luther went further than before and claimed that the Pope had no more power to interpret the Bible than anyone else. Leo ordered Luther to **recant** (take back what he said) but he refused. Next, Leo sent a **papal bull** (a formal letter and command) threatening Luther with **excommunication**. This meant he would be <u>thrown out of the Catholic Church and be unable to receive the sacraments</u>. Luther publicly burned it and was excommunicated in 1521.

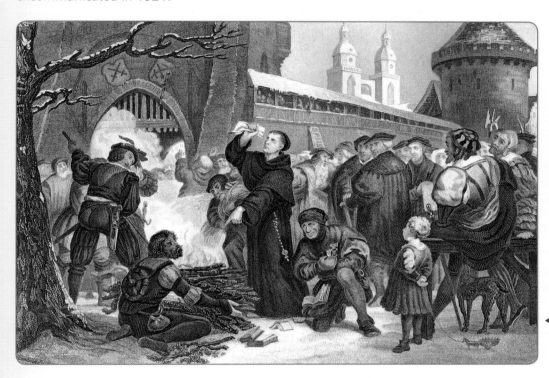

◀ Luther burning the papal bull in the square in Wittenberg

### The Diet of Worms

Luther continued to write pamphlets and give sermons rejecting the power of the Pope. The Holy Roman Emperor (the ruler of Germany) **Charles V** called a meeting (**Diet**) of German princes at **Worms** in 1521 about Luther. Luther was given safe passage there to discuss his beliefs, but he refused to change his mind, saying 'I cannot and will not recant anything, for to go against conscience is neither right or safe'.

After the Diet, Charles issued the **Edict of Worms**, making Luther an **outlaw**. Luther's supporters protested against this and afterwards became known as 'Protestants'. Luther was to be arrested and punished for **heresy** (knowingly holding a view that went against the official teachings of the Church). Fearing for him, **Prince Frederick of Saxony** arranged a fake kidnapping and hid Luther in Wartburg Castle for a year. There Luther translated the Bible into German, so that everyone could read it for themselves.

### Luther's beliefs

- The Bible – not the Pope or the Church – is the only source of guidance for Christians. There is **no need for bishops or a Church hierarchy** (structure of power).
- Therefore, each prince or king should control the Church in the area under their rule.
- Mass and the Bible should be in the **vernacular** (the language of the people) instead of Latin, so that everyone can understand them.
- 'Justification by Faith Alone.'

- The clergy should be **allowed to marry**.
- The Catholic Church has seven sacraments (baptism, confession, communion, confirmation, marriage, the last rites and ordination). However, Luther could only find two of these in the Bible, so Lutherans only believe in **two sacraments: baptism and communion**.
- Catholics believe that during communion the bread and wine is actually transformed into the body and blood of Jesus: this is called **transubstantiation**. For Luther, the bread and wine did not become the body and blood; rather, they exist side by side (**consubstantiation**).

▲ Wartburg Castle        ▲ Luther's Bible

### Later life and impact

Luther married an ex-nun, **Catherine von Bora**, and they had six children. He continued to write and preach until his death in 1546. His beliefs spread rapidly and had huge consequences for Germany and Europe:

- Many princes rejected Charles V's decision at Worms and wanted to follow Luther's teachings in their states. War broke out shortly after his death and raged until the **Peace of Augsburg** in 1555, when it was agreed that each ruler would choose the religion in his state.
- The Reformation spread throughout Europe.
- Eventually, the Catholic Church was forced to address many of the problems Luther raised, by bringing in reforms; this was called the **Counter-Reformation**.

> **DID YOU KNOW?**
>
> Luther claimed that he was often plagued by visions of the devil throughout his life. On one such occasion, while he was translating the Bible into German at Wartburg Castle, he is supposed to have thrown his inkwell at Satan!

## CHECKPOINT!

1. Explain the following terms: justification by faith alone; excommunication; heresy; vernacular.
2. How did Martin Luther protest against the sale of indulgences?
3. How did Pope Leo X respond to Luther's actions?
4. What happened at the Diet of Worms?
5. What happened to Luther after the Diet?
6. Explain Luther's beliefs on: (a) the language of Mass and the Bible; (b) the sacraments; (c) what happens at communion.
7. Name one consequence of Luther's actions.

✔ I can explain the life and beliefs of Martin Luther.

◀ TIME TO GO BACK ▶ I CAN MOVE FORWARD ➡

# 10.3: The Spread of the Reformation

In this topic, you will learn about:

❯ The spread of Protestantism around Europe

The Reformation spread quickly throughout Europe. After reading Luther's writings, many others began to question the teachings of the Catholic Church. Some came to broadly the same conclusions as Luther, but others would take a very different approach. The other major events in the Reformation were:

- 1531: **Ulrich Zwingli** launched the Reformation in Switzerland.

- 1534: **Henry VIII** established the Church of England as separate from the Catholic Church, with himself as head (you will learn more about this in chapter 11).

- 1537: **King Christian III** declared Lutheranism the official religion of Denmark and Norway.

- 1541: **John Calvin** was invited to Geneva, Switzerland to set up his version of Protestantism: **Presbyterianism** – very different to both Lutheraniam and Catholicism. He believed in predestination: that <u>God had already decided who was going to heaven before people were born</u> and nothing they did in life could affect that. He preached a strict Christianity that banned statues in churches, dancing, gambling, fancy clothes and anything else he thought might lead people into sin.

- 1571: The Netherlands became Protestant.

- 1572: **John Knox** introduced Presbyterianism to Scotland.

10<br>The Reformation

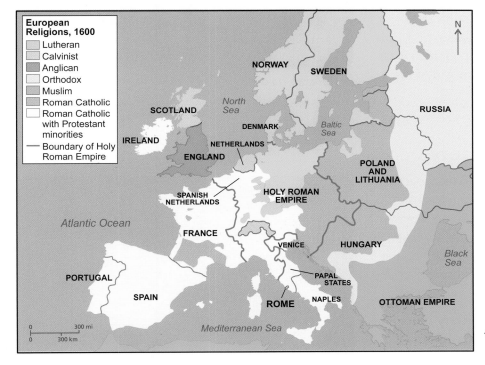

European Religions, 1600
- ▢ Lutheran
- ▢ Calvinist
- ▢ Anglican
- ▢ Orthodox
- ▢ Muslim
- ▢ Roman Catholic
- ▢ Roman Catholic with Protestant minorities
- — Boundary of Holy Roman Empire

NORWAY SWEDEN
SCOTLAND
North Sea
RUSSIA
DENMARK
Baltic Sea
IRELAND
NETHERLANDS
ENGLAND
POLAND AND LITHUANIA
SPANISH NETHERLANDS
HOLY ROMAN EMPIRE
Atlantic Ocean
FRANCE
VENICE HUNGARY
Black Sea
PORTUGAL
PAPAL STATES
SPAIN
ROME NAPLES
OTTOMAN EMPIRE
Mediterranean Sea

0  300 mi
0  300 km

Within a century of Luther publishing his theses, the Protestant challenge to the Catholic Church had spread across Europe. The continent divided along religious lines: most of the northern countries became Protestant and the south remained mostly Catholic. The Catholic Church launched the Counter-Reformation to slow or halt the growth of Protestantism.

◀ Religious divisions in Europe c.1600

## CHECKPOINT!

1. Name four European countries that became Protestant during the Reformation.
2. Explain the terms Presbyterianism and predestination. 📖❗
3. Where did John Calvin set up his church?
4. Why do you think that southern Europe remained Catholic while northern Europe became Protestant?

 I understand how the Reformation spread throughout Europe.

# 10.4: The Catholic Counter-Reformation

The Catholic Church was alarmed at the spread of Protestantism and realised that if it did not act to limit the damage, the Church could collapse. It adopted a 'carrot and stick' approach – it would use both force and persuasion to keep people inside the Church.

In this topic, you will learn about:
- ❯ The Inquisition
- ❯ New religious orders
- ❯ The Council of Trent

## 1. The Courts of Inquisition

The Church set up the **Courts of Inquisition** to arrest, try and punish anyone who they thought was a threat to Church teachings. The Inquisition used imprisonment and torture to get people accused of heresy to recant their views. People found guilty of the most serious offences could be burned at the stake (in a ceremony known as the **auto-da-fé**). These burnings were always done in public to remind people of the danger they faced if they challenged the Church. Other punishments included imprisonment, fines, confiscation of property, expulsion or the wearing of a yellow cloak (**sanbenito**). The Inquisition was quite successful in limiting the spread of the Reformation, especially in Italy and Spain.

▲ An auto-da-fé

## 2. New religious orders

The Church saw that it needed to reconnect with the faithful, and several new religious orders were founded to do this. Some, like the **Ursuline** nuns and **Capuchin** monks, worked in communities helping people and preaching the gospel. They set up schools and hospitals around Europe to help the poor.

The most important was the **Society of Jesus**, or the **Jesuits**, founded by **Ignatius Loyola** in 1534. His order was like an army, with a general at the top and priest 'soldiers' who were expected to follow orders without question. They quickly gained a reputation as being highly educated and very successful in their two main tasks:

▲ A Jesuit missionary in America

- Travelling the world, especially the newly discovered lands in the Americas and Asia, as **missionaries**. They were responsible for the conversion of the peoples of South America and for introducing Catholicism to Asia, particularly China and Japan.
- Setting up **schools** to educate the sons of the nobility or of wealthy families. They deliberately targeted these boys because they would have power and social influence when they grew up.

# 3. The Council of Trent

The **Council of Trent** was the Church's response to the attack on its teachings by the Reformers. Senior bishops and cardinals from various countries met between 1545 and 1563 in Trento, Italy.

The Council attempted to deal with the Church's existing problems and to impose discipline:

- **Simony, pluralism, nepotism, absenteeism** and **the sale of indulgences** were banned.
- **Seminaries** were set up in every diocese to train priests.
- Priests were to be **celibate** and could not marry.
- Strict rules and punishments were introduced for priests who broke these rules.
- It published a list of books that Catholics were forbidden to read **(The Index of Prohibited Books)**.

▲ A painting of the Council of Trent

It also clarified Catholic teachings and defended them against the arguments of Reformers:

- **Faith and good works** were required to get into heaven.
- There were **seven sacraments**.
- Mass and the Bible must be in **Latin**.
- They drew up a single 'rulebook' for Catholicism, the **Catechism**. This was designed to provide people with clear, simple answers to questions about their faith, and also to ensure there was consistency in how Catholicism was taught across Europe.

The Counter-Reformation was largely successful in preventing the further spread of Protestantism – but was unable to reverse it in any of the countries where it had taken hold.

## CHECKPOINT!

1. What was the Inquisition and how was it used against the Reformation?
2. How did the Jesuits try to combat the Reformation?
3. What was the Council of Trent?
4. How did it respond to problems and abuses in the Church?
5. What was the Catechism and why was it important?

 I understand the main elements of the Counter-Reformation. ← TIME TO GO BACK ◆ I CAN MOVE FORWARD →

 Go to page 63–64 of your *Sources and Skills Book* for exercises on letters from the time.

10 The Reformation

# 10.5: The Results of the Reformation

## Division and persecution

By 1650, Europe had divided into a largely Protestant north and a Catholic south. There were minority groups in most countries and these people faced persecution. Protestants were arrested and tried by the Inquisition in Catholic countries and Protestants did the same to Catholics in their countries. Many countries introduced laws that banned members of other faiths from holding public office, owning property or attending their own religious services and so on. These laws heightened the bitterness and division across Europe.

**In this topic, you will learn about:**
- ❯ Religious wars
- ❯ Power of kings
- ❯ Changes in education, art and architecture

## Religious wars

Many countries saw internal violence between Catholics and Protestants. These clashes led to full-scale civil wars in France, England, Scotland, Germany and Switzerland. Various wars broke out between countries on either side of the religious divide:

- **Spain (Catholic) and the Netherlands (Protestant)**: The Dutch fought for their independence from the Spanish crown from 1568 to 1648.

- The **Anglo-Spanish War**: As well as conflict over the New World, religion was a key reason for the war between Spain and England (1585–1604). This war saw the attempted invasion of England by the **Spanish Armada** in 1588.

- **The Thirty Years War** (1618–1648): War broke out in Germany (the Holy Roman Empire) between Catholic and Protestant states. It pulled in the rest of Europe. Historians think that roughly one-third of Germany's population died in that conflict. The **Peace of Westphalia** reinforced the earlier Treaty of Augsburg and guaranteed followers of minority religions the right to practise freely in private.

**DID YOU KNOW?**

The Inquisition was already busy in Spain before Luther wrote his theses! It began because King Ferdinand and Queen Isabella wanted to find and punish their Jewish and Muslim subjects who, when told they must convert to Christianity or leave the kingdom, stayed but kept their own religion in secret. Thousands were killed at autos-da-fé.

◀ French Protestants were massacred by Catholics in 1572; the event is known as the St Bartholomew's Day Massacre

## Power of kings

The Pope no longer had any control over countries that were now Protestant. In those countries, all Catholic Church property (churches, monasteries, estates and so forth) were seized by the Crown, which made those rulers much wealthier. It also removed a challenge to their power by giving them control over the religion of their countries. Even for Catholic countries, the Pope needed the support of the ruler to keep them Catholic, so the Church's power was much reduced.

## Education

Education became very important to both sides. Protestants wanted everyone to read and understand the Bible: that meant that everyone needed a basic education. Catholics believed that the only reason people had followed the Reformers was that they did not understand their faith. Therefore, many schools were set up to educate Catholics. Overall, this meant an increase in education levels for all the people of Europe from the 1500s onwards.

## Art and architecture

Protestants rejected the decoration of churches with statues and paintings because they saw this as being sinful, wasteful and a distraction from the study of the Bible. Their churches became very simple and plain. Catholics, on the other hand, continued to spend lavishly on the decoration of their churches to celebrate their faith and attract people into them. This gave rise to the **baroque** movement in art.

▲ Interior of a baroque cathedral, Malta

## CHECKPOINT!

1. How did the Reformation lead to the persecution of people of different faiths?
2. Name two countries that went to war with each other because of the Reformation.
3. How did the Reformation lead to a reduction in the power of the Pope?
4. What effect did the Reformation have on (a) education and (b) art?

 I understand the impact the Reformation had on Europe.

10 The Reformation

 **SUMMARY**

In this chapter, we have learned that:

- The Reformation in Europe had a number of different causes.
- The Renaissance led people to question the Church's authority.
- The incredible wealth of the Church caused resentment.
- Abuses such as nepotism, simony, absenteeism, pluralism and the sale of indulgences made many people question the Catholic Church.
- Kings wanted more control over the Church in their own countries.
- These problems came to a head when Martin Luther challenged the sale of indulgences in Wittenberg. He rejected the power of the Pope to grant indulgences and attacked the abuses of the Church. He was excommunicated, but his ideas caught on and soon he had followers all over Germany.

The Reformation spread across northern Europe from the 1520s onwards and had many important consequences:

- The Catholic Church launched the Counter-Reformation to try to stop the spread of Protestantism.
- The Inquisition tried and punished those accused of heresy.
- New religious orders (such as the Jesuits) were set up.
- The Council of Trent reformed the Church and rejected most of Luther's ideas.
- The Reformation led to the division of Europe, religiously motivated violence and the decline in the power of the Pope.

## Reflecting on... the Reformation

The Reformation shaped the history of Europe. Its challenge to authority can be seen as the beginning of the end for the absolute authority of kings. The religious divisions it unleashed can still be felt today – we have only to look at Northern Ireland, where divisions between Catholics and Protestants have played a part in creating violence between the two communities. It is an excellent example of how one minor event – in this case, the protests of one German monk – can have a profound impact on the world.

 **Understanding History**

1. Look at the causes of the Reformation. What role did (a) money and (b) power play?
2. What abuses inside the Catholic Church helped to cause the Reformation?
3. How did Martin Luther initially oppose the sale of indulgences?
4. Explain Martin Luther's beliefs on (a) justification by faith alone; (b) consubstantiation and (c) the sale of indulgences.
5. Describe the events that led to Luther being excommunicated from the Catholic Church.
6. Why did so many kings and nobles around Europe support Luther's beliefs?
7. Name three European countries and the Reformers who brought Protestantism to them.
8. How did the Catholic Church use (a) the Inquisition and (b) the Council of Trent to combat the Reformation?
9. Why did the Reformation lead to violence (a) within and (b) between European states?
10. How did the Reformation increase the level of literacy (the ability of people to read) in Europe?
11. Rewrite the various causes of the Reformation listed below in order of their importance, as you see it. Write a paragraph on why your top choice was the most important cause.

   - Influence of the Renaissance
   - Abuses in the Church
   - The wealth of the Church
   - The desire of kings for more power
   - The actions of Martin Luther

**Exploring History**

1. Imagine you were living during the Reformation in Germany. In pairs, decide who will do task (a) and who will do task (b).

   (a) Write a letter to your partner explaining why you have decided to become a follower of Luther.

   (b) Write a letter in reply to persuade your partner to remain within the Catholic Church.

3. Look at the topic on the causes of the Reformation on page 134 and pick three. Explain how they helped cause the Reformation and how that particular cause was addressed during the Reformation.

4. Write about the life of Martin Luther under the following headings:

   - His early life
   - The sale of indulgences and his Ninety-Five Theses
   - The response of the Catholic Church
   - The Diet of Worms
   - His beliefs
   - His later life

| KEY TERMS | |
|---|---|
| Protestant | at first, a supporter of reform to the Catholic Church; later, a member of the churches that broke away |
| Simony | the buying or selling of positions within the Church |
| Nepotism | the appointing of relatives to Church jobs regardless of merit |
| Pluralism | holding more than one Church job at the same time |
| Absenteeism | a priest or bishop being absent from their parish or diocese for long periods of time |
| Sale of indulgences | the selling of special prayers claimed to reduce the time a soul spent in purgatory |
| Justification by faith alone | Luther's belief that only faith in God could get you into heaven |
| Excommunication | expulsion from the Catholic Church and being unable to receive the sacraments |
| Predestination | the Presbyterian belief that God decided before a person was born whether they would go to heaven |
| Courts of Inquisition | Catholic courts set up during the Counter-Reformation to try heretics |

 Go to page 58 of your *Sources and Skills Book* for more exercises.

 Go to page 22 of your *Research Portfolio* for a task based on this chapter.

**10 The Reformation**

# Settlement in Ireland: The Plantations

LO: 2.1

| The Reformation | The Plantations in Ireland | The Age of Revolution |
|---|---|---|
| c. 1500–1700 | c. 1500–1700 | c. 1750–1850 |

The Plantations is the name given to the period of Irish history when, in the sixteenth and seventeenth centuries, Irish land was confiscated by the English Crown and then colonised by British settlers.

The Plantations set in motion major changes to Ireland and also influenced identity on the island in a lasting way. The roots of many recent events in Irish history date from this period.

# WORKING WITH THE EVIDENCE!

## Plantation towns

| Type of source | Category | Example |
|---|---|---|
| Primary | Visual | A plan for a plantation town in Ulster |
| Primary | Visual | A plan for Londonderry |

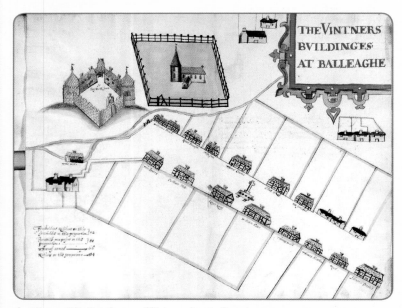

▲ Plan of Ballaghy, an Ulster plantation town

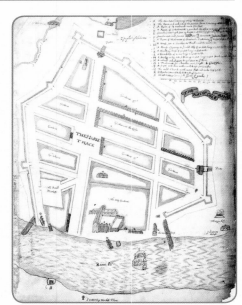

▲ Plan of Londonderry

What can these drawings tell us about how towns were planned and laid out during the Plantations?

# 11.1: Ireland in the 1500s

In the 1500s, Ireland was home to three major groups of people: the Old English, the Anglo-Irish and the Gaelic Irish. In theory, the English Crown ruled Ireland – but in reality, power in Ireland rested with these groups.

In this topic, you will learn about:
- The Old English
- The Anglo-Irish
- The Gaelic Irish

## The Old English

As you learned in chapter 7, in medieval times Dublin and its surrounding areas (known as the Pale) became the base of English power in Ireland. There, the English language, customs, dress, farming methods (mainly crop farming) and laws were practised.

- By the early 1500s, the people who lived in the Pale were mainly English merchants. They were known as the **Old English**, as they were <u>people living in the Pale who were loyal to the king</u>.

- The Reformation in England had a big impact on Ireland from the 1550s onwards. It led to an increase in tension between the Gaelic Irish and the Old English who lived in the Pale.

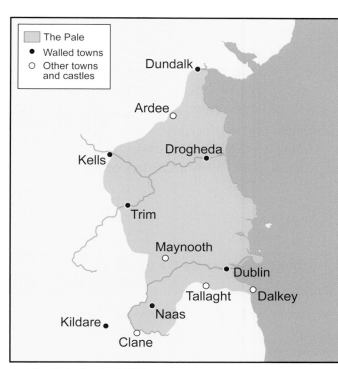

The Pale
● Walled towns
○ Other towns and castles

Dundalk
Ardee
Drogheda
Kells
Trim
Maynooth
Dublin
Tallaght    Dalkey
Naas
Kildare
Clane

▲ The Pale in the 1500s

## The Anglo-Irish

The **Anglo-Irish** were <u>descendants of the Anglo-Normans who had invaded Ireland in the twelfth century</u>.

- They were also known as the **Gaelicised Anglo-Normans**, because by 1500 they had adopted the Gaelic way of life, following the Irish traditions and laws as well as the English ones.

- By the 1500s, they had become independent of the English Crown.

▲ Kilkenny Castle, seat of the powerful Anglo-Irish Butler family

Examples of powerful Anglo-Irish families were the **Fitzgeralds of Kildare**, the **Butlers of Ormond/Kilkenny** and the **Fitzgeralds of Munster**.

- From 1468 onwards, the Lord Deputy (the king's representative in Ireland) was from an Anglo-Irish family.

# The Gaelic Irish

The **Gaelic Irish** were <u>the Gaelic chieftains who followed Irish law (known as Brehon law)</u>.

- The **Brehon laws** were <u>Gaelic Irish laws dating from the Iron Age</u>. The laws were a civil rather than a criminal code and dealt with, for example, fines for harm caused and rules about property, leadership, marriage and other contracts.
- The Gaelic Irish did not recognise the English king as ruler of Ireland.
- They feared that the Crown would try to expand its control over Ireland and therefore disliked and attacked English settlers.
- Examples of powerful Gaelic Irish families (clans) included the **O'Neills of Tyrone**, the **O'Donnells of Donegal** and the **MacCarthys of Cork**.

▲ Anglo-Irish and Gaelic Irish territories

| Brehon Law, used by the Gaelic Irish | English Common Law, used in the Pale |
|---|---|
| Courts held on hillsides | Courts held in courthouses |
| No jails or executions. Fines used as punishments | Harsh jail sentences and death by hanging given as punishments |
| Wealth measured by number of cattle owned | Wealth measured in monetary terms |
| Divorce allowed | Divorce forbidden |
| A wife kept her own name, wealth and property | A wife took her husband's name, and her property and wealth became his |
| Children born outside marriage were entitled to a share of their father's wealth or property | Children born outside marriage could not inherit any of their father's wealth or property |

## CHECKPOINT!

1. Explain the terms Old English, Anglo-Irish and Gaelic Irish. 📖
2. Name two powerful Anglo-Irish families and two powerful Gaelic Irish families.
3. What was Brehon law? Why do you think the Gaelic Irish resisted English law?
4. Why do you think tensions between the Gaelic Irish and the English in the Pale increased?

✓ I can describe Ireland in the 1500s and each of the different groups living there.

◀ TIME TO GO BACK ◆ I CAN MOVE FORWARD ▶

COLLABORATE: Work with your group to compare and contrast the Anglo-Irish and the Gaelic Irish under the following headings: laws; territory; style of dress.

**DID YOU KNOW?**

In Brehon marriage law, the groom had to pay the father of the bride in land, cattle, horses, gold or silver. Husband and wife kept individual rights to all land, livestock and household goods they each brought to the marriage.

# 11.2: Henry VIII and the Tudors

In this topic, you will learn about:
- ❯ Henry VIII and his family, the Tudors
- ❯ Surrender and regrant
- ❯ The policy of plantation

▲ Henry VIII

## Henry VIII and his family

Henry VII came to power in England in 1485. This was the beginning of the Tudor Era. His son, **Henry VIII**, became king after his father's death and was King of England **between 1509 and 1547**. Henry VIII and three of his heirs, **Edward VI**, **Mary I** and **Elizabeth I**, gradually conquered Ireland through policies such as 'surrender and regrant' and plantation.

After the death of his older brother in 1502, Henry married his brother's widow, **Catherine of Aragon**, with special permission from the Pope. Henry and Catherine had a daughter, who later became Queen Mary I. Henry still needed a male heir and Catherine was in her forties. The king wanted to marry a woman called **Anne Boleyn**, once Catherine's lady's maid, and asked Pope Clement VII to annul (cancel) his marriage. This was a problem: the Church would have had to admit that it was wrong to ever give permission, and it would anger Catherine's nephew, the Holy Roman Emperor Charles V. The Pope refused.

In 1533, with the Reformation gaining momentum in Europe, Henry VIII broke with the Church and married Anne Boleyn, who was pregnant. Their child later became Queen Elizabeth I. Henry was excommunicated by the Pope. This marked the beginning of the English Reformation and resulted in England becoming a **Protestant monarchy**. Henry VIII declared himself the **Head of the Church** (Act of Supremacy 1534), **closed down the monasteries** and **confiscated the Catholic Church's lands** (Act of Dissolution 1536). Henry went on to have six wives in total: Catherine of Aragon (mother of Mary I), Anne Boleyn (mother of Elizabeth I), Jane Seymour (mother of Edward VI), Anne of Cleves, Catherine Howard and Catherine Parr.

▲ Henry VIII's six wives

**11 Settlement in Ireland: The Plantations**

# The Tudors and Ireland

The Tudors had many reasons for wanting to fully conquer Ireland:

- To **expand their territory**. The Crown only had full control over the Pale.

- To **spread English customs, culture, laws** and so forth. These were seen as superior to those of the Gaelic Irish, who were portrayed as being barbaric and unable to look after themselves.

- To **spread their new religion**. They believed that they could enforce Protestantism in Ireland.

- To **prevent the Catholic Gaelic Irish forming an alliance** with other Catholic countries, such as Spain, and offering Ireland as a base from which to attack England.

- To **prevent further rebellions**. The Fitzgerald rebellion of 1534 was begun by the Lord Deputy's own son Thomas Fitzgerald, or 'Silken Thomas'. Hearing the rumour that his father had been beheaded in London by Henry VIII, Silken Thomas attempted to rally the lords of the Pale and even attacked Dublin Castle.

- To **save money.** Planting settlers in Ireland would be cheaper in the long term than paying soldiers to protect the English already in Ireland.

**DID YOU KNOW?**

▲ Rothe House, Kilkenny

Rothe House in the centre of Kilkenny City is the only Tudor-era house in Ireland that is intact and open to the public. It was built as three houses in 1594–1610 by the merchant John Rothe Fitz Piers to house his wife and their 12 children, as well as his business premises and a large kitchen garden and orchard.

Today you can explore the restored house and garden (growing the same plants as in the 1600s) and see how a family lived then. Archaeologists excavated the garden and their finds are in the museum on site. On the wall above a great fireplace are the antlers of the great Irish deer, which stood 2 metres high and has been extinct for the last 10,000 years. Visit the links below for photos and a 360° virtual tour!

https://educateplus.ie/go/rothe-house

https://educateplus.ie/go/rothe-house2

## Surrender and regrant

At first, Henry VIII attempted to control Ireland by peaceful means, through a policy called **surrender and regrant**. Under this policy, <u>the Anglo-Irish and Gaelic Irish rulers were to surrender themselves and their lands to Henry VIII, and he would grant their land back to them along with an English title</u>.

- Titles such as earl, lord and baron were given.
- By doing this, local rulers acknowledged Henry VIII as King of Ireland, accepted that he had a legal right to their land and promised their loyalty to him.
- Henry VIII could confiscate the lords' land if their behaviour angered him.
- <u>Land was now passed directly from father to son</u> in the English system known as **succession**. Previously, under Brehon law, a clan chose its own leader and owned all its land as a group, not divided up individually.
- This led to increased wealth and power for certain families.

◀ The Lord Deputy accepting the submission of Irish chieftains under surrender and regrant

## The policy of plantation

When Irish lands were confiscated by the king, they could be sold or rented to loyal English settlers. This was known as plantation. The **new settlers on the land** were known as **planters**.

- The planters would spread English customs and laws.
- They would defend the land from the Gaelic Irish.
- They would also spread the religion of the English Crown.

Go to page 69 of your *Sources and Skills Book* for an evidence task on a plantation estate.

### CHECKPOINT!

1. Why did Henry VIII break with the Church in Rome?
2. What were the Act of Supremacy and the Act of Dissolution?
3. Name Henry VIII's three heirs.
4. List three reasons why the Tudors wanted to conquer Ireland.
5. Explain the terms surrender and regrant and plantation.

✔ I can explain why the Tudors wanted to conquer Ireland and the policies they used.

 ⬅ TIME TO GO BACK ◆ I CAN MOVE FORWARD ➡

**11 Settlement in Ireland: The Plantations**

# 11.3: The Early Plantations

In this topic, you will learn about:

❯ The Laois-Offaly Plantation and its results

❯ The Munster Plantation and its results

▲ Edward VI

Henry VIII's son, Edward VI, became king in 1547. However, Edward was only nine then and his health was never strong. Edward died in 1553 of tuberculosis and was succeeded by his oldest half-sister, Mary. **Queen Mary I** had remained Catholic like her mother, Catherine of Aragon.

## The Laois-Offaly Plantation

The **O'Mores** and the **O'Connors** were the Gaelic Irish lords of **Laois and Offaly** in the sixteenth century. They raided the Pale frequently, mainly for cattle. Queen Mary I sent her Lord Deputy to confiscate the O'More and O'Connor lands as punishment. A plantation was then organised.

- Laois and Offaly were renamed Queen's County and King's County.
- Each county was assigned a **sheriff** to enforce English laws and customs.
- The towns of Portlaoise and Daingean were renamed Maryborough and Philipstown, after Mary and her husband Philip II of Spain.
- The confiscated land was **divided into estates** (large farms) of between 350 and 1,000 acres.
- **Land was given to Englishmen** born in England or Ireland.
- **English-style houses** had to be built.

▲ Mary I

| Results of the Laois-Offaly Plantation under Queen Mary I |
|---|
| It was a failure |
| It did not attract enough planters from England |
| Gaelic planters had to be given land |
| English customs and laws did not flourish |
| The confiscated lands were still attacked |
| It led to better planning in future plantations |

The Pale
Laois and Offaly
Earldom of Kildare, taken from the Fitzgeralds after 1537

The Pale

Maynooth

Dublin

KING'S COUNTY • Philipstown (Daingean)

Maryborough (Portlaoise)

LEINSTER

QUEEN'S COUNTY

Kilkenny

▶ The Laois-Offaly Plantation

## The Munster Plantation

Queen Mary I died in 1558, without any heirs. Her younger half-sister **Elizabeth I** then became queen. She ruled for forty-four years, famously never married and also left no heirs. She was the last Tudor.

Much of sixteenth-century Munster was ruled by the **Fitzgeralds of Desmond**, who remained Catholic. Queen Elizabeth I was Protestant like her mother, Anne Boleyn. Elizabeth encouraged Englishmen known as 'adventurers' to claim land in Munster. **Adventurers** were men who claimed to be descendants of the early Normans who had been granted land in Munster by Henry II. Elizabeth also appointed **presidents**, men who imposed English law, the English language and the Protestant religion.

The Irish lords were angered by this, and two rebellions (**the Desmond Rebellions**) followed.

- The first, in 1569, was led by **James Fitzmaurice Fitzgerald**, a cousin of the Earl of Desmond. It was put down easily and Fitzgerald fled to Europe.

- The second, in 1579, began when Fitzgerald returned to Ireland with soldiers sent by Pope Gregory XIII. He was soon killed, but his cousin the Earl of Desmond took over. The earl and his forces were finally defeated in 1583. His head was sent to Queen Elizabeth and his body was displayed in Cork.

▲ Queen Elizabeth I

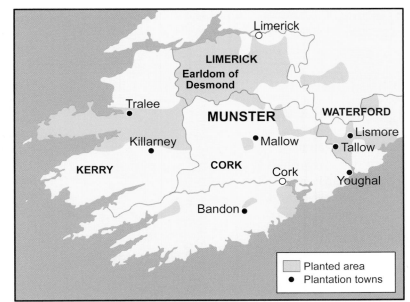

▲ Planted areas in Munster

The Desmond lands were given to **undertakers**, <u>men who undertook (agreed) to do as they were told with the land given to them</u>. The agreements included to:

- split the land into **enormous estates** of 4,000–12,000 acres.
- only **hire English** farmers, labourers and craftsmen.
- bring **their own tenants, servants, sheep, cattle and horses** from England.
- **pay rent** to the Crown.
- spread **Protestantism** and **English laws and customs**.
- **be prepared** for Catholic attacks, including a possible Spanish invasion, and construct defences.
- completely **remove the Gaelic Irish** from the land.

| The Results of the Munster Plantation under Queen Elizabeth I |
| --- |
| The Crown had hoped for 20,000 settlers, but only one-fifth of that number went |
| They still had to rent to the Gaelic Irish |
| The Gaelic Irish continued to attack the plantations |
| New towns were set up (for example, Killarney, Lismore, Youghal, Mallow and Bandon) |
| New farming methods were brought to Ireland. Tillage (crop farming) grew in popularity |
| New trades came to Ireland, such as coopering (making timber barrels) |
| Lessons were learned for future plantations |

## CHECKPOINT!

1. In what century did the Laois-Offaly Plantation and the Munster Plantation take place?
2. Explain the terms adventurer; president; and undertaker. 📖
3. Which queen was responsible for each plantation?
4. List two results of each of the plantations.
5. Why do you think the early plantations failed? Give three reasons in each case.

 I know the main events and results of the Laois-Offaly and Munster Plantations.

⬅ TIME TO GO BACK ◆ I CAN MOVE FORWARD ➡

 COLLABORATE: With a partner, discuss each of the plantations and identify two ways that its problems could have been avoided. How might that have changed the situation for the Irish there? What lessons might have been learned by the Crown?

▶ English troops collecting heads during the Desmond Rebellions

# 11.4: The Plantation of Ulster

**In this topic, you will learn about:**

- The background to the Ulster Plantation
- How the plantation was organised
- The results of the Ulster Plantation

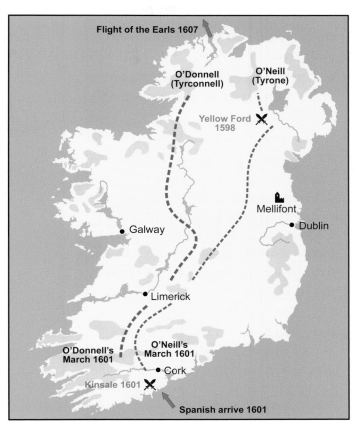

▲ Events of the Nine Years War

## Background to the Ulster Plantation

Ulster was dominated by Gaelic Irish clans, especially the powerful **O'Neills of Tyrone** and **O'Donnells of Donegal. Queen Elizabeth I** hoped to control Ulster by giving **Hugh O'Neill** the title 'Earl of Tyrone', and he had been loyal to her. However, when adventurers were planted in Ulster and sheriffs enforced Protestantism, English laws and customs, this angered Hugh O'Neill and 'Red' Hugh O'Donnell. They asked the Catholic King **Philip II of Spain** (who had been Queen Mary I's husband) for help to defend Ulster from Protestantism. He sent no troops, but the Ulster chiefs rebelled in 1594 regardless.

In the **Nine Years War** (1594–1603), the Gaelic clans in Ulster fought against the spread of English control. Hugh O'Neill won several battles, including **the Battle of the Yellow Ford**, which inspired other parts of the country to rebel. King Philip of Spain changed his mind and sent up to 4,000 soldiers to support O'Neill. The ships landed at Kinsale in Cork in 1601 but were captured by the English. O'Neill and O'Donnell tried to help but were defeated in **the Battle of Kinsale**.

In 1603 the **Treaty of Mellifont** was signed by the Ulster Gaelic clans and the English Crown to end the war. This did not stop the English trying to gain control of Ulster. O'Neill and other Ulster chiefs fled for Europe in 1607, an event known as **the Flight of the Earls**. They hoped to return with troops. However, without them there was no organised resistance to English rule in Ulster.

Queen Elizabeth I died in 1603. Her Scottish cousin James Stuart succeeded her as **King James I** and was responsible for the organisation of the Ulster Plantation.

▶ King James I

# How the Ulster Plantation was organised

In 1609 the Ulster Plantation began.

- Its area covered six counties: **Donegal, Derry, Tyrone, Armagh, Fermanagh and Cavan**.

- The land was divided into smaller estates than in Munster: none was bigger than 2,000 acres.

- The rules for the planters were more strict than on any of the other plantations.

- Estates were given to three different types of planter: undertakers, servitors and loyal Irish. **Servitors** were English or Scottish soldiers who had fought for the Crown. **Loyal Irish** were native Irish who had stayed loyal to the English during the Nine Years War.

- King James reserved the entire county of Derry for **London craft guilds**. It was renamed Londonderry, and each section of land was given to a guild, for example tailors, fishmongers and goldsmiths. They built two large towns, Derry and Coleraine. The Gaelic Irish had to live outside Derry's town walls in a boggy area known to this day as the Bogside.

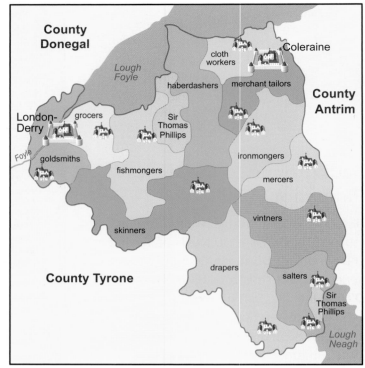

▲ Londonderry's guilds

## *Types of planter*

- The largest part of the plantation went to English or Scottish **undertakers**, who got Ulster estates of about 2,000 acres. They paid King James £5 per 1,000 acres per year. They built castles or stone houses with a bawn (courtyard) around them. They could only have English or Scottish tenants.

- Roughly 13% of the land went to **servitors**. They got estates of 1,000–1,500 acres and paid King James £8 per 1,000 acres per year. They could have Irish tenants, but they had to have strict control over them.

- **Loyal Irish** got about 14% of the land, in estates of 1,000 acres or less. They paid King James £10 per 1,000 acres and could rent land to Irish tenants. Servitors kept an eye on them for the Crown.

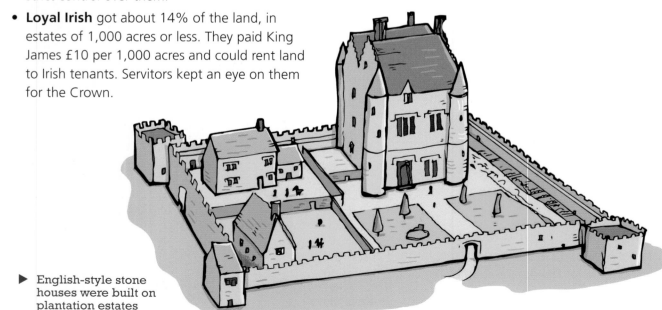

▶ English-style stone houses were built on plantation estates

# The results of the Ulster Plantation

The Ulster Plantation was more successful than both the Laois-Offaly and Munster Plantations.

◀ Tully Castle

- A very **large number of planters** arrived in a short space of time. Soon, of a total Ulster population of one million, roughly 40,000 were Scots.
- Due to the high numbers of settlers, Ulster became the plantation most **loyal to the Crown**.
- The Protestant population increased. This **new religious division within Ulster's population** followed the very same lines as the division between colonised and coloniser that we learned about in chapter 9.
- The Gaelic Irish were driven off the land they had always held. Tensions between the Catholic natives and the Protestant settlers deepened into hatred and even **violence from 1609 onwards**.

- Ulster Protestants were massacred during a **rebellion in 1641**. The English general **Oliver Cromwell** arrived in Ireland to avenge the massacre and end the rebellion. Cromwell reconquered Ireland, executed rebel leaders, confiscated Catholic-owned land across the island and gave it to Protestant planters, driving the dispossessed Catholics west. By 1652, this completed what the previous plantations had begun: very **little land remained in Catholic hands**.

- Over 20 **new towns** were founded during the Ulster Plantation and these were very well planned out. Markets were also organised in the towns to sell produce.

- English-style houses and stone castles were built on the estates.

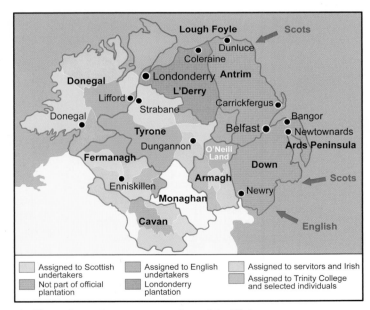

▲ How plantations were assigned in Ulster

- New **farming methods** were introduced. Crops were favoured over cattle farming.

While these results were mixed, it is clear that the Ulster Plantation was indeed very effective.

| The Results of the Ulster Plantation under King James I ||
|---|---|
| Ulster was more successful than Laois-Offaly and Munster | Cromwell reconquered Ireland and confiscated more land |
| Large numbers of English and Scottish settled in Ulster | New towns were founded and very well planned |
| Ulster became the most loyal of the plantations to the Crown | English-style houses and castles were built |
| The Protestant population grew | Crop farming began to take over from cattle farming |
| Tensions between the two groups flared (and exist to this day) | Markets were set up in plantation towns |
| Rebellions persisted | |

## CHECKPOINT!

1. What was the Nine Years War?
2. Which monarch organised the Ulster Plantation? Why?
3. How was Co. Derry's plantation organised?
4. Explain the terms servitor; Loyal Irish; and Flight of the Earls.
5. Why do you think the Loyal Irish had to pay so much more rent than the undertakers and servitors?
6. How did the Ulster Plantation affect: (a) population; (b) religion; (c) land ownership?
7. After plantation, what fraction of the population of Ulster was Scottish?
8. Name three advances that came to Ulster with the planters.

✓ I know the background to the Ulster Plantation, how it was organised and I can explain its results.

⬅ TIME TO GO BACK ◆ I CAN MOVE FORWARD ➡

▼ Recap: the Irish plantations under each of the English monarchs

**Henry VIII (1509–1547):** surrender and regrant

**Edward VI (1547–1553):** none

**Mary I (1554–1558):** Laois-Offaly

**Elizabeth I (1558–1603):** Munster

**James I (1603–1625):** Ulster

▶ Massacre at Drogheda by Cromwell's forces, 1649

# WORKING WITH THE EVIDENCE!

## The Ulster Plantation through English eyes

Read the following extract from 'A discovery of the true causes why Ireland was never entirely subdued and brought under obedience of the crown of England until the beginning of His Majesty's happy reign (1612)', written by Sir John Davies, an English nobleman who benefited from the Plantation of Ulster.

*The lands of the Irish in Ulster were the most rude and unreformed part of Ireland, and the centre of the last great rebellion. They are now better organised and established than any of the lands in the other provinces... The organisation of those lands happened with the special providence of God, who cast out those wicked and ungrateful traitors, the enemies of the Reformation in Ireland...*

*His Majesty did not utterly exclude the natives out of this plantation... but made a mixed plantation of British and Irish, that they might grow up together in one nation. The Irish were in some places transplanted from the woods and mountains into the plains and open countries, that being removed (like wild fruit trees) they might grow the milder, and bear the better and sweeter fruit.*

*When this plantation hath taken root, and been fixed and settled but a few years, with the favour and blessing of God… it will secure the peace of Ireland, assure it to the Crown of England for ever; and finally, make it a civil and a rich, a mighty, and a flourishing kingdom.*

(a) What kind of source is this?

(b) According to the author, what benefit has the plantation brought to Ulster?

(c) Who were 'those wicked and ungrateful traitors'?

(d) Why did the king not exclude the native Irish from the plantation entirely?

(e) Where were the Irish moved from?

(f) Mention two things which the author hopes will happen once the plantation has been established.

(g) What can we as historians learn about the views of the English towards the Irish from a source such as this? Give two pieces of information.

(h) List one benefit and one limitation of this source.

 COLLABORATE: In groups, make a mind map of the effects on Ireland of each of the plantations: Laois-Offaly, Munster and Ulster.

▲ Commemorative stamps of the Ulster Plantation

# 11.5: The Effect of the Plantations on Irish Identity

**In this topic, you will learn about:**

❯ The religious, political and cultural effects of the Plantations

## Religious identity

Until the Plantations, Ireland's ruling social classes, with their various loyalties and customs, were Catholic. The arrival of large numbers of Protestant planters from England and Scotland changed this. At the same time, most land that had long belonged to Catholic Irish clans passed into the hands of Protestant settlers. In Ireland, the division between coloniser and colonised (as we saw in chapter 9) matched the **new religious division**. This affected Irish identity very strongly. These effects were felt across Ireland but were most evident in Ulster, where plantation had been most successful.

Overall, the majority of Ireland's population remained Catholic, but **by 1700 Protestants owned 85% of the land**. This wealthy landlord class became known as the **Protestant Ascendancy**. Anger and mistrust grew between the communities and tensions occasionally erupted into terrible violence on both sides. This long history of conflict eventually developed into the Troubles of the late twentieth century. You will learn more about this in chapter 21.

## Political conflict

The power difference between Catholics and Protestants in Ireland led to continued conflict, especially within politics. Protestants ensured that they held on to their control, wealth and land by introducing the **Penal Laws.** These were laws which suppressed the status of Catholics in Ireland, making it very difficult to escape poverty or achieve security. The first Penal Laws came in after the Nine Years War, in 1603.

This greatly affected Irish identity and would go on to shape people's political beliefs and influence the parties they supported in the years and centuries to come. You will learn more about this in chapters 14 and 15.

**DID YOU KNOW?**

Because Catholic Mass was banned and priests were in danger, many Catholic parishes had a secret 'mass rock' somewhere far from unfriendly eyes: on a mountain, deep in the woods or tucked into a glen. The people would make their way to this place whenever a priest could appear to say Mass for them, using the rock as his altar.

▲ Mass rock near Newcastle, Co. Tipperary

| Under the Penal Laws, Catholics were forbidden to… | |
|---|---|
| buy or inherit land | marry a Protestant |
| keep weapons | work in the government |
| own a horse of good quality | vote |
| run schools or teach | attend Catholic Mass |
| attend the only university (Trinity College) | miss attending Protestant services |
| travel five miles from their home | employ a Catholic schoolmaster for their children |

# Cultural change

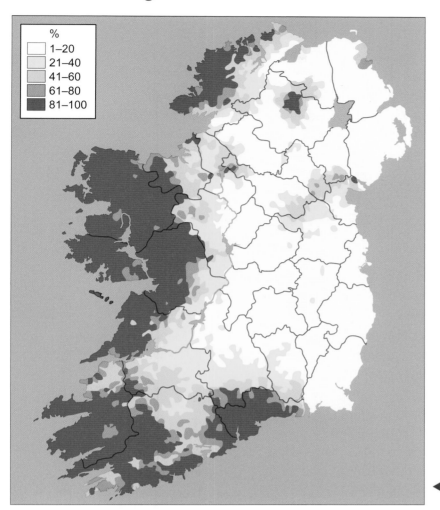

%
| | |
|---|---|
| | 1–20 |
| | 21–40 |
| | 41–60 |
| | 61–80 |
| | 81–100 |

◀ Distribution of Irish
speakers, c.1700

As the Gaelic chieftains lost power, the **culture and language of the Gaelic Irish declined**. By 1700, English was already the main language of power and of trade. The Gaelic Brehon laws were replaced by English laws. English farming methods replaced the Gaelic ways in many areas, leading to more tillage (crop farming) relative to cattle farming. Forests were cleared and land was divided into fields using hedges and ditches. More towns were built during the Plantations, leading to a more urban society. Together, these changed the Gaelic way of life and Irish culture generally.

## CHECKPOINT!

1. Explain the term Penal Laws.

2. How did the Penal Laws affect the education that Catholics could receive?

3. Give an example of how Irish identity was affected by the Plantations in terms of (a) religion; (b) politics; and (c) culture.

4. The map above shows where Irish was spoken daily around 1700. Explain why you think it looks like this.

✓ I can describe the overall results of the Plantations and explain their effect on Irish identity.

← TIME TO GO BACK ◆ I CAN MOVE FORWARD →

 **SUMMARY**

In this chapter, we have learned that:

- Dublin and its surrounding areas (the Pale) were the base of English power in Ireland. Within the Pale, the English language, customs, dress, farming methods and laws were in use.

- Most land was owned by the Anglo-Irish and the Gaelic Irish. The Anglo-Irish were descendants of the Anglo-Normans who had invaded Ireland in the twelfth century. The Gaelic Irish were the Catholic Gaelic chieftains who followed Irish laws (known as Brehon law).

- Henry VIII's family was called the Tudors. Their motives for conquering Ireland included: to expand their kingdom; to make Ireland Protestant; to stop Ireland forming alliances with Catholic monarchs; to impose English customs, culture, laws and so forth on the Gaelic Irish.

- 'Surrender and regrant' was an early policy: the Old English and the Gaelic Irish rulers were to surrender themselves and their lands to Henry VIII, and he would grant their land back to them along with an English title.

- When Irish lands were confiscated, they were sold or rented to loyal English settlers. This was known as plantation. Planting settlers was cheaper in the long term than paying soldiers to protect the English already in Ireland.

- The first plantation was the Laois-Offaly Plantation, organised by Queen Mary I. The second plantation was the Munster Plantation, organised by Queen Elizabeth I. This was slightly more successful than the Laois-Offaly Plantation, but still failed in many ways.

- The Ulster Plantation, organised by King James I, was successful. Many English and Scottish planters moved to Ulster and it became loyal to the Crown. The Protestant population grew and prospered, while the Gaelic Irish lost their land. Tensions continue to this day.

- Irish identity was affected by the Plantations in religious, political and cultural ways.

**Reflecting on... the Plantations**

The Plantations influenced identity on the island of Ireland in various ways. Ireland was changed religiously, politically and culturally. The Ulster Plantation, organised by James I, was to have the longest-lasting effect on Ireland.

 **Understanding History**

1. What was the significance of the Pale?
2. How did the policy of surrender and regrant work and how successful was it?
3. Why was the policy of plantation introduced in Ireland?
4. Put the monarchs into the order in which they ruled England: Elizabeth I, Edward VI, Mary I, James I and Henry VIII.
5. Take turns with a partner to each define five of the key terms below.

| The Pale | Gaelic Irish | Succession | Undertakers | Loyal Irish |
|----------|-------------|------------|-------------|-------------|
| Old English | Brehon Law | Adventurers | Flight of the Earls | Plantation |
| Anglo-Irish | Surrender and regrant | Presidents | Servitors | Planter |

**Exploring History**

1. Write a short paragraph about the Laois-Offaly and Munster Plantations.

2. Write an account of the Ulster Plantation and discuss its results. Why is it considered a success?

3. Ireland underwent another plantation from 1649 called the Cromwellian Plantation. Use the following links to research ten facts about this. Remember to cite correctly!

https://educateplus.ie/go/cromwell

https://educateplus.ie/go/cromwell2

| KEY TERMS | The Plantations | Irish lands confiscated by the king could be sold or rented to loyal English settlers |
|---|---|---|
| | Old English | people in the Pale who were loyal to the king |
| | Anglo-Irish | descendants of the Anglo-Normans who had invaded Ireland in the twelfth century |
| | Gaelic Irish | the Gaelic chieftains who followed Irish laws , known as Brehon laws |
| | Brehon laws | Gaelic Irish laws going as far back as the Iron Age |
| | Surrender and regrant | the Old English and the Gaelic Irish rulers were to surrender themselves and their lands to Henry VIII, and he would grant their land back to them with an English title |
| | Succession | when land was passed on from father to son in the English system |
| | Planters | the new settlers during a plantation |
| | Adventurers | men who claimed to be descendants of the early Normans granted land in Munster by Henry II |
| | Presidents | men who imposed English law, the English language and the Protestant religion |
| | Undertakers | men who undertook (agreed) to do as they were told with the land given to them |
| | The Flight of the Earls | when O'Neill and other Ulster chiefs fled to Europe in 1607 |
| | Servitors | English or Scottish soldiers who had fought for the Crown |
| | Loyal Irish | native Irish who stayed loyal to the English during the Nine Years War |
| | Penal Laws | laws that suppressed the status of Catholics in Ireland |

 Go to page 65 of your *Sources and Skills Book* for more exercises.

 Go to page 25 of your *Research Portfolio* for a task based on this chapter.

11

Settlement in Ireland: The Plantations

| The Plantations in Ireland c. 1500–1700 | The Age of Revolution c. 1750–1850 | Ireland under the Union 1800–1920 |
|---|---|---|

At the end of the eighteenth century, revolutions occurred on both sides of the Atlantic that had profound effects on the course of history. A revolution is **a rapid and significant change in society, politics, technology or the economy**. In America, France and Ireland, people rose up to overthrow the established order. They wanted to create new ways of running society where people would have a greater say over the laws that ruled their lives. The first of these revolutions took place in **North America**, where colonists fought against British rule.

# WORKING WITH THE EVIDENCE!

## The American Revolution

| Type of source | Category | Example |
|---|---|---|
| Primary | Written | Writings of the revolutionaries themselves: letters and diaries from people such as **George Washington**, **John Adams**, **Abigail Adams** and ordinary soldiers fighting on both sides<br><br>Books, pamphlets and newspapers written by political thinkers like **Thomas Paine** (e.g. *Common Sense*) |
| Primary | Written | Official documents from the **American Continental Congress** (such as the **Declaration of Independence**) and the British government |

▲ An early American newspaper

▶ Revolutionary writings

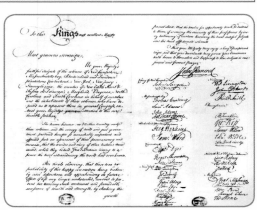

When we look at sources from the American Revolution, why do we need to be especially careful to check for bias and propaganda?

# 12.1: The Causes of the American Revolution

In this topic, you will learn about:

❷ The Age of Enlightenment
❷ Restrictions on American trade
❷ The impact of the Seven Years' War
❷ The American protests against British taxation

**DID YOU KNOW?**

The US state of Maryland was founded as a refuge for Catholics who had been persecuted in England.

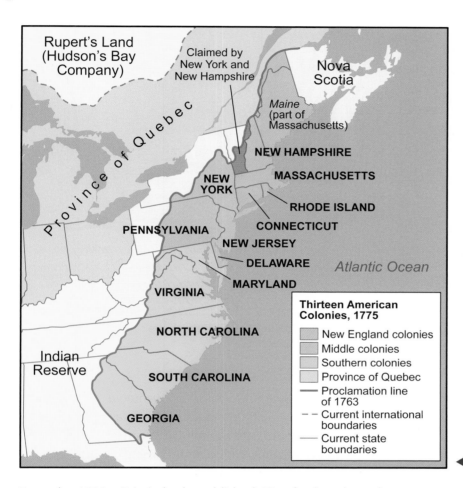

◀ The original 13 colonies, 1775

From the 1600s, Britain had established **13 colonies** along the eastern seaboard of **North America**. The colonists were from Britain and other European countries and were largely allowed to run their own affairs through their **local assemblies**. The British Crown was represented in each colony by a **governor**. Between 1650 and 1750, the population in the colonies grew to **two million** and they became very prosperous through trading in tobacco, grain, cotton and fish. Many of the colonists had left their home countries to escape religious or political persecution, while others saw the colonies as a chance to become wealthy.

By the 1760s, various factors had come together to make the colonies unhappy with British rule:

## 1. The Age of Enlightenment

During the eighteenth century, a movement called the **Enlightenment** emerged in Europe. It was a <u>movement of thinkers who valued reason and science above faith or authority as a basis for society</u>. Many of them challenged the idea that kings had a **divine right to rule** as they saw fit. Instead, they argued that power of government should be limited and the rights of the people protected.

A MAP of
the moſt INHABITED part of
VIRGINIA
containing the whole PROVINCE of
MARYLAND
with Part of
PENSILVANIA, NEW JERSEY and NORTH CAROLINA
Drawn by
Joshua Fry & Peter Jefferson
in 1751.

▲ English colonists at a dockside tobacco warehouse, from a 1751 map of Virginia above

## 2. Restrictions on trade

Relations between Britain and the colonies had become tense by the 1750s. Britain wanted **a cheap supply of raw materials** like cotton for its expanding industries and saw America as a good source for these. However, Britain did not want American competition for its industries. They wanted America as a market to sell the finished goods made by British industry using American materials. The British Parliament passed the **Navigation Acts**, which forced the colonies to sell some of their products (cotton, sugar, tobacco) to Britain alone. This meant that the British could decide the price, as the Americans had nobody else to sell to. These rules caused a lot of smuggling, which led to clashes with the British navy.

## 3. The Seven Years' War

France had also settled colonies in North America. During the **Seven Years' War (1756–1763)**, the British had defeated them and seized a lot of their territory. Huge numbers of British soldiers fought in America, and the British government wanted the colonies to contribute to the cost of the army, as it was there for their protection. The war also meant that many Americans had gained military experience through fighting with the British army.

# 4. No Taxation without Representation!

The British introduced the **Stamp Act (1765)**, requiring all legal documents, wills, newspapers, certificates and playing cards to have a government stamp – which had to be paid for – and the **Quartering Act (1765)**, which imposed taxes to cover the cost of soldiers in the colonies.

The colonists were furious. They did not want to pay more taxes and they especially resented taxes being forced upon them by a parliament in London in which they had no representatives. Opposition groups used the slogan '**No Taxation without Representation**'. There were widespread protests and violence against the Stamp Act in particular. '**Stamp men**' were beaten up and '**tarred and feathered**'. The act was withdrawn in 1766.

Groups like the **Sons of Liberty** in Boston attacked British officials, organised **boycotts** of British goods coming into America and published revolutionary pamphlets and posters demanding changes. These groups advocated (argued) for Americans to govern themselves.

▲ Opposition to the Stamp Act. The poster reads: 'England's Folly is America's Ruin'.

## CHECKPOINT!

1. What was the Enlightenment?
2. How and why did the British try to limit American trade?
3. What impact did the Seven Years' War have on the colonies in America?
4. What was the Stamp Act and how did Americans react to it?
5. Which of the causes of the American Revolution do you think was the most important? Why?

✓ I understand the causes of the American Revolution.

 TIME TO GO BACK ◀ ▶ I CAN MOVE FORWARD →

# 12.2: The Road to War

In this topic, you will learn about:

❯ The Boston Massacre
❯ The Boston Tea Party
❯ The Continental Congress
❯ The Battles at Lexington and Concord

## The Boston Massacre

After they had repealed (taken away) the Stamp Act, the British instead imposed the **Townshend Acts** in 1767, which placed taxes on goods that America imported, such as tea, glass, paint and lead. Tensions and protests continued and in 1770 a Boston mob, protesting at the Townshend Acts, confronted a group of British soldiers. The soldiers opened fire and five people were killed in the **Boston Massacre**. Exaggerated accounts soon spread, claiming the soldiers used extreme violence against the citizens. This led to even more anger among Americans.

**DID YOU KNOW?**

The soldiers were defended in court by future US President John Adams. He was able to get all of them acquitted of murder.

▲ The Boston Massacre

Go to pages 72–75 of your *Sources and Skills Book* to examine differing accounts of the Boston Massacre.

## The Boston Tea Party

After the Boston Massacre, the British withdrew all the Townshend Acts and other taxes – except a small tax on tea imports, to show they had the right to tax the colonies. However, in 1773 they passed the **Tea Act**, which exempted the East India Company from paying the tea tax. In December 1773, a group from the Sons of Liberty dressed as Native Americans and dumped 342 crates of East India Company tea into Boston Harbour, an event later known as the **Boston Tea Party**.

◀ The Boston Tea Party

In response, the British government imposed what Americans called the 'intolerable acts' on Boston and the colony of Massachusetts. The port of Boston was closed until compensation was paid for the tea, the city was put under military rule and the colony's assembly was suspended.

## The First Continental Congress

These actions worried the other colonies: if the British could do that to Massachusetts, they could do it to them. **Representatives of the colonies** met in the **Continental Congress** in September 1774. The Congress **opposed all British taxes**, urged a boycott of British goods and demanded the **removal of British soldiers**. Some demanded all-out war, but the majority were not yet willing to go that far. However, secret groups throughout the colonies began to stockpile weapons and **militias** (part-time armies) began to train and arm themselves.

## The Battles of Lexington and Concord

The British **General Gage** tried to stop these developments before they became a full-scale rebellion. In April 1775, he sent 800 troops to seize weapons at **Concord**, near Boston. An American rebel, **Paul Revere**, heard about this and organised militiamen to ride throughout the country to warn the rebels that the British were coming. At **Lexington**, on the way to Concord, a small force of American militiamen engaged the British troops. Ten Americans were killed and eight captured. When the British reached Concord, the weapons were gone. On their way back to Boston there was a larger battle and 273 British soldiers died.

## The Second Continental Congress

The violence in Massachusetts convinced many that war was now inevitable. A pamphlet written by **Thomas Paine** called ***Common Sense*** was read widely throughout the colonies. Paine argued that the British were oppressing the rights of the American people, who should become completely independent to protect those rights. When the **Second Continental Congress** met in 1776, it chose **George Washington** to be commander-in-chief of the Continental (American) Army. On 4 July 1776, the Congress issued the **Declaration of Independence** to separate the American colonies from British rule.

**DID YOU KNOW?**

The same night as Revere's ride, a 16-year-old girl named Sybil Ludington rode twice the distance Revere had through the rain to alert the Continental troops. She returned home at dawn, having averted disaster, and George Washington thanked her personally for her courage.

Go to page 76 of your *Sources and Skills Book* for an evidence task.

**CHECKPOINT!**

1. What happened at the Boston Massacre and how did Britain respond?
2. What caused the Boston Tea Party?
3. What were the 'intolerable acts' and how did the other colonies respond to them?
4. What decisions did the First Continental Congress make?
5. What happened at Lexington and Concord?
6. Why is 4 July celebrated every year in the United States of America?

 I can explain the events that led to the American Declaration of Independence.

TIME TO GO BACK ◀ ▶ I CAN MOVE FORWARD →

**12 Revolutions Option One: The American Revolution**

# WORKING WITH THE EVIDENCE!

## The United States Declaration of Independence

Read this edited extract below. Answer questions 1 to 4 on your own and questions 5 and 6 with your group.

*We hold these truths to be self-evident, that all men are created equal, that they are endowed by their Creator with certain unalienable Rights, that among these are Life, Liberty and the pursuit of Happiness. That to secure these rights, Governments are instituted among Men, deriving their just powers from the consent of the governed. Whenever any form of Government becomes destructive of these ends, it is the Right of the People to alter or to abolish it, and to institute [set up] new Government…*

*The history of the present King of Great Britain is a history of repeated injuries… all having the direct aim to establish absolute Tyranny over these States. To prove this, let Facts be known: Quartering large bodies of armed troops among us and protecting them from punishment for any murders committed on the inhabitants of these States. Cutting off our Trade with all parts of the world. Imposing Taxes on us without our Consent. Depriving us in many cases, of the benefits of Trial by Jury…*

*We, the Representatives of the United States of America, in General Congress, do, in the Name and by Authority of the good People of these Colonies, solemnly publish and declare, that these United Colonies are, and of Right ought to be Free and Independent States.*

1. What are the rights of the people and where do these come from?
2. What form of government do people have the right to alter or abolish?
3. Mention two facts given above as proof of the king's 'absolute tyranny' over the colonies.
4. What solemn declaration is made by the representatives in General Congress?
5. Is this document an example of propaganda? Who is it aimed at?
6. Using this document, describe the ideal relationship between the people and their government.

**DID YOU KNOW?**

In December 1775, the Continental Congress appointed an Irishman, John Barry from Wexford, as the captain of its first naval vessel, the *USS Lexington*. Barry is known in the US as the 'Father of the US Navy'.

▲ *Declaration of Independence*, painted by John Trumbull c. 1819

# 12.3: An American Revolutionary: George Washington

> **In this topic, you will learn about:**
> ● The life of George Washington
> ● The central events in the War of Independence

## A Life in Time: George Washington (1732–1799)

### Early life

George Washington was born in the colony of Virginia to a family of wealthy landowners. They farmed tobacco and owned a number of African slaves. He fought in the British army in the Seven Years' War. Afterwards, he was elected to Virginia's assembly. He inherited the family estates and in 1759 he married **Martha Dandridge Custis**, a wealthy widow, becoming one of the richest men in Virginia.

### The Continental Army

Washington was elected to represent Virginia at the First and Second Continental Congresses. He supported independence once he realised that there could be no compromise between the colonies and Britain. He was appointed **commander-in-chief of the Continental Army in 1775**. He received this position due to his military experience and because, as a Virginian, his appointment guaranteed the support of the largest and richest colony. Washington faced a daunting situation, as this comparison of the armies shows:

| The Continental Army | The British Army |
|---|---|
| • 20,000 men<br>• Part-time soldiers, many only serving for short periods<br>• Poorly trained and equipped: a variety of guns and other weapons, even makeshift ones from farm tools<br>• Problems of indiscipline and disease<br>• Congress was slow to pay the army<br>• The soldiers had local knowledge and could use this against the British | • 80,000 men<br>• Professional, full-time soldiers<br>• Well trained and equipped with the best weapons of the time<br>• Large navy for supplies<br>• Fighting in an unfamiliar country<br>• Treated all Americans as enemies and punished civilians, increasing support for the rebels<br>• Thousands of miles from home |

### The War of Independence

After fighting broke out in 1775, there were a number of major battles between the two sides:

- Washington lost his first battle, at **Bunker Hill**, but inflicted heavy casualties on the British.
- The Continental Army won the **Battle of Boston** and captured cannons and rifles which were needed for the war.
- After Washington was defeated at **New York** in 1776, he gained two small victories at **Princeton** and **Trenton**.
- In 1777, the British **General Howe**'s army of 18,000 men captured **Philadelphia**, America's largest city and the home of the Continental Congress. This was a huge blow: many people began to doubt that America could win and they questioned Washington's leadership.

### Turning point: Saratoga and the entry of the French

The month after the loss of Philadelphia, the American General Gates defeated a British army of 8,000 men at **Saratoga**. This victory reassured the American people and some of Britain's European rivals became interested. **France, Spain** and the **Netherlands** joined the war against Britain in 1778. French help was particularly key to the colonies' eventual victory. They sent 6,000 troops and weapons and used their fleet to disrupt British supplies. In addition, more troops had to stay behind in Britain in case of a French attack there.

▲ The Battle of Bunker Hill

### Turning point: Valley Forge

After his defeat at Philadelphia, Washington regrouped at a remote base called **Valley Forge** with his 11,000 men during the winter of 1777–1778. This was one of the harshest winters of the century. The men endured great hardship and hunger in the freezing cold. Disease was rife in the camp and by the end of February, 3,000 men had died. Hundreds more had deserted (abandoned the army).

▲ Suffering at Valley Forge

However, the army that emerged from Valley Forge at winter's end had been transformed. Washington had won the undying loyalty of his men by refusing to abandon them and sharing in their terrible conditions. During the winter, the professional Prussian soldier **Baron Von Steuben** had drilled the soldiers until they were as well trained and disciplined as any European army.

### Victory at Yorktown

Over the next few years, the balance of the war turned in favour of the Americans. They won more battles, and Washington kept the British largely confined to New York. In the decisive battle at **Yorktown** in October 1781, 7,000 British soldiers under **Lord Cornwallis** were surrounded by 9,000 American and 5,000 French troops on land and a French fleet at sea. Cut off from reinforcements and supplies and outnumbered two to one, Cornwallis surrendered to Washington. This marked the end of the war. The **Treaty of Paris** was signed between the former colonies and the British in 1783.

▲ The British surrender at Yorktown

## *Washington's later life*

After the victory in the war, Washington retired to his Mount Vernon estate. He was soon called back to serve the people as the president of the **Constitutional Convention**. This was called in 1787 to write a constitution for their new country, the **United States of America**.
A **constitution** is the set of fundamental rules for running a country that outlines the powers of government and the rights of citizens. The American constitution established a **federal republic**, a system of government where power is divided between a central government (usually headed by a president) and various regions or states.

Washington was elected the first president of the US in 1789 and was re-elected in 1792. He worked to set up the new American government and surrounded himself with the best men of his age to work with him, including **Thomas Jefferson**, **Alexander Hamilton** and **John Adams**. He retired to Mount Vernon, where in 1799 he died from pneumonia. The capital of the US was named 'Washington' in honour of the man many Americans consider 'the father of the nation'.

▲ The Washington Monument

## CHECKPOINT!

1. How did Washington become one of the wealthiest men in Virginia?
2. Why was he selected to command the Continental Army?
3. What advantages and disadvantages did the Continental Army have at the start of the war?
4. What advantages and disadvantages did the British army have at the start of the war?
5. Why was the victory at Saratoga so important to the Americans?
6. What happened at Valley Forge?
7. Give three reasons why the Americans won the war.
8. What did Washington do after the war to serve America?
9. What is a constitution?

 I understand the role played by George Washington in American history.

 TIME TO GO BACK ◀ ▶ I CAN MOVE FORWARD ➡

12 Revolutions Option One: The American Revolution

# 12.4: The Results of the American Revolution

**In this topic, you will learn about:**
- ❯ The growth of the US
- ❯ The impact on France and Ireland
- ❯ The influence of ideas

## 1. The growth of the United States of America

The most significant result of the American Revolution was the creation of the United States of America. It grew to **50 states** over the next 200 years and reached the Pacific Ocean. This expansion saw **Native American peoples and their cultures all but wiped out**. By 1900, millions of immigrants from all over the world had made America their home.

## 2. The impact on France and Ireland

News of events in America spread quickly. Newspapers, letters and returning soldiers brought the colonists' ideals to other peoples. The Americans had overthrown the rule of a king they found unjust. In France, bankrupted by the war, the rule of **Louis XVI** was beginning to collapse. People looked to the American republic for inspiration. This paved the way for the **French Revolution** in 1789 (see chapter 13).

Ireland had been under British rule since the 1100s. There, people looked at America's example and dreamed of an **independent Ireland**. This would lead to the 1798 **United Irishmen Rebellion** (see chapter 14).

## 3. The influence of ideas

The Declaration of Independence states that '**all men are created equal**', but this equality and freedom was limited to white men following the creation of the US.

- **Women** were treated as **second-class citizens** with few rights separate from those of their husbands or fathers.
- Millions of **black slaves** were kept by owners (including 'Founding Fathers' Washington and Thomas Jefferson) across the southern US.
- **Native Americans** were killed in their hundreds of thousands, were driven from their lands and saw their culture almost wiped out.

However, the ideals of the American Revolution inspired all these groups, and others who supported them, to keep fighting for their equal rights over the next 200 years.

▲ A 1787 engraving used to call for an end to slavery

---

## CHECKPOINT!

1. How did the US grow after independence from Britain?
2. What impact did the American Revolution have on (a) France and (b) Ireland?
3. How do you think the ideals of the American revolution influenced women, slaves and Native Americans in the future?

 I can explain the impact of the American Revolution, there and abroad.

 ⬅ TIME TO GO BACK ❯ I CAN MOVE FORWARD ➡

# SUMMARY

The causes of the American Revolution can be divided into long-term and short-term causes:

| Long-term causes | Short-term causes |
|---|---|
| The Age of Enlightenment | The Boston Massacre |
| British restrictions on American trade | The Boston Tea Party |
| The Seven Years' War | The Continental Congresses |
| 'No Taxation without Representation!' | The Battles of Lexington and Concord |

- The American colonies declared their independence from Britain in July 1776. Over the next five years they fought a difficult war against the British. After several early defeats, the Americans defeated the British at Saratoga. Washington retrained his army in Valley Forge in 1777–1778 and the French joined the war on the Americans' side.

- The Americans defeated the British at Yorktown in 1781 under Washington's command. This victory brought the fighting to an end and the colonies were given their independence.

- After the success of the American Revolution, the peoples of France and Ireland were inspired to follow the American example. The ideals of freedom and equality behind the revolution continue to inspire many to stand up for the rights of minorities within their own country.

### Reflecting on... the American Revolution

The American Revolution was a key event in world history. It saw the birth of a nation that would eventually become the most powerful in the world. It saw the first expression of the rights to freedom and equality for all and established the idea that governments must be answerable to those whom they govern.

# Understanding History

1. How did the Enlightenment contribute to the American Revolution?
2. Why do you think the Americans resented (a) the restrictions on their trade and (b) having to pay taxes to Britain so much?
3. How did the Americans respond to the Townshend Acts?
4. What role did the Boston Massacre and the Boston Tea Party play in the lead up to the war?
5. Compare the British and American armies during the war.
6. What were the key turning points in the War of Independence?
7. What do you think was George Washington's most important contribution to American history?
8. How did the American Revolution influence people (a) inside and (b) outside America?

9. Find out the year when the following events took place and then put them in chronological order on a timeline in your copybook, starting with the earliest.

- The Declaration of Independence
- The Battle of Yorktown
- The Stamp Act
- George Washington becomes US President
- The Townshend Acts

- The Boston Massacre
- The Battle of Saratoga
- The Seven Years' War
- The First Continental Congress
- Valley Forge

10. Copy out the table below, then sort each event or topic into its correct column.

- The Battle of Yorktown
- The Boston Tea Party
- The Sons of Liberty
- The French Revolution
- Valley Forge
- Campaigns against slavery

- The Battle of Saratoga
- The capture of Philadelphia
- The Seven Years' War
- The United Irishmen's rebellion
- The Enlightenment
- The US Constitution

| Causes of the Revolution | Course of the Revolution | Consequences of the Revolution |
|---|---|---|
| | | |

## Exploring History

1. Write an account of the life of George Washington.
2. Explain why the American colonies declared their independence from Britain in 1776.
3. Write an account of the American War of Independence and explain why the Americans won.
4. Compare the United States Declaration of Independence with the 1916 Rising Proclamation. How are the two documents (a) similar and (b) different?

| KEY TERMS | | |
|---|---|---|
| | Revolution | a rapid and significant change in society, politics, technology or the economy |
| | Enlightenment | a movement of thinkers in eighteenth-century Europe who valued reason and science above faith or authority as a basis for society |
| | Militias | part-time armies |
| | Constitution | set of fundamental rules for running a country that outlines the powers of government and the rights of citizens |
| | Federal republic | a system of government where power is divided between a central government (usually headed by a president) and various regions or states |

 Go to page 70 of your *Sources and Skills Book* for more exercises.

 Go to page 29 of your *Research Portfolio* for a task based on this chapter.

At the end of the eighteenth century, revolutions occurred on both sides of the Atlantic that would have profound effects on the course of history. A <u>revolution</u> is <u>a rapid and significant change in society, politics, technology or the economy.</u> In America and France, the people rose up to overthrow the established order. They wanted to create new ways of running society so that people could have a greater say over the laws that shaped their lives.

In 1775, Britain's colonies in North America revolted against the rule of King George III. In 1789, revolution arrived in Europe when the people of France challenged the rule of their king, Louis XVI.

## WORKING WITH THE <u>EVIDENCE!</u>

### The French Revolution

| Type of source | Category | Example |
|---|---|---|
| Primary | Written | Writings of thinkers and revolutionaries; letters and diaries by people such as **Voltaire** and **Robespierre** and ordinary people in France (especially Paris) at the time |
| | Written | Books, pamphlets and newspapers |
| Primary | Written | Official documents from various revolutionary governments and assemblies (such as the *Declaration of the Rights of Man and of the Citizen*) |

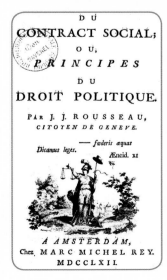

◀ Rousseau's *The Social Contract*, a book on the relationship between people and their rulers

◀ *Declaration of the Rights of Man and of the Citizen*

In what language do you think most of these sources are written? Is this a problem for some historians? How might they overcome this problem?

# 13.1: The Causes of the French Revolution

**In this topic, you will learn about:**
- France's absolute monarchy
- The Enlightenment
- Social divisions in France
- The American Revolution

There was no single cause of the French Revolution. France had many long-term problems, but few people in the 1780s imagined the fall of the monarchy and the complete change that would occur in France in the years after 1789.

## 1. France's absolute monarchy

**Louis XVI** ruled France in the late eighteenth century as an **absolute monarch**. This meant he had <u>total power over the country and claimed he had a divine (God-given) right to rule, so could do whatever he wanted</u>. This system could work when the king was a strong and competent ruler. However, Louis was weak and incompetent. His Austrian wife, **Marie Antoinette**, was unpopular with the French people. The couple lived a very extravagant and expensive lifestyle at their huge palace at Versailles. As the French economy worsened and the government's debts grew, people began to criticise the royal family.

▲ Louis XVI

## 2. The Enlightenment

During the eighteenth century, a movement called the **Enlightenment** emerged in Europe. It was <u>a movement of thinkers who valued reason and science above faith or authority as a basis for society</u>. Many of these writers were French, like **Voltaire, Rousseau and Montesquieu**. They criticised the *ancien régime* (the 'old system') of Louis' absolute monarchy. They wrote about their ideas in essays, books, pamphlets and newspapers. Many educated French people read these and wanted to change the system of government so that the king shared power with the people.

▲ Caricature of Louis XVI as a pig

# 3. Social divisions in France

The French people were divided into '**Three Estates**' or groups:

| First Estate | Second Estate | Third Estate |
|---|---|---|
| Clergy (priests and bishops) | Nobility (wealthy landowners who controlled the government and the army) | The common people: everyone from well-off doctors, lawyers, teachers and merchants to poor peasants and workers |
| Approximately 100,000 people | Approximately 400,000 people | Approximately 25 million people |
| Did not pay taxes | Did not pay taxes | Paid taxes |
| Owned 10% of the land | Owned 60% of the land | Many peasants still lived under feudal law |

The Third Estate, especially its wealthy and educated members, fiercely resented paying taxes when the other estates did not. The Third Estate had to pay all the taxes for the country. These included:

- The **taille**: a land tax
- The **gabelle**: a salt tax
- The **corvée**: members of the Third Estate had to work for free repairing roads
- The **tithe**: one-tenth of earnings or produce went to the Catholic Church

They also resented having to pay taxes while they had no say in running the country.

**13 Revolutions Option Two: The French Revolution**

## 4. The impact of the American Revolution

In **1776**, Britain's colonies in North America declared their independence. In **1778 France joined the war** in support of American independence. The success of the American Revolution influenced France in two major ways:

▼ Uniformed French solider in the American Revolution

- Firstly, many French people were inspired by the American achievements of overthrowing British rule in the name of freedom and equality.

- Secondly, France had incurred great debt by supporting the Americans during the war. By the end of the 1780s, the government's finances were in crisis and Louis urgently needed to raise taxes. When the nobility refused to pay any of the existing taxes, the king was left with no choice but to call a meeting of the **Estates General**.

▲ Marquis de Lafayette

**DID YOU KNOW?**

One man in particular ties the American and French Revolutions together: the Marquis de Lafayette. Aged 19, he bought a ship to sail west and join the American Revolution, became close to George Washington, was wounded in battle and wintered at Valley Forge with the Continental Army. On his return to France, he helped to compose the *Declaration of the Rights of the Man and of the Citizen*. He was made commander of the National Guard, but when Jacobin radicals ordered his arrest, he was captured by Austria while fleeing. Years later, Lafayette turned down the invitation to lead France himself. He is buried in Paris, under soil brought from Bunker Hill, and is known as 'the Hero of the Two Worlds'.

### CHECKPOINT!

1. What was an absolute monarch? Where did he believe his power came from?
2. How did the Enlightenment thinkers challenge the *ancien régime*?
3. What were the (a) First, (b) Second and (c) Third Estates?
4. How was the Third Estate different from the other two? Give two examples.
5. What taxes did the Third Estate have to pay and why did they resent them?
6. How did the American Revolution impact on France?

 I understand the causes of the French Revolution.

 TIME TO GO BACK ◀ ▶ I CAN MOVE FORWARD ➡

## 13.2: The Road to Revolution

In this topic, you will learn about:
- The meeting of the Estates General
- The storming of the Bastille prison

▲ Meeting of the Estates General

## The Estates General

**The Estates General** was <u>a kind of French parliament that was made up of three parts, each representing one of the three Estates</u>. It was the only body that could authorise new taxes.

On 5 May 1789, the Estates General met for the first time since 1614 at Versailles. The First Estate (with 308 members) and Second Estate (285 members) wanted to preserve their privileges, while the Third Estate (621 members) was determined to force the king to accept changes. Immediately a huge disagreement began over how the voting should work.

Nobles and clergy wanted one vote for each estate, so they could combine to outvote the Third Estate by two votes to one. The Third Estate wanted one vote per member, so that its 621 members could outvote the 593 members of the other two estates.

After six weeks of debate on this issue, the Third Estate lost patience. Declaring that they represented the French people, they named themselves **the National Assembly**. They declared that they alone had the power to pass laws. The next day, having been locked out of their meeting room, the National Assembly met on the Versailles tennis courts instead. There they swore the **Tennis Court Oath**, promising to stay together until a constitution for France was drawn up. Louis, unnerved by rumours of violent mobs in Paris, ordered the other two estates to join them within the National Assembly.

Go to page 80 of your *Sources and Skills Book* for an evidence task on the Three Estates.

▲ An artist's impression of the Storming of the Bastille

▲ The National Guard with the heads of the Bastille governor and his guards

## The Storming of the Bastille

In the summer of 1789, tensions were rising in Paris due to high food prices and shortages. A working person's diet consisted mostly of bread; when two bad harvests put its cost up to an impossible 88% of the daily wage, hunger – and anger – soon followed.

Fearing that the king would use the army to shut down the National Assembly, the citizens of Paris formed their own **militia** called the **National Guard**. On 14 July, a large, angry crowd attacked the **Bastille prison** in Paris – perhaps because they expected to find weapons there, to free prisoners, or because it symbolised the power of the *ancien régime* and the king. The governor was captured and beaten to death.

The mob in Paris became known as **sans-culottes** (literally, 'without short trousers' – theirs were long, rather than the silk knee-length breeches fashionable then). The sans-culottes were an important force in the revolution, as they continued to demand radical changes over the following years. This event is considered the start of the French Revolution. **Bastille Day** is celebrated every **14 July** as a national holiday.

### CHECKPOINT!

1. What was the Estates General?
2. In 1789, how many years had passed since it had last met?
3. Why was there a dispute over voting in the Estates General?
4. What was the Tennis Court Oath?
5. Why was there tension in Paris during the summer of 1789?
6. What happened on 14 July 1789?

 I know what the Estates General was and why 14 July is so significant. ← TIME TO GO BACK ◆ I CAN MOVE FORWARD →

### DID YOU KNOW?

On 14 July 1789, the Bastille only had seven prisoners: four forgers, two 'lunatics' and one misbehaving aristocrat. One was an Irishman who was once a military hero but now had delusions of being Julius Caesar. After a few days wandering the chaotic streets, he was placed in an asylum.

The French Revolution had both long-term and short-term causes:

| Long-term causes | Short-term causes |
|---|---|
| France's absolute monarchy | The calling of the Estates General |
| The Enlightenment | The Tennis Court Oath |
| Social divisions in France | The Storming of the Bastille |
| The American Revolution | |

Go to page 82 of your *Sources and Skills Book* for an evidence task on the Storming of the Bastille.

# 13.3: Revolution in France

## The reforms of the National Assembly

Events at the Bastille inspired the middle class, peasants and labourers around France to take action. Nobles' and bishops' houses were attacked and many of them fled abroad. The National Assembly also acted by passing sweeping reforms:

**In this topic, you will learn about:**
- ❯ How the revolutionaries changed France
- ❯ The fate of King Louis XVI
- ❯ The reaction of the rest of Europe

- They **abolished the feudal system**, all privileges of the nobility and all titles. Everyone in France was now called '**citizen**'.

- **The Declaration of the Rights of Man and of the Citizen** was passed in August 1789. This declared that:
  - All men are born free and equal.
  - All citizens have the right to liberty, property and security.
  - All citizens are equal before the law.
  - Everyone has the freedom to speak, write and print what they want.

- **The Civil Constitution of the Clergy** was passed: this abolished tithes, seized all Church property for the state, required all clergy to take an oath of loyalty to the revolution and removed the Pope's power over the French Church. This law turned many people who were devout Catholics against the revolution.

# WORKING WITH THE EVIDENCE!

## The Declaration of the Rights of Man and of the Citizen

Read this extract and answer the questions below:

> Therefore the National Assembly recognises and proclaims the following rights of man and of the citizen:
>
> - Men are born free and equal in rights.
> - The purpose of all political associations is the preservation of the natural rights of man. These rights are: liberty, property, security and resistance to oppression.
> - Liberty consists in being able to do whatever does not harm others. No man ought to be uneasy about his opinions, even his religious beliefs, provided that these actions do not interfere with the public order established by law.
> - The free communication of thought and opinion is one of the most precious rights of man: every citizen can therefore talk, write and publish freely.

1. What are the 'natural rights of man'?
2. Identify two freedoms enjoyed by the citizens of France.
3. What does liberty consist of?
4. Do you agree that 'free communication of thought and opinion is one of the most precious rights of man'?
5. The Declaration was influenced by the ideas of Enlightenment writers. Name one famous Enlightenment writer.

 **COLLABORATE:** In your group, try to find out which modern human rights are based on the rights outlined above.

## Symbols of the revolution

The aims of the revolutionaries were summed up in the slogan '**Liberty**, **Equality**, **Fraternity**':

- **Liberty:** all men are free
- **Equality:** all men are equal
- **Fraternity:** all men should treat each other as brothers

The revolutionaries also adopted a new flag for France. It was a tricolour with blue and red (the colours of Paris) on either side of the white of the royal family, to symbolise that the people were now dominant over royalty.

 COLLABORATE: Find out about the origins of the flags of the following countries and report your findings to the rest of your class: Ireland; the United Kingdom; the United States; Germany; China.

▲ Emblem of the French Revolution. It reads: 'Unity and indivisibility of the Republic. Liberty, equality, fraternity – or death'.

## The flight to Varennes

▲ The flight to Varennes

Many people in Paris feared that the king and queen, Louis and Marie Antoinette, were opposed to the revolution and would try to reverse it. In October 1789, thousands of the ordinary working women of Paris armed themselves and marched the six hours to Versailles. They forced the royal family to return to Paris, where they were confined to the **Tuileries Palace**.

Louis wanted the support of other European monarchs to crush the revolution; no monarch wanted these revolutionary ideas to spread to their countries. In particular, Louis looked to his brother-in-law, the **Emperor Leopold of Austria**, for help. He planned to escape to the Austrian-controlled Netherlands (modern Belgium) with his family. In June 1791, disguised as servants, Louis and Marie Antoinette slipped out of Paris. They were caught near the border, at the town of **Varennes**. Many people were convinced the king was conspiring with foreign powers against his own people and he was stripped of most of his powers.

## The war with Austria

Austria was seen as the main foreign threat. Believing it was only a matter of time before France was attacked, the Assembly declared war on Austria in April 1792 in an attempt to strike before the Austrians were ready. However, it was the French forces that were ill-prepared. Many army officers (who were nobles) had fled and **the army lacked good leaders**.

The Austrians were joined by the Prussians and they won several victories over the French. The sans-culottes of Paris suspected King Louis of helping France's enemies and in August they stormed the Tuileries Palace. The **royal family was imprisoned** by the National Assembly.

▲ The mob storming the Tuileries Palace

## The execution of the king

French fortunes in the war improved after an appeal was made to the people to save the revolution. Huge numbers joined the army, which then overwhelmed the invaders on the battlefield. The sans-culottes demanded more radical reforms and in September 1792 the new **National Convention** declared France a **republic** (a type of government without a king, where the people are sovereign). During the celebrations, mobs broke into various Paris prisons and executed over 1,000 people as '**enemies of the revolution**' in the **September Massacres**.

▲ The execution by guillotine of Louis XVI

Documents found in a safe in the Tuileries Palace seemed to prove Louis had been working with France's foreign enemies. He was tried by the Convention and found guilty of treason by a small majority (387 to 334). Louis XVI was executed at the **guillotine** in January 1793. Nine months later, Marie Antoinette met the same fate. These executions outraged the rest of Europe. Britain, Spain and the Netherlands declared war on France. This crisis would lead to the coming to power of **Maximilien Robespierre** and the **Committee of Public Safety**.

**DID YOU KNOW?**

The guillotine was originally invented as a more humane method of execution than hanging, but became a symbol of the brutality of the French Revolution.

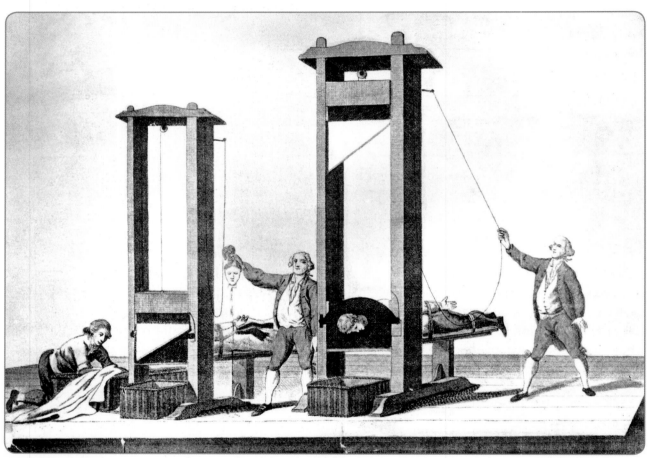

▲ Guillotine

## CHECKPOINT!

1. How did the revolution change the positions of (a) nobles and (b) clergy in France?
2. What were the main points of *The Declaration of the Rights of Man and of the Citizen*?
3. Explain the following terms: liberty; equality; fraternity.
4. What was the flight to Varennes and what were the results of it?
5. How did other European countries react to the events in France?
6. Why was Louis XVI executed?

✓ I understand the main reforms of the French Revolution and the events leading to the execution of the king.

 ◀ TIME TO GO BACK ◆ I CAN MOVE FORWARD ➤

Go to page 83 of your *Sources and Skills Book* for a newspaper report on the execution of Louis XVI.

# 13.4: Robespierre and the Reign of Terror

**In this topic, you will learn about:**
- The rise and fall of Robespierre
- The Jacobins and the Reign of Terror

## A Life in Time: Maximilien Robespierre (1758–1794)

### Early life

**Maximilien Robespierre** was born in 1758 in the small town of Arras. He trained as a lawyer and served briefly as a judge before he resigned – apparently because he could not bring himself to sentence people to death. He studied the writers of the Enlightenment, especially Rousseau. In 1789 he was elected for the Third Estate to the Estates General.

### The Jacobins

Robespierre quickly rose to prominence in the National Assembly. He was known as '**the incorruptible**' because he was considered completely honest and sincere. He was a strong supporter of all the revolution's radical changes. He argued for the revolution's ideals of liberty, equality and fraternity, voted in favour of executing the king and for the declaration of war on Austria. He was a leading member of the **Jacobins** (a radical political group) and very popular with the Paris sans-culottes. As the war worsened, he grew to believe that ruthless government and harsh punishments were necessary to protect the revolution.

### The Committee of Public Safety

After the rest of Europe declared war on France, the National Convention set up a **Committee of Public Safety** in April 1793. Its aim was to save the revolution and destroy its enemies. It had 12 members and **Robespierre** was its **president**. They faced several major problems:

- The upper classes continued to oppose the revolution
- Violent opposition to the revolution broke out in the **Vendée** region
- The war dragged on against many of Europe's strongest states
- Food prices continued to rise

In response, the Committee assumed absolute power and launched the **Reign of Terror**. Under Robespierre's direction:

1. The Committee passed the **Law of Suspects** to punish anybody even suspected of betraying the revolution. Tens of thousands were arrested, often with little evidence against them. Between June 1793 and July 1794, over 16,000 people were guillotined. Over 80% of these executions took place outside Paris.

2. The rebellion in the Vendée was put down with great savagery, killing nearly 250,000.

3. Another mass enlistment made the French army so massive (over 1 million men) that it outnumbered all their opponents put together and saved the revolution from external threats.

4. The **Law of Maximum** controlled rising prices for food and other goods. Harsh punishments (excluding execution) were used on those found to be overcharging citizens.

**DID YOU KNOW?**

Marie Tussaud was employed by the Committee of Public Safety to make wax copies of the heads of those executed during the Terror. After the Revolution, she opened a museum of waxworks in London: Madame Tussaud's.

◀ Victims of the Reign of Terror

## The fall of Robespierre

By June of 1794, the immediate danger to the revolution seemed to have passed and the military situation had improved considerably. People expected the Terror to come to an end – but instead Robespierre intensified it, targeting members of the National Convention. Many began to fear that Robespierre had too much power. The sans-culottes turned against him and he was attacked in speeches in the Convention. He was jeered with shouts of 'Down with the tyrant!' in the streets. His fellow Committee members feared they would be next – so they acted first. On 27 July

▲ Robespierre's arrest

1794, Robespierre was arrested (along with his supporters) and executed just a few hours later. The Convention elected a five-member **Directory** to run a more moderate government. This is considered to mark the end of the French Revolution.

## CHECKPOINT!

1. Why was Robespierre known as 'the incorruptible'? Based on his life, did he deserve this title?

2. Who were the Jacobins?

3. Why was the Committee of Public Safety formed?

4. Name two challenges the Committee faced and explain how it dealt with them.

5. What led to Robespierre's fall from power?

 I understand the role played by Maximilien Robespierre in French history.

 ⬅ TIME TO GO BACK ◆ I CAN MOVE FORWARD ➡

# 13.5: The Results of the French Revolution

**In this topic, you will learn about:**
➡ The impact of the French Revolution in France, Ireland and beyond

## The rise of Napoleon

The Directory was overthrown by **Napoleon Bonaparte** (1769–1821), who declared himself Emperor of France in 1804. He conquered most of Europe before he was defeated at the **Battle of Waterloo** in 1815.

## The spread of the revolution's ideals

The Revolution's slogan of 'Liberty, Equality, Fraternity' spread to other European countries and more people demanded freedom and equality. People called for more **democracy** ('rule by the people', or a say in how their countries were run) and the power of monarchs was reduced.

## The metric system

One innovation of the revolution that survived was the **metric system** of weights and measures. The metric system (and decimalisation, for currency) is based on multiples of ten; the older 'imperial system' made calculations far more complicated. However, the revolution's ten-day weeks and new calendar proved less popular.

## The rise of the middle class and armies

Across Europe the power of the nobility was reduced, as the middle classes gained more political power. This was helped by the fact that many European countries saw how successful the huge French revolutionary armies had been and copied them. As more people fought and gained military experience, they demanded more power in their countries.

▲ A revolutionary pocketwatch showing the ten days of the week

## The impact on Ireland

The ideals of the French Revolution inspired some Irishmen to fight for the liberty of Ireland and for equality between people of all religious faiths. One group, the **United Irishmen**, staged their own revolution in 1798. They received military aid from the French government. We will learn more about them in chapter 14.

### CHECKPOINT!

1. Explain the impact the French Revolution had on (a) France; (b) Europe; and (c) Ireland.

2. Which of the results of the French Revolution do you think is the most important? Explain your answer.

 I understand the results of the French Revolution.    ⬅ TIME TO GO BACK ❮ ❯ I CAN MOVE FORWARD ➡

**13 Revolutions Option Two: The French Revolution**

# SUMMARY

The causes of the French Revolution can be divided into long-term and short-term causes:

| Long-term causes | Short-term causes |
|---|---|
| France's absolute monarchy<br>The Enlightenment<br>Social divisions in France<br>The American Revolution | The calling of the Estates General<br>The Tennis Court Oath<br>The Storming of the Bastille |

- The revolution brought huge change to France: the end of the power of the nobility and the clergy; the declaration of the republic; the declaration of the rights of citizens; and a new flag.

- Other European states were alarmed by the revolution, leading to war with Austria. After the execution of Louis XVI, other European states joined the war against France.

- The war led to a crisis in France, which saw the creation of the **Committee of Public Safety** under **Maximilien Robespierre**, and **the Reign of Terror**, which saw thousands of people executed for opposing the revolution.

- The revolution had a profound effect on France and the rest of the world. It inspired others to fight for the ideals of 'Liberty, Equality and Fraternity' in their own countries.

## Reflecting on... the French Revolution

This turning point in European history ended the era of absolute monarchs and the 'divine right' of kings. It proved the power of ideas and showed that people were prepared to protest, campaign and fight for a freer and more equal world. It also had a dark side. The violence unleashed to bring down the *ancien régime* also led to the death of huge numbers of other people. These two aspects of political revolution – a passionate desire for a better world and an intense violence – would be a feature of nearly every large-scale revolution for the next two centuries.

 # Understanding History

1. Why was France's Third Estate unhappy in the 1780s?

2. Why was France in a financial crisis in the 1780s?

3. What problems occurred when Louis XVI called the Estates General in 1789?

4. What were the main reforms passed by the National Assembly?

5. Explain the significance of *The Declaration of the Rights of Man and of the Citizen*.

6. Why was Louis XVI executed?

7. What were the causes of the Reign of Terror?

8. What actions did the Committee for Public Safety take?

9. How did the Terror come to an end?

10. In your opinion, what was the most important result of the French Revolution? Explain your answer.

11. Copy out the table below, and then sort each event and topic into its correct column.

- The Storming of the Bastille
- The rise of Napoleon Bonaparte
- French aid to the Americans during their War of Independence
- The Terror
- The gabelle
- The trial of Louis XVI

- The decline in the power of kings
- The war with Austria
- The Estates General
- The Civil Constitution of the Clergy
- The 1798 Rebellion in Ireland
- The Flight to Varennes

| Causes of the Revolution | Course of the Revolution | Consequences of the Revolution |
|---|---|---|
|  |  |  |

 **Exploring History**

1. Write about the life of Maximilien Robespierre under the following headings:
   - Early life
   - The Committee of Public Safety
   - The Reign of Terror
   - His fall from power

2. Look again at the two pictures on page 180. What are the differences in the portrayal of the king between his official portrait and the cartoons in newspapers?

3. Outline the role played by the following throughout the French Revolution: (a) the sans-culottes; (b) other countries; (c) King Louis XVI.

4. Historical debate: 'The French Revolution betrayed its own ideals'. Write a speech for or against this motion. Make at least three arguments in your speech.

| **KEY TERMS** | | |
|---|---|---|
| **Revolution** | a rapid and significant change in society, politics, technology or the economy |
| **Absolute monarch** | a king who has total power over the country and claims a divine (God-given) right to rule |
| **Enlightenment** | a movement of eighteenth-century thinkers who valued reason and science above faith or authority as a basis for society |
| **The Estates General** | a kind of French parliament made up of three parts, each representing one of the three Estates |
| **Sans-culottes** | the mob of Paris, who pressured the National Assembly to take radical action during the Revolution |
| **Republic** | a type of government without a king, where the people are sovereign |
| **Democracy** | 'rule by the people'; a form of government where the people decide how the country is run and who will represent them |

 Go to page 77 of your *Sources and Skills Book* for more exercises.

 Go to page 33 of your *Research Portfolio* for a task based on this chapter.

**13 Revolutions Option Two: The French Revolution**

| The Plantations c. 1500–1700 | The Age of Revolution c. 1750–1850 | Ireland under the Union 1800–1920 |
| --- | --- | --- |

By the late 1790s, revolutions had taken place in America and France. These revolutions had been fought for freedom and equality and against the ideas that kings had the power to rule as they wished, or that people should have to live under unjust governments.

These concepts had a huge impact on Ireland. Inspired by these ideals, the **United Irishmen** emerged to challenge British rule in Ireland.

# WORKING WITH THE EVIDENCE!

## The 1798 Rebellion

| Type of source | Category | Example | |
| --- | --- | --- | --- |
| Primary | Written | Writings of the leaders of the rebellion: pamphlets, letters and diaries from people such as **Theobald Wolfe Tone** and **Lord Edward FitzGerald**<br>Newspapers from the time, such as the United Irishmen's **Northern Star**. | |
| Primary | Written | Official British government documents: (military reports, politicians' orders, debates in the parliaments in Dublin and London) and intelligence from the large **spy network** that operated amongst the rebels | |

▲ The *Northern Star* newspaper

> **Dublin Castle, 19th June, 1798.**
>
> ACCOUNTS were this day received from Brigadier-General *Barnett*, stating, that on the 17th instant a considerable Body of REBELS attacked *Kilbeggan*, but were repulsed by a Detachment of Fifty of the *Northumberland* Fencibles, under the Command of Captain *Thatcher*. One Hundred and Twenty of the REBELS were killed, and a great many wounded. The Detachment behaved with the greatest Gallantry.
>
> Brigadier General *Grose* reports from *Kilcock*, that Colonel *Irwine*, with a Detachment under his Command, had this Day engaged a Body of above 2000 REBELS, at *Ovidstown-Hill*, about one Mile from *Hortland*. The Loss of the REBELS was upwards of Two Hundred slain.
>
> The number of killed and wounded of his Majesty's Troops does not amount to more than Twenty-three.— Ensign *Inter*, of the Highlanders, was killed. Colonel *Irwine*, and Sir *Richard Steele*, were wounded; but it is hoped not dangerously. Colonel *Irwine* reports to General *Grose*, that he is highly indebted to all the Officers and Men who served under him, and that he was much benefited by the assistance he received from Colonel *Burrowes*, who volunteered on the occasion.
>
> Dublin: Printed by GEORGE GRIERSON, Printer to the King's Most Excellent Majesty;—AND CORK: REPRINTED BY A. EDWARDS.

▲ Classified document

◀ A military report made to Dublin Castle, 1798

Why are classified (secret) documents and spy reports important sources for historians?

# 14.1: The Causes of the 1798 Rebellion

In this topic, you will learn about:
> Religious divisions in late eighteenth-century Ireland
> The impact of the revolutions in America and France

◀ The Irish House of Commons in College Green, *c.*1790

## 1. The power of the Protestant Ascendancy

Since the **Plantations** of the sixteenth and seventeenth centuries and the victory of the Protestant **King William** over the Catholic **King James** at the **Battle of the Boyne** in 1690, Ireland had been under the rule of the British Crown. There was an Irish parliament in Dublin with limited powers over Irish affairs. This was controlled by the **Protestant Ascendancy** class – the wealthy land-owning minority – as only Church of Ireland members (Anglicans) could vote and become MPs (members of parliament). They owned 80% of the land but were only 15% of the population. Even though they controlled Ireland, some Anglicans resented the limited power they had in their own parliament and the unfair trading practices of the British government.

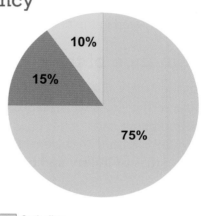

10%
15%
75%

☐ Catholics
☐ Anglicans (Church of Ireland Protestants)
☐ Presbyterians (Dissenters)

▲ Ireland's population by religion

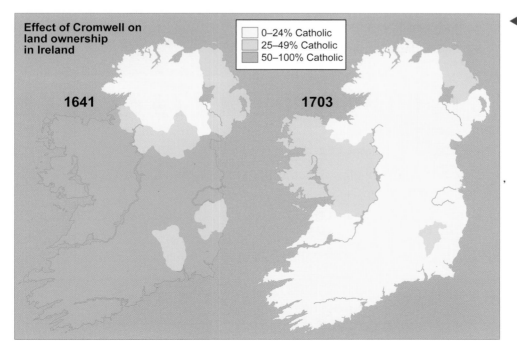

Effect of Cromwell on land ownership in Ireland

☐ 0–24% Catholic
☐ 25–49% Catholic
☐ 50–100% Catholic

1641          1703

◀ Land ownership by Catholics before and after the Cromwellian Plantations

## 2. The position of Catholics

Catholics made up 75% of the population of the island but only owned about 15% of the land. Catholics were discriminated against by the Penal Laws:

- They could not vote or sit in parliament.
- Catholic priests were banned.
- Catholics could not open or attend schools.
- Catholic-owned land had to be divided equally between all sons upon a father's death.
- They had to pay **tithes** to Church of Ireland clergy.

The laws were designed to keep them poor and powerless. While some of the worst laws were repealed in the 1770s, Catholics still had no say in how the country was run. By the 1790s, most Catholics were poor, under-educated tenant farmers who resented the high rents and tithes they had to pay. In rural areas, groups such as **the Whiteboys** attacked Protestant landlords.

## 3. The position of Presbyterians

Presbyterians (known as **dissenters** at the time, because they disagreed with the official Protestant Church of Ireland) were also not allowed to vote or sit in parliament, though they were not subjected to the harshest of the Penal Laws. They made up about 10% of the population, concentrated in the north-east of the island, around Belfast.

## 4. The influence of the American and French Revolutions

The events of the American and French Revolutions had a big impact on Ireland. They were widely reported in Irish newspapers and Irish troops brought back stories of what was happening abroad. Many Catholics and Presbyterians were excited by and attracted to the **ideas of liberty and equality** behind these revolutions.

How the British government dealt with Ireland was also affected by these revolutions. During the war in America, for fear that a similar revolt would break out in Ireland, the Irish parliament was given more power over its own affairs. During the French Revolution – especially after war was declared on France in 1793 – the British feared a rebellion in Ireland with French support, or even a French invasion to use Ireland as a base from which to attack Britain.

▶ A painting depicting drummers and a piper in the American War of Independence, entitled *The Spirit of '76*

## CHECKPOINT!

1. What was the Protestant Ascendancy?
2. What were the Penal Laws? Give two examples.
3. Why was each of the following groups unhappy about its position in Ireland by the 1790s: (a) Anglicans; (b) Catholics; (c) Presbyterians?
4. Why do you think the ideas of the American and French Revolutions appealed to many? Explain your answer.
5. Why was the British government worried about the influence of these revolutions on Ireland?

 I understand the causes of the 1798 Rebellion.

 ⟵ TIME TO GO BACK ◆ I CAN MOVE FORWARD ⟶

## 14.2: The United Irishmen

### A Life in Time: Theobald Wolfe Tone (1763–1798)

#### Early life

Theobald Wolfe Tone was born in Dublin in 1763 to a middle-class Anglican family. He studied law at Trinity College Dublin and became a barrister. At university he became interested in the writers of the **Enlightenment**, and visited Paris in 1789 to witness the events of the French Revolution at first hand. He came home inspired by his experiences and convinced that the ideas of '**liberty, equality, fraternity**' could be applied to Ireland.

▲ Theobald Wolfe Tone

◀ Tone with the United Irishmen

#### The foundation of the United Irishmen

In 1791, Tone wrote a pamphlet called ***An Argument on Behalf of the Catholics of Ireland***, which argued that Catholics should have the same rights as Protestants. He was invited to a meeting in Belfast that October by a group of Presbyterians who were also interested in the French Revolution.

This meeting founded the **Society of United Irishmen**. Along with Tone, the other founding members were **Samuel Neilson**, **Henry Joy McCracken**, **Thomas Russell** and **William Drennan**. Soon a Dublin branch was founded by Napper Tandy and other branches appeared around the country. In January 1792, they began publishing their own newspaper, ***The Northern Star***. Their original aim was peaceful reform, not violent revolution. They wanted:

- Religious equality
- Removal of British influence from Ireland (though not an independent republic)
- That all men should have the vote and the right to sit in parliament

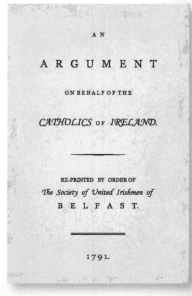

▲ *An Argument on Behalf of the Catholics of Ireland*

# WORKING WITH THE EVIDENCE!

## Extract from *An Argument on Behalf of the Catholics of Ireland*

If the odious distinction between Protestant, and Presbyterian, and Catholic were abolished, and the three great sects blended together, under the common and sacred title of Irishman, what interest could a Catholic member of Parliament have, distinct from his Protestant brother sitting on the same bench… In a word, the alternative is, on the one hand, Reform, and for the Catholics, justice and liberty; on the other, an unconditional submission to the present, and every future Administration […] while the people remain divided.

1. Use a dictionary or a thesaurus to find the meaning of (a) odious; (b) sects.
2. How did Tone want to unite Protestants, Presbyterians and Catholics?
3. What needed to happen for Catholics under reform?
4. What was the alternative to these reforms?
5. Is Tone urging a revolution in this extract? Explain your answer.

### The impact of the war with France

Tone was also the secretary of the **Catholic Committee**, a group formed by wealthy Catholics to push for reforms. Britain declared war on France in early 1793. Fearing that Catholic resentment in Ireland would lead to a revolution there, the British government decided to make concessions. They abolished most of the remaining Penal Laws and granted Catholics the right to vote – but not the right to sit in parliament.

The British government in Dublin stepped up their surveillance of groups that they considered a threat, like the United Irishmen. In 1795, a French spy named **William Jackson** was arrested and he was found to have met with Tone, who fled to the US. The government banned the United Irishmen. It became a **secret society** that was now committed to a **revolution against British rule**.

### Tone in France and Bantry Bay

Tone travelled to France in 1796 to seek military support for an Irish rebellion. In December, a French fleet of 43 ships and 15,000 men under **General Hoche** sailed to Ireland. **Storms** ensured that only 14 ships reached the landing point of Bantry Bay in Cork. After several days trying to land in the **terrible weather**, the ships turned back. Tone, bitterly disappointed, wrote in his diary: 'England has not had such an escape since the Spanish Armada'.

> **DID YOU KNOW?**
> The British government built Martello Towers along the coast to guard against a possible French invasion. Is there one near where you live?

## The governments' response

The near miss of the French invasion horrified the governments in Dublin and London. They quickly took steps to destroy the United Irishmen and their network.

- In late 1796, **General Lake** landed in Ulster, where his soldiers went from town to town demanding any weapons or information that people had. They burned houses and flogged, beat and tortured suspects. Some were given **half-hangings** (where they were hanged until they were nearly dead). Others had **pitch-cappings**: the soldiers poured tar on a person's head and set it on fire. When the tar cooled they ripped it (and the top of the scalp) off. These horrific measures were designed to terrify people and reduce support for a rebellion. They were repeated throughout Leinster.

- Part-time armies were set up: the **militia** for loyal Catholics and the **yeomanry** for loyal Protestants.

- The **Orange Order** was created to encourage unity between Anglicans and Presbyterians in opposition to Catholics.

▲ Captain Swayne pitch-capping the people of Prosperous, Co. Kildare

- Spies inside the United Irishmen passed on information that led to the arrests of most of the leaders around the country. Most significantly, the main planner of the Dublin rebellion, **Lord Edward FitzGerald**, was captured in May 1798. The remaining leadership decided to go ahead with a rebellion a week later, on 23 May 1798.

▲ The Orange Order in modern times

▲ The arrest of Edward FitzGerald

## CHECKPOINT!

1. How was Tone influenced by the French Revolution?

2. What pamphlet did he write and what did he argue in it?

3. What were the original aims of the United Irishmen?

4. How did the governments respond to concerns over (a) Catholics' loyalty and (b) plotting between France and the United Irishmen?

5. What help did Tone get from France?

6. How did the British government respond to the failed invasion at Bantry Bay? Give two examples.

 I understand the founding of the United Irishmen and the events leading up to the 1798 Rebellion.

TIME TO GO BACK ◆ I CAN MOVE FORWARD →

**14 Physical Force: The 1798 Rebellion**

# 14.3: The 1798 Rebellion

In this topic, you will learn about:

The 1798 Rebellion in:
- Dublin and surrounding counties
- Wexford
- Ulster
- Connacht

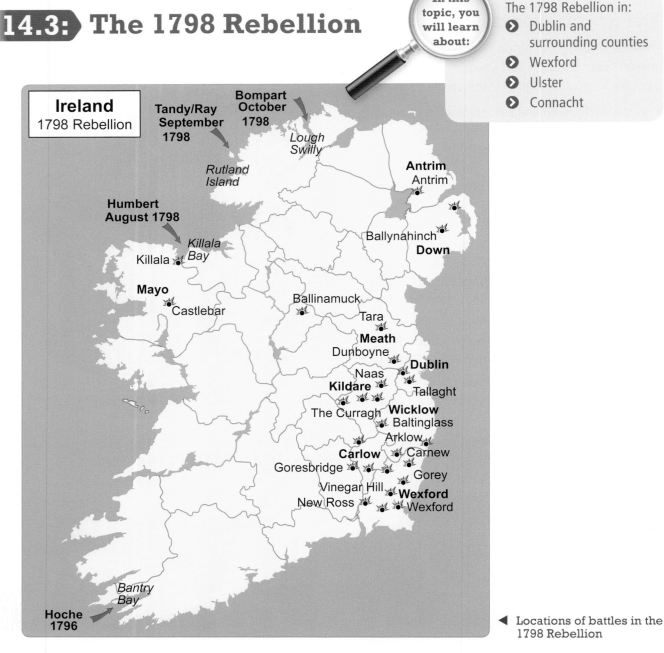

◀ Locations of battles in the 1798 Rebellion

The year 1798 marked a significant turning point in Irish history. It was the first time that **physical force nationalism** emerged on the island. This means that <u>nationalists were prepared to use violence to fight for Irish independence from Britain</u>.

## 1. Leinster: Dublin and surrounding counties

The rebels had planned that the rebellion would be signalled by the disruption of the mail coaches from Dublin. However, most of the rebels in the capital were arrested when they arrived at their assembly points, thanks to **information supplied by spies**. There were rebel attacks in Kildare, Meath, Carlow and Wicklow, but they were largely uncoordinated. They were easily defeated by the British in battles at **Carlow town** and the **Hill of Tara**.

## 2. Ulster

In Antrim, **Henry Joy McCracken** led 4,000 mostly Presbyterian rebels into battle on 6 June. The rebellion there collapsed following their defeat at Antrim town. In Co. Down, Henry Munro led 7,000 rebels to initial success at **Saintfield**, but they too were defeated over two days' fighting – the longest battle of the whole rebellion – at **Ballynahinch**.

## 3. Wexford

Wexford saw the most intensive action of the rebellion. Wexford had a more mixed population than most areas, with large numbers of Anglicans. The rebels were led by a Catholic priest, **Fr John Murphy** of **Boolavogue**, and the rebellion quickly spread throughout the county. Government troops were defeated at **Oulart Hill** and the rebels then marched on and captured **Enniscorthy** and **Wexford town**. Rebel attempts to break out of Wexford were defeated at New Ross and Arklow. The main force of the rebels, including their leaders, was surrounded and defeated at **Vinegar Hill** by General Lake on 21 June. The

▲ The massacre at Scullabogue, Co. Wexford

leaders were hanged and harsh reprisals carried out against areas that had supported the rebels.

Wexford saw the only **atrocities** committed by the rebels during the 1798 Rebellion. Some **200 Protestants** were burned alive in a barn at **Scullabogue** and another **100 were massacred in Wexford town**. In Wexford, there was deep bitterness at the Penal Laws. The harsh repression by the yeomanry provoked retaliations by the rebels against the local Protestant population. This violence was in direct contradiction of Tone's hopes of uniting 'Catholic, Protestant and dissenter' and would taint the rebellion for Ireland's Protestants.

http://1798centre.ie/

## 4. Connacht: French help arrives

Tone had been in France since the failed Bantry Bay landing of 1796. When he heard about the rebellion, he asked the French to send help. On 22 August (nearly two months after the crushing of the rebellion), 1,000 French soldiers landed at **Killala**, Co. Mayo under **General Humbert**. They overpowered a small British force at **Castlebar** but were defeated at **Ballinamuck**, Co. Longford on 8 September.

Go to pages 86–89 of your *Sources and Skills Book* for evidence tasks on the rebellion in Wexford.

◀ Battle of Vinegar Hill, Co. Wexford

**14**

**Physical Force: The 1798 Rebellion**

## The death of Tone

A final attempt was made to land more French troops in Ireland in October. Some 3,000 soldiers sailed for Donegal, led by Admiral Bompart, but they were captured by the British navy at **Lough Swilly**. Tone was on board one of the ships and was sent to Dublin for trial. After he was found guilty of treason, he asked for 'a soldier's death' (by firing squad). This was refused – but before he could be hanged, Tone tried to commit suicide by cutting his own throat. However, he was unsuccessful and five days passed before he died of these wounds.

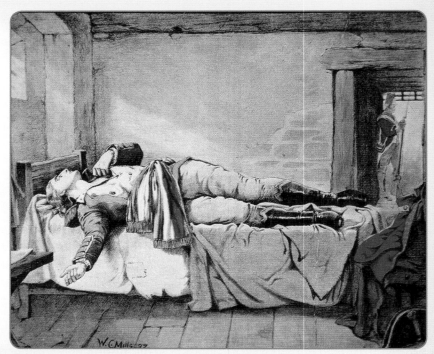

▲ The death of Tone

 COLLABORATE: Many songs were written about the events of the 1798 Rebellion. Research one: find the lyrics (and a recording if you can!) and find out about the truth behind the events described in the song. Report on your findings to the rest of your class.

| Why did the United Irishmen's rebellion fail? | |
|---|---|
| The rebels were badly organised and trained | |
| They had few decent weapons, mainly using long pikes against British rifles | |
| They received no useful French help | |
| They were infiltrated by British spies | |
| They faced much stronger government forces | |

## CHECKPOINT!

1. What was the signal for the start of the rebellion?
2. Why did the Dublin rebels fail so quickly?
3. What happened to the rebellion in Ulster?
4. How was the rebellion in Wexford different from those in other areas? Give two reasons.
5. Is it correct to describe the French help as 'too little, too late'? Explain your answer.
6. Which reason for the rebellion's failure do you think is the most important? Explain your answer.
7. What role did Tone play in: (a) the foundation of the United Irishmen; (b) getting support for the United Irishmen from abroad; (c) the events of 1798?

 I understand the main events of the 1798 Rebellion.

 TIME TO GO BACK ◀ ▶ I CAN MOVE FORWARD

# 14.4: The Consequences of the Rebellion

In this topic, you will learn about:
- Religious tensions in Ireland after 1798
- The Act of Union 1800
- The growth of Irish Republicanism

Ireland was profoundly affected by the events of the summer of 1798.

## 1. Growth of sectarianism

**Sectarianism** is <u>conflict and hatred based on a religious divide</u>. The events of 1798 intensified sectarian divisions in Ireland between Catholics and Protestants (both Anglicans and Presbyterians). News of the atrocities against Protestants in Wexford spread. The **Orange Order** claimed that the rebellion was a Catholic plot to take over the country and oppress all Protestants. Irish politics became increasingly divided on the basis of religion.

## 2. The Act of Union

After two attempted French invasions and a failed rebellion, the government in London decided to bring Ireland back under its direct control. It used a mixture of bribery and threats to get the Dublin parliament to pass the **Act of Union 1800**, which abolished the parliament in Dublin. Irish MPs went to Westminster and Ireland was run from there for the next 120 years.

Before the Union, Dublin had been a prosperous city of great importance in the British Empire. Afterwards, as the political classes moved to London and a lot of trade shifted to Belfast, Dublin became a poor, unglamorous backwater.

## 3. Irish Republicanism

Despite his failed rebellion, Tone's dream of an **independent Irish republic** based on equality between Catholics and Protestants inspired many who came after him. He became known as the 'Father of Irish Republicanism' and his ideas inspired **Robert Emmet (1803)**, the **Young Irelanders (1848)** and the **Fenians (1867)**, as well as the leaders of the **1916 Easter Rising**.

**DID YOU KNOW?**

One February morning in 1971, the Ulster Defence Association blew up the statue of Tone at the corner of St Stephen's Green in Dublin, thereby showing the considerable symbolic value he still held over 170 years later.

**14**

**Physical Force: The 1798 Rebellion**

## CHECKPOINT!

1. What is sectarianism?
2. How did the 1798 Rebellion lead to sectarian divisions in Ireland?
3. What was the Act of Union and why did the British government want it?
4. How did the Act of Union affect Dublin?
5. What impact did Tone have on Irish history?

✓ I understand the consequences of the 1798 Rebellion.

◄ TIME TO GO BACK ❯ I CAN MOVE FORWARD ➤

 **SUMMARY**

The causes of the 1798 Rebellion can be divided into long-term and short-term causes.

| Long-term causes | Short-term causes |
|---|---|
| The Protestant (Anglican) Ascendancy | The United Irishmen |
| Discrimination against Catholics and Presbyterians | War between Britain and revolutionary France |
| The influence of the American and French Revolutions | Failed invasion at Bantry Bay |
| | The repression after Bantry Bay |

- The rebellion was a military disaster. The rebels failed to take Dublin or even stop the mail coaches. The government quickly crushed the rebels in battles in Meath, Carlow, Antrim and Down.

- The rebels in Wexford had more success initially, when they seized Enniscorthy and Wexford town. They were defeated at Vinegar Hill – but not before they had slaughtered hundreds of Protestants. French help arrived after the Rebellion was already over.

- The United Irishmen had fought for an independent Irish republic which would unite Catholics and Protestants. Their defeat actually saw the end of the Irish parliament and worsened religious divisions on the island.

- The ideas of Tone inspired later generations to fight for the same cause until Irish independence was finally achieved in 1921.

### Reflecting on... the 1798 Rebellion

The 1798 Rebellion had profound consequences for Ireland. It opened the door to the use of violence to achieve political ends and forged a link between the cause of Irish freedom and violent revolution. It is a bitter irony that the sectarianism that has plagued the island for over 200 years found much of its origins in a rebellion by a group created to overcome those very differences.

 **Understanding History**

1. What were the religious divisions in eighteenth-century Ireland?
2. How did the American and French Revolutions influence Ireland?
3. Why were the United Irishmen founded?
4. What were the positive and negative effects on Ireland of the war between Britain and France?
5. What evidence is there of the effectiveness of the British spy network in Ireland?
6. Describe the events of the Rebellion (a) around Dublin and (b) in Ulster.
7. Can the events in Wexford be described as both the best and worst of the United Irishmen? Explain.
8. Give an example of sectarianism (a) during and (b) after the 1798 Rebellion.

9. Find out when the following events took place and put them in chronological order on a timeline in your copy, starting with the earliest.

- French fleet in Bantry Bay
- The founding of the United Irishmen
- Battle of Vinegar Hill
- Arrest of Lord Edward FitzGerald
- Arrest of William Jackson
- The Act of Union
- General Lake in Ulster
- Capture of Enniscorthy
- French troops land in Mayo
- Catholics get the vote
- Publication of Tone's pamphlet

10. Copy out the table below, and then sort each event and topic into its correct column.

- The French Revolution
- Battle of Vinegar Hill
- Founding of the United Irishmen
- Growth of sectarianism
- The Penal Laws
- Irish Republican rebellions in 1803 and 1848
- Atrocities in Wexford
- French navy in Lough Swilly
- General Lake's campaign of terror
- Battle of Ballynahinch
- Act of Union
- Decline of Dublin

| Causes of the Rebellion | Course of the Rebellion | Consequences of the Rebellion |
|---|---|---|
| | | |

## Exploring History

1. Write an account of the life of Theobald Wolfe Tone under the following headings:

- Early life
- Founding the United Irishmen
- Time in France
- 1798 Rebellion and death
- Legacy

2. Look at the list of reasons for the failure of the 1798 Rebellion on page 202. Write an account of the failure, backing up each reason with an example.

| KEY TERMS | | |
|---|---|---|
| | Protestant Ascendancy | the wealthy land-owning Church of Ireland minority |
| | Penal Laws | laws that discriminated against Catholics and were designed to keep them poor and powerless |
| | Dissenters | Irish Presbyterians, who 'dissented' from the official Protestant Church of Ireland |
| | Physical force nationalism | the willingness of nationalists to use violence to fight for Irish independence from Britain |
| | Sectarianism | conflict and hatred based on a religious divide |

Go to page 84 of your *Sources and Skills Book* for more exercises.

Go to page 37 of your *Research Portfolio* for a task based on this chapter.

14 Physical Force: The 1798 Rebellion

| The Age of Revolution c. 1750–1850 | Ireland under the Union 1800–1920 | Independent Ireland 1921– present day |
|---|---|---|

After the 1800 Act of Union, Britain and Ireland were united under one government in Westminster for the first time. The two islands were very different, however. Ireland was primarily an agricultural economy with many small farmers, most of whom were tenants of landlords. Revolutions in agriculture and industry during the eighteenth and nineteenth centuries had transformed Britain and it had become heavily industrialised and urbanised.

In response to the Act of Union, Irish nationalists fought campaigns seeking full equality for Catholics and the restoration of an Irish parliament.

# WORKING WITH THE EVIDENCE!

## The early nineteenth century in Ireland

| Type of source | Category | Example |
|---|---|---|
| Primary | Visual | The nineteenth century saw the invention of the first photographs and the first use of drawn illustrations in newspapers. These are very important sources. |
| Primary | Written | Official documents from the British government; speeches by political leaders; debates in the parliament in London. Newspapers became cheaper and more widely read. Letters, diaries and books written by people of the time |

◀ Leaflet scolding Dubliners for not voting

▶ Inexpensive newspapers helped to spread the news of events

What do we rely on to give us a visual image of times before photography? Why are photographs a better source?

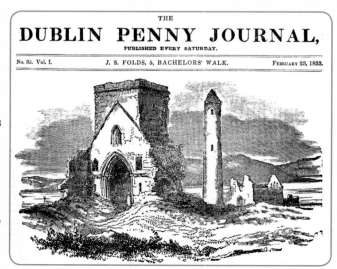

# 15.1: Ireland after the Union: Economy and Society

By 1841, the population of the island of Ireland had reached **8.2 million, up from 5.5 million in 1801**. However, the agricultural and industrial revolutions did not affect Ireland to the same extent as they did Britain.

In this topic, you will learn about:
- Industry in Ireland
- Life in Irish cities
- Agriculture in Ireland

## Industry in Ireland

Some parts of Ireland were industrialised like Britain, particularly around **Belfast** and **Dublin.**

Apart from the north-east and a handful of cities, Ireland had few factories or large industries. This was because Ireland did not have coal (to power factories) or iron resources and did not use steam engines to the extent that Britain did. Nonetheless, Ireland did have railways and canals for the transportation of people and goods.

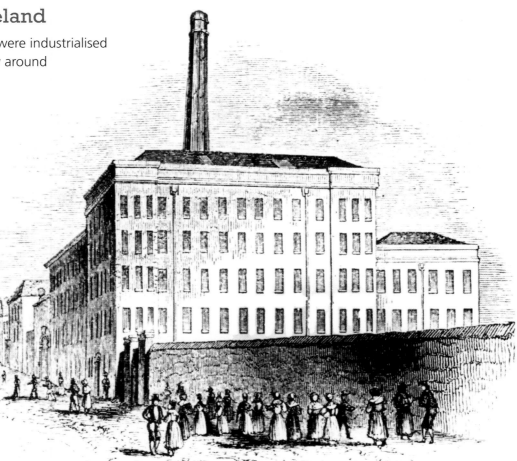

▲ A linen mill in Belfast, c.1840

### Belfast

Ulster had a thriving **textiles industry**, particularly **linen**. Irish lace and linen were considered the best in the world and were exported in large quantities through the port at Belfast. **Shipbuilding** began in the 1790s and soon flourished. These major industries allowed the city to grow rich and become the largest on the island by the middle of the century. The fact that the population around Belfast was largely Protestant meant that existing divisions in the region were further deepened by economic differences.

### Dublin

Dublin's industries included **wool** and **Guinness's brewery**. Most of rural Ireland's exports to Britain went through Dublin port. As we saw in chapter 14, Dublin went into decline after the Union, as many of its political and wealthy leaders moved to London. Many other Irish aristocrats sold their large houses in the city centre and these were turned into tenement housing, which was **massively overcrowded** and **unsanitary**. A **tenement** was a <u>building housing a large number of families in separate rooms</u>.

# Life in Belfast and Dublin

Regardless of the religious differences between the two cities, the poorest people in Dublin and Belfast (and other Irish cities) faced the same daily problems:

- Due to the rapid growth in towns and cities, **overcrowding** became a serious problem, leading to one, and sometimes two, families living in just one room.

- The water and sewerage systems could not deal with the increase, leading to **sewerage** overflows directly into the rivers where people got their water.

- Diseases such as **typhoid**, **cholera**, **smallpox**, **scarlet fever** and **tuberculosis** were common in cities and towns. Death rates amongst infants were particularly high.

- Adults and children both worked in **factories** and on **the docks** to make enough money to support their families. It was common to work from 5.30 am until 8 pm, six days a week, with only Sundays off.

- Employment was often **casual**, meaning that nobody knew if they had work from day to day, especially on the docks.

- People were prepared to work for **low wages** as there was great competition for jobs.

- Fighting and drinking became popular pastimes to help people cope with, and forget, the harshness of their lives. This led to a **high crime** rate in urban areas.

▼ A tenement in Chancery Lane, Dublin

# Ireland in the 1800s: Agriculture

In 1841, over 70% of Ireland's population was still living in the countryside, whereas the majority of Britain's population lived in towns and cities. Ireland's population had grown dramatically for a number of reasons. There had been **improvements in farming methods**, as in Britain, and food was more plentiful. Also, the Irish tended to marry young and have **large families**.

Ireland exported livestock, such as cattle, and grain to Britain. There was no real effort to develop the kind of widespread industry taking place in Britain. It was claimed that everything would work better if Ireland produced the food to feed people on both islands and Britain did the same with industrial goods. You will learn more about life in rural Ireland in the next chapter.

▲ A rural labourer's family outside their home

## CHECKPOINT!

1. By how much did Ireland's population grow between 1801 and 1841?
2. How were Belfast and Dublin different from the rest of the island?
3. Name two examples of industries that were strong in Ireland in the 1800s.
4. Why were cities so overcrowded?
5. How did this overcrowding affect people's lives? What problems did they face?
6. Why did Ireland not industrialise like Britain had?

✔ I can explain what life in Ireland was like in the 1800s.

15 Parliamentary Tradition: Daniel O'Connell

# 15.2: Ireland in the 1800s: Politics

In this topic, you will learn about:

❯ How Ireland was governed under the Union
❯ The campaigns for Catholic emancipation and repeal of the Act of Union
❯ The life of Daniel O'Connell

## The government of Ireland

When the **Act of Union** came into force in 1801, the Irish parliament ceased to exist. Ireland now sent 100 MPs to the **House of Commons in Westminster** and was represented by 32 peers in the **House of Lords**. Laws passed in London applied to Ireland.

The government of Ireland was based in Dublin Castle. The head of the government of Ireland was the **Chief Secretary**, a British politician who spent most of his time in London. The British king was represented in Ireland by the **Lord Lieutenant**.

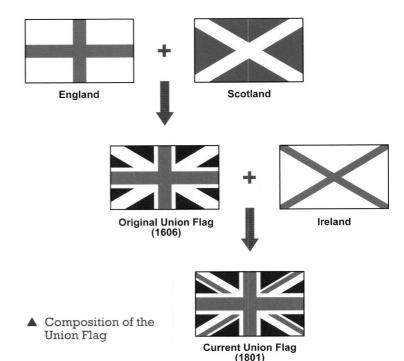

England + Scotland

Original Union Flag (1606) + Ireland

Current Union Flag (1801)

▲ Composition of the Union Flag

## 'The Catholic Question'

The biggest political issue in Ireland at this time was '**the Catholic Question**'. Many Catholics had supported the Act of Union in 1800. The British government had promised that the last of the Penal Laws would be abolished and full Catholic emancipation would be granted. **Catholic emancipation** was the goal for Catholics: that they be allowed to sit in parliament. However, all MPs had to swear an oath recognising the King of England as head of the Church. As no Catholic could swear this oath (to them, the Pope was head of the Church), they could not become MPs even if elected.

The promise to introduce emancipation after the Union had been broken. Catholics also resented paying **tithes** to the Church of Ireland. At the same time, a Catholic middle class of larger farmers, professionals and merchants was emerging who were educated and wealthy enough to campaign for change. They found their champion in a Catholic lawyer named **Daniel O'Connell**.

## CHECKPOINT!

1. How many Irish MPs represented Ireland in Westminster?
2. Who were the Chief Secretary and the Lord Lieutenant?
3. What was Catholic emancipation?
4. Why were Catholics unhappy in Ireland after the Act of Union?

 I know the main political issues that faced Ireland in the early 1800s.

 ⬅ TIME TO GO BACK ◆ I CAN MOVE FORWARD ➡

# A Life in Time: Daniel O'Connell (1775-1847) – 'The Liberator'

## Early life

**Daniel O'Connell** was born in 1775 in Cahirciveen, Co. Kerry. He was born into a wealthy Catholic middle-class family. He grew up amongst the tenant farmers of his uncle's lands and learned both Irish and English. Like most sons of well-off Catholic families, he was sent to **France** to get a university education (Catholics were not permitted to go to Trinity College Dublin). His time in Paris overlapped with the very violent phase of the French Revolution known as 'the Terror', when thousands of people were executed for supposedly being enemies of the revolution. O'Connell returned home in 1793 with **a lifelong hatred of political violence**. He supported the aims of the United Irishmen in the 1798 Rebellion, but rejected their use of violence.

## Catholic emancipation

O'Connell became a barrister. In 1811, he founded the **Catholic Board** to campaign for Catholic emancipation. This had a limited impact until he founded the **Catholic Association** in 1823 to campaign not just for emancipation, but also for the end of tithe payments and for the rights of tenant farmers. It was a mass membership organisation. The membership fee of **one penny a month** – low enough to be affordable to all but the poorest – was collected at church gates and became known as the '**Catholic Rent**'. This money funded the campaign, supported pro-emancipation MPs, paid the legal costs of those arrested for campaigning and paid for publicity material.

**DID YOU KNOW?**

Daniel O'Connell killed a man named John D'Esterre in a pistol duel in 1815!

In 1828, O'Connell stood in Clare for election to Westminster. He won the seat easily but refused to take the parliamentary oath and so was unable to take his seat. The British Prime Minister, the **Duke of Wellington** (the only British Prime Minister to have been born in Ireland), feared another rebellion in Ireland if emancipation was not granted. Westminster passed the **Emancipation Act in 1829** and O'Connell took his seat. It was O'Connell's greatest achievement and led to him being known as '**the Liberator**'. **King George IV** referred to him as '**the King of Ireland**', such was O'Connell's popularity and power after emancipation.

**15 Parliamentary Tradition: Daniel O'Connell**

### The fight for repeal

In the 1830s, O'Connell campaigned inside and outside Westminster for the **abolition of tithe payments**. In 1838 he managed to have the cost lowered and to have the tithes paid to landlords instead of to the Church of Ireland. He was elected the **first Catholic Lord Mayor of Dublin** in 1841.

▲ Daniel O'Connell speaking at a monster meeting in Co. Clare in 1828

In 1830, O'Connell set up **the Repeal Association** to campaign for the repeal (abolition) of the Act of Union. He wanted the Irish parliament restored, with the British monarch remaining as king or queen of Ireland. He used his previous tactics: people paid a **Repeal Rent** to support the campaign. There was little support for repeal in Britain and at the end of the 1830s, O'Connell started organising '**monster meetings**' around Ireland. These were huge rallies, attended by over 100,000 people. The British government grew concerned that these meetings would lead to rebellion and banned one, at **Clontarf** in 1843. Many of O'Connell's supporters wanted to defy the ban and go ahead with the meeting. Unwilling to run the risk of violence, O'Connell called off the meeting. This led to a split in the movement, with younger members setting up the **Young Irelanders**.

### Death and legacy

Just as the **Great Famine** began in 1845, O'Connell's health started to fail him. His last speech in the House of Commons in February 1847 was an impassioned plea for help for the Irish people dying of starvation. He was on a pilgrimage to Rome when he died in May 1847.

Go to pages 92–93 of your *Sources and Skills Book* for evidence tasks on Daniel O'Connell.

O'Connell's legacy has lived on after him. His approach to political action – rejecting the use of force and concentrating on the mass organisation of people – influenced people like **Mahatma Gandhi** and **Martin Luther King** in the twentieth century. In Ireland, the rejection of violence to achieve change was represented in politics by people like **Charles Stewart Parnell**, **John Redmond** and **John Hume**. **William Gladstone**, British Prime Minister in the 1870s and 1880s, described O'Connell as 'the greatest popular leader the world has ever seen'.

**DID YOU KNOW?**

Daniel O'Connell appeared on the last £20 note before the introduction of the euro in 2002.

▲ Mahatma Gandhi

▲ Martin Luther King Jr

COLLABORATE: In your group, find out about the campaign of the one of the people mentioned above and explain how their tactics were similar to O'Connell's. Report your findings back to your class.

## CHECKPOINT!

1. How did the French Revolution influence O'Connell?
2. How did the Catholic Association campaign for emancipation?
3. What happened in 1828?
4. How did the British government respond to O'Connell's election? Why did they do this?
5. What were 'monster meetings'? Why was the British government afraid of them?
6. How did O'Connell respond to the banning of the Clontarf meeting? What impact did this decision have on the Repeal movement?
7. What was O'Connell's legacy and impact on (a) Ireland and (b) the rest of the world?

I know about Daniel O'Connell's life and legacy.

◀ TIME TO GO BACK ▶ ▶ I CAN MOVE FORWARD ▶

**15 Parliamentary Tradition: Daniel O'Connell**

 **SUMMARY**

In this chapter, we have learned about conditions in Ireland in the early nineteenth century and the context in which O'Connell campaigned:

- Limited industrialisation took place around Dublin and Belfast. Most of the country remained rural and most farmers were small landholders who rented from landlords.
- Factories brought thousands of people to work in the cities, where they lived in cramped and dirty conditions. They worked long hours for low pay and were susceptible to many diseases because of poor sanitation and diet.
- Catholics were excluded from sitting in parliament. Daniel O'Connell campaigned for Catholic emancipation in the 1820s. He was successful through the use of mass protests and peaceful campaigning.
- However, he failed to achieve the repeal of the Union in the 1840s.

### Reflecting on... Daniel O'Connell

It is difficult not to see O'Connell's failure to achieve repeal of the Union as a great missed opportunity of Irish history. His commitment to peaceful means was in stark contrast to those who went before him in the United Irishmen and those who came after him in the various Irish Republican movements. The failure of non-violent mass protest convinced many of the next generation that the only solution to Ireland's problems lay in the gun.

 **Understanding History**

1. What were the differences between Dublin and Belfast in the early nineteenth century?
2. Describe life in Ireland's industrial cities.
3. Why did Ireland not have an industrial revolution?
4. Give three reasons why Irish Catholics were discontent under the Union.
5. Why do you think that King George IV called O'Connell 'the king of Ireland'?

 **Exploring History**

1. Write about the life of Daniel O'Connell under the following headings:
   - Early life
   - Repeal of the Union
   - Catholic emancipation
   - Death and legacy

2. Compare Theobald Wolfe Tone and Daniel O'Connell under the following headings:
   - Beliefs
   - Methods
   - Legacy

   Which of them do you think is the more important figure in Irish history? Give reasons for your answer.

 **KEY TERMS**

| | |
|---|---|
| Tenement | a building housing a large number of families in separate rooms |
| Chief Secretary | head of the government of Ireland, based in Dublin Castle |
| Lord Lieutenant | the British king's representative in Ireland |
| Catholic emancipation | the goal for Catholics: that they be allowed to sit in parliament |

Go to page 90 of your *Sources and Skills Book* for more exercises.

Go to page 41 of your *Research Portfolio* for a task based on this chapter.

# The Great Famine and the Irish Diaspora

**LO: 2.7**

| The Plantations in Ireland c. 1500–1700 | The Great Famine 1845–1850 | Home Rule and Cultural Nationalism 1884–1914 |

The Great Famine of 1845-1850, also known as the Great Hunger, is one of the most important events of Irish history.

Over these few years, the repeated failure of the potato crop in Ireland led to the deaths of between one and one and a half million people, while millions more emigrated to countries such as Britain, Canada, Australia and the US. This catastrophe had many far-reaching consequences and changed the course of Irish history.

## WORKING WITH THE EVIDENCE!

### The Great Famine

| Type of source | Category | Example |
| --- | --- | --- |
| Primary | Visual | Sketch of a starving boy and girl looking for potatoes |
| Primary | Visual | Illustration of the eviction of a family during the Famine |

▲ A starving boy and girl

▲ The eviction of a family during the Great Famine

What do these illustrations from newspapers of the time tell us about what life was like for people during the Great Famine?

# 16.1: Technological Change: The 1840s in Britain and Ireland

In this topic, you will learn about:
- Britain's Agricultural Revolution
- Life in 1840s Ireland

## The Agricultural Revolution in Britain

Britain's population grew quickly in the eighteenth and nineteenth centuries: **between 1801** and **1851**, the population increased from **9 million** to **22 million**. Several advances in agriculture had made more food available, which increased life expectancy. This period of change is known as the **Agricultural Revolution**.

### Advances in agriculture

**Charles Townshend**'s Norfolk system involved **a four-crop rotation cycle of wheat, turnips, oats/barley and clover/grass over four years**. Instead of leaving a field fallow every year, the important nutrients could be returned to the soil by growing turnips, clover or grass. Each crop could feed humans, animals or both.

Landlords began to insist that their tenants practise an older method called enclosure: **each tenant farmer's fields were grouped together in one small farm, fenced off, instead of in strips all across the landlord's land**.

**Robert Bakewell** developed a method known as selective breeding. **Selective breeding** is **reserving the largest or most suitable animals for breeding rather than for meat**. Larger and healthier animals were bred and meat became more widely available.

**Jethro Tull** invented the seed drill, **a machine, pulled by a horse or an ox, that sowed seeds at the right depth and in straight rows**. Before this, seeds were scattered by hand and many were wasted. This new method made sowing more efficient.

**Cyrus McCormick** invented a mechanical reaper. This was **a horse-drawn cart with a cutting blade that cut crops neatly in straight rows**. Crop harvesting became faster and cheaper.

As a result of these advances, fewer labourers were needed on farms. Thousands of people moved to cities and towns to look for work, stimulating the **Industrial Revolution. By 1850 over half of Britain's population was urban.** Conditions were not particularly good for ordinary workers.

Go to page 97 of your *Sources and Skills Book* for an evidence task on working conditions.

## Life in 1840s Ireland

In 1841, **over 70% of Irish people still lived in the countryside**, and Ireland's population had doubled in under a century to **over 8.2 million.** Reasons for this increase included:

- The Irish tended to marry young and have **large families**.

- **Enclosure** and other **improvements to farming** methods arrived in Ireland, as in Britain, and the **new machinery** produced more food than before.

Most Irish land was owned by landlords who were descendants of the planters. Irish people rented and farmed this land, growing crops to feed their families and pay their rent.

Most farmers in Ireland were **tenant farmers**. There were two types:

- **Large farmers** were farmers who rented more than 30 acres. They hired labourers to help them on the farm and grew wheat and barley to pay their rent. They also kept some cattle and sheep. Their diet consisted of meat, milk, potatoes and other vegetables.

- **Small farmers** were farmers who rented between five and 30 acres. They divided land amongst their sons. They grew wheat and barley to pay their rent. Their own diet consisted of potatoes and milk.

Poorer people worked as labourers. **Cottiers** were labourers who rented one acre from a farmer. They usually paid their rent by working for the farmer. They had a one-room thatched cottage and grew potatoes. In 1845, there were **one million Irish cottiers**. Counting their families, this made **over 4 million people** – half the population!

▼ A cottier's cottage and family

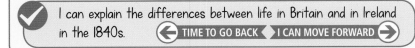

## CHECKPOINT!

1. What was the Agricultural Revolution?
2. Explain the following terms: Norfolk system; enclosure; selective breeding. 📖
3. How did technology change agriculture at this time?
4. What was a cottier?

✔ I can explain the differences between life in Britain and in Ireland in the 1840s. ← TIME TO GO BACK ◇ I CAN MOVE FORWARD →

**DID YOU KNOW?**

The potato is not native to Ireland. Sir Walter Raleigh is thought to have brought the potato to the island from the New World around 1570.

**16 The Great Famine and the Irish Diaspora**

# 16.2: The Causes of the Great Famine

In this topic, you will learn about:
- The causes of the Great Famine

The Great Famine happened across Ireland **between 1845** and **1850**. The **potato crop** failed and without other crops to feed themselves, people died of **starvation and disease** or were forced to **emigrate** (move to other countries). Several factors led to this catastrophe:

- Most Irish people were **dependent on farming**.

- With the steep **rise in population**, people had to survive on smaller plots of land.

- Tenant farmers and cottiers were very **reliant on the potato** as a source of food. Just one acre of land could grow enough potatoes to feed a family for six months. The potato was suited to Ireland's damp climate, it was easy to grow and harvest, and it stored well, unlike grain.

- Most **cottiers** worked in exchange for their rent and didn't receive money payments, so they had **no cash** to buy any other food if their potato crop failed.

- This dependence on farming and the potato made the poor vulnerable, so when **potato blight** struck, they were immediately out of options. **Potato blight** is a <u>fungus that spreads in damp and humid weather and destroys potato crops</u>.

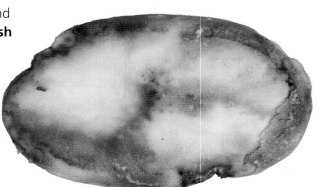

▲ Potato infected by blight fungus

| Causes of the Great Famine |
| --- |
| Rise in population |
| Widespread poverty |
| Subdivision of land, leading to ever smaller farms |
| Reliance on the potato |
| Cottiers worked in exchange for rent rather than money |
| The potato blight |

**DID YOU KNOW?**

A spray was developed in 1882 to prevent the blight fungus. It was a mix of copper sulphate and washing soda. Versions of this spray are still used by farmers today.

## CHECKPOINT!

1. When did the Famine occur?
2. Why was the rise in population so damaging for Ireland?
3. Why was the potato the main crop in Ireland?
4. What was potato blight?
5. Which of the causes of the Famine do you think was the most important? Give reasons for your answer.

 I can explain the causes of the Great Famine.

◀ TIME TO GO BACK ▶ I CAN MOVE FORWARD ➡

# 16.3: The Famine Years: 1845–1850

## The course of the Famine

The potato blight did not affect Ireland alone. Other European countries also lost their potato crops, but they were not as reliant on farming and had other available food. In Ireland, the farming poor would suffer the effects of famine for years.

- 1845: farmers noticed the **potato stalks turning black** and a strange smell from the fields. They found that the potatoes were rotten. Luckily, they had some potatoes in storage from an earlier harvest, so mass starvation was not a problem in 1845.

- 1846: **two-thirds of the crop was lost to blight** and people had used up what stores they had. The poorest began to starve. Disease spread as immune systems were weakened. People died of tuberculosis, measles and scarlet fever.

- 1847: there was virtually no potato blight but people had few seeds to plant, so the **crop was very small**. The poor continued to die of hunger and disease.

- 1848–1850: **starvation and disease worsened**. Some 40,000 more people died in 1850 than died in 1846.

- **Typhus and cholera** killed many due to bad living conditions and dirty water. People moving to towns to find work brought disease with them and it spread rapidly.

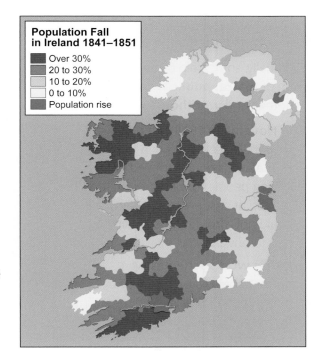

Population Fall in Ireland 1841–1851
- Over 30%
- 20 to 30%
- 10 to 20%
- 0 to 10%
- Population rise

As the Famine took hold, many tenant farmers and cottiers could not pay their rent and were faced with eviction. **Eviction** is <u>when someone is forced out of their home</u>. Cottages were sometimes burned, or the roofs pulled in, to prevent the tenants returning. Some sympathetic landlords reduced rents or let those who could not pay stay on. A few even paid passage for their tenants to emigrate. Those who could afford to leave Ireland altogether were often considered lucky, though in reality they faced a hard and uncertain journey. The ships they boarded were unsuitable and became known as **coffin ships** because so many died on board of illness or starvation.

Meanwhile, the middle and upper classes were almost untouched by hunger, homelessness and disease.

## CHECKPOINT!

1. Why was Ireland affected by the blight more seriously than other countries?
2. What diseases affected people during the Famine? Why did they spread so easily?
3. Explain the term eviction. 📖
4. Where did people evicted from their homes go to?
5. Looking at the map, which areas were the worst affected? Why do you think this was?
6. Why do you think the populations rose in Cork city and Dublin city?

✔ I understand the course of events of the Great Famine.

TIME TO GO BACK ◀ ▶ I CAN MOVE FORWARD ➡

16 The Great Famine and the Irish Diaspora

# Famine relief efforts

Help for those affected by famine was slow to arrive. The British government took a **laissez-faire** ('let it be') attitude to events, believing that <u>a government should not interfere in the economy as it would correct itself eventually</u>.

- British farmers **did not depend on the potato for food**; they had alternatives. The British government thought the situation was the same in Ireland, so they were slow to react.

- People **believed potato blight would affect only one year** of crops, so few plans were made in case blight struck again after 1845.

- The British government was so **misinformed** that it **continued to export** crops from Ireland, resulting in riots such as that in Dungarvan, Co. Waterford, where people tried to stop a grain ship from leaving port and were shot at by police.

Eventually, some help came in the form of **maize**, **public works schemes** and **workhouses**.

▲ At the gate of a workhouse

- In **November 1845** Prime Minister Sir Robert Peel sent aid in the form of **maize** – enough to feed one million people for one month. It was offered at cost price, but many still could not afford it, or sold all they had to buy the maize.

- **Public works schemes** were set up for people to earn money by building roads, walls or bridges. By 1846, 400,000 people were involved in these schemes. This was hard, physical work for people who were weak with hunger. They **earned 1 shilling per day**, but this wasn't enough as prices had risen due to shortages.

- From the early 1840s, workhouses were established for those who had nowhere else to go. A **workhouse** was <u>a large building where people worked in return for basic accommodation and food</u>. The whole family had to enter together. This was so that **landlords could clear their land of tenants who could not pay rent**. Life in the workhouse – 'the most feared and hated institution ever established in Ireland' – was meant to be harsh, so as not to encourage people to stay and to keep down the numbers entering. Despite this, the workhouses were full to **overflowing**. Inside, **families were split up**; some never met again. By 1847, there were 200,000 people in the workhouses – double what they should hold. Disease spread easily.

**DID YOU KNOW?**

One problem with the maize the British government sent was that nobody knew how to cook it. When the British government printed posters and leaflets explaining what to do, they were in English – which many of the worst affected people could not speak or read!

► Maize

Most aid came from voluntary or charity organisations, in the form of **soup kitchens** and **donations**.

• In late 1846 **the Quakers** (Religious Society of Friends) set up soup kitchens in towns such as Waterford, Enniscorthy, Limerick, Clonmel and Youghal. **Soup kitchens gave hot soup to starving people who were not in workhouses**. In mid-1847, the government set up its own **soup kitchens**.

• Money was raised by the Quakers and others to give practical and financial help to the Irish. For example, clothing was gathered from Britain for the winter of 1846– 1847 and fishermen got funding to recover the equipment they had sold to feed their families.

• Groups such as the Quakers raised awareness worldwide of Ireland's need, and **donations** came from at least 19 different countries. Queen Victoria donated money (about €172,000 today), the Ottoman Sultan sent both money and food and Pope Pius IX gave Roman coins from his private income (€19,000 today). Even the Choctaw Nation, which had recently been displaced from its homeland in the southern US and suffered great loss of life, raised money for those starving in Ireland.

▲ A Quaker soup kitchen

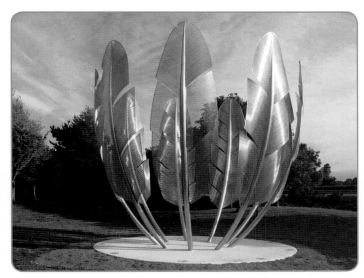
▲ 'Kindred Spirits', a memorial in Co. Cork in remembrance of the Choctaw Nation's compassion

Go to page 98 of your *Sources and Skills Book* for a visual source from the Famine years.

## CHECKPOINT!

1. Why was the British government so slow to act in response to the blight in Ireland?
2. Explain the term laissez-faire as it relates to government policy at this time.
3. How did the government try to help with (a) maize and (b) public works schemes?
4. What was a workhouse? What were the advantages and disadvantages of entering a workhouse?
5. What were soup kitchens?
6. Name some people and groups that donated money for famine relief.

✓ I can explain the various famine relief efforts and their effects.

⟵ TIME TO GO BACK ⟨⟩ I CAN MOVE FORWARD ⟶

COLLABORATE: Imagine you were a politician during the Great Famine and write down two ideas about how you would have helped people. Debate the different ideas with your group.

**16 The Great Famine and the Irish Diaspora**

# 16.4: The Impact of Famine in Ireland

**In this topic, you will learn about:**

❯ How the events of the Famine affected Ireland

The Famine years devastated Ireland's population through starvation, disease and emigration, but the Great Famine was more wide-ranging than this sad consequence. It led to deep changes in Irish society, some of which exist to the present day.

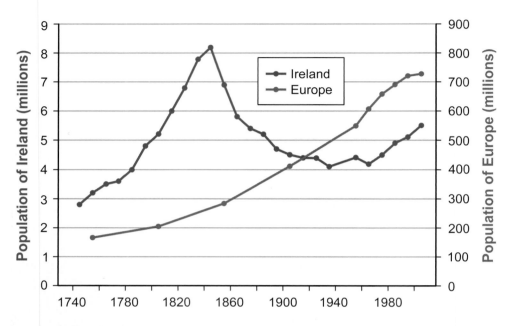

▲ Decline in Irish population relative to the change in Europe's population

- **Fall in population:** The **1841 census** showed that there were **over eight million people** on the island of Ireland. Between 1845 and 1850, the **population dropped by two million**. Roughly one million died from disease and starvation, while one million emigrated. This trend of emigration continued far beyond the 1840s. Ireland's population has **never regained its pre-Famine levels**.

- **Change in farming practices:** Though the crop failed because of potato blight, the Famine only took hold and lasted because Irish farmers were already so vulnerable. After the Famine, changes were made to ensure such a catastrophe would never happen again:

  - The Famine brought an **end to the subdivision of land**. No longer was a farm split between sons; instead, the eldest son inherited it all when his father died. This allowed larger farms, though many younger sons and daughters had to emigrate.

  - Many **landlords used their land for cattle farming after the Famine**. Ireland shifted from largely tillage/crop farming to cattle-rearing/pasture farming.

- **Rise in anti-British feeling:** Many blamed the British government for the people's suffering during the Famine. Anger over matters such as the exportation of food from Ireland fed a growing belief that Britain should not control Irish affairs and made many determined to win Irish independence. This led to **support for nationalist groups** and a desire for Home Rule and paved the way for uprisings and rebellions in the late nineteenth and early twentieth centuries.

- **Decline of the Irish language:** The predominantly Irish-speaking areas of the west and south-west of Ireland were the worst hit by both death and emigration. Over time, **people began to favour English over Irish** because it would help them find work elsewhere if they needed to emigrate.

• **New emigration trends:** In the 1881 census, the Irish population had fallen by over three million (or 37%) since 1841. This shows the continuation of emigration. The US and Britain were the main destinations for the Irish. Those who found steady work often paid for the rest of their family to follow them, so that entire families left Ireland for good.

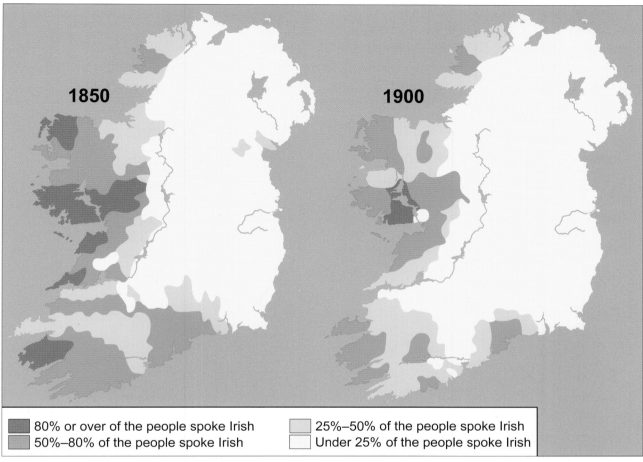

1850          1900

| | | | |
|---|---|---|---|
| ■ | 80% or over of the people spoke Irish | ▨ | 25%–50% of the people spoke Irish |
| ▨ | 50%–80% of the people spoke Irish | ☐ | Under 25% of the people spoke Irish |

▲ The decline in the number of people speaking Irish over the five decades following the Famine

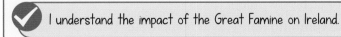 CHECKPOINT!

1. How many people either died or emigrated between 1845 and 1850? ✂
2. How did changes to farming practices contribute to continued emigration?
3. How did the British government's actions during the Famine affect political beliefs among Irish people?
4. Which areas of the island were hardest hit by the Famine?

✓ I understand the impact of the Great Famine on Ireland.  ← TIME TO GO BACK ◆ I CAN MOVE FORWARD →

 COLLABORATE: Work in pairs to find out Ireland's current population. Look at the graph on page 222 and identify two decades when it matched today's level. ✂

16 The Great Famine and the Irish Diaspora

# 16.5: The Irish Diaspora

Emigration continued after the Famine as Irish migrants settled in and brought their families to join them (**chain migration**), and sons and daughters who would no longer inherit land went abroad to seek work. This destinations included Britain, the US, Canada, Australia, South Africa and New Zealand and more. These became the **Irish diaspora**: <u>the scattering of Irish migrants and their descendants across the world</u>. Emigration from Ireland had always occurred, but from the 1840s onwards it soared. Not until the 1970s did inward migration briefly overtake emigration. Here, we will focus only on the Irish diaspora in Britain and in the US.

◀ Numbers of Irish-born immigrants living in the US and Britain. Why do you think the US numbers show a much sharper drop than those for Britain?

## The Irish diaspora in Britain

While Ireland was in the throes of famine, Britain had experienced an **industrial revolution**. For centuries, clothes and textiles had been made in people's homes; this was known as **cottage industry**. But new inventions allowed businesspeople to build factories, buy machines and hire workers to operate them.

### Inventions of the Industrial Revolution

- **John Kay** invented a machine called the **flying shuttle**, which improved looms and allowed a single weaver to weave much wider fabrics twice as fast as before.

- **James Hargreaves** invented a machine called the **spinning jenny**, which improved spinning wheels and allowed one spinner to make eight times more yarn.

- **Richard Arkwright** invented a machine called the **water frame**, a water-powered spinning machine that made stronger threads of yarn.

- **Samuel Crompton** invented the **spinning mule**, which could make forty-eight spools of thread at a time, and was a combination of the spinning jenny and the water frame.

- **James Watt** invented a **steam engine**, an engine driven by the pressure of steam from water heated by a coal fire. This engine was soon used in hundreds of different ways and demand for coal soared. By 1843, there were 130 **coal mines**, all needing workers to mine them.

- **Edmund Cartwright** invented the **power loom**, a steam-powered loom that made as much cloth as 100 weavers.

Irish emigration to British cities, especially **Liverpool**, **Manchester** and **Glasgow**, was not new. For example, shortly before the Famine 17.3% of the population of Liverpool was Irish. It was cheap to travel to Britain. People sailed on crowded steamships that were built to transport animals and grain. Many travelled on the open deck, which was cold and dangerous. Typhus travelled with some of the migrants. For some, Britain was the first stage of their journey across the Atlantic.

## Life in Britain for the Irish diaspora

- The **Irish were among the poorest**, living in the slums of Industrial Revolution Britain. Many Irish had to survive on handouts and begging. When they could get work, they accepted low wages, which made them unpopular with the British working class.

- Many died of **diseases** such as typhus, due to the unsanitary and overcrowded living conditions in the slums.

- When conditions began to improve in Britain, the Irish became part of **the industrial working class**, frequently working as publicans or shopkeepers.

- The Irish became involved in the building trade and transport, particularly as **dockers**.

- They were heavily involved in **the building of the British canal, road and rail networks** in the nineteenth century.

- Gradually the Irish **married** into the British population and moved up the social class system.

- Migration to Britain continued throughout the twentieth century. **Today, up to six million people in the UK have an Irish-born grandparent** (around 10% of the population).

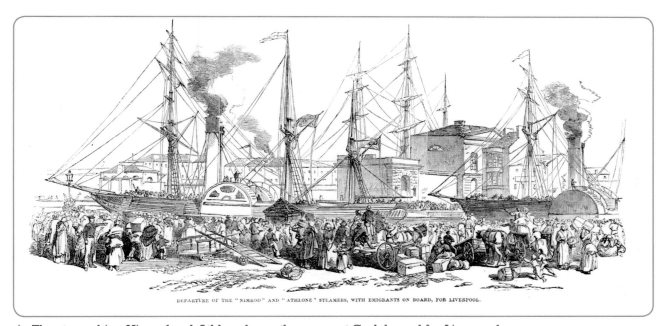

DEPARTURE OF THE "NIMROD" AND "ATHLONE" STEAMERS, WITH EMIGRANTS ON BOARD, FOR LIVERPOOL.

▲ The steamships *Nimrod* and *Athlone* leave the quays at Cork bound for Liverpool

## CHECKPOINT!

1. Explain the term Irish diaspora.
2. Why did many Irish Famine emigrants choose to go to Britain?
3. What kinds of jobs did the Irish in Britain have?
4. How did Irish emigrants impact on Britain and British people?

✓ I know the impact of Britain's Industrial Revolution and about the Irish diaspora in Britain.

 ← TIME TO GO BACK ◆ I CAN MOVE FORWARD →

# The Irish diaspora in the US

Emigration to the United States was **expensive**. The journey was long and difficult and the immigration rules were strict. The main entry for Irish people to the US was through **New York City** (although some of those who took the cheaper voyage to Canada later crossed the border into the US on foot). Until 1890, the main immigration point was at **Castle Garden**, at the southern end of Manhattan. All immigrants then went through a temporary Barge Office until the famous **Ellis Island** centre opened in 1892.

▲ Ellis Island immigration point

## *Life in the US for the Irish diaspora*

- Between 1841 and 1850, around **910,000 Irish emigrated to the US** – 250,000 in 1847 alone.

- The Famine migrants were **Catholic** and **most spoke Irish**. Their arrival was not welcomed by the large Protestant population in the US.

- Many of the Irish were uneducated. They often competed with Americans for manual labour jobs. In the 1860s, they were recruited from the docks by the US Army to serve in the **American Civil War** and afterwards to **build the Union Pacific Railroad**.

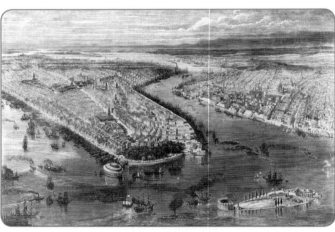
▲ Castle Garden is the circular fort on the island just off the shore of Manhattan

- The Irish suffered **discrimination** when the economy was slow. For example, in the 1850s '**No Irish Need Apply**' was a familiar feature of job advertisements.

- Because of the Famine, many Irish-Americans had a **deep hatred towards the British government** in Ireland and went on to support the Irish nationalist movement.

- Today, **over 41 million Americans claim Irish ancestry**, including several presidents (John F. Kennedy, Ronald Reagan and Barack Obama among them), writer F. Scott Fitzgerald and actors Chris Evans and Dakota and Elle Fanning.

**DID YOU KNOW?**

In 1892, Annie Moore from Co. Cork was the very first person processed at Ellis Island. She arrived on her 15th birthday with her two younger brothers. By 1924, when it closed, over twelve million people had followed her through those gates.

## CHECKPOINT!

1. What problems were faced by the Irish who emigrated to America?

2. What kinds of work did they do?

3. What impact have Irish immigrants had on America and on the American people?

 I understand what the Irish-American diaspora is and its long-term significance.

 TIME TO GO BACK ◀ ▶ I CAN MOVE FORWARD ➡

# WORKING WITH THE <u>EVIDENCE</u>!

## On board a coffin ship

Study the following witness account by Stephen de Vere, who sailed to America in the steerage (below decks) of a ship in 1847, the Famine year with the highest emigration levels.

▲ **Below decks on a coffin ship**

*Hundreds of poor people, men, women and children of all ages huddled together without light, without air, wallowing in filth and breathing a fetid atmosphere, sick in body, dispirited in heart; the fevered patients lying beside the sound, by their agonised ravings disturbing those around. The food is generally ill-selected and seldom sufficiently cooked in consequences of the insufficiency and bad construction of the cooking places. The supply of water, hardly enough for cooking and drinking, does not allow for washing. No moral restraint is attempted; the voice of prayer is never heard; drunkenness, with all its consequent train of ruffianly debasement, is not discouraged because it is found profitable by the captain who traffics in grog [watered-down rum].*

1. What type of source is this?
2. Describe the conditions on the ship to America.
3. What was the food like on board these ships? What reasons does de Vere give for this?
4. Why was drunkenness not discouraged?
5. Explain one benefit and one limitation of this source.

# SUMMARY

In this chapter, we have learned that:

- In the early nineteenth century, major changes in agriculture made more food available in Britain, increasing its population. This period of change is known as the Agricultural Revolution.

- The larger population created greater demand for goods. Businesspeople built factories, bought machines and hired workers to operate them. The resulting industrialisation of Britain is known as the Industrial Revolution.

- Ireland's population had doubled in under a century, reaching around 8.2 million by 1841.

- The Agricultural and Industrial Revolutions did not affect Ireland to the same extent as they did Britain.

- The causes of the Great Famine (1845–1850) include: a rise in population; poverty; subdivision of land; reliance on the potato; work in exchange for rent rather than cash; and potato blight.

- The British government was slow to act when the potato blight hit. Some help came eventually in the form of maize, public works schemes and workhouses. However, most help came from voluntary and charity organisations in the form of soup kitchens and donations.

- The consequences of the Great Famine include: a steep drop in population; emigration; the decline of the Irish language; the end of subdivision; changes to agriculture; and anti-British feeling.

- People emigrated to countries such as Britain, Australia, Canada and the US during and after the Great Famine, creating the Irish diaspora.

### Reflecting on... The Great Famine

Until the twentieth century, the Great Famine was the worst catastrophe in modern European history. Its impact is still felt today: Ireland continues to tend towards emigration, particularly in times of economic hardship. Perhaps due to our own experience, we have a strong tradition of donating to and working in developing countries. Though Ireland is still strongly agricultural, the Famine was a turning point; thereafter, the Irish diversified their crops and sought livelihoods outside farming. Our population has never returned to pre-Famine levels, although millions around the world claim Irish roots.

# Understanding History

1. What impact did the Agricultural Revolution have on Britain?

2. Did it have the same impact on Ireland? Explain why or why not.

3. Describe life in rural Ireland in the 1840s. Explain who owned the land, what types of farmers and labourers worked there, what they ate and how they paid their rent.

4. Draw a timeline of the events of the Great Famine from 1845 to 1850, including:
   - The first year the crops failed
   - The year farmers lost two-thirds of their crop
   - The year there was no blight, but farmers had few seeds to plant
   - The year the Quakers set up soup kitchens
   - The year the workhouse population reached 200,000

5. What were public works schemes? Were they an appropriate way to help the Irish people at the time?

6. Do you agree or disagree with the belief at the time that the British government was to blame for the Great Famine? Explain your choice.

7. What difficulties were faced by Irish people who emigrated during the Famine?

8. List and briefly explain three ways in which the Famine had a long-term impact on Ireland.

**Exploring History**

1. Write a short paragraph about the Great Famine's (a) causes and (b) consequences.
2. Write an account of the technological changes of the Industrial Revolution and how these affected society.
3. Read this statement by a witness near Louisburgh, Co. Mayo (6 March 1847) and answer the questions.

> It was melancholy and degrading in the extreme to see the women and girls withdrawn from all that was decent and proper, and labouring in mixed gangs on public roads. Not only in digging with the spade, and with the pick, but in carrying loads of earth and turves on their backs, and wheeling barrows like men, and breaking stones, are they employed. My heart often sunk within me at the obviously deteriorating effects of such occupation, while the poor neglected children were crouched in groups around the bits of lighted turves in the various sheltered corners along the line. The pay was 6d. and 7d. per day to the girls and women, and 8d. to the men ...

(a) What kind of source is this?

(b) What type of labour was involved in the public works scheme?

(c) Why might there have been different rates for men, women and children?

(d) Give one benefit and one limitation of this source.

| KEY TERMS | | |
|---|---|---|
| | **Norfolk system** | a four-crop rotation cycle of wheat, turnips, oats/barley and clover/grass over four years |
| | **Enclosure** | each tenant farmer's fields were grouped together in one small farm, fenced off, instead of in strips all across the landlord's land |
| | **Selective breeding** | reserving the largest or most suitable animals for breeding rather than for meat |
| | **Seed drill** | a machine, pulled by a horse or an ox, that sowed seeds at the right depth, in straight rows |
| | **Mechanical reaper** | a horse-drawn cart with a cutting blade that cut crops neatly in straight rows |
| | **Large farmers** | farmers who rented more than 30 acres |
| | **Small farmers** | farmers who rented between five and 30 acres |
| | **Cottier** | a labourer who rented one acre from a farmer |
| | **Potato blight** | a fungus that spreads in damp weather and ruins potato crops |
| | **Eviction** | when someone is forced out of their home |
| | **Laissez-faire** | the attitude that a government should not interfere in the economy as it would correct itself eventually |
| | **Workhouse** | a building where people worked in return for basic accommodation and food |
| | **Soup kitchens** | places that gave soup to starving people who were not in workhouses |
| | **Irish diaspora** | the spread of Irish migrants and their descendants across the world |

 Go to page 94 of your *Sources and Skills Book* for more exercises.

 Go to page 44 of your *Research Portfolio* for a task based on this chapter.

**16 The Great Famine and the Irish Diaspora**

In Ireland, the three decades between 1884 and 1914 were a time of great change. New **cultural nationalist movements** and organisations began during this period, such as the Gaelic League, the Irish Literary Revival and the GAA. Political ideas such as **Home Rule** were prominent during this time. The years 1910-1914 saw the passing of the Third Home Rule Bill, followed by the Home Rule Crisis. **World War I** broke out in 1914, suspending Home Rule and leading about a quarter of a million Irishmen, both nationalist and Unionist, to fight on Britain's side.

# WORKING WITH THE <u>EVIDENCE!</u>

## Changing Ireland 1884–1914

| Source type | Category | Example |
|---|---|---|
| Primary | Tactile | 1906 GAA County Championship medal for hurling |
| Primary | Written | *An Claidheamh Soluis* newspaper by the Gaelic League |

What do this medal and newspaper tell us about how organisations were trying to express and emphasise their 'Irishness' or nationalism? Look at the details on the medal and in the newspaper.

▲ County Championship medal

▲ *An Claidheamh Soluis*

# 17.1 A Divided Culture: North and South

## Religious divisions, north and south

The main religious denominations on the island of Ireland in the late nineteenth century were:

- **Catholics** – 77% of the population
- **Anglicans** (Church of Ireland/Protestant faith) – 12%
- **Presbyterians** (also called dissenters; Protestant) – 9%
- Other Protestant faiths, including the **Quakers**, **Baptists** and **Methodists** – 2%

The **south of Ireland** (roughly speaking, the three provinces of Connacht, Leinster and Munster) was mainly Catholic: by 1911, **89.6%** of its population was **Catholic**. In contrast, the **north of Ireland** (roughly speaking, Ulster) had a slight **Protestant** majority, at **56.33%**. Many were descended from the settlers of the Ulster Plantation.

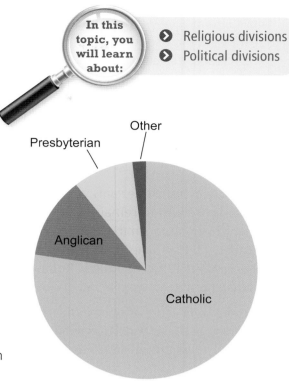

▲ The population of the island of Ireland by religion at the end of the nineteenth century

## Political divisions, north and south

At this time, Ireland was ruled entirely from Westminster. People in Ireland had varying attitudes towards this, but fell into two main political groups: nationalists and Unionists.

### Nationalists

An **Irish nationalist** is someone who believes that the Irish people are their own nation. While the majority of people in the south were nationalist, it is important to remember that there were nationalists in the north of Ireland too. At this time, two types of nationalists were on the rise: **constitutional nationalists** and **radical nationalists**.

**Constitutional nationalists** wanted to see the re-establishment of a parliament in Ireland and to achieve this through political means. They believed that the British parliament was too far removed from Irish issues to deal with them properly. **The Home Rule Party**, founded by **Isaac Butt** in 1874, was the largest nationalist political party: they won 86 of 105 seats in the 1885 general election. Under **Home Rule,** Ireland would have its own parliament in Dublin to govern local affairs, such as education and health, while Westminster could still control trade and foreign affairs. Ireland would still be part of the United Kingdom.

The leaders of the Home Rule Party (later renamed the **Irish Parliamentary Party**) in this period were:

| Charles Stewart Parnell | John Redmond |
|---|---|
| Leader, 1880–1891 | Leader, 1891–1918 |

17 Ireland 1884–1914: Politics, Culture and Sport

Radical nationalists wanted full independence from Britain and believed that they should use force if necessary to achieve this. Many of these radical nationalists belonged to the **Irish Republican Brotherhood (IRB)**. They wanted to achieve a republic. A **republic** is a country not ruled by a monarch, but instead ruled by its citizens, who choose their representatives. The IRB was founded in 1858 by James Stephens. It was a secret, oathbound society and its members were known as 'Fenians'.

▲ James Stephens

## Unionists

The majority of Irish Protestants were Unionist in their politics. A **Unionist** is someone who wants Ireland to remain part of the United Kingdom with Britain. Unionism was particularly strong in the north-east of the island, where there was a large Protestant population – but it is important to remember that there were Unionists in the south too. They believed that **'Home Rule is Rome Rule'** – that they would be discriminated against as Protestants if there were a Catholic-majority parliament in Dublin.

Unionists also feared that trade in the north could be badly affected by Home Rule. The shipbuilding and linen industries, which were very important to the north-east, relied on free access to the British market and not having taxes on their exports.

**The Unionist Party** was founded in 1905. The leaders of the Unionist Party in this period were:

| Colonel Edward Saunderson Founder: 1905–1906 | Walter Hume Long Leader, 1906–1910 | Edward Carson Leader, 1910–1921 |
| --- | --- | --- |

## Land ownership

The **Penal Laws** (from the 1600s onwards) and the **Plantations** meant that few Irish Catholics owned land, but were mainly poor tenant farmers or unskilled labourers. The Protestant Ascendancy owned most of the land in Ireland. **The Great Famine** (1845–1850) had a disproportionate impact on Irish Catholics. It reduced the number of cottiers and small farmers while allowing a new group of middle-class Catholic farmers to acquire bigger farms. In the 1800s, discontentment with this situation and with British rule would emerge in a rise in political agitation.

## CHECKPOINT!

1. Explain the terms nationalist, Unionist and republic. 📖
2. Give one example of a radical nationalist organisation.
3. What was Home Rule?
4. Give two reasons why Unionists opposed Home Rule.
5. Name one leader of the Unionist Party.
6. What three major factors had a negative effect on land ownership by Catholics?

✓ I can explain why Ireland was a divided culture north and south, religiously and politically.

 ← TIME TO GO BACK ◆ ◆ I CAN MOVE FORWARD →

# 17.2: Parliamentary Tradition: Charles Stewart Parnell and Home Rule

**In this topic, you will learn about:**
- ❯ The campaign for Home Rule
- ❯ The life and career of Charles Stewart Parnell

## A Life in Time: Charles Stewart Parnell (1846-1891)

### Early life

Charles Stewart Parnell was born on 27 June 1846 in Avondale, Co. Wicklow. His family were **Anglo-Irish** Protestant landowners. He studied at Cambridge University but never completed his studies. He was elected to parliament in 1875 as a member of the Home Rule Party in a Meath by-election.

### Parnell and the Home Rule Party

Parnell had links with the Fenians/IRB and agreed with their method of **parliamentary obstruction**. This involves deliberate interference with the progress of legislation, for example by making very long speeches to delay the passage of laws through parliament. Some Home Rule Party members distrusted Parnell because of his Fenian links.

Parnell's popularity rose because he tried to solve 'the Land Question'. With Fenians such as **Michael Davitt** and **John Devoy**, Parnell formed an organisation known as **the Land League**. The main goal was to get the British government to provide loans to tenant farmers so that they could **buy their farms** and no longer rely on renting. In the meantime he wanted to achieve **lower rents** and **prevent evictions**. This was popular with the Catholic Irish farmers who had suffered during the Great Famine.

▲ Charles Stewart Parnell

The Home Rule Party benefited from Parnell's efforts and won 63 seats in the British General Election of 1880. Parnell became leader of the Home Rule Party.

To persuade the British government to bring in reforms about land in Ireland, Parnell used the method of **political agitation**. This involves encouraging people to form local groups to demand better treatment, for example by refusing to pay rent or cooperate with local landlords. In 1881, Parnell was sent to **Kilmainham Gaol** for his political agitation and the public speeches he had made.

Violent protests took place across the country while Parnell was imprisoned. **William Gladstone**, then British Prime Minister, decided they needed to reach an agreement.

▲ Parnell entering Kilmainham Gaol

**17 Ireland 1884–1914: Politics, Culture and Sport**

In May 1882, Parnell and Gladstone signed **the Kilmainham Treaty**, which gave tenants access to land courts and helped tenants who owed money to pay their rents. Parnell promised to discourage violence. This was a triumph for Parnell and boosted the popularity of the Home Rule Party.

Four days later, a group of extreme IRB men called **'the Invincibles'** ambushed and killed two British politicians in **the Phoenix Park Murders**. This event made the radical nationalists less popular and peaceful political means were increasingly favoured.

## The fight for Home Rule

In 1882 the Home Rule Party became known as **the Irish Parliamentary Party**. In 1884, all men who owned or rented property worth £10 or more were granted the right to vote – an increase of over 300,000 voters.

## The First Home Rule Bill (1886)

In the **1885** British general election, the Irish Parliamentary Party won **86 seats**. This was important as it meant Parnell's party had enough seats to hold **the balance of power** in parliament. Parnell could either join with the Conservatives or he could form an alliance with the Liberal Party.

Parnell allied with **Gladstone** and **the Liberal Party** in January 1886, making Gladstone the Prime Minister again. As a result, the **First Home Rule Bill** was put forward by Gladstone in April 1886. The bill stated that:

- Irish MPs and Lords would leave Westminster.
- Ireland would have an elected parliament in Dublin.
- This parliament could make laws for internal affairs.
- Westminster would keep control of external affairs.
- A viceroy would represent the British monarch in Ireland.

The Conservative Party was against the First Home Rule Bill. Many felt that Home Rule would eventually lead to Ireland having full independence. The bill was defeated in June 1886, by 341 votes to 311 in the House of Commons. The Liberal Party split as a result, so another election had to take place. The Irish Parliamentary Party had an almost identical result, while the Conservatives gained and the Liberals lost a lot of votes. The Conservative Party was elected. Support for Parnell in Ireland continued to be very strong.

▲ William Gladstone

| Party | 1885 | 1886 |
|---|---|---|
| Conservatives | 247 | 317 |
| Liberals | 319 | 191 |
| Irish Parliamentary Party | 86 | 85 |
| Liberal Unionists | N/A | 77 |

▲ Election results

## False accusations

In 1887, **false accusations** of supporting violence and even of involvement in the Phoenix Park Murders were made against Parnell in *The Times* newspaper, which published a letter it claimed Parnell had written. On investigation, the letter was proved to be a forgery: Parnell's good name was cleared and he was paid compensation. This transformed Parnell into a hero in the eyes of English liberals and he received a **standing ovation** in the House of Commons. This was the peak of Parnell's career. Parnell went back to convincing Gladstone that another Home Rule Bill should be put forward if the Liberals came to power again.

### The fall of Parnell

Parnell's long relationship with a woman named **Katharine O'Shea** was to be his political downfall. Katharine was married to William O'Shea but had separated from him years before meeting Parnell, with whom she then had three children. Katharine's husband did not file for divorce until 1890, possibly because of inheritance money due to his wife. When the relationship became public due to the divorce trial, attitudes towards Parnell began to change: Catholic Ireland disapproved.

Some Liberal Party members feared that their ties to Parnell would damage them politically. Many people withdrew their support and wanted him to resign. A vote on Parnell's leadership of the Irish Parliamentary Party caused it to split in two. Parnell remained leader of one section, which became known as **the Irish National League** (INL). He continued campaigning, despite being very ill.

▲ Katharine O'Shea

Parnell married Katharine O'Shea but died of pneumonia just five months later in October 1891, aged only 45.

**DID YOU KNOW?**

Parnell was buried in Glasnevin Cemetery on top of a cholera pit holding 13,000 bodies from an outbreak in 1849. About 200,000 people attended his funeral. He had been called 'the Uncrowned King of Ireland'.

▼ Parnell's grave in Glasnevin Cemetery

## The Second Home Rule Bill

Home Rule was attempted for a second time in **1893**, when Gladstone returned to power. Again it was unsuccessful. However, this time it was passed in the House of Commons and blocked in the House of Lords. Gladstone retired in 1894, and both sides of the divided Irish Parliamentary Party entered a decline. Home Rule was not addressed properly again until **1912**.

### CHECKPOINT!

1. Explain the terms parliamentary obstruction and political agitation. 📖
2. How did Parnell gain popularity for the Home Rule Party? Give two examples.
3. Why was the First Home Rule Bill not passed in the House of Commons?
4. Why did Parnell's popularity fall following the First Home Rule Bill? Describe two factors in this.

 I can explain Parnell's role in the campaign for Home Rule and its significance.

← TIME TO GO BACK ◆ I CAN MOVE FORWARD →

**17 Ireland 1884–1914: Politics, Culture and Sport**

# 17.3: Cultural Nationalist Movements

## Cultural nationalism

In the late nineteenth and early twentieth centuries, a new type of nationalism began to emerge. **Cultural nationalism** focuses on promoting a national identity shaped by shared cultural traditions and language. Many nationalists felt that if Ireland were to achieve its own parliament, it should also set itself apart from Britain culturally. Ireland had become increasingly anglicised. **Anglicisation** was **the spreading of English culture throughout Ireland, leading to people speaking English, following English customs and playing English sports**. To boost Irish culture, various organisations and movements were founded; here we will look at **the Gaelic League** and **the Irish Literary Revival**.

> In this topic, you will learn about:
> ❯ Cultural nationalism
> ❯ The Gaelic League
> ❯ The Irish Literary Revival

## The Gaelic League

Between 1800 and 1900, the number of people who spoke only Irish plummeted from 50% to only 1%. In 1893, **Eoin MacNeill and Douglas Hyde** founded **the Gaelic League** (now **Conradh na Gaeilge**), an organisation whose aim was to promote the Irish language. They felt that Irish identity was in danger of extinction, especially the Irish language. Hyde was elected the Gaelic League's first president.

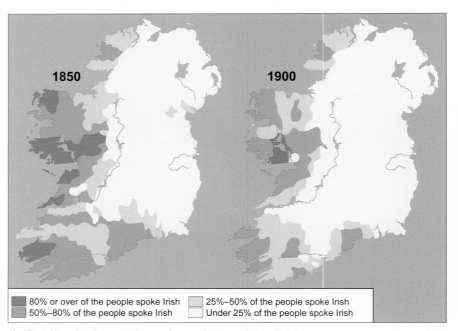

80% or over of the people spoke Irish
50%–80% of the people spoke Irish
25%–50% of the people spoke Irish
Under 25% of the people spoke Irish

▲ Decline in the number of people speaking Irish

- They founded an Irish newspaper called **An Claidheamh Soluis** ('Sword of Light') which published works in Irish such as **poems and short stories**.
- They **trained travelling teachers** called timirí to teach Irish to local communities.
- They organised feiseanna and céilidhe to encourage **Irish dancing** and **traditional Irish music**
- They aimed to increase the standard of **written Irish** throughout the country.

The Gaelic League renewed enthusiasm for the Irish language and helped to slow its decline. It contributed to the formation of Irish identity. Over time, many radical nationalists such as **Pádraig Pearse** were linked with the Gaelic League.

▶ Douglas Hyde and Eoin MacNeill

# The Irish Literary Revival

**The Irish Literary Revival** was a <u>movement that aimed to promote Irish literature and coincided with a renewed interest in Gaelic Irish cultural heritage</u>. A new form of literature emerged during the late nineteenth century. It was Irish in character but written in English, with content and themes inspired by ancient Irish myths and legends, as well as by contemporary Irish society. **William Butler Yeats** was central to the Irish Literary Revival and used Irish myths and folklore in much of his work. Politically, Yeats was sympathetic towards the IRB, but he acted only through his writing.

**Douglas Hyde** and others formed **the Irish Literary Society** in 1892 to promote new literary works. In 1899 Yeats, with other **members of the Protestant Ascendancy** such as **Lady Augusta Gregory**, **Edward Martin** and **George Moore**, established the Irish Literary Theatre (later renamed the **Irish National Theatre Society**). In 1904, this society opened **the Abbey Theatre** in Dublin. The theatre supported Irish writers and staged plays such as *Kathleen Ní Houlihan* and *The Playboy of the Western World*. Irish cultural nationalism was promoted through the popularity of the Abbey Theatre's productions and people gained a sense of an Irish identity.

▲ William Butler Yeats

▲ Lady Gregory

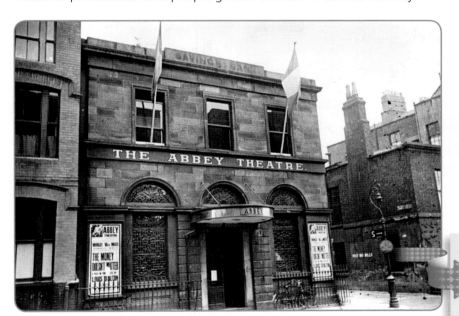
▲ The Abbey Theatre

Go to page 102 of your *Sources and Skills Book* for an evidence task on cultural nationalism.

## CHECKPOINT!

1. Explain the terms cultural nationalism and anglicisation.
2. Why was the Gaelic League founded?
3. How did the Gaelic League try to revive interest in the Irish language?
4. What was the Irish Literary Revival?
5. How did the Irish Literary Revival promote Irish writers and culture?

 I understand what cultural nationalism is and can describe the Gaelic League and the Irish Literary Revival.

◀ TIME TO GO BACK ◆ ▶ I CAN MOVE FORWARD ➡

**17 Ireland 1884–1914: Politics, Culture and Sport**

# 17.4 A Sporting Movement: The GAA

In this topic, you will learn about:

❯ The foundation, development and influence of the GAA

## The foundation of the GAA

By 1880, English sports such as tennis, cricket, soccer and rugby had become very popular in Ireland. Each was well organised and had clear rules. At the same time, Irish sports such as hurling and Gaelic football were in decline and were even unknown in some areas. They were poorly organised and people around the country played by different rules.

A man named **Michael Cusack** became particularly concerned about the state of Irish sports. He called a meeting in Hayes Hotel in Thurles, Co. Tipperary on 1 November 1884 to establish a 'Gaelic Association for the preservation and cultivation of our national pastimes'. With just seven men present, the **GAA (Gaelic Athletic Association)** was founded, encompassing sports such as hurling, Gaelic football, handball, athletics and weightlifting. The athlete **Maurice Davin** was elected president and Cusack became secretary. People such as **Charles Stewart Parnell**, **Michael Davitt** and **Archbishop Thomas Croke** became patrons of the GAA. This showed that the Home Rule Party, the IRB and the Catholic Church all supported the GAA.

▲ Michael Cusack

## The development of the GAA

- Clubs were formed all over the country and also abroad.
- Games were organised for Sundays; this had not been allowed before.
- The GAA banned people from playing Gaelic sports if they also played or attended foreign sports (rugby, cricket, soccer or tennis). Many disagreed with this decision.
- New rules were agreed for hurling, football, athletics and weightlifting in February 1885.

▲ Maurice Davin

The **IRB** saw the GAA as a perfect source of fighters for a future rebellion and infiltrated the association. While the founders of the GAA were nationalists, there was a split over the IRB's presence. Some believed in Parnell's constitutional nationalist methods, while others believed in the radical nationalism of the IRB. This divide damaged the association. The scandal about Parnell and O'Shea split the GAA as well as the Irish Parliamentary Party: many members left the GAA.

In the early 1900s the GAA became popular again. This was because:

- the IRB was not as prominent during this time
- the GAA had created links with organisations such as the Gaelic League by actively promoting the Irish language
- the new rules appealed to people
- Croke Park (named after Archbishop Croke), known as **Jones' Road** at the time, was bought in 1913, providing the GAA with new grounds for major events such as finals.

# The influence of the GAA

The GAA was instrumental in reviving Irish sports. It **linked sport and nationalism** in a way that had not been done before. This would continue throughout the struggle for Irish independence. The GAA provided a social and physical outlet for people from different social classes in towns and the countryside. Middle-class membership (teachers, clerks and so forth) rose to match that of the working class. In addition, the GAA was nationalist in its politics, supported Home Rule and served as a recruitment ground for the IRB. Many from the GAA went on to be involved in the Easter Rising and War of Independence.

| Influence of the GAA |
| --- |
| Revived Irish sports |
| Linked sport and nationalism |
| Provided a social and physical outlet for people |
| Recruitment ground for Home Rule and the IRB |
| Many members would be involved in future efforts to gain independence |

**DID YOU KNOW?**

The first all-Ireland hurling and football competitions both took place in 1887. Kilkenny has won the most All-Ireland senior hurling finals to date, while Kerry has won the most All-Ireland senior football finals.

▲ The programme for the 1913 All-Ireland hurling final

▲ The Kerry winners of the 1913 All-Ireland football final

## CHECKPOINT!

1. Briefly describe the state of sports in Ireland in the days before the GAA.
2. Where was the GAA founded and who founded it?
3. Name two significant organisations that supported the GAA.
4. How did the GAA develop? Give two examples.
5. Why did the GAA begin to decline in the final years of the nineteenth century?
6. How did the GAA influence Irish society? Give two examples.

 I understand how the GAA was founded and developed and how it influenced Irish society.

 ← TIME TO GO BACK ◆ I CAN MOVE FORWARD →

 COLLABORATE: With your group, use the various sources on this website (such as newspaper reports, photographs, medals, and videos) to gather ten other facts about the history of the GAA in your county.

https://educateplus.ie/go/gaa-centenary

17 Ireland 1884–1914: Politics, Culture and Sport

# 17.5: Political Parties and Organisations in Ireland in 1910

## The Irish Parliamentary Party

In this topic, you will learn about:

➔ Irish political parties and organisations in 1910

The **Irish Parliamentary Party** declined in popularity after the Parnellite split but was reunified under **John Redmond** in 1900. It had little power in the early 1900s but had steady support as there was no real alternative. Its **constitutional nationalist** aims were unchanged:

- to achieve Home Rule or self-government by having a parliament in Dublin to deal with internal affairs. Westminster could look after external affairs

- the King/Queen of England to be the King/Queen of Ireland.

## Sinn Féin

**Sinn Féin**, meaning 'we ourselves', is a nationalist political party founded in 1905 by **Arthur Griffith**, a Catholic Dublin-born journalist. He wanted Ireland to win independence and establish its own parliament. It started off as a small party but later grew in size. **Arthur Griffith** and Sinn Féin wanted:

- **a dual monarchy**, where the King/Queen of England would also be the King/Queen of Ireland

- to **develop Irish industry** by having tariffs put on goods transported across international borders

- to achieve these by using **parliamentary abstention**, meaning that Irish MPs would withdraw from the Westminster parliament they entered in the 1801 Act of Union to set up their own parliament in Dublin

- the **Dublin parliament** would deal with Ireland's internal affairs.

▲ Arthur Griffith

## The IRB

The **Irish Republican Brotherhood** had been founded in 1858 and was a secret radical nationalist organisation whose members believed in the use of **physical force**. In 1910 the IRB was a small organisation and was only starting to grow again in support since the 1880s. The IRB wanted:

- complete independence from Britain

- to make Ireland a republic

- to use physical force to achieve this.

## The Unionist Party

Unionists wanted to retain the Act of Union and keep their strong link with Britain. **Edward Carson** was the leader of the Unionist Party between 1910 and 1921. He was a Dublin-born Protestant lawyer. Carson and the Unionist Party wanted:

- the parliament in Westminster to continue to make laws for Ireland
- the British government and the Crown to still have representatives in Ireland.

**DID YOU KNOW?**

The Crown's representative in Ireland was called the Lord Lieutenant. The house in the Phoenix Park built as his summer residence (he lived in Dublin Castle otherwise) is now known as Áras an Uachtaráin and is the residence of the President of Ireland.

▲ Edward Carson

## CHECKPOINT!

1. How had the Irish Parliamentary Party recovered from the Parnellite split by 1910?

2. What were the aims of Sinn Féin?

3. How did they differ from those of the Irish Parliamentary Party?

4. Explain what is meant by dual monarchy. 📖

5. What were the political goals of the IRB? Give two examples.

6. What did the Unionist Party want to achieve?

 I can describe the aims of each of the main political groups in Ireland in 1910.

◀ TIME TO GO BACK ◀ ▶ I CAN MOVE FORWARD ▶

▲ Anti-Home Rule poster

AGAINST HOME RULE HANDS UP!

▲ Pro-Home Rule poster

ERIN UNFURLS HER FLAG

HOME RULE

With the free, green flag above thee,
And beneath kind friends who praise
Oh ERIN, lovely ERIN,
This is thy day of days.

# WORKING WITH THE EVIDENCE!

## Home Rule posters

1. What does each of these posters tell you about the views of Unionists or nationalists towards the idea of Home Rule?

2. Describe the details and symbols you notice in each of the posters.

3. What are (a) the benefits and (b) the limitations of posters as sources?

## 17.6: The Home Rule Crisis (1912–1914)

In this topic, you will learn about:
- The Parliament Act 1911
- The Third Home Rule Bill 1912
- Unionist opposition
- Nationalist reaction

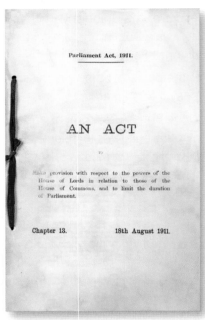

▲ The Parliament Act of 1911

### The Parliament Act of 1911

The Conservative Party had been in government from 1895 to 1906. It and the Unionists had always supported each other to ensure a majority. While the Conservatives were in power, Home Rule would not be passed. In 1906 the **Liberal Party** was voted into government and had enough votes that it did not need outside support.

However, in 1910 the Liberals again needed the help of the Irish Parliamentary Party to stay in government. Until this point, the House of Lords could block (**veto**) any laws or bills passed by the House of Commons. In 1911, the Liberals passed a law that changed this: the Parliament Act. It stated that the **House of Lords could not fully veto any bill and could only delay laws from passing for two years**. This meant that Home Rule was a possibility in the near future.

### The Third Home Rule Bill of 1912

The Liberals had tried to pass a Home Rule Bill twice before, in 1886 and 1893. Both times it had been vetoed by the House of Lords. In 1912 the leader of the Liberals was **Herbert Asquith**. He put forward the **Third Home Rule Bill** to the House of Commons and House of Lords. It was similar to the other Home Rule Bills:

- Ireland would have its own parliament in Dublin to deal with internal affairs.
- The parliament in Westminster would deal with external affairs such as foreign policy and taxation.

Due to the Parliament Act, the House of Lords could not veto the Home Rule Bill even though the Conservatives and the Unionist Party both opposed it – so Home Rule would become law in **1914**.

► Herbert Asquith

# Unionist reaction to the Third Home Rule Bill

Unionists were opposed to Home Rule because they believed **'Home Rule is Rome Rule'** and they felt that trade would be greatly affected. Unionists believed the government would not enforce Home Rule if opposition was strong enough. They:

- organised **demonstrations and protests** against Home Rule

- made a declaration called the **Ulster Solemn League and Covenant**, which stated that Unionists would 'use all means to defend the present conspiracy to set up a Home Rule Parliament in Ireland'. This was signed by over 200,000 men on 28 September 1912. Some even signed it in their own blood. Roughly 250,000 women signed a similar, separate declaration

- founded the UVF (or **Ulster Volunteer Force**) in January 1913 as **paramilitary resistance**. A **paramilitary force** is <u>an unofficial military-style organisation of amateur soldiers</u>. Some 100,000 joined the UVF, led by former army officers

- bought arms and ammunition from Germany for the UVF. **The Larne gun-running** took place in April 1914, when 35,000 guns and five million rounds of ammunition were smuggled into Ulster.

> **DID YOU KNOW?**
>
> The first three signatories of the Ulster Solemn League and Covenant were Edward Carson, Lord Londonderry (former Viceroy of Ireland) and James Craig.

## Ulster's Solemn League and Covenant.

Being convinced in our consciences that Home Rule would be disastrous to the material well-being of Ulster as well as of the whole of Ireland, subversive of our civil and religious freedom, destructive of our citizenship and perilous to the unity of the Empire, we, whose names are underwritten, men of Ulster, loyal subjects of His Gracious Majesty King George V., humbly relying on the God whom our fathers in days of stress and trial confidently trusted, do hereby pledge ourselves in solemn Covenant throughout this our time of threatened calamity to stand by one another in defending for ourselves and our children our cherished position of equal citizenship in the United Kingdom and in using all means which may be found necessary to defeat the present conspiracy to set up a Home Rule Parliament in Ireland. ¶ And in the event of such a Parliament being forced upon us we further solemnly and mutually pledge ourselves to refuse to recognise its authority. ¶ In sure confidence that God will defend the right we hereto subscribe our names. ¶ And further, we individually declare that we have not already signed this Covenant.

The above was signed by me at _____
"Ulster Day," Saturday, 28th September, 1912.

_____

—— God Save the King. ——

▲ Solemn League and Convenant declaration document

▼ Carson inspecting the UVF, 1914

17 Ireland 1884–1914: Politics, Culture and Sport

# Nationalist reactions to Unionist opposition

**Eoin MacNeill** of the Gaelic League suggested in a November 1913 article that nationalists should follow the Unionists' example by forming their own paramilitary force and pressuring the British government to make sure Home Rule did indeed happen.

▲ The Howth gun-running

- The IVF (**Irish Volunteer Force**) was officially founded at the Rotunda in Dublin in November 1913. MacNeill was made chief of staff. By 1914 the IVF had almost 100,000 volunteers, including all types of nationalist: members of the Home Rule Party, the IRB and Sinn Féin.

- Germany also sold arms and ammunition to the IVF. **The Howth gun-running** took place in July 1914, when 900 rifles and 25,000 rounds of ammunition were landed in Howth in north Co. Dublin on a ship called the **Asgard**.

With both groups now armed and Home Rule still causing disagreement in the government, civil war had become a real possibility.

However, on 4 August 1914 Britain declared war on Germany, beginning **World War I**. The Home Rule Bill became law on 18 September but was immediately suspended because of the war.

▲ Mary Spring Rice and Molly Childers aboard the *Asgard* with rifles and ammunition

 COLLABORATE: With your group, use this website to find out whether anybody with your surname (or any other local name) signed the Solemn League and Covenant. You can learn where they lived in 1912, where they signed the declaration and you can even see their signature.

https://educateplus.ie/go/ulster-covenant

## CHECKPOINT!

1. What change was brought in by the Parliament Act of 1911?
2. When was the Third Home Rule Bill meant to come into effect?
3. What does UVF stand for?
4. List two ways the Unionists tried to convince the British government to stop Home Rule.
5. What does IVF stand for?
6. List two ways the nationalists tried to make sure Home Rule happened.

 I can explain the Home Rule Crisis 1912–1914.

 TIME TO GO BACK   I CAN MOVE FORWARD

## A Life in Time: Edward Carson (1854–1935)

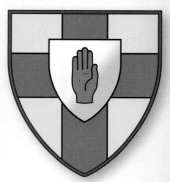

▲ The Red Hand of Ulster

◄ Carson addressing an Orange Order demonstration in Belfast

### Early life

Carson was born in Dublin on 9 February 1854, into a middle-class Protestant family, and studied law at Trinity College. His political career began in 1892, when he was appointed Solicitor-General for Ireland. He was elected a **Unionist MP** for Trinity College (1892–1918). Carson was a brilliant orator and his public speeches attracted large crowds.

### Carson and Home Rule

In February 1910, Carson agreed to become leader of the Irish Unionist Parliamentary Party and in June 1911 he led the Ulster Unionists. He believed the union between Britain and Ireland was in the best interests of his fellow countrymen; he was an Irish patriot, but not a nationalist. During the Home Rule Crisis, he spoke against the Third Home Rule Bill in the House of Commons and organised rallies in Ireland. He was the first signatory of **the Ulster Solemn League and Covenant**. He was uneasy about the decision to establish an Ulster Volunteer Force and to run guns through Larne. However, he accepted the UVF as a means of applying additional pressure to the British government. By 1914, he had come to support Irish partition as a solution, accepting that Home Rule was inevitable.

### Later career

When **the Government of Ireland Act 1920** was introduced, Carson advised his party to work for the exemption of six Ulster counties from Home Rule as the best compromise (an idea he had previously rejected). This proposal passed and as a result the Parliament of Northern Ireland was established. Carson remained as **Unionist leader until 1921** and retired in October 1929. He died in 1935 and is buried in St Anne's Cathedral, Belfast.

https://educateplus.ie/go/edward-carson

# 17.7: Ireland and World War I

## The split in the Irish Volunteer Force

Carson and the Unionists supported the British war effort and encouraged people to join the British army. They felt it would help to maintain their union with Britain and they hoped to receive special treatment after the war. Thousands of Ulster Unionists joined the British army to show their loyalty.

With the nationalists and the IVF, things were not so clear-cut. **John Redmond** of the Irish Parliamentary Party made a speech in **Woodenbridge**, Co. Wicklow in which he asked IVF members to join the British army. He **hoped that this would benefit Ireland** when it came to the Home Rule negotiations after the war. The Irish Volunteer Force split over the issue of whether or not to support Britain in World War I. At the time, people thought the war would be short and that Home Rule would soon be in place. However, the war lasted for four eventful years.

Go to pages 103–104 of your *Sources and Skills Book* for evidence tasks on the recruitment of Irish soldiers.

In this topic, you will learn about:
- The split in the Irish Volunteer Force
- Irish soldiers in World War I

▶ Army recruitment poster depicting John Redmond

| The Irish Volunteer Force split | |
| --- | --- |
| **National Volunteers** | **Irish Volunteers** |
| 175,000 agreed with Redmond and felt that supporting Britain would benefit Home Rule. | 11,000 disagreed and were led by Eoin MacNeill. They wanted to stay and make sure Home Rule happened. |

## The Irish soldiers of World War I

About **250,000** Irishmen fought on Britain's side in World War I, and between 30,000 and 50,000 died. Nationalists and Unionists fought on the same side, but for different reasons. Many Irishmen fought in World War I not only because of their political beliefs, but because times were hard at home and it was a good opportunity to earn money to send home to their families.

Nationalists joined **the 16th (Irish) Division**, which contained regiments such as the Irish Guards, the Royal Dublin Fusiliers and the Royal Munster Fusiliers. Unionists joined **the 36th (Ulster) Division**. Some of the battlefield engagements where Irish soldiers fought were **the Battles of the Somme** in France, **Passchendaele** in Belgium and **Gallipoli** in Turkey.

▲ The 16th (Irish) Division

**DID YOU KNOW?**

During Easter week of 1916 – while at home the Rising against British rule was underway, using German guns – the 16th (Irish) Division of the British army at Hulluch in northern France underwent several horrific German gas attacks. More Irish people died at Hulluch alone than in the Rising. Sadly, many Irish survivors of the war were made unwelcome at home in its aftermath. Ireland had changed in their absence.

## CHECKPOINT!

1. Why did (a) Unionist and (b) nationalist leaders encourage their supporters to fight in World War I?
2. Why did the IVF split?
3. What groups did it split into and what was the difference between them?
4. How many Irishmen fought in World War I?
5. Why did so many enlist to fight?

 I understand the effect that the outbreak of World War I had on Ireland.

 TIME TO GO BACK ◀ ▶ I CAN MOVE FORWARD ➡

**17 Ireland 1884–1914: Politics, Culture and Sport**

 **SUMMARY**

In this chapter, we have learned that:

- Irish nationalists at this time fell into two camps: constitutional nationalists (seeking change through peaceful politics) and radical nationalists (prepared to use violence for political change).
- Charles Stewart Parnell campaigned for tenants' rights and Home Rule and his party was immensely popular in the 1880s. However, the First (1886) Home Rule Bill failed during Parnell's time and the Second (1893) Home Rule Bill failed soon afterwards.
- The Gaelic League, the GAA and the Irish Literary Revival were at the forefront of cultural nationalism at this time.
- During this period, the GAA's ties to various nationalist groups were extremely close. The IRB sought new members within the local GAA clubs.
- In 1910 the important political groups in Ireland were the Irish Parliamentary Party, Sinn Féin, the IRB and the Unionist Party.
- The Parliament Act of 1911 meant that the House of Lords could only delay (not veto) laws. This Act made Home Rule possible.
- The Third Home Rule Bill was presented to the British government in 1912.
- Unionists responded to the Third Home Rule Bill by: holding demonstrations, founding the UVF, creating the Ulster Solemn League and Covenant and sourcing arms and ammunition.
- Nationalists reacted to this by founding the IVF and likewise buying arms and ammunition.
- Unionists supported Britain in World War I (1914–1918). Nationalists had mixed opinions, causing the IVF to split into the National Volunteers and the Irish Volunteers.
- About 250,000 Irishmen fought on Britain's side in World War I, and 30,000–50,000 died. Some Irish regiments were the Irish Guards, the Royal Dublin Fusiliers and the Royal Munster Fusiliers.

## Reflecting on... Ireland 1884–1914

The years 1884–1914 saw significant change in Ireland. Politically, the divisions that had existed on the island since the Plantations became sharper as the competing ideas of Home Rule and Unionism emerged. The formation of the armed UVF and IVF threatened to cause wide-scale violence between the communities.

In the meantime, a revival of uniquely Irish culture was taking place, as the Gaelic League tried to save the Irish language from decline, the GAA linked sports and nationalism across the island and the Irish Literary Revival looked to Ireland's past to encourage a sense of separate 'Irishness'.

The hardening of lines between the two communities would eventually see the island split in two and shape the twentieth century in Ireland.

 **Understanding History**

1. Why were the religions so unevenly distributed on the island of Ireland at this time?
2. What are the differences between a constitutional nationalist and a radical nationalist?
3. Explain what Home Rule would involve, referring to the First Home Rule Bill of 1886.
4. Give three reasons why cultural nationalism emerged.
5. How did the Irish Parliamentary Party/Home Rule Party and Sinn Féin differ in 1910?
6. What were the details of the Third Home Rule Bill?
7. How did the Third Home Rule Bill create a crisis?
8. Why was Home Rule not achieved in this period (1884–1914)?

**Exploring History**

1. Write a short paragraph on: the Home Rule Campaign; the Gaelic League; the Irish Literary Revival; and the GAA.
2. Write an account of the life and career of Charles Stewart Parnell.
3. Write a paragraph about the effect of World War I on Ireland.
4. Write an account of the life and career of Edward Carson.
5. Create a timeline of the events that happened during the Home Rule Crisis 1912–1914, with the Parliament Act of 1911 as your starting point.

**KEY TERMS**

|  |  |
|---|---|
| Irish nationalist | someone who believes that the Irish people are their own nation |
| Constitutional nationalists | wanted to see the re-establishment of a parliament in Ireland and wanted to achieve this through political means |
| Home Rule | Ireland would remain part of the United Kingdom but have its own parliament in Dublin to govern local affairs, while Westminster would control trade and foreign affairs |
| Radical nationalists | wanted full independence from Britain and believed that they should use force if necessary to achieve this |
| Republic | a country not ruled by a monarch, but instead ruled by its citizens, who choose their representatives |
| Unionist | someone who wants Ireland to remain part of the United Kingdom |
| Parliamentary obstruction | deliberate interference with the progress of legislation, for example by making very long speeches to delay the passage of laws through parliament |
| Political agitation | encouraging people to form local groups to demand better treatment, for example by refusing to pay rent or cooperate with local landlords |
| Cultural nationalism | focuses on promoting a national identity shaped by shared cultural traditions and language |
| Anglicisation | the spreading of English culture throughout Ireland |
| The Gaelic League | an organisation whose aim was to promote the Irish language |
| The Irish Literary Revival | a movement that aimed to promote Irish literature and coincided with a renewed interest in Gaelic Irish heritage |
| Parliamentary abstention | Irish MPs would withdraw from the Westminster parliament they entered in the 1801 Act of Union to set up their own parliament in Dublin |
| Paramilitary force | an unofficial military-style organisation of amateur soldiers |

 Go to page 99 of your *Sources and Skills Book* for more exercises.

 Go to page 48 of your *Research Portfolio* for a task based on this chapter.

**17 Ireland 1884–1914: Politics, Culture and Sport**

# 18 Ireland 1916–1923: The Struggle for Independence

## LO: 2.4

| Home Rule and Cultural Nationalism 1884–1914 | The Easter Rising and the Irish Civil War 1916–1923 | The Emergency in Ireland 1939–1945 |

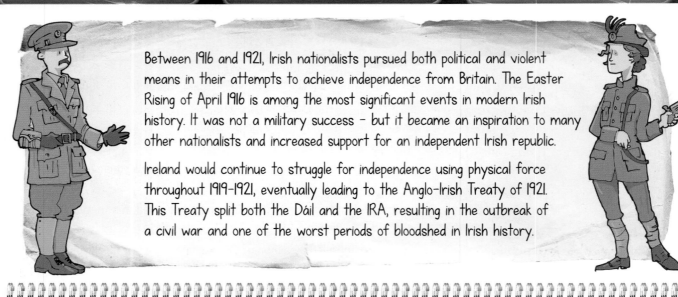

Between 1916 and 1921, Irish nationalists pursued both political and violent means in their attempts to achieve independence from Britain. The Easter Rising of April 1916 is among the most significant events in modern Irish history. It was not a military success – but it became an inspiration to many other nationalists and increased support for an independent Irish republic.

Ireland would continue to struggle for independence using physical force throughout 1919–1921, eventually leading to the Anglo-Irish Treaty of 1921. This Treaty split both the Dáil and the IRA, resulting in the outbreak of a civil war and one of the worst periods of bloodshed in Irish history.

# WORKING WITH THE EVIDENCE!

## The Struggle for Independence

| Type of source | Category | Example |
|---|---|---|
| Secondary | Written | A history book about the Easter Rising |
| Primary | Visual | A photograph of Cork city, burned by the Black and Tans |
| Primary | Written | A newspaper headline from the Irish Civil War |

◀ The Burning of Cork

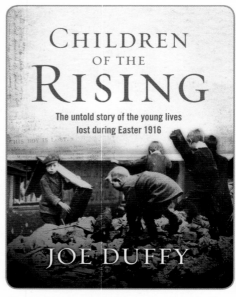

What information can we gather from these sources about Ireland's struggle for independence?

▲ Children of the Rising by Joe Duffy

## 18.1: Planning the Rising

In this topic, you will learn about:
- The plans for a rising
- The involvement of the Irish Volunteers
- How it went wrong

### Preparations

The **Irish Republican Brotherhood (IRB)** had infiltrated many organisations in Ireland, including the GAA, Sinn Féin and the IVF. Soon after the outbreak of World War I, the IRB leaders began to plan a rising. Home Rule had been put on hold and the IRB believed that **'Britain's difficulty was Ireland's opportunity'** – that Britain was distracted elsewhere and this would be the perfect time to strike.

The IRB formed a **secret Military Council** to organise the Rising. Its members included **Thomas Clarke**, **Seán Mac Diarmada**, **Pádraig Pearse**, **Joseph Plunkett**, **Éamonn Ceannt** and **Thomas McDonagh**. The council was secret due to the danger of infiltration by spies for the British government.

The Military Council needed weapons. Funds for these came largely from Irish-Americans. Joseph Plunkett and the Irishman and former British diplomat **Sir Roger Casement** used the money to buy arms and ammunition from Germany, Britain's enemy in World War I. It was decided that the Rising would begin on Easter Sunday, 23 April 1916 – not only because Easter was a holiday period, but also because Pearse believed in blood sacrifice: that they would give up their lives for the good of the future of Ireland. This was symbolically linked to Christ's sacrifice on the cross during Easter.

The council learned that **James Connolly**, the socialist leader of an organisation called **the Irish Citizen Army**, set up to protect workers during the **Strike and Lockout of 1913**, was also preparing for a rising. Connolly had co-founded **the Labour Party** in 1912. In January 1916, the Military Council convinced Connolly to join it in a rising.

▲ From top, left to right: Thomas Clarke; Seán Mac Diarmada; Pádraig Pearse; Joseph Plunkett; Éamonn Ceannt; Thomas McDonagh

▲ Roger Casement      ▲ James Connolly

18

Ireland 1916–1923: The Struggle for Independence

## The involvement of the Irish Volunteers

**Eoin MacNeill** and most of the Irish Volunteers, who had no idea of the planned Rising, continued to drill and parade as normal. MacNeill was not a member of the IRB and had been opposed to the idea of a rebellion. He believed that the Irish Volunteers could only justify fighting if they were first attacked by the British government. The Military Council knew that for the Easter Rising to be a success, they would need MacNeill and the Irish Volunteers. They showed MacNeill a forged document stating that the British government planned to disarm the Irish Volunteers. The document was on Dublin Castle paper, so it became known as **the Castle Document**. MacNeill gave the Irish Volunteers permission to take part in the Easter Rising.

▲ The *Aud*

## The plans go wrong

The Easter Rising was planned as a nationwide rebellion. Arms and ammunition were to land in Co. Kerry with **Roger Casement** on board **the Aud** and be distributed to Irish Volunteer groups throughout the country. However, the plans soon began to go wrong.

The *Aud* was captured by the British navy in Tralee Bay on the Friday before Easter. It was sunk by its captain and all 20,000 rifles were lost. Casement, who had been travelling in a German submarine, was captured. Eoin MacNeill found out that the Castle Document was a **forgery**. He cancelled the participation of the Irish Volunteers by placing a notice in the *Sunday Independent* newspaper.

Any chance of success was fading. However, the Military Council decided to go ahead with the Rising.

▶ Eoin MacNeill's cancellation notice in the *Sunday Independent*

**NO PARADES!**

**Irish Volunteer Marches Cancelled**

A SUDDEN ORDER.

The Easter manoeuvres of the Irish Volunteers, which were announced to begin to-day, and which were to have been taken part in by all the branches of the organisation in city and country, were unexpectedly cancelled last night.

The following is the announcement communicated to the Press last evening by the Staff of the Volunteers:—

April 22, 1916.

Owing to the very critical position, all orders given to Irish Volunteers for to-morrow, Easter Sunday, are hereby rescinded, and no parades, marches, or other movements of Irish Volunteers will take place. Each individual Volunteer will obey this order strictly in every particular.

EOIN MACNEILL,
Chief of Staff,
Irish Volunteers.

 **COLLABORATE:** Work together to research five facts about Roger Casement's career before the 1916 Rising.

## CHECKPOINT!

1. Explain the term blood sacrifice.
2. What was the role of the Military Council in planning the Rising?
3. What support from outside Ireland did the rebels get?
4. Describe the purpose of the Castle Document.
5. How did the plans for the Rising fall apart during Easter week?

✓ I can explain how the Easter Rising was planned and what went wrong.

 ← TIME TO GO BACK ◆ I CAN MOVE FORWARD →

# 18.2: The 1916 Easter Rising

In this topic, you will learn about:
- ❯ The course of the Rising
- ❯ Britain's response to the Rising
- ❯ Why the Rising failed

▲ Irish Volunteers inside the GPO, 1916

## The Rising goes ahead

The Military Council went ahead with the Rising on **Easter Monday, 24 April 1916**. Pearse felt that the British would not expect this after the loss of the *Aud*. As it was a bank holiday Monday, many British soldiers based in Dublin had the day off. Only Dublin Volunteers could be gathered on such short notice, so the Rising was now mainly confined to the capital. By now the rebels knew it would be a military failure, but hoped that their blood sacrifice would inspire people.

On Easter Monday morning, about 1,500 Volunteers and members of the Irish Citizen Army marched from Liberty Hall to various city centre buildings. The buildings they occupied included the **General Post Office (GPO)**, **Jacobs Factory**, **Boland's Mill**, **the Four Courts**, **the South Dublin Union**, **the Mendicity Institution**, **St Stephen's Green** and **the Royal College of Surgeons**. Pearse and Connolly occupied the GPO and made it the headquarters of the Rising. Outside the GPO, Pearse read **the Proclamation of the Irish Republic** aloud – announcing that they were setting up a provisional (temporary) government replacing Britain's control in Ireland. At the time, many people walking by did not grasp the importance of this event; some even thought that it was a play.

**COLLABORATE: In your** group, research some other places in Ireland where the Rising also went ahead, for example Co. Galway, Co. Meath and Co. Wexford.

**DID YOU KNOW?**

About 30 original copies of the Proclamation still exist: one can be viewed in the National Print Museum in Dublin.

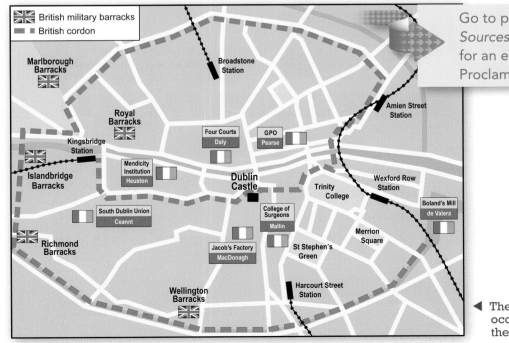

Go to page 109 of your *Sources and Skills Book* for an evidence task on the Proclamation.

Map key:
- 🇬🇧 British military barracks
- British cordon

Marlborough Barracks
Broadstone Station
Amien Street Station
Royal Barracks
Kingsbridge Station
Four Courts — Daly
GPO — Pearse
Mendicity Institution — Heuston
Islandbridge Barracks
Dublin Castle
Trinity College
Wexford Row Station
Boland's Mill — de Valera
South Dublin Union — Ceannt
College of Surgeons — Mallin
Merrion Square
Richmond Barracks
Jacob's Factory — MacDonagh
St Stephen's Green
Harcourt Street Station
Wellington Barracks

◀ The Rising in Dublin: occupied locations and the leader at each

**18** Ireland 1916–1923: The Struggle for Independence

# Britain's response

The British government was indeed taken by surprise. Only 400 British soldiers were on duty that Easter Monday. However, **extra soldiers** were quickly brought in from **the Curragh barracks** in Co. Kildare and from England **through ports such as Dún Laoghaire**. By Tuesday evening, British soldiers outnumbered the rebels by 5,000. On Wednesday, the gunboat the **Helga** was brought up the Liffey and shelled the GPO.

As the week went on, the British gained control, with **pockets of rebels surrounded** within buildings and spaces such as St Stephen's Green. At **Mount Street Bridge** on Wednesday, however, 13 rebels in several positions held up some 1,750 soldiers for hours, killing or wounding 231 before being overwhelmed.

By Friday, it was clear that the rebels had been defeated. The city centre was in ruins, the rebels were surrounded and looting was occurring all over the city. Civilian casualties were very high – 54% of total deaths were civilians, while just 16% were rebels. **Pearse surrendered unconditionally** on Saturday. A nurse named **Elizabeth O'Farrell**, who had tended to the injured inside the GPO, went as messenger to the British general. News of the surrender spread and the Rising was over everywhere by Monday 1 May 1916.

| Why the Rising failed |
|---|
| Lack of weapons and ammunition |
| Small number of Irish fighters |
| Confusion leading up to the Rising |
| Britain had greater numbers of soldiers and better weapons |
| The rebels based themselves in areas that could be easily surrounded |
| Many civilians did not realise the significance of the events until afterwards |
| It was not the countrywide rebellion that was intended |

Visit **www.educateplus. ie/resources/artefact** for a video on a historical repository on the Easter Rising at the GPO Witness History Exhibition

◀ View from the south side of O'Connell Bridge in the aftermath of shelling from the *Helga*

## CHECKPOINT!

1. Why was the decision taken to go ahead with the Rising?
2. Look at the map on page 253. What do you think the rebels were trying to achieve with the buildings they occupied? Look at their names and locations.
3. Who read the Proclamation of the Irish Republic outside the GPO?
4. Give two examples of the British response to the Rising.
5. Look at the table above on why the Rising failed. Which of these reasons do you think is the most significant? Explain your answer.

 I can describe how the Rising went ahead, how the British reacted and why the Rising failed.

 ◀ TIME TO GO BACK ◀ ▶ I CAN MOVE FORWARD ➔

# 18.3: The Consequences of the Easter Rising

In this topic, you will learn about:
❯ The consequences of the Easter Rising

▲ Taking up the Easter sacrifice symbolism, this poster declares the executed rebel leaders 'martyrs'

In military terms, the Easter Rising was a failure, but it set in motion events that led to the independence of most of the island from Britain.

- About **500** people were **killed** and about 2,500 were injured. Those lost included 300 civilians, 40 of whom were children.

- **Damage to buildings and property** throughout the city amounted to nearly €4 million in today's money. This initially angered Dublin citizens, who jeered the captured rebels as they were marched through the city.

- Almost **3,000 people were sent to British prisons**, such as **Frongoch** in Wales. These prisons were perfect places for revolutionary ideas to spread and were later called '**universities of republicanism**'.

- **Ninety leaders of the Rising were sentenced to death**. Between 3 and 12 May 1916, 15 rebels were shot in **Kilmainham Gaol**, Dublin, including all members of the Military Council. James Connolly was unable to stand due to severe injuries and so was shot while seated. The executions began to turn popular opinion in favour of the rebels, at home and abroad, and so they were halted. However, in London Roger Casement was hanged for treason on 3 August 1916.

- The newspapers at the time referred to **'the Sinn Féin Rising'** and so Sinn Féin's popularity surged. Sinn Féin were not officially involved in the 1916 Rising, however.

**DID YOU KNOW?**

About 250 women were involved in the Easter Rising. Most belonged to Cumann na mBan, the women's branch of the Irish Volunteers, and fought in Dublin. Some were members of James Connolly's Irish Citizen Army, including: Connolly's daughters, Ina and Nora; Constance Markievicz; and trade unionists Winifred Carney and Rosie Hackett. Dublin's newest bridge was named for Rosie Hackett in 2014.

## CHECKPOINT!

1. What damage was done by the Rising?
2. How did the British treat (a) the rebels and (b) their leaders after the Rising?
3. Why were the executions stopped?
4. Why do you think the executions changed public opinion?

 I can explain the consequences of the Easter Rising.

 ⬅ TIME TO GO BACK ◀ ▶ I CAN MOVE FORWARD ➡

18 Ireland 1916–1923: The Struggle for Independence

## A Life in Time: Pádraig Pearse (1879–1916)

### Early life

Pádraig Pearse was born to a family of stonemasons on Great Brunswick Street (now Pearse Street), Dublin on 10 November 1879. He was educated by the Christian Brothers at Westland Row and won a scholarship to the Royal University (University College Dublin), where he studied law.

### The Gaelic League and St Enda's school

From his youth, Pearse was very interested in Irish language and culture. He joined the Gaelic League in 1895, became editor of its paper, *An Claidheamh Soluis*, and later sat on its committee. He lectured in Irish at UCD. To advance his vision of a free Gaelic Ireland, Pearse set up a bilingual school for boys, St Enda's, in 1908. Pearse believed that the key to reviving the Irish language was education. In 1910, the school moved to Rathfarnham, where it now hosts the Pearse Museum.

> https://educateplus.ie/go/st-endas

### Role in the Irish Volunteer Force

At first Pearse supported Home Rule, but his outlook became more radical. He was elected to the Irish Volunteers' provisional committee in 1913 and later became its Director of Organisation. In July 1914, Pearse was involved in the **Howth gun-running**, and hid the stash at St Enda's. His graveside oration at the 1915 funeral of Fenian leader O'Donovan Rossa ended: 'Ireland unfree shall never be at peace'.

### The Easter Rising and Pearse's execution

As a founding member of the Irish Volunteers, a member of the Military Council and one of the signatories, Pearse read the Proclamation of the Irish Republic on the steps of the GPO. He was present in the GPO throughout the Rising as commander-in-chief of the Irish forces. On Saturday 29 April, he surrendered unconditionally on behalf of the rebels in order to prevent further civilian deaths. Pearse was executed on 3 May 1916 at Kilmainham Gaol, and was buried in quicklime at Arbour Hill. His younger brother William was executed the next day.

◄ The family shopfront on today's Pearse Street

## 18.4: Commemorating the Easter Rising

**In this topic, you will learn about:**

> Why we commemorate events such as the Easter Rising

The year 2016 was the **centenary** (100-year anniversary) of the Easter Rising. Many commemorative events were held throughout the year all around Ireland to remember the people and events connected with the Rising. A **commemoration** is <u>a ceremony in which a person or an event is remembered</u>. Although the Rising took place mostly in Dublin, communities elsewhere also marked the occasion, since men and women from their villages or towns took part in the Rising in Dublin and elsewhere.

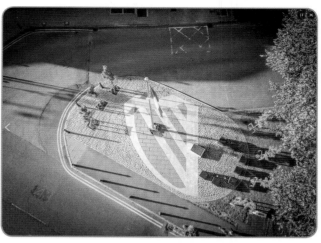

▲ 1916 memorial in Dunboyne, Co. Meath

When we commemorate, we remember **important events and people from our past that have helped to shape who we are today.** Commemorations can be controversial, especially when the events were violent or destructive, and above all when lives were lost. It is important to find the right tone when marking an event of this kind: it is not a celebration, but a respectful recognition that the event has a special meaning for us and our lives.

The Easter Rising is commemorated because the efforts of the rebels and the reaction of the British helped convince many more people to turn against British rule and seek full independence for Ireland. The Easter Rising came to be seen as the first stage in a long and difficult process which transformed Ireland, paving the way to our independence and all that has resulted from it over the past century.

▲ President Michael D. Higgins, laying a wreath at the Garden of Remembrance at the centenary of the Rising

### CHECKPOINT!

1. Explain the terms centenary and commemoration.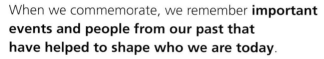
2. Why was the Rising commemorated in 2016?
3. Do you think there might be any downsides in commemorating 1916?

✓ I can explain why we commemorate events in our history, such as the Easter Rising. ⬅ TIME TO GO BACK ◀ ▶ I CAN MOVE FORWARD ➡

COLLABORATE: Work with your group to think of any other events that will be (or should be) commemorated in Ireland over the next few years. Discuss ways in which they could be commemorated.

**18 Ireland 1916–1923: The Struggle for Independence**

# 18.5: The Rise of Sinn Féin and the First Dáil

In this topic, you will learn about:
- ❯ The rise of Sinn Féin
- ❯ The 1918 General Election
- ❯ The first Dáil

## The rise of Sinn Féin

Sinn Féin's popularity rose after the Easter Rising for a number of reasons:

- Sinn Féin was given the recognition and **credit for the Easter Rising** in newspapers at the time. Many younger people became drawn to the party and felt that the Irish Parliamentary Party (IPP) was outdated.

- People were **angered by the executions** of the leaders of the Easter Rising. Many became convinced that **Home Rule would not be enough**, and so support for the IPP declined.

- Sinn Féin changed its aims in 1917. The new aim was to achieve '**the international recognition of Ireland as an independent Irish Republic**'.

- Sinn Féin began to win **by-elections** in 1917 and 1918, filling seats that were empty due to retirements and deaths during World War I. Elections had not been held since the outbreak of war. One example was in East Clare in 1917, when Éamon de Valera won the by-election to replace the IPP MP Willie Redmond (brother of John Redmond), who had been killed in World War I.

- **Éamon de Valera** took over from Arthur Griffith as Sinn Féin leader in 1917. De Valera was the only surviving commander from the Easter Rising and benefited from people's growing admiration for the rebels. De Valera also became the new President of the Irish Volunteers.

- In 1918, the British government planned to introduce conscription to Ireland. This became known as the **Conscription Crisis**. Conscription is when it is made compulsory for men aged 18 and over to join the military for a period of time. All Irish parties at the time were opposed to conscription, but Sinn Féin organised its opposition very well. When the British government dropped its plans, Sinn Féin received most of the credit for it.

- The **German Plot** was when members of Sinn Féin were arrested by the British government for allegedly plotting with Germany. There was no evidence to support this, which again increased Sinn Féin's popularity.

▲ A Sinn Féin by-election poster

▲ Éamon de Valera

## ANTI-CONSCRIPTION PLEDGE.

The following is a copy of the Pledge:—

"Denying the right of the British Government to enforce Compulsory Service in this Country *we pledge ourselves solemnly to one another to resist Conscription* by the most effective means at our disposal."

▲ An anti-conscription poster

## The 1918 General Election

A general election was held in December 1918, after the war ended. Of 105 seats in Ireland, Sinn Féin won 73 and the Unionist Party won 23, while the IPP won only 6. These election results made it clear that people no longer wanted a Home Rule parliament, but instead favoured a republic with complete independence from Britain. Sinn Féin decided to **abstain** from the parliament in Westminster and **to form a government in Dublin** instead, which they would all attend. From there they would work to achieve a republic. The Sinn Féin MPs called themselves **teachtaí dála (TDs)**.

## The First Dáil

Sinn Féin formed a government in Dublin, in **the Mansion House**, Dawson St, on **21 January 1919**. They named it **Dáil Éireann** ('meeting of Ireland'). At the first meeting, only 27 TDs were present because the remainder were in jail or on the run due to such events as the German Plot. The Irish Parliamentary Party and the Unionists refused to attend and continued attending Westminster. **Cathal Brugha** was chosen as president/leader of the Dáil, due to Griffith and de Valera being in jail. At its first meeting the Dáil issued a **Declaration of Independence**, saying that they would establish 'an Irish Republic and pledge ourselves and our people to make this declaration effective by every means at our command'.

At an April meeting, when more TDs were present after being released (or having escaped!) from jail, the new ministers were selected.

Éamon de Valera
President of the Dáil

Arthur Griffith
Minister for Home Affairs

Cathal Brugha
Minister for Defence

Michael Collins
Minister for Finance

Constance Markievicz
Minister for Labour

W.T. Cosgrave
Minister for Local Government

Eoin MacNeill
Minister for Industries

**18 Ireland 1916–1923: The Struggle for Independence**

◄ The First Dáil Éireann,
21 January 1919

The Sinn Féin government began to make changes in Ireland to try to establish control.

- They gained control of **local government**.
- They founded **Sinn Féin/Dáil courts** to deal with people's court cases and crimes.
- They organised **loans** to help run the new Dáil: Michael Collins raised **a loan from the general public** of over £300,000. De Valera went to the US to get recognition for the Dáil, and raised nearly $5 million from the supportive **Irish emigrant population**.

The Dáil was declared illegal by the British government in late 1919. The British parliament passed the **Government of Ireland Act 1920** in which there would be a Home Rule parliament in Ulster and one for the rest of Ireland, to try keep both Unionists and nationalists happy. Sinn Féin rejected this compromise and continued to demand independence for the whole island.

## CHECKPOINT!

1. Explain the terms conscription and TD. 📖❗
2. How did Sinn Féin become associated with the Rising?
3. What evidence is there that Sinn Féin became popular afterwards?
4. How did the proposed plan for conscription impact on Ireland?
5. Draw a pie chart to show the results of the 1918 General Election.
6. When did the First Dáil take place?
7. What does 'Dáil Éireann' mean? 📖❗
8. Name three ministers and give their positions in the First Dáil.
9. How was money to run the Dáil sourced?
10. How did the Dáil try to establish its control of the country?
11. What was the Government of Ireland Act?

✓ I can describe Sinn Féin's rise in popularity and the formation of the First Dáil.

◄ TIME TO GO BACK ▶ I CAN MOVE FORWARD ➡

 COLLABORATE: Work in a group to research the other ministers appointed to the First Dáil and write down two facts about each of them.

# 18.6: The War of Independence, 1919–1921

In this topic, you will learn about:

- ❯ How the War of Independence began
- ❯ The tactics of the IRA and the British forces
- ❯ The key events of the War of Independence
- ❯ The end of the War of Independence

## The outbreak of the War of Independence

The War of Independence began on **21 January 1919** – the very same day that the First Dáil met – when a **Royal Irish Constabulary** (RIC) patrol was ambushed in **Soloheadbeg in Co. Tipperary**. Two RIC constables were killed by the group of volunteers, led by **Dan Breen** and **Séan Treacy**. The ambush was not authorised by the Dáil.

Since the Rising, the Irish Volunteers had been infiltrated by members of the IRB. Many members of the First Dáil, including Michael Collins, belonged to the Volunteers and the IRB. At this point, the Irish Volunteers became known as the **Irish Republican Army** (IRA), as the Dáil had declared them the official army of the Irish Republic.

## The methods of the IRA

- The IRA used **guerrilla warfare** tactics against the British forces (mainly the RIC). **Guerrilla warfare** is <u>a tactic involving ambushes and hit-and-run methods</u>. RIC barracks were attacked and raided for their arms and ammunition.

- **Michael Collins**, as Director of Intelligence, organised an **intelligence network** of spies to gather information from a wide range of people such as secretaries, cleaners, policemen and even people working within Dublin Castle. He formed a Dublin group called **the Squad**, or sometimes the 'Twelve Apostles'. These were assassins whose job was to kill spies and British detectives. They received a salary for their work and were effective at preventing the British from gaining information.

- Local units called **flying columns** were set up as numbers in the IRA increased. They took part in large-scale ambushes, raided local police stations for arms and helped organise the IRA in rural areas. They were fed and sheltered by local people, which made them hard for the British to locate.

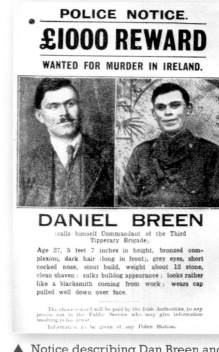

▲ Notice describing Dan Breen and offering a reward for information

▲ Michael Collins, 1916

## The methods of the British

- The British government under **David Lloyd George** needed to take action and bring in reinforcements to help the RIC. This led to the formation of the **Black and Tans** in the spring of 1920. They were made up of ex-British soldiers and named for the colours of their uniforms, a mix of army and RIC uniforms.

- Later, ex-army officers were recruited to help. They were known as the **Auxiliaries** and were ruthless. By the end of 1920 the British police force and army had grown to 40,000, compared to the IRA's 10,000.

- Terrible reprisals were carried out by the Black and Tans and the Auxiliaries. A **reprisal** was <u>an act of retaliation against local people in revenge for attacks on British organisations</u>. This only had the effect of increasing support for the IRA.

▲ Black and Tans search a suspected Sinn Féin member at gunpoint, November 1920

## Key events of the War of Independence

- 20 March 1920: British forces murdered the Lord Mayor of Cork, **Tomás MacCurtain**, who had led the Cork Volunteers in the Rising.

- 25 October 1920: **Terence MacSwiney** (Lord Mayor of Cork after Tomás MacCurtain) died in Brixton Prison, London after 74 days on hunger strike.

- 1 November 1920: **Kevin Barry** (18) was hanged for taking part in an ambush in Dublin in which a British soldier was killed.

- 21 November 1920: Collins's Squad killed 13 British intelligence agents in the dawn hours. In retaliation, the Auxiliaries entered Croke Park during a Dublin vs. Tipperary football match and opened fire on the crowd, killing 12 people, including Tipperary player Michael Hogan. This event became known as **Bloody Sunday.**

▲ Kevin Barry

cumann na gcleas lúit ngaedealac
(GAELIC ATHLETIC ASSOCIATION)

GREAT CHALLENGE MATCH
(FOOTBALL)

Tipperary v. Dublin

AT CROKE PARK

On SUNDAY, NOVEMBER 21, 1920

MATCH AT 2.45 P.M.

ADMISSION ∴ ∴ ∴ ∴ 1/-

◄ Match ticket for Bloody Sunday

- 28 November 1920: **Tom Barry** and the West Cork Brigade ambushed and killed 18 Auxiliaries in **Kilmichael, Co. Cork**. In retaliation, Auxiliaries burned Cork city centre.
- 25 May 1921: the IRA burned Dublin's **Custom House**. The fire lasted for five days and destroyed records going back for centuries. Eighty IRA men were killed or captured.

## The end of the War of Independence

Both the British and the Irish government recognised that peace was needed. The war was costing Britain £20 million a year, and the Irish were running out of arms and ammunition. The British government was also being criticised at home and abroad for the actions of the Black and Tans and the Auxiliaries against civilians. When de Valera returned from America he agreed to a truce with Lloyd George. The truce began on **11 July 1921**.

# CHECKPOINT!

1. When and how did the War of Independence begin?
2. Explain the term guerrilla warfare.
3. What methods did the IRA use during the War of Independence in (a) rural areas and (b) urban areas?
4. Who were the Black and Tans and the Auxiliaries?
5. What was a reprisal? Give an example from the War of Independence.
6. Why was a truce declared in July 1921?

✓ I can describe the main events and details of the War of Independence.

◀ TIME TO GO BACK ◀ ▶ I CAN MOVE FORWARD ▶

▼ Black and Tans observing Henry Street, Dublin, 1921

# 18.7: The Anglo-Irish Treaty, 1921

In this topic, you will learn about:

- The Treaty negotiations
- The terms of the Anglo-Irish Treaty
- The Dáil debates

## The Treaty negotiations

After the truce was agreed, negotiations began in London. Sinn Féin selected a delegation to represent Ireland in the negotiations. The Irish delegation included **Arthur Griffith**, **Michael Collins**, **Robert Barton**, **Éamonn Duggan** and **George Gavan Duffy**. **Erskine Childers** also went to London as a secretary. De Valera did not go, as he wanted information to be brought back to him before any decisions were officially made. He also wanted to be in Ireland to deal with groups like the IRA if needed.

▶ A British newspaper announces the signing of the Anglo-Irish Treaty

▲ The Irish delegation. Seated, from left: Arthur Griffith; E. J. Duggan; Michael Collins; Robert Barton. Standing, from left: Erskine Childers; George Gavan Duffy; John Chartres

The British delegation included **Lloyd George**, **Winston Churchill**, **Austin Chamberlain** and **Lord Birkenhead**. They were very experienced in politics and negotiation, having just negotiated the **Treaty of Versailles** at the end of World War I.

| The Irish delegation wanted: | The British delegation wanted: |
|---|---|
| a republic completely independent of Britain | to keep Ireland within the British Empire |
| no border/partition between north and south | to protect the Ulster Unionists |

The negotiations lasted for two months, from **October to December 1921**. It became obvious to the Irish delegation that a compromise with Britain was necessary. They were in regular contact with de Valera and the government at home, but were pressured by Lloyd George to accept a deal, with the threat of war if they refused.

De Valera had met with Lloyd George four times between the truce and the Treaty negotiations. Their discussions had covered most of what would eventually become the terms of the Treaty. Collins and Griffith felt at the time that de Valera had set them up, knowing that an unpopular compromise lay in store. They believed that Ireland could not continue fighting and had to accept the deal.

▲ David Lloyd George

Go to page 110 of your *Sources and Skills Book* for an evidence task on the negotiations.

## The terms of the Anglo-Irish Treaty

On **6 December 1921** the 'Treaty between Great Britain and Ireland' (the **Anglo-Irish Treaty**) was signed. The main terms were:

- Ireland would not be a republic but a **dominion**. A **dominion** is <u>a self-governing country within the British Empire</u>. It would have its own parliament but the British king would remain the head of state.
- Ireland would be called **the Irish Free State**.
- A governor-general would be the king's representative in the Free State.
- All TDs would have to take an **oath of allegiance to the British Crown**.
- Britain would keep three naval ports in Ireland – **Cobh, Berehaven and Lough Swilly**.
- Northern Ireland would continue to stay in Britain and have its own parliament, as decided in the Government of Ireland Act 1920.
- A **boundary commission** would be set up to decide a border between the north and south of Ireland.

## The Dáil debates

Public opinion on the Anglo-Irish Treaty was divided. While many were happy any agreement had been reached that would end the fighting, others saw the Anglo-Irish Treaty as a sell-out. The Dáil debated the Treaty from December 1921 until January 1922, splitting into pro- and anti-Treaty sides.

| The Pro-Treaty Side<br>Included Arthur Griffith, Michael Collins and W. T. Cosgrave | The Anti-Treaty Side<br>Included Éamon de Valera, Cathal Brugha and Austin Stack |
|---|---|
| **Main arguments:** | **Main arguments:** |
| <ul><li>They could not fund a war against Britain any longer.</li><li>The Treaty could be built on over time and was a stepping stone to full independence.</li><li>The Treaty was an improvement on Home Rule.</li><li>The Treaty guaranteed immediate peace with Britain.</li></ul> | <ul><li>They had not achieved the republic that they had fought for and died for.</li><li>They should have achieved better terms.</li><li>Irish TDs should not have to swear an oath of allegiance to the Crown.</li><li>The Treaty left Ireland partitioned.</li></ul> |

The Treaty debate in the Dáil ended on 7 January 1922 with a vote resulting in the Anglo-Irish Treaty being **accepted by 64 votes to 57**. De Valera resigned as President of the Dáil and left, along with his supporters. Arthur Griffith was elected President of the Dáil in his place. A provisional government was set up to put the Treaty in place.

### CHECKPOINT!

1. Who were the members of the Irish delegation? What important figure did not attend?
2. Who were the members of the British delegation? What advantage did they have over the Irish negotiators?
3. When was the Treaty signed?
4. What is a dominion? How was this more than Home Rule but less than a republic?
5. What were the other main terms of the Anglo-Irish Treaty?
6. What arguments were made by people who a) supported and b) opposed the Treaty?

 I can explain the terms of the Anglo-Irish Treaty 1921 and what happened during the Treaty negotiations.

 TIME TO GO BACK ◀ ▶ I CAN MOVE FORWARD

 Go to page 112 of your *Sources and Skills Book* for an evidence task on the oath of allegiance.

 COLLABORATE: With your group, write a speech either for or against the Treaty and deliver it to your class.

# 18.8: The Irish Civil War, 1922–1923

## The Pro-Treaty and Anti-Treaty divide

Sinn Féin had split down the middle over whether to accept the Anglo-Irish Treaty. A **provisional government** was set up and Arthur Griffith was elected President of the Dáil. The provisional government oversaw the withdrawal of British troops from Ireland and set up a new government.

In this topic, you will learn about:

❯ The pro-Treaty and anti-Treaty divide

❯ The outbreak of the Irish Civil War

▲ British troops leaving their barracks in Dublin

After the Dáil debates and vote, divisions between pro-Treaty and anti-Treaty sides deepened. Even families and friends were divided over the issue. As it had Sinn Féin, the Treaty also divided the IRA: IRA supporters of the Treaty became known as the **Irish Free State Army** or **Regulars** and the IRA members who were against the Treaty became known as **Irregulars**. Both sides began to take over the now-empty British barracks around the country.

In April 1922, **Irregulars led by Rory O'Connor** occupied **the Four Courts** and other buildings in Dublin in protest against the Dáil's acceptance of the Treaty. Michael Collins, now the commander-in-chief of the pro-Treaty **Free State Army**, was reluctant to attack his former colleagues and friends and wanted to hold off until the general election in June 1922.

Sinn Féin put forward both pro-Treaty and anti-Treaty candidates. The results (92 pro-Treaty candidates to 36 anti-Treaty candidates elected) clearly showed that a large majority of the people supported the Treaty. This put the government in a strong position.

| General election results, June 1922 | |
|---|---|
| Sinn Féin (Pro-Treaty) | 58 |
| Sinn Féin (Anti-Treaty) | 36 |
| The rest (including the Labour Party) Pro-Treaty | 34 |
| Total Pro-Treaty | 92 |
| Total Anti-Treaty | 36 |

## The fighting begins

In the same week, a leading British Unionist named **Henry Wilson** was assassinated and General O'Connell of the Free State Army was kidnapped. Collins was forced to act. On **28 June 1922**, Collins began to attack the Four Courts with artillery borrowed from Britain. The Civil War had officially begun.

Within two days, the Irregulars in the Four Courts had surrendered and within the week had yielded the other buildings in Dublin city. **Sixty-four people died in Dublin**, including Cathal Brugha. Rory O'Connor was captured and replaced by Liam Lynch as the Chief-of-Staff of the Irregulars. **De Valera condemned the government's actions** and supported the anti-Treaty side of the IRA.

The Irregulars retreated to Munster, where they had a lot of support. They had control of many of the old RIC barracks and used guerrilla warfare tactics against the Free State Army. South of the Limerick–Waterford line became known as the **Munster Republic**. A recruitment drive meant that the Free State Army grew to 60,000, greatly outnumbering the Irregulars. They drove them out of the barracks they had taken over. Cork fell to the Free State Army on 12 August. The Irregulars retreated to the countryside.

▲ The Free State Army shells the Four Courts, occupied by the Irregulars

▲ Destruction in Dublin during the Civil War

 COLLABORATE: Work together to research whether your local area has any connection to the Civil War and present your information to the class.

## CHECKPOINT!

1. How did the Treaty affect Sinn Féin?
2. Who were (a) the Regulars and (b) the Irregulars?
3. What were the results of the 1922 election? What did they mean?
4. What event sparked the fighting in the Civil War?
5. Describe the events in Dublin.
6. What was the Munster Republic?

 I can explain the divisions that followed the Anglo-Irish Treaty and describe the main events of the Civil War.

⬅ TIME TO GO BACK ◆ I CAN MOVE FORWARD ➡

# 18.9: The End of the Civil War

On 12 August 1922, Arthur Griffith died of a brain haemorrhage at just 51 years of age. He had founded Sinn Féin, was one of the chief negotiators with the British and had been instrumental in building the new Irish government. His death was a shock and a great loss.

Just ten days later, Collins was killed in an ambush in **Béal na Bláth** between Bandon and Cork city while inspecting the Free State Army. His body was transported to Dublin by ship. His funeral, on 28 August, was a huge public event, with up to half a million attendees. He was buried in Glasnevin cemetery, like Griffith.

Griffith and Collins were mourned deeply by members of both the pro-Treaty and anti-Treaty sides. Collins's death in particular had an effect on people who had once fought with him against the British. Some people, such as de Valera, believed that the bloodshed needed to end. After Collins's death, the Free State government took a harder line against the Irregulars.

**In this topic, you will learn about:**

- The deaths of Arthur Griffith and Michael Collins
- How the Civil War drew to an end
- The legacy of the Civil War

**DID YOU KNOW?**

Long before he became passionate about Irish independence, Erskine Childers fought for the British in South Africa (and wrote a famous spy novel). He used his yacht, the *Asgard*, to deliver guns to Howth in 1914, attended the Treaty negotiations in 1921 and was executed in 1922 for the possession of an unlicensed revolver given to him by Michael Collins. His son later became Ireland's fourth president.

▼ Crowds at Michael Collins's funeral

Go to page 112 of your *Sources and Skills Book* for an evidence task on the death of Collins.

**18 Ireland 1916–1923: The Struggle for Independence**

269

# A Life in Time: Michael Collins (1890–1922)

## Early life

Michael Collins was born at Woodfield near Clonakilty, Co. Cork, on 16 October 1890, the youngest of eight children. He was given the nickname 'the Big Fellow'. He was influenced by his father and his teachers, who taught him patriotic ballads and poems.

## Sinn Féin and IRB membership

Collins was a member of Sinn Féin and joined the IRB in 1909. In 1914 he became an Irish Volunteer and was the administrative assistant to Joseph Plunkett in the GPO, but did not take part in the fighting. After the Rising, Collins was a prisoner of war in Stafford Prison (England) and Frongoch Prison (Wales), where his qualities as a leader emerged within the 'universities of republicanism'. He was elected a Sinn Féin MP/TD in 1918.

## The War of Independence

As Director of Intelligence, Collins was a key figure during the War of Independence. He organised the Squad – the group of assassins who targeted British spies and detectives – and also had spy networks throughout the country.

## The Anglo-Irish Treaty

Collins was a member of the Irish delegation sent to negotiate with Britain after the War of Independence. Collins considered the Treaty no more than a step towards obtaining a 32-county republic – 'the freedom to achieve freedom' – and signed it with 'great reluctance'. He subsequently wrote: 'I tell you this – early this morning I signed my own death warrant'.

## The Civil War

In April 1922, a group of anti-Treaty IRA men took control of the Four Courts building in Dublin. Using artillery on loan from London, Collins's order to attack marked the beginning of civil war in Ireland. Collins took charge as commander-in-chief of the pro-Treaty, Free State army. His campaign was successful.

## The death of Collins

On 22 August 1922, Collins was killed in an ambush in Co. Cork. He lay in state for three days at City Hall before the funeral procession left for Glasnevin cemetery. The *Irish Independent* reported it as the 'greatest pageant of sorrow ever seen in Dublin: a cortège three miles long'.

For more about Michael Collins, visit the link below.

https://educateplus.ie/go/michael-collins

## The end of the Civil War

The president of the Dáil was now **W. T. Cosgrave**, and **Kevin O'Higgins** became Minister for Home Affairs (including law and order). In October 1922, the Free State government passed the **Special Powers Act**, which allowed its forces to arrest, try and imprison IRA members for a number of offences and even execute them. As a result, 12,000 Irregulars were arrested.

▲ W. T. Cosgrave

▲ Kevin O'Higgins

Fighting continued into 1923. Unlike the British during the War of Independence, the Free State Army had the advantage of knowing the countryside well. Liam Lynch was killed in April 1923. De Valera and the new Chief-of-Staff of the Irregulars, **Frank Aiken**, persuaded members of the IRA to agree to a ceasefire on 24 May 1923.

## The legacy of the Civil War

The Civil War was to have a lasting legacy for Ireland:

- **Death and damage to property**: Up to 1,500 people are thought to have been killed during the Civil War. Roughly €38 million of damage was caused to property. The centre of Dublin had to be rebuilt.

- **A divided country**: Families and friends had split across pro-Treaty and anti-Treaty lines, solidified by the Civil War and its atrocities. This created bitter, sometimes permanent, rifts.

- **Political developments after the Civil War**: W. T. Cosgrave and the pro-Treaty side renamed themselves **Cumann na nGaedheal** ('the Union of the Irish') early in 1923. A **constitution** was written for the Irish Free State (called 'Saorstát Éireann'). A parliament called the **Oireachtas**, made up of the Dáil and the Seanad, was set up, as were **an Garda Síochána** and a reorganised **courts system**.

- Under the **boundary commission**, the border between north and south was left unchanged, displeasing many.

- The two largest political parties in Ireland today have their roots in the Treaty politics of that time. Cumann na nGaedheal (later became **Fine Gael**) arose from the pro-Treaty side and **Fianna Fáil** was formed from the anti-Treaty side. Sinn Féin was no longer Ireland's main political party.

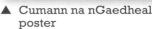
▲ Cumann na nGaedheal poster

▲ Fianna Fáil poster

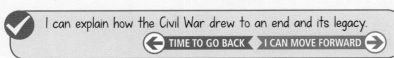

## CHECKPOINT!

1. How did the deaths of Griffith and Collins affect the Civil War?
2. Who replaced Arthur Griffith as president of the Dáil?
3. What was the Special Powers Act?
4. What was Cumann na nGaedheal? Name three of its achievements.
5. Why did the Civil War have a long legacy for Ireland?

✔ I can explain how the Civil War drew to an end and its legacy.
← TIME TO GO BACK ◆ I CAN MOVE FORWARD →

COLLABORATE: Work with your group to research the successes and failures of the Cumann na nGaedheal government.

# 18.10: Northern Ireland

In this topic, you will learn about:
- How Northern Ireland was established
- Sectarianism
- Gerrymandering

## The establishment of Northern Ireland

While nationalists in the south of Ireland were trying to achieve independence, northern Unionists wanted to remain in the United Kingdom.

The new state of Northern Ireland was set up under the Government of Ireland Act 1920. It had a form of Home Rule with its own parliament, later based at Stormont, Belfast. It was in control of internal affairs such as education and health care. This **separation of the north and south of Ireland into two different states** was called **partition**.

**James Craig** became Northern Ireland's first prime minister in 1920. The Unionists refused to join the Irish Free State in 1921. Northern Ireland sent 12 MPs to Westminster from 1920, while its Northern Ireland parliament was dominated by the Unionists. Nationalists in Northern Ireland, led by **Joseph Devlin**, would not take their seats for six years in protest against the new state. This left the Unionist Party without any opposition.

▲ James Craig

▲ Joseph Devlin

▼ Stormont

# Sectarianism

- Many Unionists were also members of **the Orange Order**. The Orange Order is an organisation dedicated to keeping Northern Ireland British. They did this by holding rallies and parades.

- A police force called the **Royal Ulster Constabulary (RUC)** was set up in Northern Ireland. It was made up mainly of Protestants.

- Other part-time forces, notably the **B-Specials**, were also mainly Protestant.

- These forces continued to be Protestant-dominated because they rapidly became associated with anti-Catholic bias and Catholics didn't want to join them.

- A combination of all the above led to sectarianism and sectarian violence. <u>Sectarianism is conflict and hatred based on a religious divide</u>.

▲ The Orange Order on parade in the 1920s

▲ The Royal Ulster Constabulary in the 1920s

# Gerrymandering

When local elections were held in Northern Ireland, each part of a city or town was divided into wards. The Unionist Party made sure that the boundaries for the divisions were drawn up specially to give Unionist candidates the advantage over nationalist candidates. This <u>rearrangement of voting districts to benefit one political party</u> is known as **gerrymandering**. For example, Derry had a largely Catholic population, but the Unionist Party still held the majority of council seats. Gerrymandering meant that throughout Northern Ireland, most councillors in the wards were Unionists. This resulted in discrimination against nationalists in regard to housing, jobs, schools, local facilities and more.

**DID YOU KNOW?**

The Orange Order holds a parade every year on 12 July to commemorate the victory of King William of Orange at the Battle of the Boyne in 1690.

---

## CHECKPOINT!

1. How was Northern Ireland established?
2. Name the first prime minister of Northern Ireland.
3. How did Unionists maintain their control of Northern Ireland?
4. Explain the term gerrymandering. 📖

✓ I can describe the establishment of Northern Ireland.

⬅ TIME TO GO BACK ◆ I CAN MOVE FORWARD ➡

---

 COLLABORATE: Work together to gather information about James Craig's life and career.

**18** Ireland 1916–1923: The Struggle for Independence

# SUMMARY

In this chapter, we have learned that:

- The 1916 Rising was organised by a secret military council while Britain was absorbed by World War I. The 'Castle Document' was forged to convince Eoin MacNeill to involve the Irish Volunteers.

- Arms from Germany were lost when the *Aud* was sunk while evading capture by the British navy.

- The Rising still went ahead, but in fewer locations, with fewer people and weapons than planned, and on Easter Monday instead of Sunday. It was based mainly in Dublin city centre.

- The British brought soldiers in from the Curragh and England and used a gunboat called the *Helga* to shell the GPO from the Liffey.

- Pádraig Pearse surrendered on behalf of the rebels: the Rising was over by Monday 1 May 1916.

- About 500 people were killed and about 2,500 injured, and buildings and property suffered heavy damage. Almost 3,000 people were sent to prisons in Britain, 90 leaders were sentenced to death, and 15 of these were shot between 3 and 12 May in Kilmainham Gaol.

- Sinn Féin rose in popularity and won 73 of 105 seats in the 1918 General Election.

- Sinn Féin abstained from attending Westminster and formed a Dublin government (Dáil Éireann) in the Mansion House, Dawson St, on 21 January 1919.

- The War of Independence began on 21 January 1919, with the ambush of an RIC unit in Tipperary. The Irish used guerrilla warfare, the Squad and flying columns. The British brought in the Black and Tans and the Auxiliaries. A truce was called on 11 July 1921.

- Negotiations began in London in October 1921. The Irish delegation was led by Arthur Griffith and Michael Collins, while the British delegation included David Lloyd George and Winston Churchill. On 6 December 1921 they signed the Anglo-Irish Treaty.

- The Dáil debated the Treaty from December 1921 until January 1922 and split into a pro-Treaty side and an anti-Treaty side. On 7 January 1922, the Treaty was accepted by 64 votes to 57.

- The IRA also split into pro-Treaty members (known as the Irish Free State Army, or Regulars) and anti-Treaty members (Irregulars).

- The Irish Civil War began on 28 June 1922 when Michael Collins shelled the Four Courts, then occupied by the Irregulars under Rory O'Connor.

- Arthur Griffith and Michael Collins both died in August 1922. They were mourned by members of both the pro-Treaty and anti-Treaty sides.

- W.T. Cosgrave became President of the Dáil and Kevin O'Higgins became Minister for Home Affairs, including law and order. The Public Safety Act allowed a sharp crackdown.

- The Civil War ended on 24 May 1923. It had caused many deaths and bitter local divisions, and would shape Irish political divisions into the future.

### Reflecting on... the Struggle for Independence

Nationalism and Unionism both continued their rise between 1914 and 1923, and had a huge impact on Irish life and politics. Nationalism went from the goal of Home Rule via the Easter Rising, a declaration of statehood and the War of Independence to Sinn Féin in the Dáil, showing the growth of nationalist ideas during this time. Unionists had a form of Home Rule as a result of the Government of Ireland Act 1920 and the Unionist Party remained in power in Northern Ireland.

- Northern Ireland was created in 1920 under the Government of Ireland Act. Its first prime minister was James Craig. The parliament was Unionist-dominated.

- Sectarianism and gerrymandering had serious effects on Catholics living in Northern Ireland.

## Understanding History

1. Do you believe the rebels were right to go ahead with the Rising? Why or why not?

2. How significant do you think the fighting at Mount Street Bridge was for the Irish?

3. Put the following Easter Rising events in the correct column/date: buildings occupied by rebels; arrival of the *Helga*; city in ruins; reading of the Proclamation by Pearse; surrender by Pearse; Mount Street Bridge; arrival of British soldiers.

| Monday 24 April | Tuesday 25 April | Wednesday 26 April | Thursday 27 April | Friday 28 April | Saturday 29 April |
|---|---|---|---|---|---|
| | | | | | |
| | | | | | |

4. How would you describe the long-term effect of the Easter Rising on Ireland?

5. Which events do you believe were the most important in the rise of Sinn Féin?

6. Why do you think the IRA was so successful during the War of Independence?

7. Create a timeline of the following events from the Struggle for Independence: the First Dáil; ambush in Soloheadbeg; Government of Ireland Act; 1918 General Election; War of Independence truce; Treaty debates; the Conscription Crisis; Bloody Sunday; the execution of Kevin Barry; the Treaty's acceptance in the Dáil.

8. Give two reasons why some people were against the Treaty and some people were for the Treaty. Which side would you have supported? Give a reason for your choice.

9. Give two reasons why the Civil War began.

10. Give two reasons why the Free State Army won the Civil War.

11. How did the Civil War come to an end?

12. How did gerrymandering impact on Catholics in Northern Ireland?

## Exploring History

1. Write a paragraph about each of the following: (a) the planning; (b) the course; (c) the consequences of the Rising.

2. Write an account of the life and career of Pádraig Pearse.

3. Write a paragraph about each of the following: (a) the rise of Sinn Féin; (b) the War of Independence; (c) the Treaty negotiations.

4. Write a paragraph about each of the following: (a) pro-Treaty and anti-Treaty divisions; (b) the main events of the Civil War; (c) the legacy of the Civil War.

5. Write an account of the life and career of Michael Collins.

6. Write an account of the establishment of Northern Ireland.

18 Ireland 1916–1923: The Struggle for Independence

**7.** Name five things the Treaty would give Ireland, according to this source. From your study of this topic, give two reasons why people would have disagreed with this poster.

# THE TREATY
## GIVES IRELAND

1. A PARLIAMENT RESPONSIBLE TO THE IRISH PEOPLE ALONE.
2. A GOVERNMENT RESPONSIBLE TO THAT PARLIAMENT.
3. DEMOCRATIC CONTROL OF ALL LEGISLATIVE AFFAIRS.
4. POWER TO MAKE LAWS FOR EVERY DEPARTMENT OF IRISH LIFE.
5. AN IRISH LEGAL SYSTEM CONTROLLED BY IRISHMEN.
6. AN IRISH ARMY.
7. AN IRISH POLICE FORCE.
8. COMPLETE FINANCIAL FREEDOM.

9. A NATIONAL FLAG.
10. FREEDOM OF OPINION.
11. COMPLETE CONTROL OF IRISH EDUCATION.
12. COMPLETE CONTROL OF HER LAND SYSTEMS.
13. POWER AND FREEDOM TO DEVELOP HER RESOURCES AND INDUSTRIES.
14. A DEMOCRATIC CONSTITUTION.
15. A STATE ORGANISATION TO EXPRESS THE MIND AND WILL OF THE NATION.
16. HER RIGHTFUL PLACE AS A NATION AMONG NATIONS.

### DUBLIN CASTLE HAS FALLEN !
### BRITISH BUREAUCRACY IS IN THE DUST !
### IS THIS VICTORY OR DEFEAT ?

# SUPPORT THE TREATY

## KEY TERMS

| | | |
|---|---|---|
| **Blood sacrifice** | the rebels would give up their lives for the good of the future of Ireland |
| **Commemoration** | a ceremony in which a person or an event is remembered |
| **Conscription** | when it is made compulsory for men aged 18 and over to join the military for a period of time |
| **Guerrilla warfare** | a tactic involving ambushes and hit-and-run methods |
| **Reprisal** | an act of retaliation against local people in revenge for attacks on British organisations |
| **Dominion** | a self-governing country within the British Empire |
| **Regulars** | IRA supporters of the Treaty, also called the Free State Army |
| **Irregulars** | IRA members who were against the Treaty |
| **Partition** | separation of the north and south of Ireland into two different states |
| **Sectarianism** | conflict and hatred based on a religious divide |
| **Gerrymandering** | the rearrangement of voting districts to benefit one political party |

Go to page 105 of your *Sources and Skills Book* for more exercises.

Go to page 52–58 of your Portfolio to complete tasks based on this chapter.

**18 Ireland 1916–1923: The Struggle for Independence**

| The Struggle for Independence 1916–1923 | The Emergency in Ireland 1939–1945 | World War II 1939–1945 |

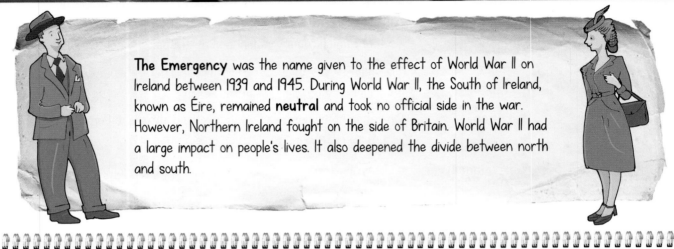

**The Emergency** was the name given to the effect of World War II on Ireland between 1939 and 1945. During World War II, the South of Ireland, known as Éire, remained **neutral** and took no official side in the war. However, Northern Ireland fought on the side of Britain. World War II had a large impact on people's lives. It also deepened the divide between north and south.

## WORKING WITH THE EVIDENCE!

### The Emergency

| Type of source | Category | Example |
|---|---|---|
| Primary | Visual | Clery's advertisement for clothing and furnishings during the Emergency |
| Primary | Written | De Valera's speech on neutrality, from Dáil records |

▲ Clery's advertisement in the *Irish Times* on 3 December 1942

'Over 20 years ago another peril brought the country to one magnificent unity. The leaders of all Parties, the Church and the people combined for a great and noble purpose – to save our young men from being forced into a war against the nation's will. Can I not ask for the same unity to-day to resist being brought into a war in which our State has declared its desire and its intention not to be involved? There is but one line of safety for us, to be ready to resist to the utmost whosoever may attack us.'

▲ Extract from de Valera's speech on neutrality

What information do these sources provide about the Emergency?

## 19.1: Ireland on the Eve of World War II

**In this topic, you will learn about:**
- ❯ Changes in Ireland before 1939
- ❯ Cumann na nGaedheal
- ❯ Fianna Fáil

### A change in government

Cumann na nGaedheal remained in power until 1932, having faced many challenges since the Civil War – not least restoring law and order after years of bitter conflict. They set up **an Garda Síochána** in 1925. They also began to modernise the country by building a **hydroelectric scheme at Ardnacrusha** on the River Shannon in 1929, founding the **ESB** (Electricity Supply Board). However, they had become increasingly unpopular for a number of reasons:

- The country was still heavily **reliant on agriculture** and had little industry.
- From 1929, the **economic Great Depression** was to affect the whole Western world severely for over a decade, increasing unemployment, poverty and emigration.
- The party had made **no progress in dismantling the terms** of the Anglo-Irish Treaty.
- It continued to introduce unpopular **Public Safety Acts** to support law and order.

**Fianna Fáil** was set up by Éamon de Valera in 1926 after he left Sinn Féin. Other Sinn Féin members such as Frank Aiken and Seán Lemass joined him. Fianna Fáil were highly organised and on the rise. Kevin O'Higgins was assassinated in 1927 and W.T. Cosgrave introduced **the Electoral Amendment Act**. This act stated that all elected TDs had to take the oath of allegiance or give up their seats in the Dáil. De Valera and Fianna Fáil decided to take the oath of allegiance.

| Fianna Fáil | 72 seats |
|---|---|
| Cumann na nGaedheal | 56 seats |
| Labour Party | 7 seats |
| Others | 18 seats |

▲ Results of the 1932 General Election

Cosgrave called an election in 1932 and with the help of Labour, Fianna Fáil entered into government.

▲ A 1932 election poster for Cumann na nGaedheal

MR. COSGRAVE WILL THINK MORE ABOUT THE UNEMPLOYED AFTER THE ELECTIONS— HE'LL BE ONE OF THEM.

▲ A 1932 election poster for Fianna Fáil

**19** Ireland during World War II: The Emergency

# Fianna Fáil in power (1932–1948)

By 1939 Fianna Fáil had achieved progress on several fronts:

- **Dismantling the Anglo-Irish Treaty**:
  - They removed the **oath of allegiance in 1933**: the **Statute of Westminster** allowed Commonwealth countries to pass laws without interference from Britain.
  - They sidelined the position of governor-general.
  - References to the British monarch were removed from the Irish Constitution in 1936.

- A new constitution, **Bunreacht na hÉireann**, was passed in 1937 and Douglas Hyde became the first President of Ireland. The constitution stated that:
  - the country was now to be called Éire or Ireland; Irish was the official language; the head of the country was to be a President; the prime minister was to be called the Taoiseach; and it claimed **the right to assert control over the island of Ireland**.

- De Valera decided to stop paying Britain **land annuities** – the <u>repayments of loans given to Irish farmers by Britain to buy their farms</u>. In response, Britain placed a tariff (tax) of 20% on all Irish agricultural goods. This caused great hardship for Irish farmers, as 83% of their exports went to Britain. De Valera retaliated by putting a 5% tariff on British goods entering Ireland. This was known as **the Economic War**. It lasted from 1932 to 1938 and ended with the signing of the Anglo-Irish Agreement, resulting in:
  - The land annuities being abolished; the Irish government paid a once-only fee of £10 million.
  - Tariffs were reduced.
  - The Treaty ports of **Cobh**, **Lough Swilly** and **Berehaven** were returned to Ireland.

- **Welfare payments** were introduced for widows and orphans in 1933 and unemployment assistance was introduced in 1935.

- **Ten thousand more houses** were built than during Cumann na nGaedheal's government.

- The **IRA was banned** in 1936 and 500 members were imprisoned in 1939 after they began bombing Britain.

## CHECKPOINT!

1. Why had Cumann na nGaedheal become less popular? Give three reasons.
2. Who founded Fianna Fáil? Why did he do this?
3. How did Fianna Fail dismantle the Anglo-Irish Treaty?
4. What changes did Fianna Fail introduce into Ireland?
5. Explain the term land annuities.

I can describe the changes that had happened in Ireland by 1939.

TIME TO GO BACK | I CAN MOVE FORWARD

COLLABORATE: Work together to list all the Presidents of Ireland and research one fact about each.

# 19.2: Neutrality and the Emergency Powers Act

In this topic, you will learn about:
❯ Ireland's neutrality in World War II
❯ The Emergency Powers Act

## Ireland's neutrality in World War II

World War II broke out in September 1939. Ireland declared itself to be a neutral country. **Neutrality** involves **not fighting in a war and not supporting either side**. Ireland was neutral because:

- Ireland wanted to continue to show its independence from Britain.
- Ireland was ill-prepared to fight in a war.
- Ireland's economy was weak and would be further damaged by war.
- Staying out of World War II was a popular decision with all political parties.

However, while Ireland was officially neutral, the government did favour the **Allies – Britain, France and the United States**. This can be seen in the fact that:

- Ireland allowed Allied planes to fly over Donegal from Northern Ireland.
- German airmen were imprisoned if caught, while British and Americans were allowed to 'escape' over the border.
- Irish fire brigades went to Belfast to help with the destruction after German bombings.
- Around 50,000 Irishmen joined the British army.

## The Emergency Powers Act

This period in Ireland was named 'the Emergency' after a law called the **Emergency Powers Act** passed by the government in 1939. Under it, the government could go to great lengths to ensure that Ireland stayed neutral. Newspapers were strictly censored: they could not share any news that might show a bias towards any side. Plays, poetry and books were also **censored**. Even people's post could be opened and examined if the government felt the need to do so.

▲ 'Éire' cut into the Irish coastline so that German bombers would not mistake it for Britain

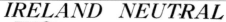

**IRELAND NEUTRAL**

**Oireachtas Is Unanimous For Emergency Measures**

**GERMANY'S NEUTRALITY ATTITUDE TO IRELAND**

**MINISTERS TAKE OVER NEW DUTIES**

▲ Newspaper report stating Ireland's neutrality

---

## CHECKPOINT!

1. Explain the term neutrality. 📖
2. Why did Ireland stay neutral during World War II?
3. What evidence is there that Ireland favoured the Allied side?
4. What changes were introduced by the Emergency Powers Act 1939?
5. Why do you think that strict censorship was introduced during World War II in Ireland?

 I can explain Ireland's neutrality in World War II and the Emergency Powers Act. ⬅ TIME TO GO BACK ◆ I CAN MOVE FORWARD ➡

**DID YOU KNOW?**

Winston Churchill suggested to de Valera that a united Ireland might come about in return for Ireland's support in World War II.

 COLLABORATE: Research which other countries were neutral during World War II and what their reasons were for this.

 Go to page 116 of your *Sources and Skills Book* for an evidence task on the Emergency.

# 19.3: Life in Éire during the Emergency

> **In this topic, you will learn about:**
> ❯ Life in Éire during World War II
> ❯ Shortages and rationing
> ❯ Fuel and the glimmer men

## Shortages and rationing

Ireland relied on imports of food, fuel and other items. This was a problem during World War II as German submarines were stopping British ships bringing supplies to and from Britain, affecting imports and exports to Ireland. **Seán Lemass** was appointed **Minister for Supplies** during the war. He had to make sure Ireland had enough essentials to keep functioning in wartime. To achieve this he needed supplies, and so he set up the **Irish Shipping Company** to transport goods to Ireland in 15 cargo ships. Fuel and some foods remained in short supply, however. Lemass also introduced the **Compulsory Tillage Scheme**, which meant that all farmers had to till a certain amount of land and sow a certain acreage of wheat.

> **DID YOU KNOW?**
>
> Ireland was bombed by the Germans during World War II, probably by accident. Bombs were dropped in Campile, Co. Wexford, killing 3 people, and also on the North Strand in Dublin, killing 28 people.

Rationing of food, clothes, footwear and so forth was introduced due to the shortages. People were given ration books, which contained coupons that could be exchanged for goods in shops. This method of **rationing** limited the goods people could buy to a fixed amount. Tea, flour, butter, sugar and other essentials were hard to get. People dried out and reused their tea leaves.

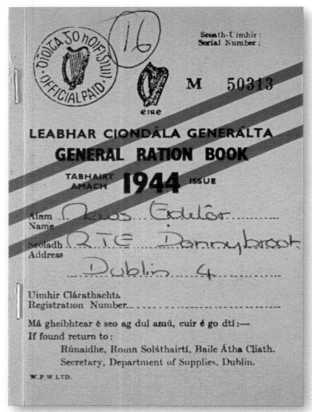

▲ A ration book

▲ Seán Lemass

## Fuel shortages and the glimmer men

Electricity and gas were in short supply and had to be rationed. Government inspectors called glimmer men called to houses in towns and cities to check that people were not overusing their gas supplies. If you were using more than your allowed amount, you could be cut off or prosecuted in the courts.

Petrol was extremely limited, and was only really used by doctors and priests. Ireland had imported a lot of its coal from Britain, and this was hard to do during the war. Turf replaced coal as a fuel. The army was put to work cutting **turf** from the bogs around Ireland.

▲ Turf-cutting in the Emergency

Trains had to run on turf and took longer to get to their destinations as a result. Irish industry was greatly affected by the fuel shortages. Factories had to lay off workers, so emigration from Ireland increased. People moved to Britain to work in the busy factories there. Agriculture was also affected by a lack of products such as fertilisers and animal feeds.

# CHECKPOINT!

1. Explain the terms rationing and glimmer man.
2. What role did Seán Lemass play during the Emergency?
3. What was the purpose of the Irish Shipping Company?
4. How were people's lives affected by (a) rationing of food and (b) shortages of fuel?

✔ I can describe what life was like in Ireland/Éire during the Emergency.

◀ TIME TO GO BACK ❯ ❯ I CAN MOVE FORWARD ▶

▼ The aftermath of the North Strand Bombing

**19 Ireland during World War II: The Emergency**

# WORKING WITH THE EVIDENCE!

## A 1944 Ration Book

iv

### YOUR RATION BOOK.

**Types of Ration Books.**—Two main types of General Ration Books are being issued. The ordinary General Ration Book is for use by all persons except the Heads of Households. General Ration Books with diagonal red bars on the covers are provided for the Heads of Households. The coupons in both books (pages 1 to 47) are similar. The only point of difference is that Householder's Folders (pages 49 to 51) are included in the General Ration Books issued to Heads of Households. This folder is provided for commodities which may be rationed on a household instead of on an individual basis.

**Have you got the right Ration Book ?**—You should examine your ration book when you receive it to make sure that you have got the right one. If you are not the Head of a Household and have received a ration book with Householder's Counterfoils (pages 49 to 51), you should cut out the folder immediately along the line indicated on left-hand margin on page 49. You should then insert (in block letters) on the folder your name, full address and post the folder to the Department of Supplies, Ballsbridge, Dublin.

If you are the Head of a Household and you receive a ration book not containing Householder's Folder (pages 49 to 51), you should write immediately to the Department of Supplies, Ballsbridge, Dublin, for the folder, giving (in block letters) your name, full address and the registration number on the front of your ration book.

**Head of Household.**—For rationing purposes, the Head of a Household means a person who holds or occupies a house, or part of a house, whether separately valued or not, as his or her own dwelling and that of his or her household, including family, servants and guests (including paying guests and boarders).

The Head of a Household is not normally regarded as including any person residing in a ship, vessel, boat, hotel, club, hostel, boarding school, residential educational establishment, religious institution, county home, public or private hospital, convalescent or nursing home, mental hospital, institutions for the blind, deaf and dumb or other residential charitable institutions,

v

prison, industrial and reformatory school, lock-up or other place of detention, military barracks, garda station, or any establishment or institution similar to those mentioned.

**Changes in household.**—Where the Head of a Household dies or leaves the household the Householder's Folder in his or her ration book should be cut out and used by the person who succeeds him or her as Head of the Household. Where in any case the household breaks up, the Householder's Folder should be returned to the Department of Supplies, Ballsbridge, Dublin, enclosing, at the same time, name, full address (in block letters) and registration number on front of ration book.

**New Households.**—Where a new household is set up, e.g., on marriage, the Head of the Household should apply to the Department of Supplies, Ballsbridge, Dublin, for Householder's Counterfoils, giving (in block letters) his or her name, full address and the registration number on the front cover of his or her ration book and a statement as to the circumstances in which the application is being made.

### How to Use Coupons.

**Sugar, Tea and Butter.**—You must register with a shopkeeper in order to draw your rations of sugar ; registration is necessary also to obtain rations of tea and butter. To register you should enter your name and address and the date on the appropriate page of coupons in the space indicated. Bring or send the ration book to the shopkeeper. The shopkeeper will cut out the page of coupons and he should insert the date, the number of the page detached and sign his name and insert his address on the first vacant line on the inside of the cover (front or back) of the ration book. Directions will be given by the Department of Supplies in the public Press from time to time as to the appropriate pages of coupons to be used in drawing sugar, tea and butter rations.

**Soap.**—Every time you purchase soap you should hand your ration book to the shopkeeper to enable him to cut out the appropriate coupon.

**Clothing.**—When you go into a shop to buy any rationed article of yarn, cloth or clothing (or footwear) you should hand your ration book to the shopkeeper to enable him to cut out the appropriate coupons. When ordering goods by post, do not send your ration book. Cut coupons out, sign your name, address and registration No. clearly on the back and then send the coupons with your order.

1. What type of source is this?

2. According to the source, where was the Department of Supplies based?

3. How is the head of a household defined?

4. What should happen to the ration book if the head of the household dies?

5. What food items are mentioned in the source?

6. What should you do if buying soap or clothing?

7. Give two benefits of a source such as this for historians.

## A Life in Time: Éamon de Valera (1882–1975)

### Early life

Éamon de Valera was born in Manhattan, New York on 14 October 1882 to a Spanish father and an Irish mother. He was sent to live with his grandmother in Limerick at the age of two after his father died. He attended school in Blackrock College, Co. Dublin from the age of 16. He graduated in 1904 with a mathematical degree from UCD and went to teach at Belvedere College.

### Role in Ireland's struggle for independence

De Valera joined the Gaelic League in 1908 and the Irish Volunteers in 1913, having been sworn into the IRB by Thomas MacDonagh. During the 1916 Rising, he commanded the garrison at Boland's Mills. He was sentenced to death, but this was changed to life in prison and he was released in June 1917. It is uncertain whether this was because of his American citizenship, or because the change in public opinion had alarmed the British. From June 1919 to December 1920, de Valera raised $6 million from Irish-Americans to support an Irish government. He returned to Ireland towards the end of the War of Independence.

### Sinn Féin

De Valera accepted British proposals for a truce in July 1921 and sent a delegation to London to negotiate a peace settlement. He was president of Sinn Féin from 1917 to 1926. He opposed the Anglo-Irish Treaty and resigned when the Dáil passed it. Sinn Féin split as a result.

### Fianna Fáil

De Valera left Sinn Fein to found Fianna Fáil in 1926. In 1932 they won the general election and were in power for 16 years. The 1937 Constitution, *Bunreacht na hÉireann*, was mainly de Valera's work. While in power, de Valera dismantled the Anglo-Irish Treaty. He declared a state of emergency in 1939 and kept Ireland neutral during World War II. He was Taoiseach from 1937 to 1948, again from 1951 to 1954, and finally from 1957 to 1959, when he was elected President of Ireland.

### Later life

De Valera was President from 1959 to 1973. He died on 29 August 1975 and is buried in Glasnevin cemetery. His granddaughter Síle de Valera and grandson Éamon Ó Cuív have both served as TDs in recent years.

For more about Éamon de Valera, visit the links below.

> https://educateplus.ie/go/de-valera

> https://educateplus.ie/go/de-valera2

**19 Ireland during World War II: The Emergency**

# 19.4: Life in Northern Ireland during World War II

**In this topic, you will learn about:**
- Life in Northern Ireland during World War II
- Industry and agriculture
- Northern Ireland as a base for troops
- Attacks on Belfast

## Industry and agriculture

As part of the United Kingdom, Northern Ireland fought on Britain's side. Conscription was not compulsory, but **rationing** was. After World War I, Northern Irish industries had struggled, but from 1939 they boomed. Companies such as **Harland and Wolff** (a shipyard) and **Short Brothers** (an aircraft factory) played key roles in the war. Between 1939 and 1945, Belfast produced 140 warships, 123 merchant ships and 1,600 aircraft. Parachutes, ropes, uniforms, tanks and shells were produced in Northern Ireland. **Unemployment levels dropped** by 20% to only 5%.

Agriculture in Northern Ireland benefited from World War II as well. Prices were guaranteed for food on the British market. In 1941, over 17,000 gallons of milk were being exported to Britain every day. **Compulsory tillage farming** led to an increase in the acreage being used for growing flax, oats and potatoes. Even some golf courses were used for tillage farming.

## Northern Ireland as a base for troops

Planes and boats were based in Northern Ireland to **patrol the Atlantic** and search for German U-boats. They helped **protect supplies being transported** between the islands. Northern Ireland became an important **base for American troops** once they entered the war in December 1941. They were either protecting trade across the Atlantic or preparing for the Allied invasion of Normandy. Roads and ports had to be improved to cope with the added traffic of American troops – at one stage there were **120,000 American troops** based in Northern Ireland.

▲ An advertisement for Harland & Wolff during World War II

*Builders of* **WARSHIPS** *and* **MERCHANT VESSELS**

*Engineers*

*Shiprepairers*

**HARLAND & WOLFF**
LIMITED

▲ Short Brothers aircraft manufacturers during World War II

▲ American troops in Northern Ireland

## Attacks on Belfast

Due to the amount of industry in Belfast, it was one of the major target cities for the Germans. It was not well defended because the government thought it was too far away for the **German bombers (Luftwaffe)** to reach. Belfast city was bombed four times in April and May of 1941. This period was called the **Belfast Blitz**. Factories such as Harland and Wolff were seriously damaged, about 1,100 people were killed and over 56,000 homes were destroyed. Great numbers of people left the city to move to towns outside of Belfast, and some even took refuge south of the border.

▼ Aftermath of the Belfast Blitz

**DID YOU KNOW?**

During World War II the workforce of Harland and Wolff tripled to approximately 35,000 workers.

19 Ireland during World War II: The Emergency

## CHECKPOINT!

1. How did World War II affect (a) industry and (b) agriculture in Northern Ireland?
2. Why were American soldiers stationed in Northern Ireland?
3. Why was Belfast attacked by the Luftwaffe?
4. What impact did the bombing have on Belfast?

 I can describe what life was like in Northern Ireland during World War II.

 ← TIME TO GO BACK ◆ I CAN MOVE FORWARD →

 COLLABORATE: Work in groups to gather information about the Harland and Wolff shipyard and the Short Brothers factory during World War II.

# 19.5: Post-war Divide between North and South

## North and south move further apart

The experience of World War II for Northern Ireland was completely different to that of the rest of the island.

- The south did not suffer **heavy bombing and huge loss of life**, as the north had.

- The **economy** in the south suffered during the war, whereas the economy in Northern Ireland improved. Only several years after the war was over could rationing be ended in the south.

- The contribution of Northern Ireland to the war effort meant that its **ties to Britain became even stronger**.

- The fact that Éire had stayed neutral created a bigger gap between north and south. It demonstrated the South's independence, but **damaged relations** between Éire and Britain/Northern Ireland.

- It took years for the south's **trade links** to return to normal.

- When Franklin D. Roosevelt died on 12 April 1945, de Valera expressed his **condolences**. However, he did the same to the German people **when Hitler died** on 30 April. This action was **criticised by many** as it appeared that de Valera (and Ireland) did not recognise the horrors that had been committed by Hitler and the Nazis.

In this topic, you will learn about:

❯ How World War II widened the north–south divide

▲ Memorial to Irish merchant seamen near Dublin's docks

### DID YOU KNOW?

Over 150 Irish merchant seamen died during World War II transporting supplies to and from Ireland. Éamon de Valera, in his speech to the nation in 1945, said: 'To the men of our mercantile marine who faced all the perils of the ocean to bring us essential supplies, the nation is profoundly grateful'.

## CHECKPOINT!

1. How did World War II affect the economies of Ireland, north and south?

2. Why do you think the link between Northern Ireland and Britain was strengthened by the war?

3. Why did the war push the two parts of Ireland further apart?

4. How do you think the war impacted on relations between Ireland and Britain? Give reasons for your answer.

 I can explain how a bigger division was created between north and south as a result of World War II.

⟵ TIME TO GO BACK ◀ ▶ I CAN MOVE FORWARD ⟶

 **SUMMARY**

In this chapter, we have learned that:

- Cumann na nGaedheal were in government until 1932. They had become increasingly unpopular. Fianna Fáil and Labour formed the new government in 1932. Fianna Fáil began to dismantle the Anglo-Irish Treaty. The Irish Free State became Éire/Ireland.

- Ireland declared itself neutral when World War II broke out. The government created the Emergency Powers Act in 1939, which meant they were able to go to great lengths to ensure that Ireland stayed neutral, for instance, through censorship.

- Many items were in short supply in Ireland, which led to rationing. The Irish Shipping Company was set up to bring supplies to and from Ireland. Inspectors called glimmer men were employed to check people's fuel usage. Irish turf was used instead of imported coal.

- Northern Ireland's industry and agriculture improved during World War II. It was attacked by German bombers due to its factories in industrial areas such as Belfast, and was also used as a base for American troops.

- After the war, the divide between the north and south of Ireland was even wider than before. Northern Ireland's industries had grown and its relationship with Britain had become stronger.

> ### Reflecting on...
> ### Ireland in World War II: The Emergency
>
> World War II had a large impact on the lives of Irish people, north and south. The two parts of the island had very different experiences of World War II, with the relationship between Northern Ireland and Britain strengthening, and the independence of Ireland from Britain becoming clearer.

 **Understanding History**

1. Why did Fianna Fáil finally decide to take the oath of allegiance?
2. Why did Cosgrave call a general election in 1932?
3. What was the economic war? How was it resolved?
4. How did the government respond to the outbreak of World War II in 1939?
5. What measures were put in place to ensure that Ireland could survive the Emergency?
6. How were Irish relations with the (a) British and (b) Germans during the war?
7. Explain how the war widened the divide between the north and south of Ireland.
8. Explain how the war brought Britain and Northern Ireland closer together.

# Exploring History

1. Write a paragraph about each of the following:
   - why Cumann na nGaedheal lost popularity
   - the achievements made by Fianna Fáil by 1939.

2. Write an account of World War II in Éire.

3. Write an account of World War II in Northern Ireland.

4. Look at this cartoon, published by *Punch* magazine in 1940.

   (a) Describe what you see in the cartoon.

   (b) What image does this present of Ireland and its decision to stay neutral in World War II?

EAMON DEFYING THE LIGHTNING

| KEY TERMS | | |
|---|---|---|
| **Land annuities** | the repayments of loans given to Irish farmers by Britain to buy their farms |
| **Neutrality** | involves not fighting in a war and not supporting either side |
| **Rationing** | limiting the goods that people could buy to a fixed amount |
| **Glimmer men** | inspectors in towns and cities who checked that people were not using too much fuel |

Go to page 114 of your *Sources and Skills Book* for more exercises.

Go to page 59 of your *Research Portfolio* for a task based on this chapter.

| The Emergency 1939–1945 | Ireland in the 1960s | The Troubles 1969–1998 |
|---|---|---|

The 1960s was a decade of huge change for Ireland. It was a period of political change, as one generation of leaders handed over to another; economic change, as Ireland abandoned the policies of protectionism; and social change, with the coming of RTÉ, Vatican II and free education. It was the decade when the modern Irish state was born.

# WORKING WITH THE EVIDENCE!

## Ireland in the 1960s

| Type of source | Category | Example |
|---|---|---|
| Primary | Written | Newspapers, official records, diaries and speeches from the 1960s |
| Primary | Oral | Interviews with people who lived through this time of change, many of whom are still alive |
| Primary | Visual | RTÉ began broadcasting on New Year's Eve 1961 and is an invaluable record for events in Ireland from the 1960s onwards |

◀ Newspaper marking the 50th anniversary of the Rising

▶ An RTÉ studio during the 1960s

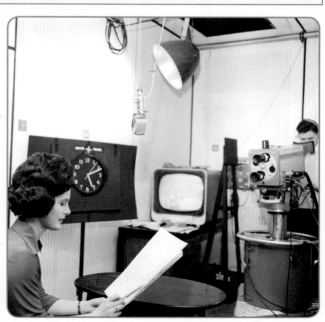

Why is the launch of RTÉ such an important event for historians? How did television change how we view the past?

# 20.1: The 1950s: Ireland's Lost Decade

**In this topic, you will learn about:** the problems Ireland faced in the 1950s:
- ❯ Economic
- ❯ Political
- ❯ Social

▲ A 1950s Irish company that is still in business today

## Economic crisis

In the years after World War II, Ireland faced many problems. Governments since the 1930s had followed **protectionism**. This meant that they used <u>high tariffs (charges) on goods coming into Ireland to protect Irish businesses from foreign competition</u>, so imported goods were very expensive. Also, because they were protected by the tariffs, Irish businesses were quite inefficient and badly run. There was little money available to invest in the economy. These things combined to create **high unemployment**.

## Social problems

As there were very few jobs available in Ireland, people **emigrated** from Ireland in large numbers – 44,000 per year in the 1950s. By 1961, the population had fallen to its lowest levels since the Famine. This led to **rural depopulation**, where <u>young people left rural areas to find work and increasingly only older people remained</u>.

▲ Elderly people in a 1950s Irish village

## Political instability

Ireland in the 1950s was still being led by men such as **Éamon de Valera** and **Richard Mulcahy**, who had fought in the War of Independence 30 years before. They continued to follow old ideas and ways of doing things. This problem was made worse by a series of weak governments in the late 1940s and 1950s. Elections were held in 1948, 1951 and 1954. After each election, a weak government of either Fianna Fáil or a coalition of parties was formed. This meant that no majority existed in the Dáil and the government was unable to act to tackle the problems Ireland faced.

### CHECKPOINT!

1. What is protectionism and what impact did it have on Ireland?
2. Give two examples of the political problems Ireland faced in the 1950s.
3. How many people were leaving Ireland every year in the 1950s?

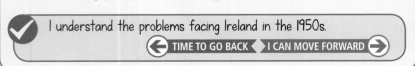

I understand the problems facing Ireland in the 1950s.

⬅ TIME TO GO BACK ❯ I CAN MOVE FORWARD ➡

▲ Éamon de Valera

# 20.2: Changes in Politics and the Economy

**In this topic, you will learn about:**
- The life of Seán Lemass
- Economic change in the 1960s
- New relations with Northern Ireland
- New openness to the world

## A Life in Time: Seán Lemass (1899–1971)

### Early life and career

Seán Lemass was born in Dublin in 1899. He fought in the 1916 Rising and the War of Independence. He was one of the founding members of Fianna Fáil in 1926. He served as **Minister for Industry and Commerce** and as **Minister for Supplies** during World War II. He became Taoiseach and leader of Fianna Fáil in 1959 after de Valera retired.

### Economic change

Lemass was convinced that radical changes in economic policy were needed to save the country. He worked with the Secretary-General of the Department of Finance, **T. K. Whitaker**, to produce and implement the **First Programme for Economic Expansion** in 1959. The main aims were:

▲ Seán Lemass

- **Free trade**: Ireland would reduce tariffs on imports to encourage trade and reduce prices.

- **Encourage foreign investment**: taxes were reduced on foreign companies that set up in Ireland and they were given grants to create jobs.

- **Grants to business and farmers**: £220 million was given to help them modernise so they could increase production and be more efficient.

The programme was a huge success. The economy grew at 4% per year during the 1960s – double its target. Unemployment had fallen by a third by 1961. Emigration fell from 44,000 a year to 16,000 a year in 1961 and to 11,000 a year by 1971.

### New relationship with Northern Ireland

▲ T. K. Whitaker

Since partition in 1921, the governments in Belfast and Dublin had had little contact. Lemass was determined to change this. While he continued to want a united Ireland, he thought the two parts of the island should be 'good neighbours'. In January 1965, he travelled to Belfast and met the Northern Irish Prime Minister, **Terence O'Neill**. O'Neill visited Dublin too. They agreed to cooperate on non-controversial matters such as tourism, education and agriculture. Trade increased between the two parts of the island.

Go to page 119 of your *Sources and Skills Book* for an evidence task on Ireland's economy.

## Opening Ireland to the world

Under Lemass's leadership, Ireland began to engage with the world much more. Ireland had joined the **United Nations** in 1955 but became more active in the 1960s and was even elected to the **UN Security Council** (its highest body) in 1962. Irish soldiers served in **UN peacekeeping missions** in the Congo, Cyprus and the Middle East.

▲ Irish UN peacekeepers

In 1961, Ireland applied to join the **European Economic Community (EEC)**, along with Britain. Lemass decided to do this because Britain was Ireland's biggest export market and he hoped to gain new markets for Irish goods in Europe and grow the economy. When France stopped the British application (they worried the British were too close to the US), Ireland withdrew its application. Ireland and Britain would eventually join the EEC in 1973.

Ireland's openness to the world was marked in June 1963, when the US President **John F. Kennedy** (the first Catholic President of the US) became the first foreign head of state to visit. His visit drew the **international spotlight** and let Ireland show the world how much it had changed in recent years.

▼ US President John F. Kennedy visiting Ireland

**DID YOU KNOW?**

President Kennedy often told his family how much he had enjoyed his visit to Ireland. When he was assassinated in November 1963, his wife Jacqueline requested that Irish army cadets be part of the burial service.

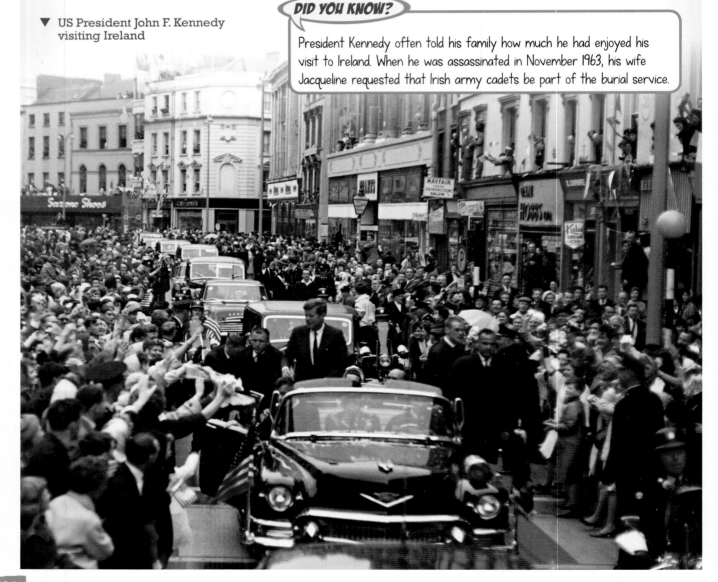

## Leadership change

Lemass led Fianna Fáil to victory in the 1961 and 1965 general elections. He appointed young TDs like **Charles Haughey**, **George Colley** and **Patrick Hillery** as government ministers. They would dominate Irish politics for the next 30 years. He presided over the **1966 50th anniversary celebrations of the Easter Rising**. Saying it was time for a new generation to take over, Lemass resigned at the end of 1966. He was succeeded by **Jack Lynch**, who, at 49, was the first Taoiseach of the generation to have grown up in an independent Ireland. Lemass died in 1971.

## ////// CHECKPOINT! //////

1. What were the main points of the First Programme for Economic Expansion?
2. Was it a success? Give reasons for your answer.
3. How did Lemass change relations with Northern Ireland?
4. In what way did Ireland become active in the United Nations?
5. Why did Ireland apply to join the EEC in 1961 and was this application successful?
6. Who succeeded Lemass as Taoiseach?

✓ I can explain the changes Seán Lemass introduced as Taoiseach.

 ← TIME TO GO BACK ◇ I CAN MOVE FORWARD →

 COLLABORATE: In your group, research the 1966 commemoration of the Easter Rising and answer these questions:

1. What events were organised to commemorate the 1916 Rising in 1966?
2. What message do you think the government was trying to send out about Ireland in 1966?
3. What impact did the 1966 commemoration have on Ireland, north and south?
4. How was 1916 commemorated in 2016?
5. What were the main differences between the 1966 and 2016 events?

▼ Cars undergo a final inspection at the Ford factory in Cork during the mid-1960s

# 20.3: Social Change in the 1960s

**In this topic, you will learn about:** how Irish society changed in the 1960s via:
- ❯ RTÉ
- ❯ The Catholic Church
- ❯ Education

## RTÉ

Until the 1960s, Ireland had no domestic television service. This was seen as another example of Ireland lagging behind the rest of the world. In 1960 the government passed the **Broadcasting Authority Act**, which set up an independent authority to run radio and television in Ireland. **Telefís Eireann** (later RTÉ) launched on 31 December 1961. By the 1970s, more than 50% of the homes in the country had a TV and most received only the one RTÉ channel. Television was key in changing Irish society over the following decades. It did so in the following ways:

▲ Gay Byrne on the set of *The Late Late Show* in 1966

- **Foreign influences**: People saw shows from the US and the UK and news from around the world. They could compare their lives to other people's and ask why Ireland was different.

- **Debating controversial topics**: Programmes like **The Late Late Show**, under **Gay Byrne**, regularly discussed topics like marriage breakdown, contraception, women's rights, religion, sex, homosexuality and the Traveller community, and over time helped to shift society's attitudes on these topics.

- **Challenging the powerful**: On RTÉ, people saw political leaders, senior Catholic bishops and other important people in authority being openly challenged for the first time and having to defend their actions and answer questions.

**DID YOU KNOW?**

The *Late Late Show*, which has been on air since 1962, is the longest running chat show in the world!

 COLLABORATE: Watch an episode of the RTÉ series *Reeling in the Years* on the 1960s on the RTÉ Player or YouTube. Write down:
- three things you learned about Ireland in that year.
- three things that surprised you about Ireland in that year.
- three things that are different about Irish life now.

Compare your list with others in your group and make a presentation to your class on your findings.

 Go to page 120 of your *Sources and Skills Book* for an evidence task on RTÉ.

# WORKING WITH THE EVIDENCE!

Read this account of RTÉ's early years by Gay Byrne in *RTÉ Off Camera: Images from the Early Years of RTÉ Television* (2004) and answer the questions.

> When we got television, admittedly only one-channel television, I recall the importance and significance that everybody seemed to attach to everything that appeared on the screen. It cannot be overstated … it was the home-made programmes that caused the real stir… New ideas and new terms flowed into every living room in the country. In rapid succession we learned about poverty and illiteracy and subjects that had been taboo and were not mentioned in polite society like divorce and contraception. The first time we mentioned the remotest possibility of divorce in Ireland on *The Late Late Show* some of the audience walked out in protest.
>
> Television seeped into the slow, orderly Irish world of received authority, dutiful newspaper reporting, and practically no social comment outside the four walls of a public house near closing time. Not everybody was delighted with this innovation. Television bypassed the newspapers and they did not like it.

1. How many channels were initially broadcast?
2. Which programmes caused the most 'stir'?
3. What controversial topics were discussed?
4. How did some people react to the discussion of divorce?
5. Who was opposed to television? Why do you think this was?

## The Catholic Church

In 1962, **Pope John XXIII** called the **Second Vatican Council** to reform the Catholic Church and make it better suited to the modern world. **Vatican II**, as it became known, was made up of senior Catholic clergy from around the world and made radical changes to the Church:

- The Mass was to be said in the **vernacular** (native language) instead of Latin, and the priest would face the congregation.

- Laypeople (non-priests) were given a greater role in the Church.

- The Bible was to be published in the vernacular, people were encouraged to read it themselves and all Church teachings were to come from the Bible.

- **Ecumenism** sought more understanding and cooperation between the various different Christian Churches around the world.

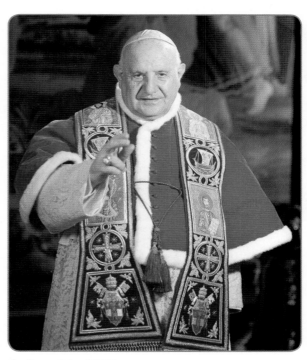

▲ Pope John XXIII

After Vatican II, more people began to question the teachings and authority of the Church. This would begin the gradual lessening of its influence on Irish society.

 COLLABORATE: In a group, compare the decisions of Vatican II with the beliefs of Martin Luther in the 1500s. What similarities do you find?

20 An Important Decade: Ireland in the 1960s

## Education

In 1966 the Minister for Education, **Donogh O'Malley**, wanted to expand the educated workforce so that Ireland would be more attractive to foreign businesses. He introduced major reforms to the education system, including:

- **free schooling** up to the Intermediate Certificate (the old name for the Junior Cycle).
- **free transport** for students to schools.
- **grants** to build more schools.
- **Regional Technical Colleges** (the old name for Institutes of Technology) were opened.

The impact of these reforms was huge: the numbers sitting the Leaving Certificate rose from 8,600 in 1961 to 24,000 in 1972. The practice of Irish children leaving education after primary school was ended by the early 1970s.

▲ Donogh O'Malley

▼ An Irish classroom in the late 1960s

## CHECKPOINT!

1. When did RTÉ start broadcasting?
2. Name two ways in which RTÉ affected Irish society.
3. Why did Pope John XXIII call the Second Vatican Council?
4. Name two reforms of the Catholic Church introduced by the Second Vatican Council.
5. How did Donogh O'Malley reform Irish education in 1966?
6. Which do you think was the most important change in Irish society: RTÉ, Vatican II or the education reforms? Give reasons for your answer.

✓ I understand the changes within Irish society in the 1960s.

TIME TO GO BACK ◀ ▶ I CAN MOVE FORWARD

 **SUMMARY**

In this chapter, we have learned that:

Like the rest of the world, Ireland experienced rapid and far-reaching changes during the 1960s. Nearly all the changes were initiated by governments led by Seán Lemass. In some cases, like the economy, the impact was immediate. In other cases, like the launch of RTÉ or Vatican II, the effect would take longer to be felt in society.

- Economics: Ireland dropped protectionism in favour of free trade and foreign investment.

- Northern Ireland: Lemass met with Terence O'Neill to forge better relations on the island.

- Internationally: Ireland became more active in the UN, applied for EEC membership and welcomed US President Kennedy on a state visit.

- Politics: a new generation of leaders took over the running of the state.

- RTÉ: Irish television meant that people were exposed to more outside influences, debates about controversial topics and the questioning of those in positions of power.

- Vatican II: the Catholic Church introduced changes to its practices and teaching.

- Education: free schooling meant that more children than ever before finished secondary school.

### Reflecting on... the 1960s in Ireland

It would be wrong to see Ireland as being a completely different place at the end of the 1960s. Social change came gradually in the years and decades that followed. But the impact of RTÉ, Vatican II, economic change, international openness and access to education would be felt for decades to come. That is why many historians consider the 1960s to mark the birth of modern Ireland.

 **Understanding History**

1. What economic problems did Ireland face in the 1950s?
2. What were the causes of these problems?
3. How did these problems impact on Irish society?
4. Explain why the First Programme for Economic Expansion was so important for Ireland.
5. How did Lemass seek to change Ireland's relationship with (a) Northern Ireland; (b) Europe; and (c) the United Nations?
6. Why was RTÉ set up and what impact did it have?
7. What was the Second Vatican Council and what did it decide?
8. How did Donogh O'Malley reform Irish education?

**20** An Important Decade: Ireland in the 1960s

# Exploring History

1. Write about the life of Seán Lemass under the following headings:
   - Life before 1959
   - Economic policies
   - Foreign policies
   - Legacy

2. Explain how and why Ireland changed in the 1960s in: (a) the economy; (b) politics; and (c) society.

3. Copy out the table below. For each effect, suggest at least one cause from the changes that Ireland saw in the 1960s. Remember, some might have more than one cause.

| Cause | Effect |
|---|---|
| | Ireland became richer |
| | Irish people became better educated and well informed |
| | Better north–south relations |
| | Decline in the power of the Catholic Church |
| | President Kennedy's visit to Ireland |
| | Irish women demanded more equal treatment |

4. Does this photograph date from before or after 1962? Explain your answer.

**KEY TERMS**

| | |
|---|---|
| **Protectionism** | using high tariffs (charges) on goods coming into a country to protect native businesses from foreign competition. |
| **Rural depopulation** | young people left rural areas to work and increasingly only older people remained. |
| **Free trade** | the removal of tariffs and other restrictions on trade between countries. |
| **Ecumenism** | the attempt to promote more understanding and cooperation between the various different Christian Churches around the world. |

 Go to page 117 of your *Sources and Skills Book* for more exercises.

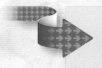 Go to page 63 of your *Research Portfolio* for a task based on this chapter.

# The Troubles in Northern Ireland

## LO: 2.5

**21**

| Independent Ireland 1922–present day | The Troubles in Northern Ireland 1969–1998 | European Integration 1973–present day |
| --- | --- | --- |

Since its creation in 1921, Northern Ireland had been a divided society. Sectarian divisions between the Protestant majority and the Catholic minority meant the new state discriminated against Catholics. The resulting injustices led to protests and eventually to the outbreak of violence by paramilitary groups. Over 3,500 people lost their lives during the Troubles.

# WORKING WITH THE EVIDENCE!

## The Troubles

| Type of source | Category | Example |
| --- | --- | --- |
| Primary | Written | Newspapers, official records, diaries and speeches from the people involved on all sides |
| Primary | Oral | Interviews with people who lived through the Troubles, many of whom are still living today |
| Primary | Audiovisual | RTÉ and BBC news reports and investigations into the Troubles |
| | Visual | The two communities expressed their views by painting murals. These are a unique source on Northern Ireland and give us an insight into how the people most affected by the violence saw it |

Find one example of a republican/nationalist mural and one loyalist/Unionist mural from the Troubles. In your group, do a presentation on the two murals. Explain who the people are and what the symbols mean. If historical events are shown, explain what happened then and why it is important to that community.

◀ Newspaper headlines the day after Bloody Sunday, 1972

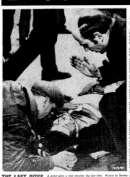

▶ Republican mural

https://educateplus.ie/go/troubles

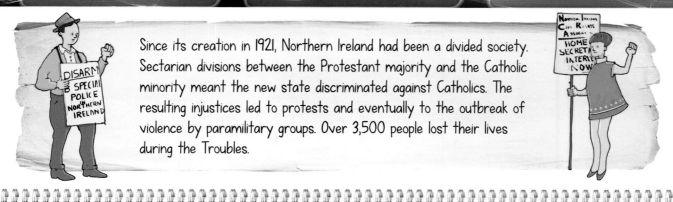

# 21.1 Northern Ireland, 1920–1963

In this topic, you will learn about:
- ❯ The establishment of Northern Ireland
- ❯ Discrimination against Catholics
- ❯ The welfare state

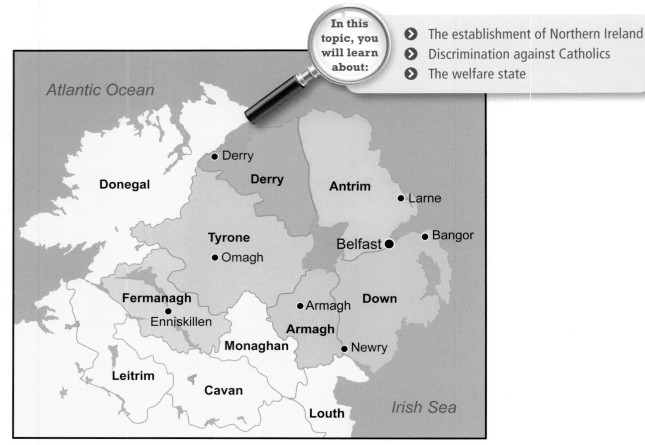

▲ Counties and major towns of Northern Ireland shown in colour

## The Government of Ireland Act 1920

As you learned in chapter 18, Ireland was partitioned into two states under the **Government of Ireland Act 1920**. The six counties of Armagh, Antrim, Down, Derry, Tyrone and Fermanagh became Northern Ireland. The population of the six counties was split: two-thirds were Protestants, most of whom were **Unionists**. The other third were Catholics, who were mostly **nationalists**. Northern Ireland had its own parliament in Stormont outside Belfast to deal with local issues like policing and education. They also sent MPs to Westminster, which had power over things like defence and foreign affairs. The Unionist government saw the minority-nationalist population as a threat and was determined to keep them from gaining political or economic power.

## The sectarian state

The new Northern Irish state was a sectarian one that actively discriminated against Catholics:

- **Gerrymandering**: Electoral constituencies were drawn to ensure that **Unionists always won elections**, even in majority-nationalist areas. Notoriously, Derry City Council always had a Unionist majority, although 70% of the city's population was Catholic.

- **Multiple votes**: In addition, owners of property and businesses received additional votes in local council elections. As most business and property was owned by Protestants, they had far more votes in elections than Catholics.

- Jobs: **Catholic unemployment** was double that of Protestants. Highly paid jobs in the civil service did not go to Catholics, and Unionist ministers urged businesses to 'wherever possible employ Protestant lads and lassies'.

▲ The RUC

- Policing: The **Royal Ulster Constabulary (RUC)** was an almost exclusively Protestant armed police force. It had part-time special constabulary units, such as the '**B-Specials**', who became notorious for their **violence against Catholics**.
- Housing: Catholics were passed over in favour of Protestants when **public housing** was being allocated.
- Education: **Catholic schools received less funding** from the government.

## World War II and the welfare state

As a part of the UK, Northern Ireland was fully involved in World War II. Belfast was heavily bombed during the **'Belfast Blitz'**, but overall the North's economy benefited from the war, with demand high for food and machinery produced in the province. After the war, the British Labour government under **Clement Attlee** included Northern Ireland in its new **welfare state**. This was a new programme of social spending by the government that made education and health care free to everyone, built more public housing and increased social welfare payments.

One of the most important effects of the welfare state on Northern Ireland was that it greatly expanded the funding available to Catholic schools. Many children who would have left school at 12 now went on to complete their secondary education and go to university. This **first well-educated generation of Northern Irish Catholics** would emerge in the 1960s to challenge the discrimination their community faced.

## CHECKPOINT!

1. What did the Government of Ireland Act 1920 do to Ireland?
2. What was the population make-up of Northern Ireland?
3. How did the Unionists use the police to help them retain control?
4. How were Catholics discriminated against in (a) education; (b) housing; and (c) employment?
5. Name one important impact on Northern Ireland of (a) World War II and (b) the welfare state.

 I understand how Northern Ireland was set up as a sectarian state.

 TIME TO GO BACK  I CAN MOVE FORWARD

# 21.2: The O'Neill Years, 1963–1969

In this topic, you will learn about:
- ❯ Terence O'Neill's economic reforms
- ❯ His outreach to Catholics
- ❯ Unionist opposition to his reforms
- ❯ The Civil Rights Movement

In 1963, **Terence O'Neill** became Prime Minister of Northern Ireland. He was a young man, part of a new generation of politicians. He set out, in his own words, to '**build bridges between our two communities**'. His leadership was an opportunity to create a fairer Northern Ireland.

## O'Neill's economic policies

The North's economy had slowed in the 1950s as the ship building and linen industries declined. O'Neill used **tax breaks and grants** to attract new industries and foreign businesses to the province. He was successful, creating **65,000 new jobs** by 1970. However, most of the investment was in the heavily Protestant east. The Catholic west remained underdeveloped and poor.

## Relations with Catholics

O'Neill tried to improve relations with Catholics. He was the first Northern Ireland Prime Minister to visit Catholic schools and hospitals. When the Pope died in 1963, he ordered flags to be flown at half-mast. In 1965, he met with the Republic's **Taoiseach Seán Lemass**, the first time the heads of government on the island had met since 1920.

▲ Terence O'Neill

Catholics began to hope for widespread change in Northern Ireland and an end to discrimination. However, O'Neill was slow to follow these symbolic gestures with concrete changes in housing or employment policies.

▶ Lemass and O'Neill

## Unionist opposition to O'Neill

By 1965, Unionist opposition to O'Neill's policies was growing, even though no real change to Northern Irish society had been attempted. Some members of his own party, such as **Brian Faulkner**, were wary of his attempts to reconcile with Catholics and the Republic, believing these things would undermine the position of Unionists. **Reverend Ian Paisley** of the **Free Presbyterian Church** attacked O'Neill for betraying the Union and the Protestants of Northern Ireland. Paisley launched an '**O'Neill Must Go**' campaign. This opposition made it difficult for O'Neill to respond positively to growing pressure from Catholics for change.

▲ Ian Paisley

### CHECKPOINT!

1. What were Terence O'Neill's economic policies?
2. How did they worsen the divisions in Northern Ireland?
3. What steps did O'Neill take to reach out to Catholics?
4. What impact did these have on Catholics?
5. Why did Unionist opposition to O'Neill emerge?

✓ I can explain the main events of O'Neill's time as Prime Minister.

← TIME TO GO BACK ◆ I CAN MOVE FORWARD →

**DID YOU KNOW?**

The first major event of the Northern Irish civil rights movement took place in 1968: a march protesting against the allocation of housing to a young unmarried Protestant woman over a Catholic family with four children.

## The Civil Rights Movement

Catholics became increasingly frustrated by the lack of progress in Northern Ireland and decided to campaign more actively for a change in their status. In the late 1960s, a new generation of Catholic and nationalist leaders emerged. These included **Gerry Fitt**, **John Hume**, **Austin Currie** and **Bernadette Devlin**. The **Northern Ireland Civil Rights Association (NICRA)** was formed in 1967. Its demands were:

- to disband the B-Specials
- an end to discrimination in housing and employment
- 'one man, one vote' in voting for local elections
- an end to gerrymandering.

▼ A civil rights march in Northern Ireland

◀ Members of NICRA on hunger strike outside 10 Downing Street, protesting internment. From left to right: John Hume, Austin Currie, Paddy O'Hanlon and Bernadette Devlin.

NICRA was not concerned with the question of partition or a united Ireland. Essentially, it demanded '**British Rights for British Citizens**' and won the support of many Protestants. However, many Unionists, pointing at the nationalist politicians involved in NICRA, dismissed it as a 'republican plot' against Northern Ireland and therefore refused all of their demands.

NICRA was committed to peaceful means to achieve change. It modelled itself on the Civil Rights Movement of African-Americans led by Dr **Martin Luther King** in the US. NICRA organised marches, petitions, legal aid for people discriminated against, boycotts of businesses and so on. The RUC and the government banned marches, claiming a risk of violence between NICRA and extreme Unionist counter-marches led by Ian Paisley.

In October 1968, a march that had been banned went ahead. It was attacked by the RUC and the images were captured by television cameras. That night in Derry and Belfast there was mass rioting and violent clashes between Catholic youths and the RUC.

## The end of O'Neill

The British government forced the Unionists in Stormont to announce some changes to housing and voting. In December, after more marches and rioting, O'Neill made a speech saying 'Northern Ireland is at a crossroads' and appealed for calm to allow the reforms to work. There was more violence in January, when a civil rights march was attacked by extremists. O'Neill was eventually forced to resign by his party in April 1969 and was replaced by **James Chichester-Clark**.

# ////////////// CHECKPOINT! //////////////

1. Why was NICRA set up?
2. What were its aims?
3. What were its methods? Why did its members choose these methods?
4. How did Unionists respond to it?
5. How did violence break out in 1968?
6. Do you think O'Neill was a success or a failure as Prime Minister of Northern Ireland? Give reasons for your answer.

 I know about the Civil Rights Movement in Northern Ireland.  ◀ TIME TO GO BACK ◆ I CAN MOVE FORWARD ➔

# 21.3: The Beginning of the Troubles

In this topic, you will learn about:
- The Battle of the Bogside
- The introduction of the British army
- New political parties and terrorist groups
- Internment
- Bloody Sunday

▲ The Battle of the Bogside

## The Battle of the Bogside

Violence continued on the streets throughout 1969. In August, there were riots when a march by the Unionist **Apprentice Boys** passed through the Catholic **Bogside** area of Derry. The rioters drove the RUC out of the Bogside, throwing stones and home-made firebombs (nicknamed Molotov cocktails). They raised barricades across the streets and declared the area '**Free Derry**'. This became known as the **Battle of the Bogside**. The violence spread to Belfast, where Unionist rioters attacked Catholic homes. To end the violence, the British government ordered the British army onto the streets. The Catholic community initially welcomed the soldiers as their protectors from Unionist attacks. This positive attitude would not last.

## The violence escalates

There were soon clashes between rioters on both sides and the soldiers. In the midst of the violence, new terrorist (or paramilitary) groups sprang up. **Terrorism** is the use of fear and acts of violence to try to change society or government policy for a political or ideological purpose. In Northern Ireland, terrorists targeted both the security forces (the RUC and army) and innocent civilians.

- **The IRA**: In 1969, seeing the crisis as a chance to push for a united Ireland, the Northern members broke away from their Dublin-based command. This new group was called the Provisional IRA, or 'Provos'. They carried out attacks on the RUC and the army, planted bombs in Britain and Northern Ireland and killed innocent civilians who they claimed were working for the British. Their political wing was **Sinn Féin**, which was led by **Gerry Adams** from the mid-1980s.

- **Loyalists**: On the other side, the **Ulster Volunteer Force (UVF)** and the **Ulster Defence Association (UDA)** were set up. **Loyalists** are Unionists who are willing to use (or support the use of) paramilitary violence to defend the Union. They attacked Catholic civilians as reprisals for IRA attacks.

Go to page 124 of your *Sources and Skills Book* for an evidence task on the Battle of the Bogside.

▲ British troops on the streets of Northern Ireland

## New political parties

- The **Social Democratic and Labour Party (SDLP)** was founded as a new nationalist political party in 1970 by the leaders of the Civil Rights Movement. It was led first by **Gerry Fitt** and then by **John Hume**. It rejected the use of violence to solve the North's problems and was more concerned with improving people's lives than with gaining a united Ireland.

- The **Democratic Unionist Party (DUP)** was founded by **Rev. Ian Paisley** in 1971. It opposed any compromise with nationalists and demanded harsh measures to deal with IRA violence.

▲ SDLP leaders Gerry Fitt and John Hume

## Internment

In 1970 and 1971, the IRA carried out gun attacks on the security forces and organised youths in Catholic areas to throw stones and riot. In response, the army held house searches in these areas, which cost them the support of Catholic communities.

In August 1971, as the violence worsened, the new Prime Minster **Brian Faulkner** introduced the policy of internment. **Internment** is <u>the arrest and imprisonment of people without trial</u>. Faulkner wanted to round up the IRA leadership in order to stop the violence. However, this tactic was an absolute disaster:

- A lot of innocent people were arrested and held, while most of the IRA leaders escaped to the Republic.

- Only Catholics were arrested, even though loyalists had been attacking Catholic communities for two years. More people joined the IRA as a result of the internment policy.

▲ Marchers arrested on Bloody Sunday

## Bloody Sunday

On **30 January 1972**, NICRA organised a march to protest against internment in Derry. It was banned but 15,000 people marched anyway. The British army was sent into the Bogside following reports of an IRA sniper. When Catholic youths on the march threw stones at an army barricade, soldiers opened fire on the crowd, killing 14 and injuring 13 more. The soldiers claimed they were fired upon, but no one else heard shots and no guns were found. There were protests around the world at the shootings. In Dublin, protesters burned down the British Embassy.

▲ Fr Edward Daly with a dying marcher

## CHECKPOINT!

1. Describe the Battle of the Bogside.

2. Why were British troops sent onto the streets on Northern Ireland in 1969?

3. What is terrorism?

4. Explain who these groups are: the IRA; the UDA; the SDLP; the DUP.

5. What was internment?

6. What happened on Bloody Sunday 1972?

 I understand how the violence escalated in the early years of the Troubles.

 ◀ TIME TO GO BACK ◆ I CAN MOVE FORWARD ▶

21 The Troubles in Northern Ireland

# 21.4: The Sunningdale Agreement

**In this topic, you will learn about:**

- ❯ The suspension of the Stormont government
- ❯ The signing of the Sunningdale Agreement
- ❯ The Ulster Workers' Council Strike

## Stormont parliament suspended

In the aftermath of Bloody Sunday, the British government saw that the Unionist government was failing to deal with the crisis. It decided to introduce direct rule from London. The Stormont parliament was suspended in March 1972 by British Prime Minister **Edward Heath**. He appointed **Willie Whitelaw** to act as Secretary of State for Northern Ireland. Whitelaw wanted this to be a temporary measure and tried to restore local control as quickly as possible.

## The signing of the Sunningdale Agreement

◀ The Sunningdale Agreement being signed

In 1973, elections took place for a new Northern Ireland Assembly. Afterwards, Whitelaw invited the party leaders to talks. He wanted to set up a **power-sharing government**, where nationalists and Unionists would govern together. Eventually, in December 1973, the leaders of the Unionist Party (**Brian Faulkner**), the SDLP (**Gerry Fitt**), the British government (**Edward Heath**) and the Irish government (**Liam Cosgrave**) signed the **Sunningdale Agreement**.

- A **power-sharing executive** would be established between the Unionist Party, the SDLP and a small Unionist party, the Alliance.

- A **Council of Ireland** was to be set up, consisting of politicians from the North and the Republic. It would promote cross-border cooperation in areas such as the economy, farming and policing. This was an attempt to undermine the IRA by showing that peaceful means could bring Ireland closer together.

Go to page 126 of your *Sources and Skills Book* for a visual evidence task.

## The Ulster Workers' Council strike

The executive took office in January 1974. It faced opposition on both sides:

- The IRA continued its campaign of violence, claiming that the Sunningdale Agreement did not bring about a united Ireland, while Unionist voters could see little good in a deal that would not end the violence.

- Unionist opposition was widespread. Members of Faulkner's own party and Ian Paisley's DUP opposed power sharing with nationalists and especially the Council of Ireland. They claimed it would undermine the Union and lead to a united Ireland.

In May 1974, the Unionist **Ulster Workers' Council** organised a general strike. Goods could not be transported, factories were shut down and the electricity supply was shut off. The executive resigned and the Sunningdale Agreement collapsed. Direct rule from Westminster was re-imposed.

◀ Ulster Workers' Council strikers blockading Stormont

### CHECKPOINT!

1. Why did the British government suspend Stormont in 1972?
2. Why did the British government think that power sharing would be a solution to the problems in Northern Ireland?
3. What was agreed as part of the Sunningdale Agreement?
4. Who were the leaders who signed the Sunningdale Agreement? Why do you think it was important that all these leaders supported it?
5. Why did (a) the IRA and (b) some Unionists oppose the Sunningdale Agreement?
6. How did the Ulster Workers' Council bring about the end of the Sunningdale Agreement?

 I understand the Sunningdale Agreement and why it failed.  ⬅ TIME TO GO BACK ❱ I CAN MOVE FORWARD ➡

 COLLABORATE: Divide the class into either four or eight groups. Each group takes one of the following positions: (a) Unionist supporters of Sunningdale; (b) Unionist opponents of Sunningdale; (c) nationalist supporters of Sunningdale; (d) nationalist opponents of Sunningdale.

Research the arguments of your side and make a speech to the rest of the class arguing for or against Sunningdale from that perspective.

21 The Troubles in Northern Ireland

# 21.5: Stalemate

## Terrorist groups

▲ IRA paramilitaries

▲ Loyalist paramilitaries

While a political solution was being pursued, there was near-constant violence on the streets of Northern Ireland and also **IRA attacks within Britain**. The IRA adopted a tactic they called '**spectaculars**': staging large-scale attacks on the British mainland to make Britain want to exit Northern Ireland. For example, the **Birmingham Pub Bombings** of November 1974 killed 21 and injured 182 people. Attacks such as these led to a lot of anti-Irish feeling in Britain.

In addition, the IRA carried out frequent attacks in Northern Ireland which they claimed targeted the RUC and the army. However, many innocent civilians were killed. In all, the IRA was responsible for **over half of the 3,500 deaths** that occurred during the Troubles.

**Loyalist terrorist groups** also engaged in brutal attacks on civilians. They did not have the IRA's funding, bomb-making skills or resources. Most of their attacks focused on killing Catholic civilians in Northern Ireland in supposed retaliation for IRA actions. These attacks were intended to terrify the Catholic population. The **Dublin and Monaghan Bombings** of May 1974 killed 33 civilians and injured 300 when a series of car bombs went off during rush hour. The UVF later claimed responsibility.

The security forces (RUC and army) also killed civilians while attempting to find and stop terrorists on both sides.

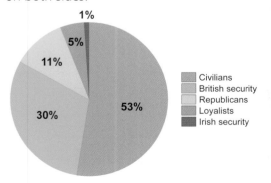

1%
5%
11%
30%
53%

Civilians
British security
Republicans
Loyalists
Irish security

▲ Deaths during the Troubles

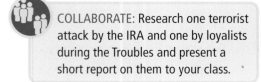

COLLABORATE: Research one terrorist attack by the IRA and one by loyalists during the Troubles and present a short report on them to your class.

▲ An IRA man patrols as children walk to school in Belfast

## The hunger strikes

In the late 1970s, IRA prisoners in the **Maze Prison** outside Belfast demanded 'political status': <u>to be treated as political prisoners rather than as ordinary criminals</u>. They wanted to wear their own clothes and have more visits and contact with the outside. **Margaret Thatcher's** government rejected these demands. In 1981, prisoners led by **Bobby Sands** went on **hunger strike**, which meant <u>they refused all food until their demands were met</u>.

The hunger strike generated sympathy around the world, especially in the Republic. People admired the strikers' bravery in being willing to die for their beliefs. Considerable anti-British feeling arose. Tensions rose between the Irish and British governments, as the Irish urged Thatcher to concede to some of the strikers' demands. During the strike, Sands was elected a Westminster MP. However, Thatcher refused to back down and Sands died after 66 days on hunger strike. Nine more prisoners died before the IRA called off the hunger strike.

International attention had been drawn to the Troubles. Sands' election also showed the IRA that it could pursue a **political strategy as well as a military one**. Its political wing, **Sinn Féin**, began to take part in electoral politics and tried to win support on the basis of its policies and arguments.

▲ People marching in support of the hunger strikers

▲ Bobby Sands' election poster

**DID YOU KNOW?**

The IRA came very close to killing Margaret Thatcher when they detonated a bomb at the Conservative Party conference in 1984. While she survived, five other people were killed.

▲ Margaret Thatcher, British Prime Minister 1979–1990

## CHECKPOINT!

1. What tactics were employed by the IRA during the Troubles?
2. What tactics were employed by the loyalists?
3. What percentage of people killed during the Troubles were civilians?
4. Why did IRA prisoners go on hunger strike in 1981?
5. What was the British reaction to the hunger strikes? Why do you think this was?

✓ I understand the use of violence and the role of the hunger strikes in the Troubles.

← TIME TO GO BACK ◄► I CAN MOVE FORWARD →

**21 The Troubles in Northern Ireland**

# 21.6: The Search for Peace, 1985–1998

In this topic, you will learn about:
- The Anglo-Irish Agreement 1985
- The IRA and loyalist ceasefires
- The Good Friday Agreement 1998

## The Anglo-Irish Agreement 1985

By 1985, the British and Irish governments were looking for a new way to work together on Northern Ireland. As the violence continued and Sinn Féin gained support, Taoiseach **Garret FitzGerald** wanted to show that the political process could work to deliver change. In the **Anglo-Irish Agreement** of 1985, he and **Margaret Thatcher** agreed to increase security cooperation, and that the Republic would have a role in the running of Northern Ireland. The Irish government would have the right to be consulted and put forward proposals through an **inter-governmental conference**.

▲ FitzGerald and Thatcher signing the Anglo-Irish Agreement

Unionists were outraged by the agreement. To them, the idea of the Republic having any role in Northern Ireland was a betrayal. They staged huge demonstrations against it, with over 100,000 people marching in Belfast. Thatcher refused to back down and ignored their protests. The SDLP leader **John Hume** welcomed it and used his relationship with the Irish government to pressure the British through the new conference.

## The IRA and loyalist ceasefires

In the following years, the two governments worked hard to bring the parties in Northern Ireland together to agree a new power-sharing relationship. They also engaged in secret talks with Sinn Féin and the IRA to try to bring the violence to an end. This process of talks eventually resulted in the **Downing Street Declaration** in December **1993**. This declaration set out the terms for all-party talks on the future of Northern Ireland. Most importantly, **only parties committed to peace could be involved**. This meant that Sinn Féin could only take part in talks if the IRA ended its terrorism campaign. On the basis of the Declaration, the IRA called a ceasefire in August 1994. Loyalist groups followed with their own ceasefire in October 1994.

▶ The *Irish Independent* announcing the ceasefire

# The Good Friday Agreement 1998

After the ceasefires came four years of difficult talks and negotiations. The IRA ceasefire even broke down at one stage over the slow rate of progress. Eventually, direct talks began under the chairmanship of US Senator **George Mitchell**. The main players were:

| Ulster Unionists | SDLP | Sinn Féin | Irish government | British government |
|---|---|---|---|---|
| David Trimble | John Hume | Gerry Adams | Bertie Ahern | Tony Blair |

The hardline Unionists, led by Ian Paisley's DUP, refused to engage in talks with Sinn Féin and so did not take part. Just before Easter 1998, the parties and governments reached agreement on the **Good Friday Agreement**. This was an attempt at a comprehensive deal **to secure a sustainable peace** for Northern Ireland. Its main terms included:

- power sharing between all the main political parties
- cross-border bodies to link the north and south
- that the Republic would give up its constitutional claim on Northern Ireland
- the release of IRA and loyalist prisoners from jail
- **decommissioning** (surrendering) of weapons by terrorist groups
- the reform of the RUC and gradual withdrawal of most British soldiers

In a **referendum** on both sides of the border, the agreement was accepted by 71% of people in Northern Ireland and 94% in the Republic. Putting the agreement into practice was difficult and neither side quite kept its part of the deal. Despite this, there was **never a return to violence** by the main terrorist groups, and in 2005 the IRA announced the end of its armed campaign.

▲ Paisley and McGuinness in 2007

In 2007, **Ian Paisley** of the DUP and **Martin McGuinness** of Sinn Féin – once sworn enemies – were elected as First and Deputy First Minister of Northern Ireland. This showed how far Northern Ireland had come since the end of the Troubles.

**CHECKPOINT!**

1. What did the two governments agree in the Anglo-Irish Agreement in 1985?
2. What was the Unionist reaction to the Anglo-Irish Agreement?
3. What was the Downing Street Declaration?
4. When did (a) the IRA and (b) the loyalists call ceasefires?
5. Who were the main leaders involved in the talks in the late 1990s?
6. What were the main terms of the Good Friday Agreement of 1998?
7. Did the Good Friday Agreement enjoy strong public support? Give a reason for your answer.

 I understand how the Troubles were finally brought to an end. 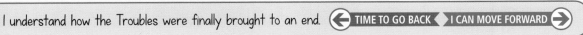 ← TIME TO GO BACK ◆ I CAN MOVE FORWARD →

21 The Troubles in Northern Ireland

# A Life in Time: Northern Ireland Peacemaker John Hume (1937- )

## Early life

John Hume was born in Derry City in 1937. He worked as a teacher and became active in the local community. He helped to found the Derry Credit Union, campaigned for better housing in the city and for a university to be established in Derry.

## Civil rights activist

Hume became involved with the **Civil Rights Movement** after the failure of his housing and university campaigns due to Unionist opposition. He was a founder member of NICRA and believed it should only pursue peaceful means. Hume was elected to Stormont in 1969. In 1970 he helped found the **SDLP** to give a new voice to nationalists. As the violence worsened throughout the early 1970s, he repeatedly rejected the use of force as a means of achieving change.

## The search for peace

As a senior member of the SDLP, Hume was appointed Minister for Commerce in the **Sunningdale Power-Sharing Executive**. After the collapse of the Sunningdale Agreement, he began working closely with the Irish government. He became leader of the SDLP in 1979. He strongly supported the Anglo-Irish Agreement in 1985. He then began holding talks with Gerry Adams, the leader of Sinn Féin. He was harshly criticised for this, as the IRA were still killing people. However, Hume insisted he was willing **'to talk to anyone, any time'** to find a peaceful solution to the conflict. His work paid off with the IRA ceasefire in 1994 and the **Good Friday Agreement** in 1998. He retired as leader of the SDLP in 2004.

## Legacy

Along with the Ulster Unionist Party leader David Trimble, Hume was awarded the **Nobel Peace Prize** in 1998 for his work during the peace process. Hume belongs to the same tradition in Irish history as O'Connell and Parnell: men who believed Ireland's problems could only be resolved peacefully.

▶ Hume (right) receiving the Nobel Peace Prize with David Trimble

# SUMMARY

In this chapter, we have learned that:

- After partition in 1921, Northern Ireland was established. The Unionist Party, which represented the majority-Protestant population, created a state which actively excluded Catholics and sought to keep them from gaining any power.

- Catholics were discriminated against in housing, employment and politics. Unionists used gerrymandering and multiple votes to stay in power, even in majority-Catholic areas.

- By the 1960s, Catholics had benefited from improved education through the welfare state. The new Prime Minister, Terence O'Neill, started to reach out to Catholics but failed to follow up his gestures with concrete reforms.

- Catholics set up NICRA to campaign for civil rights through peaceful means. When their marches began to be banned and attacked, violence broke out in the streets.

- The British army was sent into Northern Ireland after the Battle of the Bogside in 1969. They quickly became the target of attacks by the IRA.

- Following Bloody Sunday in 1972, the British government suspended the Stormont parliament. The 1973 Sunningdale Agreement aimed to get the moderates on the nationalist and Unionist sides to share power. It collapsed under Unionist opposition to power sharing and to the Council of Ireland.

- Violence continued throughout the 1970s and 1980s. The British and Irish governments worked together closely to find ways to end the fighting. This led to the Anglo-Irish Agreement in 1985 and the Downing Street Declaration in 1993.

- The IRA and loyalists called ceasefires in 1994. Talks then began and eventually the Good Friday Agreement was signed between the governments and the main political parties in 1998.

- In the course of the Troubles some 3,500 people were killed.

## Reflecting on... the Troubles

The long relationship between Britain and Ireland has often been one of conflict. The violence during the three decades of the Troubles should be seen in the historical context of religious discrimination dating back to the plantations of the 1600s and the advent of physical force nationalism in 1798.

Northern Ireland was, and is, a divided society: each community feels it has grievances against the other. Three decades of violence did little to improve this, but the failure of that violence to change the status of Northern Ireland did highlight the futility of terrorism.

**21 The Troubles in Northern Ireland**

# Understanding History

1. Why was Ireland partitioned in 1921?
2. Explain the difference between Unionists and nationalists.
3. How did Terence O'Neill try to change Northern Ireland?
4. Why were some Unionists so opposed to civil rights and how did they respond to NICRA's campaign?
5. What happened during the Battle of the Bogside?
6. What was the Sunningdale Agreement and why did it fail?
7. How did the hunger strikes affect Northern Ireland?
8. What were the main terms of the Anglo-Irish Agreement?
9. What events led to the IRA ceasefire in 1994?
10. How did Northern Ireland develop after the Good Friday Agreement?
11. Find out when the following events took place and put them in order on a timeline in your copy, starting with the earliest. Write the year and one sentence beside each.

   - The Downing Street Declaration
   - The Battle of the Bogside
   - Terence O'Neill meets with Seán Lemass
   - The Sunningdale Agreement
   - NICRA founded
   - The IRA hunger strikes
   - The IRA ceasefire
   - British troops arrive in Northern Ireland
   - The Good Friday Agreement
   - The Government of Ireland Act

 # Exploring History

1. Write about the life of John Hume and his role in bringing peace to Northern Ireland.
2. Outline the causes of the Troubles.
3. What were the similarities and differences between the Sunningdale Agreement (1973) and the Good Friday Agreement (1998)?
4. How did the Irish and British governments work together to find a solution to the Troubles?

| **KEY TERMS** | | |
|---|---|---|
| | **Welfare state** | a programme of social spending by the British government to provide free education, free health care, public housing and increase social welfare payments |
| | **Terrorism** | the use of fear and acts of violence to try to change society or government policy for a political or ideological purpose |
| | **Loyalists** | Unionists who are willing to use (or quietly support the use of) paramilitary violence to defend the Union |
| | **Internment** | the arrest and imprisonment of people without trial |
| | **Power-sharing government** | nationalists and Unionists governing Northern Ireland together |
| | **Political status** | the demand by prisoners that they be treated as political prisoners rather than as ordinary criminals |
| | **Hunger strike** | the refusal of all food until demands are met |
| | **Decommissioning** | the surrender or destruction of weapons by terrorist groups |

 Go to page 121 of your *Sources and Skills Book* for more exercises.

 Go to page 67 of your *Research Portfolio* for a task based on this chapter.

| Ireland under the Union 1800–1922 | Twentieth-Century Ireland 1900–1999 | Ireland in the 1960s 1960–1969 |
| --- | --- | --- |

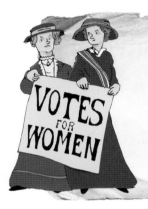

As Ireland embarked on its struggle for independence, and later, throughout the difficult birth and early years of the Irish state, another struggle for rights was ongoing – those of Irish women. Women had few rights in 1900: no vote, limited access to education and limited employment opportunities. Over the next 100 years, this would change dramatically, largely due to actions taken by women themselves.

# WORKING WITH THE EVIDENCE!

## The changing lives of women

| Type of source | Category | Example |
| --- | --- | --- |
| Primary | Written | Using the **census records**, we are able to track the progress of women in areas like level of employment and education |
| | | Political records of changes in the laws that affected women and news reports on the social movements and campaigns for greater equality |
| Primary | Aural/oral | Interviews with women who lived through this time of change, many of whom are still alive today |

Speakers at the Dublin meeting to organise a Women's Right to Choose Campaign were Patricia Mac Mahon (U.S./Catholics for a Free Choice), Ann Connolly, Dublin, and Jan Parker, Britain.

### Women campaign for the right to choose

A GROUP of Dublin women formed a Women's Right to Choose Campaign because they see 'there is an urgent need to change the law on abortion in this country'. An estimated 9,000 women go from Ireland every year to have abortions in Britain.

A survey of 300 women who went to England this year shows the sensation-seeking press image of young, single and irresponsible users of contraceptives is far from being the whole story.

Nearly a third of the women already had children, so had first hand knowledge of what it means to go ahead with a pregnancy in Ireland. Almost half of women — "a staggering 42% — had never used any contraception at all, a fact the Campaign sees as a severe indictment of the difficulty and expense of obtaining contraception here. Well over half, 63%, were working women which lends support to the claim that a "child-bar" is rapidly replacing the old "marriage-bar" against women holding down jobs. "Saddest of all," say the women campaigners, "30% of all these women gave their main reason for seeking an abortion as their parents, a hypocrisy that calls to mind the Victorian era rather than 1980."

The Campaign for a Woman's Right to Choose held a well supported meeting over the summer. In spite of being called in the middle of the holiday period a hundred people — mostly women — came along. And women's groups in the north have combined to reform the abortion law more along the lines of the British 1967 Act. At present the old British Act of 1929 allows Northern Ireland doctors to terminate pregnancies in very limited circumstances, so like their southern sisters most northern women travel to Britain for abortions. In the Republic of Ireland the 1861 Offences against the Persons Act allows life sentences for having or performing an abortion.

◀ Newspaper article on campaign for reproductive rights

Ask one of your female relatives (mother, aunt or grandmother, for instance) what changes in their lifetimes they think have been the most important for women.

▲ Interviewing a female relative

# 22.1: The Early Twentieth Century: Women as Second-Class Citizens

In this topic, you will learn about:

- ❯ The vote
- ❯ Education
- ❯ Employment
- ❯ The struggle for Irish independence

THE

**IRISH CITIZEN**

AUGUST 15. 1914. - ONE PENNY

VOTES FOR WOMEN

NOW!

DAMN

YOUR WAR!

▲ *The Irish Citizen front page*

## Getting the vote

In 1900, women were legally inferior to men. They could not vote, their rights to property and education were limited and discrimination in the workplace was entirely legal. Women across the world saw getting the vote as the key to advancing women's rights in other areas. The campaign for voting rights was called **suffrage** and the women who campaigned were called suffragettes.

In 1908, **Hanna Sheehy-Skeffington** founded the **Irish Women's Franchise League (IWFL)**. It campaigned for votes for women by copying the tactics of the suffragettes in Britain: parades, attacks on property and hunger strikes in prison.

Women Smash Windows of Dublin Castle
Leading Militant Suffragettes Are Put in Jail

WOMEN BEGIN NEW REIGN OF TERROR

Suffragettes Smash Hundreds of Show Windows in the London Stores.

TRY TO INVADE COMMONS.

Rowdies Attack Demonstrators and Police Fight Hard to Protect Them.

▲ Headlines report the actions of Irish suffragettes

## Education

While the numbers of girls attending school had increased in the 1800s, thanks largely to the efforts of Catholic religious orders, it was only in 1908 that all universities in Ireland were opened to women. In the years afterwards, about 10% of university students were women, but only those from wealthy and middle-class backgrounds.

Alice Oldham spearheaded the campaign for the admission of female students to Trinity College, which was finally achieved in 1904. There is now a student prize in her name.

▶ Early graduates from Irish universities

## Employment

In the early part of the twentieth century, women were expected to marry and have children. Their husbands would provide for them, so there was no need for them to work. **Some women worked before they got married** (45% of national school teachers were women) but they had to give up those jobs on marriage. Most middle-class women did not go out to work but supervised their servants, who did the housework and took care of the children.

Poorer women, especially single ones, often worked outside the home as **domestic servants** (maids, cooks, nannies), as **street traders** in larger cities and in the Belfast **mills**, where they were paid **lower wages than men**. In rural areas, they were expected to help on the farm as well as run the household and often look after animals.

▲ Domestic servants of a Mr Austin, early twentieth century

Go to page 131 of your *Sources and Skills Book* for an evidence task on women living in poverty.

## Women in the independence movement

Women were excluded from active involvement in the Home Rule movement, but a women's organisation, **Cumann na mBan**, was founded in 1914 to support the independence movement. In 1916, Cumann na mBan became an auxiliary force to the Irish Volunteers. During the Easter Rising, several women fought, including **Countess Constance Markievicz**, **Dr Kathleen Lynn** and **Margaret Skinnider**, while others acted as messengers between the rebel bases and nurses inside them, such as Elizabeth O'Farrell. Markievicz would go on to become the first woman elected to Westminster in 1918 (she did not take her seat) and later served as Minster for Labour during the First Dáil.

The contributions of women during the struggle for independence were often ignored or denied after 1922. Many were refused military pensions that were granted to men who fought the British.

Go to pages 132–134 of your *Sources and Skills Book* for tasks on women and Irish nationalism.

► Rose McNamara of Cumann na mBan

## CHECKPOINT!

1. What is suffrage and what did Irish women do to win it?
2. How was Irish women's access to education limited in the early twentieth century?
3. What were employment prospects like for Irish women?
4. How were women involved in the struggle for Irish independence?

 I can explain the barriers faced by women in early twentieth-century Ireland.

◀ TIME TO GO BACK ◀ ▶ I CAN MOVE FORWARD ▶

**22 Women in Twentieth-Century Ireland**

# 22.2: Independent Ireland

## Women and politics

The **1922 Constitution of the Irish Free State** gave the vote to all women and men over the age of 21. At this time, the voting age for British women was 30, but only for particularly privileged women. Very few women were elected to the Dáil in the first decades of the state and those who were made little to no impact. No woman was appointed as a government minister until 1979, when **Máire Geoghegan-Quinn** became Minister for the Gaeltacht. The new Irish state was very conservative, with the Catholic Church holding a dominant position. The view that a woman's place is in the home was widespread and accepted by most men and women.

In this topic, you will learn about:
❯ Women in political life
❯ Women and employment

- Divorce and contraception were banned.
- Women could not sit on juries.
- The 1937 Constitution recognised a woman's special role 'within the home'.

# WORKING WITH THE EVIDENCE!

 With your group, look at the following excerpt from the 1937 Constitution and answer the questions that follow:

## Bunreacht na hÉireann (Constitution of Ireland, 1937)

### Article 41.2.1

In particular, the State recognises that by her life within the home, woman gives to the State a support without which the common good cannot be achieved.

### Article 41.2.2

The State shall, therefore, endeavour to ensure that mothers shall not be obliged by economic necessity to engage in labour to the neglect of their duties in the home.

### Article 45.4.2

The State shall endeavour to ensure that the strength and health of workers, men and women, and the tender age of children shall not be abused and that citizens shall not be forced by economic necessity to enter avocations [casual work] unsuited to their sex, age or strength.

1. What do women give to the State through their 'life within the home'?
2. To protect women's place within the home, what does the State have to do?
3. How might article 45.4.2 be used to exclude women from certain professions?
4. How do these articles reflect the attitude of the time towards women?
5. Come up with (a) two arguments in favour of and (b) two arguments against the removal of these sections from the Constitution.

**DID YOU KNOW?**

Women who became pregnant outside marriage could be sent to **Magdalene laundries** by their families to avoid public shame. These were run by Catholic nuns and the women were expected to work for no pay until their children were born – and sometimes beyond. Very often the children were put up for adoption without their mothers' permission. The last Magdalene laundry closed its doors in 1996 and the Irish state formally apologised to the 'Magdalene women' in 2013.

## Employment for women

After independence, many women continued to work as domestic servants or in low-paid jobs – always for lower pay than men.

▲ Women at work in Jacob's biscuit factory, Dublin, c.1910

- In 1932, a '**marriage bar**' was introduced: this meant that women automatically lost their jobs in the public service (for example as teachers or government officials) when they got married. Many employers followed suit and it became accepted that most women would give up work when they married.

- In 1936, the government passed the **Conditions of Employment Act**, which limited the number of women in any industry.

- When unemployment rose, the first ones to lose their jobs in any industry were almost always women. Trade unions often encouraged employers to pay men more and fire women first.

The result of these measures was that in 1946, **only 2.5% of married Irish women were in employment, as opposed to 25% in Britain**. It is perhaps no surprise that women emigrated from Ireland at much higher rates than men in the 1940s and 1950s.

## CHECKPOINT!

1. When did women receive the vote in Ireland?

2. What evidence is there that Ireland after independence was a conservative society in terms of women's rights?

3. How did governments in the 1930s restrict women's access to employment?

4. Why do you think that women were forced to give up their jobs when they got married?

5. How did these policies affect women in employment?

6. What do you think was the overall impact on Irish women of all the restrictions mentioned in this section?

 I know about the restrictions on Irish women in the decades after independence.

 ⬅ TIME TO GO BACK ◆ I CAN MOVE FORWARD ➡

# 22.3: Moves towards Equality

## The 1960s: Gradual change

As we saw in chapter 20, the 1960s was a decade of great change for Ireland and saw the beginnings of positive changes for women. As the **economy expanded**, more workers were needed. Many of these jobs went to women, who made up 25% of the workforce by 1970. **Free education** and increased access to universities also benefited women. **New careers** were opened to women in professions requiring high-level qualifications (for example, as doctors, lawyers or engineers). RTÉ was also influential. Shows like *The Late Late Show* debated controversial topics like marriage breakdown and contraception and this helped to change attitudes over time.

In this topic, you will learn about:

- ❯ The impact of the 1960s on Irish women
- ❯ The Irish feminist movement
- ❯ Changes for women in the 1970s and beyond
- ❯ The life of Mary Robinson

## The Irish feminist movement

◀ The Irish Women's Liberation Movement arriving back from Belfast, 1971

Worldwide, the 1960s saw many marginalised groups fighting for more rights, for example African-Americans in the US, Catholics in Northern Ireland and black South Africans. The feminist movement was part of this wider struggle for rights. **Feminism is the movement aimed at achieving gender equality, based on political, social and economic equality between men and women**. Irish feminists such as **Nell McCafferty**, **Mary Kenny** and **Nuala O'Faolain** founded the **Irish Women's Liberation Movement** in 1971. They pressured politicians, held protest marches and organised events to draw attention to the inequality of Irish laws.

- On one occasion a group took the train to Belfast and brought back contraceptives to protest against the law banning them in the Republic. As it happened, they could not get the contraceptive pill, so they bought aspirin instead and swallowed that in front of the cameras, aware that nobody in the Republic would know the difference!

- On another, a group went into a pub and ordered 30 whiskeys and one pint of Guinness. When the barman refused to serve them a pint (as many pubs would not do for women), they refused to pay for the whiskeys and left.

## Changes in the 1970s

In 1972, the **Commission on the Status of Women** recommended the removal of most of the legal barriers to equality. Ireland also came under pressure from the **European Community** (which it had joined in 1972) to introduce laws to promote equality. Progress continued into the 1980s and 1990s:

- The 'marriage bar' was abolished.

- The **Anti-Discrimination Act of 1974** banned paying men more for the same work.

- The **Employment Equality Act of 1977** outlawed discrimination on the basis of sex or marital status.

- The ban on contraception was lifted gradually in 1978 and 1985 and abolished altogether in 1993.

- Divorce was introduced in 1996.

## The position of women at the end of the century

By 2000, women made up over 40% of the workforce but were far more likely to hold low-paid positions. A low percentage of employed women held high-paid executive positions. However, women did make up 55% of university students in 2000 and were more likely to pursue professional careers in law, medicine, business or education than their mothers had been.

In politics, there has been some progress towards equality. **Mary Robinson** was elected President in 1990, followed by another woman, **Mary McAleese**. In 2011, **Susan Denham** became Ireland's first female Chief Justice of the Supreme Court. In 1993, **Mary Harney** became the first woman to lead a political party, the **Progressive Democrats**, and also the first female Tánaiste in 1997. Three other women have served as Tánaiste: **Mary Coughlan** (2008–2010), **Joan Burton**, who was also leader of the Labour Party (2014–2016), and **Frances Fitzgerald** (2016–2017). However, there has not yet been a female Taoiseach.

Women have made significant advances in other areas too. **Olivia O'Leary** became a prominent broadcaster in RTÉ news programmes in the 1980s, opening the door for other women. In sport, athlete **Sonia O'Sullivan** and boxer **Katie Taylor** won medals in the World Championships and the Olympics.

These (and many other) women's recognised excellence in their fields paved the way for younger generations to strive for success and to expect the same opportunities and respect as men.

▲ Mary McAleese

▲ Olivia O'Leary

▲ Sonia O'Sullivan

22 Women in Twentieth-Century Ireland

## A Life in Time: Mary Robinson (1944– )

### Early life

Mary Robinson (née Bourke) was born in Ballina, Co. Mayo, in 1944. She studied law at Trinity College, King's Inns and Harvard Law School, and became a Reid Professor in Trinity College in the 1960s.

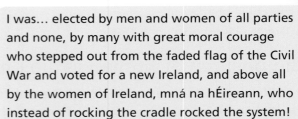

### Political and legal career

Robinson was elected to **Seanad Éireann** as an independent in 1969. She campaigned on women's rights and worked to remove the ban on contraceptives and the marriage bar. She supported the introduction of divorce and opposed the 1983 anti-abortion amendment to the Constitution. As a leading barrister, she brought cases to the Irish and European courts that established the right to free legal aid, gay rights and the protection of the Viking site at Wood Quay.

> I was… elected by men and women of all parties and none, by many with great moral courage who stepped out from the faded flag of the Civil War and voted for a new Ireland, and above all by the women of Ireland, mná na hÉireann, who instead of rocking the cradle rocked the system!

### The presidency

Robinson was the **Labour Party's candidate** for the presidency in 1990, though she was initially given little chance against the Fianna Fáil and Fine Gael candidates. Robinson campaigned all over the country for months and, after controversy overcame her rival Brian Lenihan, she won. Her victory was seen as a huge symbolic step forward for Irish women as well as for the liberalisation of Irish society.

As President, she opened up the office, visiting groups all over the country and inviting others to Áras an Uachtaráin. She reached out to marginalised groups at home and abroad: the Traveller community, LGBT people, Irish emigrants, the homeless and African victims of famine and war. She helped the Northern peace process by meeting Sinn Féin's Gerry Adams and was the first Irish President to meet Queen Elizabeth II. In 1997 she was appointed the **UN High Commissioner for Human Rights**. Mary Robinson has been one of The Elders (an international group of public figures devoted to peace and human rights worldwide) since 2007 and also founded a climate justice organisation.

▲ Robinson being sworn in as president

## CHECKPOINT!

1. How did Irish women benefit from the changes of the 1960s?

2. What is feminism and how was Ireland influenced by it?

3. What legal changes occurred for Irish women in the 1970s?

4. What impact do you think Mary Robinson's election as president in 1990 had on Irish women?

5. How did she change the presidency?

 I understand the progress towards equality made by Irish women in the late twentieth century.

 ← TIME TO GO BACK ◀▶ I CAN MOVE FORWARD →

 **SUMMARY**

In this chapter, we have learned that Irish women's lives changed in profound ways in the course of the twentieth century.

- Up until 1922, women had little say over their lives or their country, as they did not have the vote, were relegated to poorly paid jobs and had little access to education.
- Despite playing an important role in the independence struggle and winning the vote in 1922, women were discriminated against by a series of Irish laws, and even the Constitution declared their proper place to be 'in the home'.
- This situation did not start to change until the 1960s, when greater employment and educational opportunities opened up for women.
- The feminist movement in Ireland pushed for change and achieved important legal reforms in the 1970s and 1980s.
- The 1990s saw important symbolic firsts in politics, with women elected as party leaders, as presidents and as Tánaistí.

### Reflecting on... Women in Twentieth-Century Ireland

The history of Irish women over the last century is an illustration of a lesson often repeated in wider world history: marginalised groups cannot wait for their rights to be handed to them, but must fight for them themselves. Legal changes may happen relatively quickly (for example, getting the vote) but it takes far longer to change society.

 **Understanding History**

1. In the years before 1922, how did Irish women try to improve their position?
2. Why do you think that so many women became involved in the struggle for Irish independence?
3. Why do you think their contribution was largely ignored in the years after independence?
4. What ways were women's lives (a) improved and (b) limited in the Irish Free State?
5. What is feminism?
6. How did the IWLM campaign for equality in Ireland?
7. In which of the following areas do you think the most progress has been made for women in the twentieth century: education, employment, or politics? Give reasons for your answer.
8. Why do you think that employment and education are so important for the progress of women's rights?

 **Exploring History**

1. Write an account of the life of Mary Robinson under the following headings:
   - Early life and education
   - Political career in the Seanad
   - Legal career
   - The presidency of Ireland
2. Write an account of how women's lives changed in Ireland in the twentieth century in terms of (a) education; (b) politics; and (c) employment.

| KEY TERMS | Suffrage | the campaign for voting rights. Campaigners specifically for votes for women were called suffragettes |
|---|---|---|
| | Feminism | the movement aimed at achieving gender equality, based on political, social and economic equality between men and women |

 Go to page 129 of your *Sources and Skills Book* for more exercises.

 Go to page 71 of your *Research Portfolio* for a task based on this chapter.

22 Women in Twentieth-Century Ireland

| Ireland: The Easter Rising | World War I | Russia: The October Revolution |
|---|---|---|
| 1916 | 1914–1918 | 1917 |

The twentieth century saw extraordinary advances in science and technology that would transform people's lives. However, it was without comparison in human history for the sheer scale of destruction and misery that people inflicted upon each other in war.

Over the four years of World War I, 18 million people died and there were profound changes in governments, societies and technology. The war's aftermath shaped a world which would see even more devastating conflicts.

## WORKING WITH THE EVIDENCE!

### World War I

| Type of source | Category | Example | |
|---|---|---|---|
| Primary | Visual | World War I was the first conflict to be extensively photographed and filmed by both the media (journalists) and private soldiers | |
| Primary | Written | Official documents from the governments at war: war reports, speeches by political leaders. Newspapers carried detailed coverage of the war from reporters at the front | |
| | | Letters, diaries and books written by people of the time. Writers like Siegfried Sassoon, Ernest Hemingway and Wilfred Owen wrote memoirs, poetry and novels that portrayed the lives of ordinary soldiers | |

▲ A soldier photographs the reality at the front

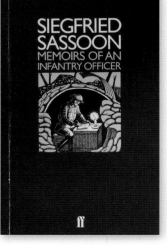

What are the advantages and disadvantages of using poetry or fictionalised accounts of a soldier's life?

◀ A novel presenting a fictionalised account of Sassoon's own experiences at the front

# 23.1: The Causes of World War I

In this topic, you will learn about:
- The causes of World War I
- The two sides in the war

| | |
|---|---|
| Central Powers | |
| Entente Allies | |
| Neutrals | |
| Front line | |

◀ Map of Europe in 1914 with the Western and Eastern Fronts marked in red

In the years before 1914, Europe was dominated by empires that were competing for power and territory. A number of issues were driving European countries apart:

- **disagreements over colonies** in Africa and Asia
- **military arms races**, especially between Germany and Britain over their naval fleets
- competition between Austria and Russia for **influence in the Balkans** (south-east Europe) as the Ottoman Empire slowly collapsed and new states (such as Serbia) emerged

These issues saw the creation of a **system of alliances** between states. An **alliance** is an agreement between states to aid each other in wartime.

On **28 June 1914** the heir to the Austro-Hungarian Empire, the **Archduke Franz Ferdinand**, was assassinated in **Sarajevo** (the capital of Bosnia). The Austrians blamed the Serbian government for his death and declared war on them in August. Russia, an ally of Serbia, declared war on Austria. Germany, who had encouraged its Austrian ally to take a hard line on Serbia, declared war on Russia. France, an ally of Russia, went to war with Germany. When Germany's army invaded Belgium to get to France, Britain (which had promised to protect Belgium) declared war on Germany.

▼ Alliances in World War I

| The Entente Powers | The Central Powers |
|---|---|
| Britain (and Ireland) | Germany |
| France | The Austro-Hungarian Empire |
| Russia (until October 1917) | The Ottoman Empire |
| Italy (from 1915) | |
| The United States (from 1917) | |

## CHECKPOINT!

1. Why were there tensions between European states in the years before World War I?
2. What is an alliance?
3. What event sparked the outbreak of war in 1914?
4. Which countries were on either side in the conflict?

 I can explain how World War I began.

 ← TIME TO GO BACK ❯ I CAN MOVE FORWARD →

**23** World War I and its Consequences

# 23.2: World War I

**In this topic, you will learn about:**

- Trench warfare
- New military technology
- How the war came to an end

▲ French infantry advancing across no man's land

## In the trenches

Both sides had expected the war to be over within months. British soldiers told their families they would be home by Christmas. However, the war quickly developed into a **stalemate**: neither side could win. The Germans, who almost defeated the French in the first few weeks, had to split their forces between the Eastern Front (in Russia) and the Western Front, and so could not defeat either. Nor could the British and French drive the German army out of northern France. Along the **Western Front**, soldiers dug networks of **deep trenches** to protect themselves from enemy fire. The strip of land between the opposing armies was called **no man's land**. There, the ground was soon churned up, and in many locations a deep, sticky, dangerous mud lasted for the entire war. Trenches and shell craters were often full of foul water.

To take the enemy trenches, soldiers had to climb out of their trenches (go '**over the top**') and march across **no man's land**. However, they were met by barbed wire, machine-gun fire and shelling. This made World War I battles incredibly bloody. For example, in 1916 1.1 million people were killed over five months at the **Battle of the Somme** alone.

## A new era in warfare

World War I also saw the introduction of **new military technology**, including the first use of **aeroplanes** for reconnaissance, aerial combat and bombing. German **submarines, or U-boats**, attacked any ships, military or civilian, in enemy waters. The British invented the **tank** to try to break the stalemate on the Western Front. **Mines and grenades** were widely used. World War I also saw the **first use of chemical weapons** (by both sides): chlorine, mustard and phosgene gas.

Warfare had been transformed: never before could so many be killed, at a distance and in so many ways. Sadly, the generals were slow to adjust their tactics to this new reality.

### DID YOU KNOW?

Within six months, medics observed a set of symptoms among soldiers in the trenches – extreme anxiety, tremors, confusion, memory loss, nightmares, sudden sight or hearing loss – that they named 'shell shock'. Today, doctors would call it PTSD (Post-Traumatic Stress Disorder). Some 80,000 soldiers in the British army alone were diagnosed with shell shock, including the poets Siegfried Sassoon and Wilfred Owen, who became friends at the hospital where they had been sent to recover. Sassoon's poem 'Survivors' and Owen's poem 'Mental Cases' address shell shock.

## The end of the war

The bloody conflict dragged on for over four years. Attempts by the Entente Powers to break the stalemate by attacking Turkey in 1915 failed. The Russian government was overthrown in October 1917 by the **Bolsheviks** (communists) led by **Vladimir Lenin**; this ended Russian involvement. However, the US entered the war on the Entente's side in 1917, and the arrival of one million American troops eventually turned the tide in their favour. **Germany and its allies surrendered** in November 1918.

▲ A reconstruction at an Australian memorial, entitled 'Man in the Mud'

▲ A World War I tank

Go to page 137 of your *Sources and Skills Book* for an evidence task on a soldier's life during World War I.

## CHECKPOINT!

1. Why was there a stalemate during much of World War I?
2. What were trenches and no man's land in World War I?
3. How were battles fought on the Western Front?
4. Why did these battles have so many casualties?
5. What new technology was introduced to warfare during World War I?
6. How did the war end?

 I understand how World War I was fought.

 TIME TO GO BACK ◀ ▶ I CAN MOVE FORWARD ➡

23 World War I and its Consequences

# 23.3: The Paris Peace Conference

**In this topic, you will learn about:**

❯ The leaders of the victorious powers in World War I

❯ What they wanted

❯ The outcome of the conference

The Entente Powers dictated the terms of the peace treaty to Germany and its allies. They met for a peace conference at Versailles, outside Paris, throughout 1919. There were three main leaders (known as the **Big Three**):

- **Woodrow Wilson** (US President)
- **Georges Clemenceau** (French Prime Minister)
- **David Lloyd George** (British Prime Minister)

Each of the three wanted different things.

- **Wilson** wanted **a just peace to prevent future wars** and had outlined his views in his **'Fourteen Points'** speech when the US entered the war. He sought to reduce the size of armies to preserve the peace. He also believed in the **'right to self-determination'**, the right of a people or nation sharing a common language and culture to govern themselves independently. He wanted a new organisation, **the League of Nations**, set up to keep peace between nations.

▲ Left to right: Lloyd George, Clemenceau and Wilson

- **Clemenceau** blamed the Germans for starting the war and therefore wanted to punish Germany. France had lost 1.4 million men in the war and suffered billions in damages; it demanded **compensation**. Clemenceau was also determined to secure France against future German attacks and **to prevent Germany ever being a threat again**.

- **Lloyd George** also wanted Germany punished to appease people at home in Britain. He saw the peace treaty as an opportunity **to expand the British empire and boost the British economy**, both at the expense of Germany.

After six months of negotiations, the **Treaty of Versailles** was agreed in June 1919. The German representatives were not given a chance to seek any changes to the text. They were told to agree or else there would be a return to war. The **main points of the Treaty** were:

1. The **War Guilt Clause** placed blame solely on Germany for starting the war.

2. Germany would pay £6.6 billion (£300 billion in today's money) in **reparations** (<u>compensation payments paid by the loser to the victors after a war</u>) to Britain, France and other countries. This debt was finally cleared in 2010.

3. Germany **surrendered all its colonies** in Africa and Asia to Britain and Japan.

4. Germany lost **territory in Europe** to France, Denmark and Poland.

5. The German armed forces were reduced to 100,000 men and only six naval ships and they were **banned** from having an **air force, tanks or submarines**.

6. Germany and Austria were forbidden to unite.

7. To protect France's security, Germany was banned from putting any troops in the Rhineland, the border area between the two countries. It became a **demilitarised zone**.

8. The **League of Nations** was set up.

Legend:
- Formerly Austria-Hungary
- Territory lost by Germany
- Territory lost by Russia
- Demilitarised area

◀ Map of the Central Powers' territorial losses and newly created countries

Go to page 138 of your *Sources and Skills Book* for an evidence task on the Treaty of Versailles.

**23** World War I and its Consequences

## CHECKPOINT!

1. Who were the Big Three at the Paris Peace Conference?

2. What did each of them want from the negotiations?

3. What was the War Guilt Clause?

4. What were reparations?

5. What territories did Germany lose after World War I?

6. What happened to the German armed forces?

7. How do you think the German people felt about the Treaty of Versailles?

 I can explain the Treaty of Versailles.

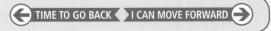 TIME TO GO BACK ◀ ▶ I CAN MOVE FORWARD ➡

# 23.4: The Consequences of World War I

## 1. New states

The Austro-Hungarian and Ottoman Empires were abolished and new states were created in Central and Eastern Europe and the Middle East. This was due to Wilson's belief in the **right to self-determination**. These new states included Poland, Czechoslovakia, Yugoslavia, Turkey and Finland.

## 2. Resentment

The Treaty was deeply unpopular in Germany, where people felt it was unduly harsh. They rejected the idea that they were solely responsible for the war and resented the humiliating loss of territory and limitations on their military. They felt betrayed by their government for signing the treaty.

In Italy, there was a lot of anger that they did not receive all the land they had been promised when they entered the war. In both countries, this anger and resentment would lead to many people supporting the new extreme nationalist ideologies of **Nazism** and **fascism**.

▲ British and Belgian infantry retreating from the Front

## 3. Economic problems

The reparations imposed on Germany crippled its economy. There was **mass unemployment**. As Germany was Europe's largest economy, wider Europe also took a long time to recover. This ongoing **economic hardship** added to the bitterness felt at the end of the war.

## 4. The rise of communism

Russia had been devastated by the war and its army's defeat to the smaller German army. In 1917 the Russian tsar (emperor) was overthrown and the world's **first communist government** came to power under **Vladimir Lenin**. Russia would try to spread communism across Europe and beyond.

## 5. The League of Nations

Wilson had hoped that the League of Nations would prevent future wars by settling disputes peacefully and encouraging collective security. This meant working together to stop aggression. However, the US refused to join, and Germany and Russia were not allowed to join. This meant that some of the world's most powerful states were not members, making it difficult for the League to operate with authority.

## CHECKPOINT!

1. How did World War I lead to the creation of new states? Give three examples.
2. Why did the people of (a) Germany and (b) Italy resent the Treaty of Versailles?
3. Where was the world's first communist government?
4. What problems did the League of Nations face?

 I understand the consequences of World War I.

 TIME TO GO BACK ◆ I CAN MOVE FORWARD ➡

 **SUMMARY**

In this chapter, we have learned that:

- World War I broke out in August 1914. The long-term cause of the war was the rivalry between powerful European states over colonies, armaments and the Balkans. The assassination of Archduke Franz Ferdinand brought the system of European alliances into play.
- The war was mainly fought along two fronts, west and east. In the trenches of the Western Front, the opposing armies faced each other across no man's land. Over 18 million people were killed between 1914 and 1918.
- After the war, the leaders of the victorious allies met at Versailles to negotiate a peace deal to impose on Germany.
- The Treaty of Versailles blamed Germany for starting the war, imposed significant reparations, limited the size of its military and removed some of its territory.

### Reflecting on... World War I

The wars of the nineteenth century were limited to armies and battlefields – but in 1914, war became 'total'. Civilians were directly targeted by bombings and blockades. Soldiers died in their millions and many survivors were left physically and emotionally damaged. Technological advances allowed people to kill each other with far greater efficiency and detachment.

World War I changed the world: empires fell, millions died, states were created, revolutions broke out and the seeds of an even more devastating conflict were sown.

 **Understanding History**

1. Why did war break out in Europe in the summer of 1914?
2. Why did so many die during World War I?
3. Why do you think the French and US leaders had such different aims during the Paris Peace Conference?
4. What effect did World War I have on (a) France; (b) Germany; and (c) Russia?
5. How did World War I give rise to new political ideologies such as (a) fascism and (b) communism?

 **Exploring History**

1. Write an account of World War I under the following headings:
   - Causes
   - Style of warfare
   - Peace talks

2. The Treaty of Versailles has been described as 'both unjust and foolish'. Do you agree or disagree with this statement? Give reasons for your answer, referring to the terms of the Treaty.

| KEY TERMS | | |
|---|---|---|
| | **Alliance** | an agreement between states to aid each other in wartime |
| | **No man's land** | the strip of land between the trenches of the opposing armies |
| | **Right to self-determination** | the right of a people or nation sharing a common language and culture to govern themselves independently |
| | **Reparations** | compensation payments paid by the loser to the victors after a war |

 Go to page 135 of your *Sources and Skills Book* for more exercises.

 Go to page 75 of your *Research Portfolio* for a task based on this chapter.

**23**

World War I and its Consequences

| World War I | Stalin's Russia | World War II |
|---|---|---|
| 1914–1918 | 1924–1953 | 1939–1945 |

After World War I, under the leadership of Vladimir Lenin, Russia became the first communist state. Josef Stalin took over from Lenin and used terror and propaganda to keep control and ensure that communism remained strong in Russia.

Within a generation, Russia was transformed from a backwards, agricultural, peasant society to a more modern, industrial, urban one. However, the Russian people paid a high price for this transformation.

# WORKING WITH THE EVIDENCE!

## Stalin's Russia

| Type of source | Category | Example |
|---|---|---|
| Primary | Visual | Propaganda poster |
| Primary | Visual | Stalin monument, Prague (destroyed in 1962) |

▲ The Stalin Monument, Prague

ВЕЛИКИЙ СТАЛИН-ЗНАМЯ ДРУЖБЫ НАРОДОВ СССР!

▲ Propaganda poster

What image of Stalin and Russia is being presented by each of these sources? What can historians learn from sources such as these?

# 24.1: Communism and the Bolsheviks

In this topic, you will learn about:
- ❯ Communism
- ❯ The Bolsheviks and the civil war

## Communism takes root in Russia

Russia's poor performance in World War I prompted riots and strikes; **Tsar (Emperor) Nicholas II** was forced to step down in February 1917. The provisional government that replaced him was overthrown in the **October Revolution of 1917**, when **Vladimir Lenin** came to power. The tsar and his family were imprisoned in a house far from the capital.

Lenin and his followers were called **Bolsheviks**. The Bolshevik Party believed in the ideas of **Karl Marx**, a German political thinker who said that the working classes should stage revolutions to end private ownership and distribute wealth, making society 'classless'. This was **communism**: a system of government where the state controls all aspects of the economy (property, business and jobs) and of society, with limited rights for individuals. In addition, religion was discouraged and Church property was seized.

> 'Workers of the world, unite! You have nothing to lose but your chains'
> – Karl Marx

Russia became the world's first communist state. All political parties other than the Bolshevik Party were banned. The government took control of the banks and factories. Lenin negotiated a peace treaty with Germany that ended Russia's involvement in World War I.

▲ Vladimir Lenin

▲ Karl Marx

**24 Life in Communist Russia**

# The Russian Civil War

Many Russians were worried by these events. In 1917, civil war broke out. The Bolsheviks' **Red Army**, under the command of **Leon Trotsky**, fought the **White Army** (an alliance of various anti-communist groups). In July 1918, Tsar Nicholas II, his wife and five children were executed by the Bolsheviks in the house where they had been imprisoned.

▲ Tsar Nicholas II and family (Romanovs)

By 1921, Lenin and the Bolsheviks had gained control of the country and the last clusters of the White Army were defeated in 1922. Russia was renamed **the Union of Soviet Socialist Republics (USSR)**. 'Soviet' originally meant a workers' council.

**DID YOU KNOW?**

The Bolsheviks' secret police was called the Cheka. During the civil war they 'removed' any person who was an 'actual or potential threat' to the government – so-called 'enemies of the state'. In St Petersburg alone, the Cheka killed 800 people. This time became known as 'the Red Terror'.

## CHECKPOINT!

1. Explain the following terms: communism; Bolsheviks; the Cheka.
2. Who was (a) Karl Marx; (b) Vladimir Lenin; (c) Leon Trotsky?
3. How did Lenin come to power in 1917?
4. List two changes Lenin and the Bolsheviks made once in power.
5. What was the outcome of the Russian Civil War?

I can explain communism and how Russia became a communist state.

 COLLABORATE: With your group, research Karl Marx and write down ten points on his ideas about communism.

# 24.2: Stalin's Rise to Power

**In this topic, you will learn about:**
- Lenin's death
- The Bolshevik power struggle
- Stalin's rise to power

## Lenin's death

Lenin suffered two strokes in 1922 and knew he was weakening, so he wrote his **Testament**, a document outlining his vision for the future of communism. It also contained his thoughts on each of his colleagues. He was very critical of **Josef Stalin**, who had been appointed **General Secretary** of the Communist Party in 1922. He wanted Stalin removed from his position. Lenin died on 21 January 1924 without a named successor. A power struggle began among the senior members of the party: **Lev Kamenev**, **Grigory Zinoviev**, **Nikolai Bukharin**, **Leon Trotsky** and **Josef Stalin**.

▲ Lenin lying in state

## Stalin's rise to power

Leon Trotsky was the frontrunner for the leadership of the Communist Party. He was well liked by the ordinary party members and had been successful during the civil war. In his *Testament*, Lenin had also described Trotsky as the 'most capable'. Many leaders in the party, however, saw Trotsky as arrogant and worried that he already controlled the Red Army and would have too much power as leader. Stalin took control of Lenin's funeral arrangements and gave the speech there; this led people to believe that he was to be Lenin's successor.

▲ Leon Trotsky

Stalin played the various party members off against each other. He used Kamenev and Zinoviev to expel Trotsky from the party and the country. He then turned on them, forced them out of their government positions and replaced them with his supporters.

Stalin announced his policy **Socialism in One Country**: the plan to first strengthen communism in the USSR before spreading it further afield. By 1928, Stalin was the absolute ruler of the USSR. He would enforce his rule ruthlessly in the years ahead.

▲ Josef Stalin

  CHECKPOINT!

1. What was Lenin's *Testament*?
2. Why was Trotsky seen as the likely successor to Lenin? Why were some people opposed to him?
3. How did Stalin eventually seize power?
4. What was Socialism in One Country?

 I can explain how Stalin rose to power.

← TIME TO GO BACK  ◆ I CAN MOVE FORWARD →

**DID YOU KNOW?**

Trotsky was exiled from the USSR in 1929. Ten years later, Stalin ordered his assassination. In August 1940, Trotsky was attacked in his Mexican home with an ice-axe and died the following day from head injuries.

24 **Life in Communist Russia**

Go to page 141 of your *Sources and Skills Book* for an evidence task on Lenin's *Testament*.

## 24.3: Life in Stalin's Russia

In this topic, you will learn about:
- Economic policies
- The use of terror and propaganda
- Educational policies
- Women's lives

### Economic policies

Stalin's economic policies greatly affected the lives of millions of people.

- In 1927, Stalin started a scheme called collectivisation. **Collectivisation** was the joining of small, unproductive farms together to create large, state-owned farms. Workers would be hired to run them or farmers could collectively own all the land and equipment. However, the farmers refused to surrender their farms. By late 1929, Stalin began to use force to get them to cooperate. Over 2.5 million **kulaks** (wealthy independent farmers) were simply removed and sent to **gulags**, or forced labour camps. By 1936, 90% of farmland had been collectivised.

- Stalin launched three Five-Year Plans to boost industrialisation. A **Five-Year Plan** was a set of targets (and policies designed to meet them) over a period of five years. He believed that the USSR was up to 100 years behind other industrialised countries.

  - The **First Five-Year Plan (1928–1932)** focused on heavy industry and the production of coal, oil, steel and electricity. The targets were mostly unrealistic but improvements were made.

  - The **Second Five-Year Plan (1933–1937)** had a continued focus on industry and also on transport and the production of consumer goods. The Moscow underground was built, as were canal and rail links.

  - The **Third Five-Year Plan (1938–1941)** was cut short due to the 1941 invasion by Germany. Instead, the focus switched to the production of arms and ammunition.

- Shortages of everyday goods were widespread and food had to be rationed. Some regions were devastated by **famines**.

- **Rewards** such as higher wages were given to the most productive workers.

- Many workers were provided with **an apartment, free schooling** and **free basic healthcare**.

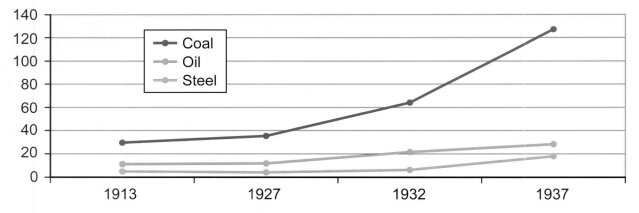

▲ Industrial output under the Five-Year Plans (in millions of tonnes)

# Terror

Stalin wanted to keep his grip on power. He was a **dictator**: someone who has gained almost total control over their country and uses a variety of means, especially terror and propaganda, to hold on to power. Stalin's use of terror became a part of life in the USSR.

- In 1934 the **Cheka (secret police)** were reorganised and renamed **the NKVD**. They arrested (and sometimes tortured or executed) so-called '**enemies of the state**'. Suspicion and fear reigned, as people were encouraged to report anybody that they suspected to the NKVD.

- The NKVD ran the gulags. Up to **30,000 gulags** existed throughout the Soviet Union, but the largest camps lay in the most extreme geographical and climatic regions of the country, such as Siberia. Prisoners were forced to carry out manual work such as felling trees, mining or building railroads. The combination of violence, extreme climates, hard labour, poor food rations and unsanitary conditions led to **extremely high death rates**. Over one million people died in the gulags from 1934 to 1953.

▲ Gulag workers digging a canal system

- Stalin became increasingly paranoid that people were trying to overthrow him. In 1934, he began a **purge** of his party, removing all those who he believed were challenging his authority. That year alone, almost one million members were expelled from the Communist Party.

- Stalin organised three show trials between 1936 and 1938. A **show trial** was a staged trial held in public to influence popular opinion. It was a method of propaganda, so the press were invited to attend. The defendants had been tortured for their confessions. Their families were also threatened with arrest and torture.

– The **first show trial** was held in **August 1936**. It was known as **the Trial of the Sixteen** because 16 Communist Party leaders (including **Zinoviev** and **Kamenev**) were tried for the assassination of a man called Sergei Kirov and for trying to overthrow the government. All were executed within hours of the verdict, despite Stalin saying that they would not be executed if they pleaded guilty.

▲ A show trial

– The **second show trial**, in **January 1937**, was called **the Trial of the Seventeen**. It saw 17 current and former leading Bolsheviks tried. Thirteen were executed and the others were sentenced to ten years in the gulags.

– The **third show trial**, in **March 1938**, was known as **the Trial of the Twenty-One**. Stalin used it to get rid of his last potential rivals, such as **Nikolai Bukharin** and the **head of the NKVD, Genrikh Yagoda**. They were accused of plotting to assassinate both Lenin and Stalin. Bukharin took three months to confess, only doing so when threats were made against his family. All but three of the defendants were executed.

• **The Red Army** was **purged** in **1937**. Stalin did not trust anyone who had served under Trotsky. A secret military trial took place of eight army commanders: all confessed and were executed. A more widespread purge of the Red Army happened afterwards. Almost 30,000 Red Army officers were either fired or executed.

> **DID YOU KNOW?**
>
> Stalin is rumoured to have watched the show trials from behind a screen.

## CHECKPOINT!

1. Explain the following terms: collectivisation; gulags; kulaks; Five-Year Plan. 📖
2. How was collectivisation carried out in the USSR?
3. What happened under the (a) First, (b) Second and (c) Third Five-Year Plans?
4. Were Stalin's attempts to industrialise the USSR successful? Give reasons for your answer.
5. What is a dictator? 📖
6. What was the NKVD and who did it target?
7. What was a show trial? How did Stalin ensure the conviction of the defendants?
8. What happened to the Red Army in 1938? Why did this happen?
9. How did Stalin use terror to achieve total control of the USSR?
10. Why do you think dictatorships need to use terror as a tactic?

 I can describe Stalin's economic policies and the use of terror in the USSR.

 ← TIME TO GO BACK ◆ I CAN MOVE FORWARD →

## Propaganda

Stalin used propaganda to keep control of the USSR, and its messages loomed large in people's lives. Events such as the show trials were propaganda, and many other examples existed.

▲ A propaganda poster showing happy workers

- The Communist Party newspaper was called **Pravda** ('Truth'). In it, Stalin was praised and his rivals or enemies were criticised.

- Posters and works of art had to present the idea of a successful country with a happy workforce, demonstrating the greatness of the USSR and the success of communism.

- Stalin became a godlike figure: posters and statues of him were everywhere in the USSR.

- Cities and streets were named after Stalin, for example **Stalingrad** and **Stalinsk**.

- Stalin was referred to as '**the Brilliant Genius of Humanity**' and '**the Father of Nations**'.

- Those declared enemies of the state or killed in purges were sometimes even airbrushed out of photographs or removed from all records, as if they had never existed.

▲ Photograph of Stalin with Yezhov (head of the NKVD after Yagoda) at his side

▲ The same picture, doctored after Yezhov's fall from favour and execution (1940)

## Education

- Propaganda was also used in schools. Textbooks were rewritten to make Stalin's role in the October Revolution and the Russian Civil War look more impressive. The roles of others, such as Trotsky, were downplayed or erased completely.

> 'Education is a weapon whose effect depends on who holds it in his hands and at whom it is aimed'
> – Josef Stalin

- Stalin made **attending school compulsory** to combat illiteracy and improve efficiency in the workplace. He also brought back exams, which had been removed during Lenin's rule.

- Before the revolution, literacy rates in Russia were roughly 28% overall (only 13% for women). Records claim that literacy rates soared to 56% in 1924 and to 75% by 1937.

- Children were to learn how to be of the greatest possible service to their country.

- Youth organisations such as the **Young Communists** and the **Komsomol** were founded. Both worked to convince the youth of the importance of communism, so that they would ensure it continued into future generations.

24 Life in Communist Russia

## Women's lives

- Marx had insisted on the equality of men and women in communist society. Under Lenin, the **status of Russian women improved** a lot: they got the vote and the right to an education; they could access contraception and divorce; legally, they could be head of the household; all jobs were open to women (in theory).

- Cheap dining halls, laundries and childcare were provided by the state so that traditional responsibilities would not prevent women working or getting involved in this new society.

- Stalin was more conservative: he wanted the birth rate to be high, because the USSR would need many children to build up its workforce and army.

- Parents received a **child allowance** from the state, but only if married. Divorce was discouraged and contraception was made illegal again.

- Women who had six or more children were paid 2,000 roubles per year for five years as a reward from the state. Mothers of nine or more children also received a medal.

- In 1935 women made up 44% of the workforce of the USSR, and by **1937** it was **50%**.

### CHECKPOINT!

1. What is propaganda? Give three examples of how it was used by Stalin.
2. Why do you think that dictatorships need to use propaganda?
3. Name two ways that Stalin's educational policies benefited the USSR.
4. What policies did Stalin introduce to encourage large families?
5. Do you think that Stalin's ideas about women reflected those of Marx? Explain your answer.

I understand the use of propaganda and can discuss education and women's lives in Stalin's USSR.

TIME TO GO BACK ◀ ▶ I CAN MOVE FORWARD →

## WORKING WITH THE EVIDENCE!

Joseph E. Davies, US Ambassador to the USSR, 1936–1938, reflects on the second show trial of January 1937:

The most extraordinary part of this trial, from a Western outlook, is that there should have been such a trial at all. The accused had all entered the plea of guilty. There remained nothing for a court to do but to hear possible pleas for clemency and to adjudge the fact and sentence the accused. But here a so-called trial was held which lasted for six days and in which presumably all proof was produced that the prosecutor could possibly adduce – from our point of view an entirely useless proceeding.

The occasion was dramatized for propaganda purposes. It was designed: first, as a warning to all existing and potential plotters and conspirators within the Soviet Union; second, to discredit Trotsky abroad; and third, to solidify popular national feeling in support of the government against foreign enemies – Germany and Japan. During the trial every means of propaganda was employed to carry to all parts of the country the horrors of these confessions. The newspapers were filled not only with reports of the testimony but also comments of the most violent and vituperative character as to the accused. The radio also was working overtime.

1. What type of source is this?
2. Explain what the writer finds 'most extraordinary' about the trial of January 1937.
3. What does the writer mean when he suggests that the trial was 'dramatized for propaganda purposes'?
4. What three propaganda messages does the writer believe the trial was designed to send?
5. What means were used to spread these messages?
6. Give one benefit and one limitation of this source for historians.

# A Life in Time: Josef Stalin (1878–1953)

## Early life

Josef Stalin was born near Tiflis in Georgia on 8 December 1878. His father was a cobbler and his mother was a housemaid. He had smallpox scars on his face from childhood, which he had airbrushed in photos. At 16 he was in training to be a priest, but was expelled for his radical Marxist ideas.

## Role in the Bolshevik Party

For joining the Bolsheviks, Stalin was arrested and sent to Siberia in 1904. In the years that followed, Stalin grew close to Lenin and Bukharin, joining the Bolshevik central committee in 1912. He had a minor role in the October Revolution of 1917. During the Russian Civil War, he organised the 'Red Terror' and gained a reputation for brutality.

## Seizing power

Stalin became the Communist Party general secretary in 1922 and gradually gained power by appointing his loyal supporters to positions of responsibility. When Lenin died in 1924, Stalin was ready to seize power, making the arrangements for Lenin's funeral and increasing his hold on the leadership. In 1928, he had Trotsky expelled from the party and exiled.

▲ Stalin as a young man

**DID YOU KNOW?**

Stalin means 'man of steel'; his original, Georgian name was Iosif Vissarionovich Dzhugashvili.

## Industrialisation of the USSR

Stalin intended to transform the Soviet Union into an industrial giant through his Five-Year Plans. He believed that the USSR was 50–100 years behind other industrialised countries. He organised the combination of small farms into larger 'collective farms'. Better-off farmers (kulaks) resisted surrendering their lands and were persecuted or eliminated.

## The purges

The purges of the 1930s saw Stalin targeting anyone who he believed posed a threat to his power. The show trials were intended to frighten his opponents. He later purged the Red Army: first the officers and then the soldiers.

## World War II

In August 1939, Stalin signed a 'non-aggression pact' with Germany. When Germany invaded the Soviet Union in 1941, Stalin appealed to the patriotism of its citizens to defend 'Mother Russia' in what became known to Russians as the 'Great Patriotic War'. He created an alliance with Britain and France to defeat the Germans. After the war, the USSR emerged as a superpower. By the time of Stalin's death in 1953, the USSR was taking part in the 'Cold War'.

https://educateplus.ie/go/stalin

https://educateplus.ie/go/stalin2

# SUMMARY

In this chapter, we have learned that:

- Vladimir Lenin created the first communist state after the October Revolution of 1917. His political party was called the Bolsheviks.

- Lenin did not name a successor. When he died, a power struggle took place between Kamanev, Zinoviev, Bukharin, Trotsky and Stalin. Josef Stalin rose to power.

- Stalin aimed to industrialise and modernise the USSR. He began a method called collectivisation. He also created three Five-Year Plans to increase production in the USSR.

- Stalin used terror tactics to intimidate the Russian people, for example through purges, the secret police (Cheka/NKVD), the gulags and the show trials. He used propaganda to control information and to project a strong, forward-looking image of the USSR to the outside world. Examples include the posters and statues, the youth groups, the party newspaper *Pravda*, and the rewriting of fact in textbooks and through altered photographs and records.

### Reflecting on... Stalin's Russia

The October Revolution of 1917 created the world's first communist state. Lenin and Stalin set up a system to be a beacon to the rest of the world and encourage the spread of communism. The USSR industrialised rapidly and access to education and healthcare was improved. However, its people lived in fear of the state. The conflict between communism and other political ideologies – first fascism and later Western democracy – would dominate the twentieth century.

# Understanding History

1. How did the Bolsheviks come to power in Russia?

2. What changes did they introduce after the revolution?

3. Explain the struggle for power after Lenin's death.

4. What did Stalin want to do when he came to power in the USSR? Give three examples of the policies he introduced.

5. What was collectivisation and how did it affect the USSR?

6. What were the Five-Year Plans and what was their impact on the USSR?

7. How did Stalin use terror to ensure his control of (a) the Communist Party and (b) ordinary people's lives?

8. How was propaganda used to secure Stalin's power?

9. What changes did Stalin bring to education and why did he make these changes?

10. What was life like for women in the USSR?

# Exploring History

1. Write a paragraph about: (a) Stalin's economic policies; (b) the use of terror in Stalin's Russia; and (c) the use of propaganda in Stalin's Russia.

2. Write an account of the life and career of Josef Stalin.

3. Read the following quotes about Stalin. Write down your reaction to each of them, stating whether you agree or disagree, and then give your own opinion on Stalin.

   – *'Stalin was the most violent of leading Bolsheviks... He had reached dominance in the Party before [anyone]... knew what happened.'* Robert Service

   – *'Joseph Stalin was a great man; few other men of the twentieth century approach his stature.'* W.E.B. Du Bois

   – *'Stalin is the saviour of all the oppressed.'* Chairman Mao Zedong

   – *'Every Party member must raise his revolutionary qualities in every respect to the same level as those of Marx, Engels, Lenin and Stalin.'* Nelson Mandela

| KEY TERMS | | |
|---|---|---|
| | **Communism** | a system of government where the state controls all aspects of the economy (property, business and jobs) and of society, with limited rights for individuals |
| | **Collectivisation** | the joining of small, unproductive farms together to create large, state-owned farms |
| | **Kulaks** | wealthy independent farmers |
| | **Gulags** | Soviet forced labour camps |
| | **Five-Year Plan** | a set of targets (and policies designed to meet them) over a period of five years |
| | **Dictator** | someone who has gained almost total control over their country and uses a variety of means, especially terror and propaganda, to hold on to power |
| | **Show trial** | a staged trial held in public to influence popular opinion |

Go to page 139 of your *Sources and Skills Book* for more exercises.

Go to page 79 of your *Research Portfolio* for a task based on this chapter.

**24 Life in Communist Russia**

| World War I | Fascist Germany | World War II |
|---|---|---|
| 1914–1918 | 1933–1945 | 1939–1945 |

After World War I, under the leadership of Benito Mussolini, Italy became a fascist dictatorship. Fascism spread to Germany in the form of the Nazi Party. Adolf Hitler had become the leader of the Nazi party by 1921 and he was elected German chancellor in 1933. Hitler used terror, anti-Semitism and propaganda to ensure that he remained in power. He enforced new economic policies to improve Germany's employment levels.

## WORKING WITH THE EVIDENCE!

### Nazi propaganda posters

| Type of source | Category | Example |
|---|---|---|
| Primary | Visual | Nazi poster |
| Primary | Visual | Poster for the Hitler Youth |

▲ A Nazi poster with the slogan 'Long live Germany!'

▲ A Hitler Youth Poster

What image of Hitler and Germany is being presented in these propaganda posters? What can historians learn from sources such as these?

# 25.1: Fascism

In this topic, you will learn about:
- ❯ Fascism
- ❯ Mussolini and fascist Italy

## Fascism in Europe: Italy

In World War I, Italy lost 600,000 soldiers. Italy was not rewarded with land that it had been promised at the Paris Peace Conference of 1919. Many Italians were angered by this. The country was also in debt as a result of the war and unemployment was high. As a result of all this, governments in Italy did not last long. There were five different governments between 1918 and 1922. Many believed that the democratic parties were getting them nowhere and they needed something different. Some people became interested in communism. However, another political ideal became popular in Italy. This was **fascism**.

In 1919 **Benito Mussolini** founded a new political party called the Fascist Party. Mussolini believed that a **dictatorship** was needed to solve Italy's problems. He was prepared to use violence if necessary. He wanted a one-party state with complete control, like Stalin's dictatorship in chapter 24. **Fascism is a form of government that is a one-party dictatorship**. Fascists are against democracy and are **nationalistic**

▲ Benito Mussolini in the early 1920s

(believe that their nation is superior). Fascism is centred around a single leader and uses propaganda and fear to ensure control of the state. The first two fascist leaders were Mussolini and Hitler.

Mussolini was made prime minister on 28 October 1922 by the King of Italy, who had lost faith in democracy and the current government. Under Mussolini, the **Acerbo Law** was passed in 1923 to say that the party with the most votes would get two-thirds of the seats in government. After he used violence and bribery to win the 1923 election, Mussolini started to **rule by decree**. This meant that **he could make laws without going through parliament**. His political opponents were arrested and Mussolini stayed in complete control of Italy until his death in 1945. He was known as **Il Duce** ('the leader').

**DID YOU KNOW?**

The fascist symbol is based on the Roman fasces. It is a bundle of rods and an axe, to represent the strength of the state and to remind people of when Italy was strong during the Roman Empire.

## CHECKPOINT!

1. List two reasons why fascism became popular in Italy after World War I.
2. Explain the terms fascism and dictatorship. 📖
3. Who founded the Fascist Party?
4. In what two countries did the first two fascist leaders come to power?
5. How did Mussolini maintain his control over Italy after 1922?

 I can describe what fascism is and how fascism began in Italy.

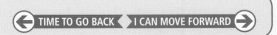
← TIME TO GO BACK ◄ ❯ I CAN MOVE FORWARD →

# 25.2: Hitler's Rise to Power

**In this topic, you will learn about:**
- The Weimar Republic
- The Nazi Party
- Hitler's rise to power
- Creating a dictatorship

## The Weimar Republic

After World War I, Germany became a democracy, named '**the Weimar Republic**' after the town where it was founded. The Weimar government was in power when **the Treaty of Versailles** was signed. Many Germans blamed these politicians for failing to restore Germany's greatness – and even for defeat in World War I, because they signed the armistice ending the war in November 1918. They were nicknamed '**the November criminals**'. For much of the 1920s, Germany was in economic crisis, with very high levels of unemployment and inflation. This further undermined people's confidence in the Weimar Republic.

## The Nazi Party

The **National Socialist German Workers' Party (NSDAP)**, or **Nazi Party** for short, was founded in 1919 and was originally small. The Nazis wanted to speed up German recovery by scrapping the Treaty of Versailles.

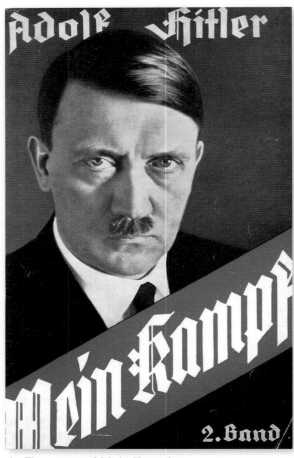

▲ The cover of *Mein Kampf*

They were extremely anti-communist. After World War I, Adolf Hitler worked as a spy for the German army. While spying on Nazi Party meetings, he grew impressed by their ideas and later joined them. Hitler was a **gifted speaker** and he was soon chosen as party leader.

Hitler and the Nazi Party organised a rebellion in Munich in November 1923, commonly known as **the Beer Hall Putsch** because it began in a beer hall. It was quickly stopped and Hitler and other Nazis were sent to prison. Hitler was released after nine months of his four-year sentence. While in prison, Hitler wrote ***Mein Kampf*** ('My Struggle'), which outlined the core Nazi beliefs and his vision for the future of Germany. In it, he claimed that Jews and communists in particular were major threats to Germany. This marked the beginning of his persecution of the Jews. He also put emphasis on '**racial purity**' and demanded an end to the humiliating Treaty of Versailles and more territory for Germany in Central Europe – which he called **Lebensraum** (meaning 'living space' for ethnic Germans).

Hitler admired Mussolini's Fascist Party and adopted many of its methods, including the fascist salute, an army – the **SA** or **Sturmabteilung (stormtroopers)**, also called '**Brownshirts**' – and an emblem. Hitler chose to use the **swastika** instead of the fasces emblem used by Mussolini and made it the country's official flag.

▲ Swastika

# The rise of the Nazi Party

Several factors helped Hitler and the Nazi Party to rise to power:

- **The unpopularity of the Weimar government**: Many blamed the Weimar government for Germany's defeat, for the harshness of the Treaty of Versailles and the hard times afterwards.

- **The Great Depression**: The German economy was on its knees after World War I. Germany took out loans from the US during the 1920s to try to recover. However, in 1929 the US experienced the **Wall Street Crash**, <u>when the value of shares in the New York stock exchange suddenly collapsed, throwing the US and connected economies into chaos</u>. The international Great Depression that followed lasted over a decade. US banks withdrew their loans from Germany. Banks and factories closed and unemployment soared.

- **Hitler's leadership and policies**: The Beer Hall Putsch, though unsuccessful, showed that Hitler was trying to bring about change. His public speaking skills were of great benefit to the Nazi Party. Hitler opposed the Treaty of Versailles and promised to fix the economy, something people desperately needed. His nationalism appealed to a defeated people because it encouraged them to take pride in their nation and reassured them that he could restore Germany to greatness. He was also anti-communist, and the wealthy feared communism, so his party had their support.

- **Propaganda**: Hitler used propaganda to his advantage. He used short simple slogans so everyone could understand. He played on people's emotions, particularly in relation to the Treaty of Versailles, unemployment and communism.

- **Increased popularity in elections**: The Nazi Party gained more seats in parliament (**the Reichstag**) with each general election. In 1928 it had 12 seats. By 1932, it had 230 seats. Soon, the Nazi Party had become the largest party in Germany.

On 30 January **1933**, Hitler was appointed **Chancellor** (Prime Minister) of Germany by President Hindenburg. He began to form his dictatorship.

▼ Passersby watching the Reichstag as it burns, February 1933

# Creating a dictatorship

- In **February 1933** the **Reichstag** building was set on **fire**, allegedly by a Dutch communist. This provided Hitler with an excuse to ban the Communist Party and give extra powers to his SA.

- Hitler called a general election in March 1933. Hitler's SA, along with his bodyguards known as the Waffen SS (**Schutzstaffel**), attacked opponents and voters. Votes for the Nazis soared, but they failed to win an overall majority.

- Hitler created a law called **the Enabling Act** in March 1933. This allowed him **to rule by decree**, meaning he could make laws without going through parliament first – creating a dictatorship. Hitler was now known as **der Führer** ('the leader').

▲ The Waffen SS

## CHECKPOINT!

1. What was the Weimar Republic? What problems did it face?
2. What was the Beer Hall Putsch? Why was it important in Hitler's rise to power?
3. What beliefs did Hitler write about in *Mein Kampf*?
4. How was Hitler influenced by Mussolini?
5. What was the Wall Street Crash? Why was it important in Hitler's rise to power?
6. How did Hitler use propaganda?
7. How did Hitler establish a dictatorship after 1932?

 I can explain how Hitler rose to power.

 ◀ TIME TO GO BACK ❯ I CAN MOVE FORWARD ➔

 Go to page 145 of your *Sources and Skills Book* for an evidence task on *Mein Kampf*.

# 25.3: Life in Hitler's Germany

In this topic, you will learn about:
- Economic policies
- Education
- Women's lives
- Propaganda
- Anti-Semitism
- Terror

▲ The Volkswagen car at a Nazi rally

## Economic policies

Hitler had promised to eliminate unemployment. In 1933, six million people were unemployed; roughly 11% of the population. Between 1933 and 1939, the Nazis dramatically transformed Germany's economy.

- **Independent trade unions** were abolished and strikes were made illegal.

- **Public works schemes** were created to build motorways (called Autobahnen) and the Olympic stadium. Many unemployed people found work on projects such as these.

- **Rearmament**, in violation of the Treaty of Versailles, began to take place. This involved ships, submarines, planes, arms and ammunition being manufactured again for the German military.

- The motor industry also expanded. A new car called **Volkswagen** ('the people's car') was designed and manufactured in 1937. It was priced at the same cost as a small motorcycle, so most people could afford one.

- Hitler cut taxes to encourage **private industry**. Many companies benefited from this, such as Krupps (steel), Siemens (electronics) and Mercedes-Benz (motors).

## Education

- Hitler concentrated on the young, aware that they would be the future of the Nazi Party. **Nazi youth groups** were set up, including the **Hitler Youth** and the **League of German Maidens**. There, children were indoctrinated (brainwashed) with Nazi ideas.

- In schools, **textbooks** were **rewritten** to glorify Germany and Hitler. *Mein Kampf* became the official history book.

- Teachers had to be members of the Nazi Party.

- Loyalty to the Führer was taught at every level of education and a portrait of Hitler was displayed in every classroom.

▲ A classroom in Nazi Germany, with Hitler's portrait on the wall

25 Life in Fascist Germany

## Women's lives

- Women were expected to stay at home and look after the family. Female doctors, teachers and civil servants were forced to **give up their careers**. Even near the end of the war, women were not asked to serve in the armed forces.

- Women's job was to keep the home nice for their husband and family – a woman's life was to revolve around '**the three Ks**': **Kinder, Küche, Kirche** (children, kitchen, church). 'The three Ks' were promoted within propaganda and made clear what German women's roles should be.

- Hitler wanted a **high birth rate**, so that the population would grow. Mothers who had more than eight children were awarded a gold medal.

- The Nazi ideal of wholesome German womanhood was reflected in **fashion**. Women were supposed to wear traditional peasant costumes with flat shoes, and have their hair in plaits or buns. They were not supposed to wear make-up or trousers, dye their hair or smoke in public.

▲ A poster showing an idealised Aryan family and encouraging people to turn to their local Nazi Party group

## CHECKPOINT!

1. How did the Nazis try to reduce unemployment?
2. How did industry expand under the Nazis?
3. How did the Nazis use education to their advantage? Why did they target young people?
4. What roles were women supposed to have in Nazi Germany? How was this promoted?
5. How was a German women meant to dress and style herself? Why?

 I can explain what life was like in Hitler's Germany in relation to economics, education and the lives of women.

 TIME TO GO BACK ◀ ▶ I CAN MOVE FORWARD ➡

## Propaganda

Nazi propaganda was used to control which information reached the public and to influence popular opinion.

- **Joseph Goebbels** was made Minister for National Enlightenment and Propaganda. He was in complete **control of the press, radio, cinemas, theatres and art**. Books by Jews were banned, along with any books disagreeing with Nazism. **Book burnings** took place to rid the country of such books.

- Goebbels organised the production of cheap radios, called '**the people's radio**', so that Hitler's speeches could reach every home. Loudspeakers were installed along streets.

- Posters were put up all around Germany presenting Hitler as a godlike figure, as we saw in Russia with Stalin. People had to celebrate Hitler's birthday and '**Heil Hitler!**' or 'Hail Hitler!' was a common greeting. The **Nazi salute** was made compulsory.

▲ Joseph Goebbels

- The Nazis held party rallies in Nuremberg, Bavaria. The **Nuremberg Rallies** had a different theme each year. In 1934, the 'Rally of Unity and Strength' was held. It is the best remembered because the documentary-maker **Leni Riefenstahl** recorded the event and made the propaganda film *Triumph of the Will* from it, promoting the cult of the Führer.

- The **1936 Olympics** were held in Berlin. This was an opportunity to show off the great achievements of Nazi Germany and present it as a flourishing nation to the outside world.

## Terror

Hitler used terror to hold onto power and control his critics.

- In 1933, the **Gestapo**, or <u>secret police</u>, was set up by Hermann Göring and led by Heinrich Himmler. People were encouraged to report opponents or communists to the secret police.

- By 1934, Hitler began to believe that his SA were a threat to him, particularly their leader **Ernst Röhm**. Hitler had set up the SS as his personal bodyguards and they were led by Heinrich Himmler. On 30 June 1934, in a two-day purge known as **the Night of the Long Knives**, the SS killed the leaders of the SA and others they suspected of being a threat.

- From as early as 1933, critics of the regime or people who were considered undesirable in Nazi Germany were sent to **forced labour camps**, similar to Stalin's gulags. Among them were journalists and political prisoners (including communists), LGBT people, Roma people, people with disabilities, Catholic priests, Jehovah's Witnesses and a great many Jews.

**25 Life in Fascist Germany**

# Anti-Semitism

Jews were seen as outsiders in many European countries. Hitler's hatred of Jews was evident in his book *Mein Kampf*. **Anti-Semitism** is <u>a hatred of, or prejudice against, Jewish people</u>. Hitler used anti-Semitism to gain popular support.

- The **Nuremberg Laws** were passed in 1935. They were made 'for the protection of German blood and honour'. These laws removed the rights of Jews: to be German citizens; to vote; to own property; to hold certain jobs (such as teachers, civil servants, soldiers and doctors); and to marry non-Jewish citizens. The Nazis believed that <u>Germans and other Nordic peoples were a superior 'master race'</u>, called **Aryans**. Jews had to wear a six-pointed yellow star, the **Star of David**, on their clothing to mark them out as Jewish.

- Hitler's treatment of the Jews worsened. In November 1938, a Jewish teenager murdered a German diplomat in Paris. This was followed by a two-day riot across Germany and parts of Austria called the **Night of the Broken Glass (Kristallnacht)**. Thousands of Jewish-owned buildings, including businesses, synagogues and cemeteries, were destroyed and at least 100 Jews were killed. Thousands more were sent to concentration camps and their homes and belongings were confiscated.

As a result of the Nuremberg Laws and Kristallnacht, half of Germany's Jewish community fled the country. The Jewish population was to suffer enormously during World War II. You will learn about this in chapter 28.

▲ An anti-Semitic poster reading 'The war is *his* fault!'

▲ A scene of destruction in the aftermath of Kristallnacht

## CHECKPOINT!

1. What role did Joseph Goebbels play in Nazi propaganda?
2. What were the Nuremburg Rallies?
3. What was the Gestapo?
4. How was terror used to ensure Nazi control of Germany? Give two examples.
5. What were the Nuremburg Laws? How did they affect Jews living in Germany?
6. What was Kristallnacht?

 I can describe life (terror and propaganda) when Hitler was in power.

 ← TIME TO GO BACK ◆ I CAN MOVE FORWARD →

◄ A Nuremberg rally

# WORKING WITH THE EVIDENCE!

An extract on the 1933 Nuremberg Rally from the *Irish Times*, 29 August 1933:

> Hundreds of thousands of Nazis, all wearing their brown shirt uniforms, all with arms raised to support their leader... this is the scene which will greet spectators at Nuremberg on Sunday, when Nazis are expected to give the greatest demonstration of the physical power of the movement yet witnessed. In their masses they will pass in review before Hitler. The event is to mark the last day of the first convention of the Nazi Party since Hitler assumed power… Every known method of making an impression on the masses has been pressed into service for this convention. There will be military parades, illuminated streets, gaily-decorated houses and shops, a gigantic display of fireworks, lectures on Nazi endeavours and achievements, and three speeches by Hitler.

1.  What type of source is this?
2.  How does the writer describe the scene that will greet visitors who come to Nuremberg for the 1933 rally?
3.  According to the source, what was the special significance of the 1933 rally?
4.  According to the source, 'making an impression on the masses' was a key purpose of the rallies. What methods of achieving this does the writer give in relation to the 1933 rally?
5.  Give one benefit and one limitation of this source for historians.

## DID YOU KNOW?

The first Nazi book burning took place on 10 May 1933 opposite Berlin's oldest university. Students carried thousands of books by authors with 'an un-German spirit' from the library to the fire. Today there is a small, simple memorial and a plaque with a prophetic warning written by the German poet Heinrich Heine in 1820: 'That was just a prelude; where they burn books, they will eventually burn people too'.

## A Life in Time: Adolf Hitler (1889–1945)

### Early life and World War I

Adolf Hitler was born on 20 April 1889 in Braunau am Inn, Austria. Hitler's father was a customs official and had a poor relationship with his son. Hitler grew up Catholic. He was expelled from a couple of schools before he moved to Vienna in 1905 to pursue his dream of becoming an artist. Hitler found that he did not have much artistic talent and he soon became very poor. His mother died in 1907. In 1914, Hitler moved to Munich, where he hoped to become an architect. He joined the German army when World War I broke out. He was a messenger during the war and was decorated with the Iron Cross for bravery.

### Rise to power

After the war, Hitler joined the National Socialist German Workers' Party (NSDAP) or Nazi Party.

By 1921, he had become the leader of the Nazi Party. While in prison for the failed revolution known as the Beer Hall Putsch, Hitler wrote *Mein Kampf* or 'My Struggle'. He revived the Nazi Party after his release. Hitler was an incredibly persuasive speaker and

▲ Hitler in his World War I uniform

also used propaganda to great effect. He founded the SS and the Gestapo to remove any threats to his power. Opponents were either killed or sent to hard labour camps. In 1933, Hitler became German Chancellor. When President Hindenburg died in August 1934, Hitler abolished the presidency and declared himself Führer, leader of Germany.

### Beliefs and methods

Hitler's anti-Semitism led to the creation of the Nuremberg Laws and, ultimately, to the Holocaust. He forced Jewish people to go to concentration camps, where six million Jews were killed during World War II. Hitler believed in a 'master race' and had so-called 'inferior' groups of people imprisoned, exiled or killed. He wanted to unite German-speaking peoples into an empire called the 'Third Reich', expanding its territory under a policy he named 'Lebensraum', meaning 'living space' for ethnic Germans.

**DID YOU KNOW?**

Hitler was nominated for the Nobel Peace Prize in 1939! However, the nomination was made by a Swedish democratic MP in the spirit of sarcasm and spoke of Hitler's 'glowing love for peace'.

### World War II

Hitler directly defied the Treaty of Versailles by joining with Austria (the Anschluss) and remilitarising the Rhineland. Germany's 1939 invasion of Poland on his orders marked the outbreak of World War II. After five years of war, as the Red Army surrounded Berlin, Hitler married his girlfriend Eva Braun. On 30 April 1945, the couple took their own lives before they could be arrested by the Red Army.

https://educateplus.ie/go/hitler

https://educateplus.ie/go/hitler2

# SUMMARY

In this chapter, we have learned that:

- World War I and the Treaty of Versailles had a large impact on Italy and Germany.
- Fascism began in Italy in 1919 under the leadership of Benito Mussolini.
- The National Socialist German Workers' Party (NSDAP), a fascist party, was founded in 1919. It was generally known as the Nazi Party. Hitler became a member and soon became its leader.
- In November 1923, Hitler and the Nazi Party organised a rebellion in Munich now commonly known as the Beer Hall Putsch. While in prison he wrote a book called *Mein Kampf*.
- Several factors helped the Nazis to rise to power: the public's loss of faith in the Weimar government; the Great Depression; Hitler's leadership and policies; Nazi propaganda.
- In January 1933, President Hindenburg appointed Hitler Chancellor (Prime Minister) of Germany.
- Hitler used terror and propaganda to ensure that he kept control over Germany. The SS and the Gestapo enforced terror. Examples of propaganda included posters, the Nuremberg Rallies, rewritten textbooks, youth groups and the Berlin Olympics.
- Hitler improved the economy of Germany by boosting private industry, introducing public work schemes and promoting the Volkswagen car.
- Hitler used education to influence German youth. Nazi youth groups included the Hitler Youth and the League of German Maidens. History books were rewritten and a portrait of Hitler was put in every classroom.
- Women were expected to stay at home and look after the family. Their life was to revolve around the three 'Ks': *Kinder, Küche, Kirche* (children, kitchen, church).
- Hitler was deeply anti-Semitic. In the early years of his regime, this was evident in *Mein Kampf*, the Nuremberg Laws and Kristallnacht.

## Reflecting on... Hitler's Germany

Hitler's policies had a positive effect on the economy and so for many people, everyday life improved. Poverty and unemployment were greatly reduced. However, Nazi propaganda and terror used to keep control of Germany impacted on people's lives in a negative way. Anyone who belonged to a supposedly 'inferior' group or who criticised Nazi policy was in great danger. Hitler used education to influence and shape the beliefs of young Germans. Women's lives were narrowed by Nazi policies, as they were expected to stay at home and raise large families.

**25 Life in Fascist Germany**

**Understanding History**

1. Why did fascism begin in Italy?
2. How did Mussolini gain control of Italy?
3. How did Hitler rise to power?
4. How successful were Hitler's economic policies? Explain your answer.
5. What methods did Hitler take to influence the young, and what effect did this have?
6. Why was it important to Hitler that women raised and looked after a family?
7. How successful was Hitler's use of propaganda? Explain your answer.
8. How did Hitler use terror to control the German population?

 **Exploring History**

1. Write a paragraph about each of the following:
   - Hitler's economic policies
   - terror in Hitler's Germany
   - anti-Semitism
   - Nazi propaganda

2. Write an account of the life and career of Adolf Hitler.

3. Read the following quotes about Hitler. Write your reaction to each of them, stating whether you agree or disagree, and then give your opinion on Hitler.

   – 'One may dislike Hitler's system and yet admire his patriotic achievement. If our country were defeated, I hope we should find a champion as indomitable to restore our courage and lead us back to our place among the nations' – Winston Churchill

   – 'If there had been a strong democratic sentiment in Germany, Hitler would never have come to power… [Germans] deserved what they got when they went round crying for a hero' – A.J.P. Taylor (historian)

   – 'The irony was that Hitler's ambition to impose his will on others did perhaps more than anything to ensure that his enemies' will to win burned brighter still. The Allies were united by nothing so much as a fundamental desire to smash Hitlerism' – Richard Overy (historian)

| **KEY TERMS** | | |
|---|---|---|
| | **Fascism** | a form of nationalistic government that is a one-party dictatorship |
| | **Rule by decree** | the ability to make laws without going through parliament |
| | **Lebensraum** | 'living space' – the plan to expand Germany's territory |
| | **Wall Street Crash** | when the value of shares in the New York Stock Exchange suddenly collapsed, throwing the US and connected economies into chaos |
| | **Kinder, Küche, Kirche** | 'Children, kitchen, church' – the Nazi view of a woman's role in society |
| | **Gestapo** | Hitler's secret police |
| | **Anti-Semitism** | a hatred of, or prejudice against, Jewish people |
| | **Aryans** | Germans and other Nordic peoples, considered a 'master race' by the Nazis |

 Go to page 142 of your *Sources and Skills Book* for more exercises.

 Go to page 83 of your *Research Portfolio* for a task based on this chapter.

| World War I | Fascist Germany | World War II |
|---|---|---|
| 1914–1918 | 1933–1945 | 1939–1945 |

During his rise to power, Adolf Hitler had promised that he would do away with the Treaty of Versailles, make Germany strong and expand its territory. In the years 1933-1939, Hitler moved gradually into a position of strength and readiness, while Western Europe watched uneasily but hesitated to act. His foreign policies were to lead to the outbreak of World War II.

## WORKING WITH THE EVIDENCE!

### The approach to war

| Type of source | Category | Example |
|---|---|---|
| Primary | Oral | A speech by Chamberlain to the House of Commons on 1 September 1939 on having to use force against Germany |
| Primary | Written | Newspaper reports |

This morning the British Ambassador in Berlin handed the German Government a final Note stating that, unless we heard from them by 11 o'clock that they were prepared at once to withdraw their troops from Poland, a state of war would exist between us. I have to tell you now that no such undertaking has been received, and that consequently this country is at war with Germany.

You can imagine what a bitter blow it is to me that all my long struggle to win peace has failed... I know you will play your part with calmness and courage.'

▲ Neville Chamberlain's speech to the House of Commons, 1 September 1939

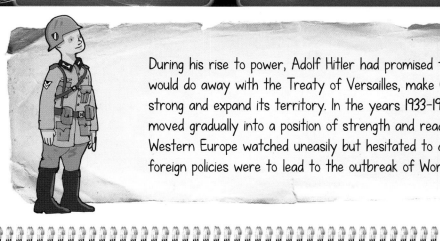

▲ Front page of a London newspaper on 1 September 1939

What can you learn about the causes of World War II from the above sources?

# 26.1: Hitler's Foreign Policies

## Hitler's main aims

The **Treaty of Versailles** had weakened Germany terribly. Its restrictions were unacceptable to Hitler, and he planned to defy them and reclaim Germany's power and territory by:

- rebuilding the German army and navy
- re-occupying the Rhineland
- regaining the territory lost after World War I
- expanding further into a 'greater Germany' by uniting all German speakers under a policy called **Lebensraum**, meaning **'living space' for ethnic Germans**. This German Empire would be known as **the Third Reich**, or 'third regime or empire'.

Hitler knew that Britain and France would be anxious to avoid another war. Nor was Germany strong enough – yet. He was careful to only push a little at a time.

> **In this topic, you will learn about:**
> - Hitler's main aims
> - Rebuilding the army and navy
> - Re-occupation of the Rhineland
> - The Anschluss
> - The Sudetenland

> **DID YOU KNOW?**
>
> The First Reich was the medieval Holy Roman Empire, which lasted until 1806. The Second Reich corresponded to the German Empire from 1871–1918. By declaring itself the Third Reich, Hitler's Germany (1933-1945) was associating itself with a powerful imperial past.

## Rebuilding the German army and navy

The Treaty of Versailles had restricted the German army to 100,000 men and banned it from having an airforce, tanks or submarines. In 1933 Hitler withdrew Germany from the League of Nations.

However, in 1935 **the Anglo–German Naval Agreement** was signed, regulating the size of the German navy in relation to the British navy. The British had made this agreement without consulting France or Italy and it actually granted Germany the right to expand its navy beyond the limits set by the Treaty of Versailles. This gave Hitler confidence.

In 1935, Germany reintroduced **conscription** and soon the army had grown beyond its Treaty limits. Hitler then increased the size of the navy and created an airforce, called **the Luftwaffe**. No steps were taken by Britain or France to halt Germany's dramatic military expansion.

▼ **An early Luftwaffe plane**

## Occupation of the Rhineland

German troops had been forbidden to occupy the region bordering France called the **Rhineland** (see map on page 333). In March 1936, Hitler sent troops into the Rhineland with orders to retreat if France sent its army to meet them. The German troops were greeted by cheering crowds as they crossed the River Rhine. Once again, Britain and France did not react.

## The Anschluss

First on the list for Lebensraum was **Austria**: a German-speaking country, Hitler's birthplace, and somewhere the Nazi Party had strong support. The Treaty of Versailles had specifically forbidden Germany and Austria to unite.

◀ Rhineland citizens welcoming the German troops

In February 1938, Hitler threatened the Austrian Chancellor with war unless he let Austrian Nazis into his government. The Chancellor tried to limit the Nazis' grasp on power and was replaced by a Nazi chancellor, who immediately invited German troops to enter Austria. An agreement was then signed absorbing Austria into the Third Reich. This event was known as the **Anschluss**, the joining together of Germany and Austria. Hitler entered the Austrian capital Vienna, greeted by cheering crowds. Britain and France did not interfere.

**DID YOU KNOW?**

Hitler and Mussolini made an agreement together in 1936 called the Rome-Berlin Axis, linking the two countries and stating that they would support each other.

26 The Causes of World War II

## The Sudetenland

Hitler noted Europe's lack of authority and realised that he could go further. His next aim was to absorb the German-speakers in **Czechoslovakia** into the Reich. **The majority German-speaking regions of Czechoslovakia** were together called the **Sudetenland**. The Germans living there were encouraged to campaign for independence. Nazi propaganda made it look as though the Czechoslovakian state had been mistreating the Sudeten Germans.

▶ Sudetenland Nazi propaganda poster reading 'We did it! Alch [the area shown on the map] is free! Heil Hitler!'

| Sudetenland: Czech territory given to Germany at Munich, 30 September 1938 | Czech territory annexed by Poland 1 November 1938 |
| Czech territory given to Hungary by Germany and Italy at Vienna, 2 October 1938 | Remainder of Czechoslovakia, annexed by Germany, 15 March 1939 |

◀ The gradual takeover of Czechoslovakia

## CHECKPOINT!

1. What were Hitler's foreign policy aims?

2. What was Lebensraum? 📖!

3. How did Hitler try to dismantle the Treaty of Versailles?

4. What occurred in the Rhineland in 1936? Why is this an important milestone on the road to war?

5. What was the Anschluss? How was it achieved?

6. What was the Sudetenland? 📖!

7. How did Britain and France react to Hitler's foreign policy? Explain your answer using at least two examples.

✓ I can explain Hitler's foreign policies and how he carried them out.

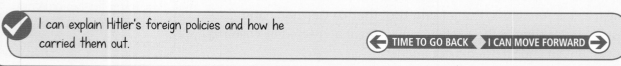

◀ TIME TO GO BACK ◆ I CAN MOVE FORWARD ▶

# 26.2: Appeasement

**In this topic, you will learn about:**

❯ The attitude of France and Britain

❯ Appeasement

## The attitude of France and Britain

So far, both France and Britain had stood by with no response while Hitler rebuilt the German army and navy, entered the Rhineland and joined with Austria. There were a number of reasons for this:

- France **did not want to risk a war** with Germany over the Rhineland, especially as the size of the German army was unknown.
- France believed that its system of fortification along its eastern border with Germany, called the **Maginot Line**, would be enough to prevent a German attack.
- Many British people felt that the Treaty of Versailles had actually been **too harsh** on Germany and were sympathetic towards its people.
- The **memory of World War I** was still strong in Britain and the thought of another war so soon was terrible.
- France, Britain and others were **very concerned about Stalin and the threat of communism**. They knew that the new German regime was strongly anti-communist.

## Appeasement

Awareness of all the lives lost in the horrors of World War I was very fresh in British minds. In the **'Peace Ballot'** of 1934–1935, millions of British people voted for a pacifist (pro-peace) approach, and since then appeasement had been British foreign policy. **Appeasement** involved <u>agreeing to Hitler's demands in the hope of avoiding war</u>. The British Prime Minster in 1937 was **Neville Chamberlain**, who said 'We should seek by all means in our power to avoid war, by analysing possible causes, by trying to remove them, by discussion in a spirit of collaboration and good will'. Hitler saw Britain's reluctance to engage assertively and took advantage of this.

▶ Neville Chamberlain

 COLLABORATE: Divide the class into two sides, one in favour of appeasement and one against. Come up with arguments for your position and present these to the class.

## CHECKPOINT!

1. Why did France want to avoid war with Germany?
2. Why was Britain opposed to using force in response to German actions?
3. What was the policy of appeasement?

 I can describe France and Britain's attitude towards Hitler and explain the policy of appeasement.

 ◀ TIME TO GO BACK ❯ I CAN MOVE FORWARD ➡

**26**

**The Causes of World War II**

# 26.3: The Munich Conference and the Nazi–Soviet Pact

**In this topic, you will learn about:**
- The Munich Conference
- The effect on Czechoslovakia
- The Nazi–Soviet Non-Aggression Pact

## The Munich Conference

In September 1938, Neville Chamberlain, Adolf Hitler, Benito Mussolini and Édouard Daladier (of France) met for the **Munich Conference** to discuss the issue of Czechoslovakia and **the Sudetenland**. They agreed to make Czechoslovakia surrender the area of the Sudetenland to Germany. Notably, Czechoslovakia was not part of the talks. Hitler promised the other leaders that **he would not demand any more territory**. Chamberlain returned to Britain to cheering crowds, claiming to have achieved '**peace for our time**'.

▲ Mussolini, Hitler, Daladier and Chamberlain at the Munich Conference

In **March 1939**, Hitler broke the Munich Agreement and **took over the rest of Czechoslovakia**. Now nobody could deny that appeasement had been a failure. Britain started to rearm itself, reintroduced conscription and began to make agreements with other countries, such as France and Poland, against Hitler. Britain and France promised Poland that they would come to its aid if Germany invaded. They hoped that Stalin would agree to the same, but talks with him broke down.

## The Nazi–Soviet Non-Aggression Pact

Fascism and communism were natural enemies and Hitler had sworn to eliminate communism. It was therefore a shock for European leaders when Hitler and Stalin signed the **Nazi–Soviet Non-Aggression Pact** in August 1939 (also called the Molotov–Ribbentrop Pact). Under this, they agreed upon:

- a ten-year period when they would not attack each other or help each other's enemies

- a **secret clause**: an agreement to partition Poland between them, and also that Romania and the Baltic states (Finland, Estonia, Latvia and Lithuania) would belong to a Russian 'sphere of influence'.

This pact led Stalin to believe that he was safe from German attack. The Red Army was not ready for war; it had recently lost thousands of senior officers to Stalin's purges.

▲ Hitler and Stalin greet each other with false politeness over the body of Poland

Hitler was planning to invade Poland and this pact meant that he need not worry about the USSR reacting aggressively from the east. By taking western Poland, he would gain the strategically important port city of Danzig (modern Gdansk) and reclaim the **'Polish Corridor'** and a lot of former German territory.

On **1 September 1939**, **Germany invaded Poland**. Two days later, Britain and France declared war on Germany. World War II had begun.

▲ The division of Poland agreed under the Nazi–Soviet Pact

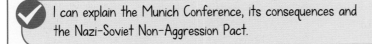 **CHECKPOINT!**

1. Who attended the Munich Conference? Why did it take place?

2. What was agreed there?

3. What was the result of the Nazi takeover of Czechoslovakia?

4. What did Hitler and Stalin agree in the Nazi–Soviet Non-Aggression Pact?

5. How did World War II begin?

 I can explain the Munich Conference, its consequences and the Nazi-Soviet Non-Aggression Pact.

◀ TIME TO GO BACK ◆ I CAN MOVE FORWARD ➔

Go to page 148 of your *Sources and Skills Book* for an evidence task on the Nazi–Soviet Pact.

26 The Causes of World War II

# WORKING WITH THE <u>EVIDENCE!</u>

The statement by Neville Chamberlain on his return from the Munich Conference, 30 September 1938:

> We, the German Führer and Chancellor and the British Prime Minister, have had a further meeting today and are agreed in recognizing that the question of Anglo–German relations is of the first importance for our two countries and for Europe.
>
> We regard the agreement signed last night and the Anglo–German Naval Agreement as symbolic of the desire of our two peoples never to go to war with one another again. We are resolved that the method of consultation shall be the method adopted to deal with any other questions that may concern our two countries, and we are determined to continue our efforts to remove possible sources of difference, and thus to contribute to assure the peace of Europe...
>
> My good friends, for the second time in our history, a British Prime Minister has returned from Germany bringing peace with honour.
>
> I believe it is peace for our time... Go home and get a nice quiet sleep.

1. What type of source is this?
2. According to the source, what were the agreements symbolic of?
3. What method would be used to deal with any other questions in the future?
4. According to the source, what had Chamberlain achieved?
5. Name one benefit and one limitation of this source for historians.

# SUMMARY

In this chapter, we have learned that:

- To restore Germany's strength as a nation, Hitler defied the Treaty of Versailles by: rebuilding the German army and navy; remilitarising the Rhineland; and seeking to unite all German-speakers into a greater German Empire, the Third Reich.

- In March 1938, Hitler absorbed Austria into the Third Reich in an event called the Anschluss.

- Hitler invaded the Sudetenland in the autumn of 1938. In March 1939 he invaded the rest of Czechoslovakia, breaking the promise he had made in Munich to France, Britain and Italy.

- At the Munich Conference, Britain and France had used the policy of appeasement in the hope that Hitler would be content with Austria and the Sudetenland and war could be avoided.

- Hitler and Stalin signed the Nazi–Soviet Non-Aggression Pact in March 1939.

- On 1 September 1939, Hitler invaded Poland. World War II was declared two days later.

### Reflecting on... the Causes of World War II

In his determination to restore Germany to strength, Hitler was willing to act gradually. He defied the Treaty of Versailles step by step and made strategic pacts and alliances, so that the other powers would not move against him before Germany was ready for a full-scale war. In hindsight, the policy of appeasement would seem naïve. Its noble intention was to prioritise peace and save lives, but it came up against the Nazi vision of a Third Reich that was theirs for the taking.

**26 The Causes of World War II**

▲ Hitler's expansionism in stages numbered 1 to 5

# Understanding History

1. What was Hitler's first open breach of the Treaty of Versailles?
2. Why did Britain and France adopt the policy of appeasement?
3. Why was there controversy over which countries did and did not attend the Munich Conference?
4. What were the benefits of the Nazi–Soviet Non-Aggression Pact for (a) Hitler and (b) Stalin?
5. Why did this pact increase the likelihood of war?

# Exploring History

1. Write a paragraph about each of the following: appeasement, the Munich Conference and the Nazi–Soviet Non-Aggression Pact.
2. Who was more responsible for the outbreak of World War II: Germany, or Britain and France? Explain your answer, referring to both.
3. On 3 September 1939 King George VI called upon '…my people at home and my peoples across the seas… I ask them to stand calm, firm and united in this time of trial. The task will be hard. There may be dark days ahead and war can no longer be confined to the battlefield. But we can only do the right as we see the right and reverently commit our cause to God.'

   (a) According to the source, what did King George VI ask people to do?

   (b) Why will the task be hard?

   (c) What are the benefits of a source like this for historians?

| KEY TERMS | | |
|---|---|---|
| | Lebensraum | 'living space' for ethnic Germans; the policy behind the expansion of German territory |
| | Anschluss | the joining together of Germany and Austria in the Third Reich |
| | Sudetenland | the majority German-speaking regions of Czechoslovakia |
| | Appeasement | agreeing to Hitler's demands in the hope of avoiding war |

 Go to page 146 of your *Sources and Skills Book* for more exercises.

 Go to page 87 of your *Research Portfolio* for a task based on this chapter.

| World War I | World War II | The Cold War |
|---|---|---|
| 1914–1918 | 1939–1945 | 1945–1991 |

World War II was declared in September 1939. The two opposing sides were the Allied powers (Britain, France and Poland, later joined by the USSR and the US) and the Axis powers (Germany, Italy and Japan).

While World War I had been fought almost entirely along two fronts, this war would spill across all of Europe and beyond, from Belfast to the USSR, from Scandinavia to north Africa, and from 1941 also throughout the Pacific region. Major developments in technology changed the nature of combat on land, at sea and in the air – and affected civilians like never before. World War II resulted in the deaths of over 60 million people, while approximately 40 million more were refugees when the war ended.

## WORKING WITH THE EVIDENCE!

### World War II

| Type of source | Category | Example |
|---|---|---|
| Primary | Visual | A poster trying to rally the Allies against Nazi Germany |
| Primary | Visual | A *Punch* magazine cartoon from 1940 |

▲ An Allied poster rallying support

Leslie Illingworth, 1940.

▲ A *Punch* magazine cartoon from 1940

What can you learn from these sources about the Allies' attitude towards World War II?

# 27.1: Technological Change: A New Kind of War

In this topic, you will learn about:
- ❯ Advances in wartime technology
- ❯ The impact of the new technology

## New wartime technology

Both the Allied and Axis powers created, then refined, new weapons and technology to gain an advantage over their enemies.

### At sea

- Better **submarines** and **torpedoes** were developed and research went into anti-submarine technology – most importantly **ASDIC (sonar)** and **radar**, so that ships could scan the ocean for hidden threats.

- **Aircraft carriers** helped to control the seas. They were seagoing air bases with a flight deck and facilities for carrying, arming, deploying and recovering aircraft.

▲ An aircraft carrier

### On land

- By now, tanks were an important part of warfare. Germany had developed various **Panzer tanks** in defiance of the Treaty ban. The heavily armoured **Tiger tank** weighed 54 tonnes, had an 8.8 cm gun and had a top speed of 45 km/h. The Allies developed **dummy tanks** to trick the Germans, as well as **amphibious tanks**, which were capable of crossing water.

- Improvements were also made to **grenades, pistols, rifles** and **machine guns**. The Germans invented a machine gun called the **MG 42** that could fire 1,200 rounds per minute.

▲ Panzer, Tiger model

### In the air

- The British **Hurricane** and **Spitfire** aircraft were powered by Rolls Royce engines. The American **B-29 Superfortress** was a long-range bomber developed in 1942. In 1944, Germany invented the first jet fighter, called the **Messerschmitt ME 262**.

- Long-range rockets were developed during the war by German scientists. The **V1** was the first flying rocket. It flew at speeds of 400km/h. The **V2** flew at supersonic speed, with a top speed of 5,760 km/h.

▲ Spitfires flying in formation

▲ The 'mushroom cloud' produced by the testing of an atomic bomb in the Pacific

## The atomic bomb

- The US feared that Germany would be the first to develop the atomic bomb, so it began an intensive research programme codenamed **the Manhattan Project**. The first working atomic bomb was tested in the New Mexico desert. In 1945 the US air force dropped atomic bombs on the Japanese cities of **Hiroshima** and **Nagasaki**, killing at least 129,000 people.

**DID YOU KNOW?**

Albert Einstein's only involvement in the development of the atomic bomb was a letter urging the US to research it, warning that the Germans had the potential to develop one themselves.

## The impact of new wartime technology

- Fighting no longer had to be confined to particular areas as in World War I. The new technology was **highly mobile** and so units and 'fronts' could move very rapidly.

- War came to civilian populations in a way it never had before. While an estimated 7 million civilians died in World War I, this was dwarfed by the estimated **38–55 million civilian deaths** of World War II. Numerous cities were destroyed, for example Coventry, Warsaw, Dresden and Leningrad.

- The technological advances by countries such as Britain and the US made all the difference in their eventual defeat of the Axis powers. However, the **destructive power** of this technology was far greater than ever before: while World War I cost 10 million soldiers their lives, roughly 15–20 million soldiers died in World War II.

 COLLABORATE: Work together to research the Manhattan Project. Lay out the information you find in a brainstorm.

## CHECKPOINT!

1. How did technology change warfare (a) at sea; (b) on land; (c) in the air?
2. Why was the atomic bomb developed?
3. Describe how new technology impacted on (a) civilians and (b) soldiers.

 I can explain the advances in World War II technology and how this changed the nature and impact of the war.

 TIME TO GO BACK ◀ ▶ I CAN MOVE FORWARD ➡

27 People and Nations: World War II

# 27.2: The Fall of Poland and France

**In this topic, you will learn about:**

> Blitzkrieg
> The invasion of Poland
> The Phoney War
> The invasion of France and Operation Dynamo
> Vichy France

## The invasion of Poland

Hitler resented the fact that Poland had received former German provinces under the Treaty of Versailles. He also wanted **the Polish Corridor**, a strip of land that gave access to the Baltic Sea, and the use of Poland's resources to help feed and fuel the war effort.

The German army used a new tactic when it invaded Poland: **Blitzkrieg**, or 'lightning war'. **Blitzkrieg is a tactic of surprise attack beginning with heavy bombing of an area by the German air force (Luftwaffe), followed closely by Panzer tanks and finally by the infantry**. Hitler would use this tactic again against France and the USSR.

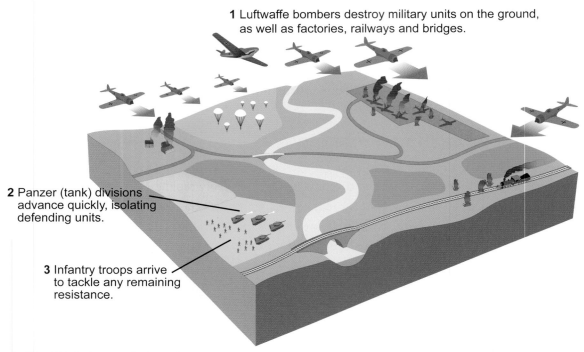

**1** Luftwaffe bombers destroy military units on the ground, as well as factories, railways and bridges.

**2** Panzer (tank) divisions advance quickly, isolating defending units.

**3** Infantry troops arrive to tackle any remaining resistance.

▲ The Blitzkrieg tactic in action

- Luftwaffe bombers destroyed most of the Polish air force on the ground before it had a chance to fight back. The success of Blitzkrieg depended on this element of surprise.
- The Luftwaffe also destroyed Polish transportation lines such as roads, railways and bridges.
- German Panzers cut the Polish army off from its supplies and reinforcements.
- The German infantry (foot soldiers) defeated the weakened Polish army.

Within **five weeks**, Poland had been defeated. The **Soviet Union then invaded** from the east. Hitler and Stalin split Poland between them, as they had secretly agreed in their pact of that August.

## The invasion of France

Britain and France expected Germany to attack the west and did not act to assist Poland. After World War I, the French had built **the Maginot Line**, a series of fortifications along the French–German border. For eight months, they and the **British Expeditionary Force (BEF)** faced the Germans, who waited behind their own fortification, the Siegfried Line. Since no fighting took place, this was nicknamed **the Phoney War**. In April 1940 Germany occupied Denmark and Norway to gain control of air bases and prevent an Allied invasion. Neville Chamberlain resigned and was replaced as Prime Minister by **Winston Churchill**.

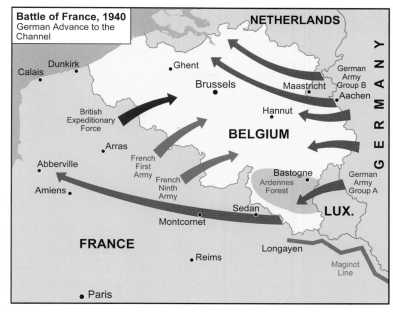

▲ The German advance through Belgium and into France

On 10 May 1940, the attack on Belgium, the Netherlands and France finally began, using Blitzkrieg tactics. The Germans avoided the Maginot Line by using Panzers to roll through the wooded, hilly terrain of **the Ardennes**, which the French had thought impossible to cross. This sudden advance drove a wedge between the BEF and the French army.

The BEF soldiers were pushed back to the coastal town of **Dunkirk**, where they became trapped. For nine days, over 900 boats were involved in the Allied evacuation of about 350,000 soldiers from the beaches at Dunkirk, also known as **Operation Dynamo**.

Meanwhile, the French forces collapsed as the Germans advanced. At this point, Italy declared war on France. German forces entered Paris unopposed on 14 June.

Germany occupied the northern half of France. In the unoccupied 'free zone', **a puppet government** (controlled by the Nazis) was set up in the town of Vichy with the elderly **Phillippe Pétain** as leader. This regime, known as **Vichy France**, was very conservative and cooperated with the Nazis' anti-Semitic policies.

▲ Operation Dynamo: the evacuation from Dunkirk

## CHECKPOINT!

1. Explain the term Blitzkrieg.
2. How was Poland conquered so quickly?
3. What was the Phoney War?
4. What was the Maginot Line?
5. Describe how Germany invaded France.
6. Why was France so easily defeated in 1940?
7. What was Operation Dynamo?
8. What was Vichy France?

✔ I can describe how Poland and France fell to German forces.

## 27.3: The Battle of Britain and the Blitz

**In this topic, you will learn about:**

- The Battle of Britain
- The Blitz

### The Battle of Britain

Poland and France had both fallen to the Nazis. Of the Allied powers, only Britain remained. Hitler suggested peace talks, but Churchill refused.

Hitler planned a full invasion of Britain, codenamed **Operation Sea Lion**. He used submarines (U-boats) to attack shipping routes to Britain and to damage radar bases. For any invasion to succeed, the British **Royal Air Force** (RAF) had to be destroyed or badly weakened. The **campaign of aerial attacks on Britain by the Luftwaffe** became known as **the Battle of Britain**. On the first day, 13 August 1940, 1,485 German bombers attacked RAF bases, including airfields and radar stations. These raids continued for a month. RAF pilots in Hurricanes and Spitfires were in constant **dogfights** (**close combat between military aircraft**) with the German **ME 109s** and **ME 110s**.

By mid-September 1940, the British had won the Battle of Britain. This was the first time Hitler had suffered a defeat. Some reasons for this were:

- The Germans moved their focus to London, which gave the RAF time to reorganise.
- Radar gave the British **advance warning** of German air raids.
- The British **Spitfires were better** than the German planes.
- German planes could not stay long in British airspace: they had to return to the Third Reich to refuel.
- German losses were greater: 1,700 Luftwaffe planes were shot down and nearly 3,500 airmen were killed or captured.

▼ The Battle of Britain

## The Blitz

The Luftwaffe switched its strategy to one of <u>**bombing British cities at night-time**</u>: this was **the Blitz**. During the Blitz, the Germans dropped explosive and incendiary (designed to start fires) bombs on London and other cities. Hitler's main targets were ports, power stations and factories. The British used anti-aircraft guns to defend their cities.

The air raids killed 43,000 civilians and lasted for eight months, until May 1941. One infamous example was Coventry on 14 November 1940, when 500 German bombers dropped 500 tonnes of high explosives and nearly 900 bombs in ten hours of relentless bombing.

▲ People walk to work in Coventry past the charred and smoking results of the previous night's air raids

Go to page 154 of your *Sources and Skills Book* for an evidence task on evacuation.

## Life in wartime Britain

Thousands of homes were destroyed in the air raids. Whenever warning sirens were heard, people took shelter. Up to 130,000 slept in the London Underground stations. <u>**Children from the cities were sent to stay with families in the countryside**</u>, where it was safer: this was known as **evacuation**.

Approximately **seven million women entered the workforce** during World War II. On farms, in factories and on the railways, canals and buses, women filled roles that had been left vacant when men went to war. In addition, women worked in wartime industries such as munitions and aircraft factories and in the armed forces, carrying out clerical duties and vehicle repairs.

Before the war, Britain had imported two-thirds of its food supplies. Now merchant ships were under attack by U-boats. Foods such as sugar, butter and bacon became rare and **ration books** were introduced for every citizen. By 1942, tea, milk, eggs and cheese were also rationed. A campaign called '**Dig for Victory**' encouraged people to grow their own food on any available land.

The public was also asked to donate old pots and pans to be melted down to make materials for aircraft. In fact, they were never used for this, but it boosted people's morale to feel that they were helping with the war effort.

---

### CHECKPOINT!

1. What was Operation Sea Lion?
2. Name the German and British aircraft used during the Battle of Britain.
3. Give three reasons why Britain won the Battle of Britain.
4. Explain the term the Blitz.
5. Describe what life was like for people in wartime Britain.

 I can explain the Battle of Britain and the Blitz and describe life in wartime Britain.

 ← TIME TO GO BACK ◆ I CAN MOVE FORWARD →

**27** People and Nations: World War II

## 27.4: The Invasion of the USSR and the Battle of Stalingrad

In this topic, you will learn about:
- Operation Barbarossa
- The Battle of Stalingrad

### Operation Barbarossa

Hitler wanted to expand the Third Reich's Lebensraum to the east – including the USSR, which was rich in resources such as oil. He also wanted to destroy communism and saw Slavic peoples as inferior. He expected to defeat the Red Army quickly and even delayed the invasion by a month to cover fighting elsewhere. On 22 June 1941, **Operation Barbarossa** began. Germany invaded the Soviet Union in a rapid three-pronged attack towards the most important cities – **Moscow**, **Leningrad** and **Kiev**. Blitzkrieg tactics were very successful at first.

Stalin was shocked when Hitler invaded. He had dismissed warnings of a possible attack. Aided by propaganda, he called on his people to fight what was known as **the Great Patriotic War** against Germany. As it retreated, the Red Army used a scorched earth tactic, destroying anything useful to the enemy (such as crops, roads, bridges, railways and communication lines). Stalin also moved his factories further east so that the production of tanks and weapons could continue.

By the end of September, Kiev had fallen, Leningrad was under siege and the German army was approaching Moscow. However, conditions were incredibly tough. Heavy rain in October 1941 turned roads into seas of mud, making transport very difficult. Then as winter set in, the Germans discovered that they were not prepared for the extreme temperatures – as low as **–40 °C**. Petrol froze and engines would not start. Many German soldiers froze to death. The Red Army seized this advantage to launch a counterattack that stopped the German army short of Moscow.

▼ German troops advancing eastwards under Operation Barbarossa

# The Battle of Stalingrad

In late summer 1942, the German forces that had taken Kiev advanced towards the oilfields of the Caucasus and the city of **Stalingrad**, led by **General Paulus**.

The city had been heavily bombed and large parts of it were in ruins. Rubble blocked the streets to tanks and snipers waited at windows. The Red Army was told to defend Stalingrad at all costs. The German Sixth Army and the Red Army fought each other for each building, sometimes hand-to-hand.

As the freezing winter of 1942–1943 set in, the Russians began to encircle the Germans to cut them off from their supplies. Russian supplies were being ferried in across the River Volga each night. On top of the deathly cold, the German forces began to starve. The Luftwaffe attempted to airdrop supplies, but only a fraction of what they needed reached the soldiers. Hitler denied General Paulus's request to retreat, insisting they continue to fight for Stalingrad 'to the last soldier and the last bullet'.

In **February 1943**, 91,000 starving, frozen and surrounded soldiers of the **Sixth Army finally surrendered**.

▲ Fighting in the ruins of Stalingrad

▲ Monument in Volgograd (once Stalingrad) today

The exact number of casualties will never be known. However, it is estimated that over 800,000 Axis soldiers (German, Italian, Romanian or Hungarian) and 1.1 million Russians were either killed, wounded, missing or captured at Stalingrad. Many historians regard the Battle of Stalingrad as the **main turning point of World War II**.

## CHECKPOINT!

1. What was Operation Barbarossa?
2. Why did Hitler invade the USSR?
3. What effect did the winter of 1941 have on the German invasion?
4. Describe the Battle of Stalingrad.
5. Why was the Battle of Stalingrad a major turning point in the war?

 I can explain what happened during Operation Barbarossa and the Battle of Stalingrad.

 ← TIME TO GO BACK ◆ I CAN MOVE FORWARD →

**27 People and Nations: World War II**

# 27.5: The War Beyond Europe

**In this topic, you will learn about:**

- The US entering World War II
- War in North Africa and the surrender of Italy
- The Battle of the Atlantic

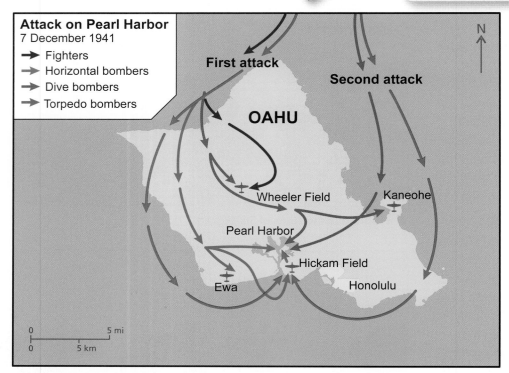

**Attack on Pearl Harbor**
7 December 1941
➜ Fighters
➜ Horizontal bombers
➜ Dive bombers
➜ Torpedo bombers

First attack

Second attack

OAHU

Wheeler Field

Kaneohe

Pearl Harbor

Hickam Field

Ewa

Honolulu

0    5 mi
0    5 km

N

▲ Pearl Harbor on the island of Oahu, Hawaii

## The US enters World War II

Although the US had provided the Allies with weapons and supplies, **until 1941 it had officially remained neutral**.

Japan had become an ally of Germany in 1936. Japan wanted to gain territory and resources in eastern Asia and the Pacific Ocean – but the US had obstructed this. On 7 December 1941, without declaring war, Japan attempted to destroy the entire American Pacific fleet at **Pearl Harbor** in Hawaii. In just two hours, 3,000 people were killed. Japan and the US were immediately at war. Within four days, Japan's Axis partners, Germany and Italy, had declared war on the US. President **Franklin D. Roosevelt** marshalled the US forces to fight Japan and also agreed to send troops and weapons to help fight the Axis powers in Europe and North Africa. He agreed with Churchill that defeating Hitler should be the top priority.

## War in the Mediterranean

Between October and November 1942, the British defeated the German Afrika Korps at **El Alamein in Egypt**, under Field Marshal Montgomery and armed with US weapons. In November, the US and Britain joined to launch **Operation Torch**: the invasion of Vichy France-controlled **North Africa**. The Axis powers were encircled in Tunisia and surrendered in May 1943. Over 275,000 prisoners were taken.

Britain and the US then planned **Operation Avalanche**: the invasion of Italy. They liberated **Sicily** between July and August. **Mussolini was toppled from power** and when the Allies invaded mainland Italy in September, Italy surrendered. The German-controlled, mountainous north of Italy was not as easy to conquer and fighting persisted there. Allied troops did not take Rome until June 1944.

## The Battle of the Atlantic

The US had sent food and military supplies to Britain across the Atlantic Ocean since the outbreak of war. In just six months in 1940, **German U-boats** (submarines) sank over three million tonnes of Allied shipping, with great loss of life. From 1941, the US navy shared the guarding of Atlantic shipping and added resources, men and supplies to the war effort.

New **radar and sonar technology** helped, as did the evolving art of codebreaking. The German navy used **the Enigma code** to communicate with its U-boats; once this code was cracked, Allied ships knew where the U-boats would be and could avoid or attack them.

**DID YOU KNOW?**

The British government recruited mathematicians, translators, chess players and people gifted at solving cryptic crosswords to do top-secret work as codebreakers. At Bletchley Park outside London, the mathematician Alan Turing designed a machine to help decipher the Enigma code. By early 1945, some 10,000 people worked there (75% were women) reading up to 4,000 coded messages a day.

▲ This 1941 German painting shows a U-boat crew watching a torpedoed British cargo ship as it sinks

## CHECKPOINT!

1. What happened at Pearl Harbor and what effect did it have?
2. Who was the US President at this time?
3. What was the Battle of the Atlantic?
4. What was the impact of the US entering the war?

 I can explain why the US entered World War II and the impact that it had.

 ← TIME TO GO BACK ◆ I CAN MOVE FORWARD →

27 People and Nations: World War II

# 27.6: The D-Day Landings

In this topic, you will learn about:
- D-Day
- Air raids on Germany
- The final offensives

## D-Day

Stalin needed Churchill and Roosevelt to attack from the west to ease the pressure on the Red Army. In **Operation Overlord**, <u>US, British and Canadian troops would land in Normandy</u>, France – but they fed the Germans false plans that they were to land further east, at Calais. The five beaches were given codenames: **Utah**, **Omaha**, **Juno**, **Gold** and **Sword**. **General Eisenhower** led the largest seaborne invasion in history, with over 7,000 ships and landing craft, on 6 June 1944, now known as **D-Day** or **Deliverance Day**.

Most of Germany's troops were stationed in Calais, where they expected the invasion. The Allies landed around 156,000 troops to the west while 10,000 planes protected them from overhead. They broke down German defences on the beaches, built artificial harbours to bring in tanks and trucks and established a pipeline for fuel. By August, the Allies had stopped the Germans at Falaise, and **Paris was liberated on 25 August**.

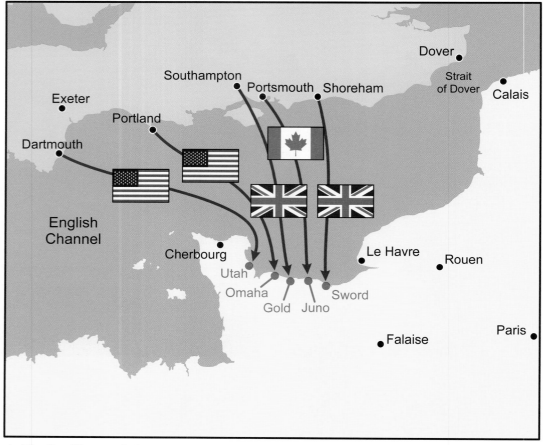

▲ The five Normandy beaches where the D-Day Landings took place, and Calais to the north-east

## Air raids on Germany

The Allies bombed Germany by day and night, targeting the large cities such as **Hamburg** and **Berlin** and also the industrial centre in the **Ruhr Valley**, to damage war production.

**Dresden** underwent some of the worst bombing. In four raids on 13–15 February 1945, over 3,900 tonnes of high-explosive bombs and incendiary devices were dropped by the RAF and the **US Army Air Forces** (USAAF), causing an immense firestorm. About 25,000 people died, most of whom were civilians.

# The final offensives

After D-Day, between June and August 1944, the Red Army launched a massive offensive, **Operation Bagration**, and drove the Germans from the USSR. In December 1944, Germany launched its **final offensive: the Battle of the Bulge**, a repeat of their 1940 attack through the Ardennes. However, they were exhausted and were defeated by January 1945. To the east, the USSR resumed its offensive and crossed the Oder River into Germany, heading for Berlin. Red Army soldiers inflicted terrible **revenge on German civilians** as they went.

## CHECKPOINT!

1. Explain the term Operation Overlord.
2. Describe the D-Day landings. Why were they successful?
3. What other successes did the Allies have after the liberation of Paris?
4. What effect did the bombings have on Germany?
5. What was the Battle of the Bulge? Why did the Germans think it would be a success?

✓ I can explain the D-Day landings and the closing stages of the war.

 ← TIME TO GO BACK ◆ I CAN MOVE FORWARD →

▼ Dresden in the aftermath of the Allied fire-bombing

**27 People and Nations: World War II**

# 27.7: The War's End and Impact

> **In this topic, you will learn about:**
> - How World War II came to an end
> - The impact of World War II

▲ Hiroshima after the atomic bomb

## The end of World War II

By 1945, major German cities such as Berlin and Dresden had been destroyed. German soldiers were still fighting but were unable to halt the Russian and Allied troops. In March 1945, the Allies crossed the River Rhine in western Germany.

The USSR began to attack Berlin. **Hitler committed suicide** in his bunker when the Red Army was just streets away and was succeeded by Admiral Dönitz, who surrendered. **Victory in Europe Day (VE Day)** is celebrated on 8 May 1945.

Japan surrendered on 15 August 1945, now known as **Victory over Japan Day (VJ Day)**, after the US had dropped two atomic bombs on the cities of Hiroshima and Nagasaki.

| Reasons why the Allies were victorious |
| --- |
| • The alliance of the 'Big Three' – Britain, the US and the USSR – meant they had more troops, weapons and equipment. |
| • Germany was weakened as it was fighting a two-front war. |
| • The Allies gained control of the air. |
| • The Red Army defeated the German army on land. |
| • Hitler sacked many of his advisers and interfered too much in Germany's military tactics. |

## The impact of World War II

World War II had both immediate and long-term consequences.

- In total, over **60 million people died** in World War II. Most of those killed were civilians. Roughly 40 million more were displaced inside their own country or became refugees elsewhere. Many survivors had seen their homes destroyed, gone hungry, lost loved ones, or experienced terror and violence.

- Many **cities were destroyed by bombing**. Whole industries, vast areas of farmland, roads, railways, communications and so forth also had to be rebuilt.

- The countries of Eastern Europe came under **USSR control** and became communist.

- **Trials** of Nazi war criminals took place in Nuremberg; some were executed.

▲ Londoners celebrating Victory in Europe Day

- The US and the USSR were now the two **most powerful countries** in the world. Tensions between the two developed into the Cold War. You will learn more about this in chapter 29.

- **Britain and France were weak** after the war. Their colonies began to demand independence.

- The **United Nations** was established in 1945 to prevent another war. It replaced the League of Nations.

- The **EEC** was set up in 1957 to encourage greater closeness and cooperation between European states.

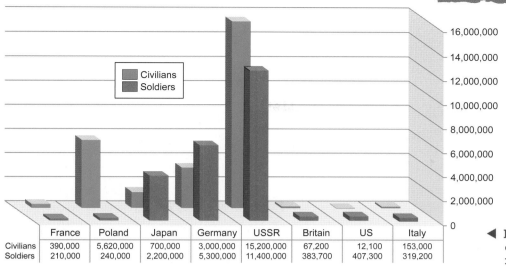

| | France | Poland | Japan | Germany | USSR | Britain | US | Italy |
|---|---|---|---|---|---|---|---|---|
| Civilians | 390,000 | 5,620,000 | 700,000 | 3,000,000 | 15,200,000 | 67,200 | 12,100 | 153,000 |
| Soldiers | 210,000 | 240,000 | 2,200,000 | 5,300,000 | 11,400,000 | 383,700 | 407,300 | 319,200 |

◀ Death figures of combatant countries, including war-related disease and famine

## CHECKPOINT!

1. How did World War II draw to an end?

2. Why did the Allies win the war?

3. Look at the graph above. What was the proportion of civilian to military deaths in (a) Poland and (b) the USSR? Which countries had the highest casualties?

4. How did World War II impact on (a) Germany; (b) Europe; (c) the US and USSR; (d) the wider world?

✔ I can describe the impact of World War II.

 ⬅ TIME TO GO BACK ◆ I CAN MOVE FORWARD ➡

# WORKING WITH THE EVIDENCE!

Study the following extract from a speech delivered by Winston Churchill to the House of Commons on 4 June 1940.

> The British Empire and the French Republic, linked together in their cause and in their need, will defend to the death their native soil, aiding each other like good comrades to the utmost of their strength.
>
> Even though large tracts of Europe and many old and famous States have fallen or may fall into the grip of the Gestapo and all the odious apparatus of Nazi rule, we shall not flag or fail.
>
> We shall go on to the end, we shall fight in France, we shall fight on the seas and oceans, we shall fight with growing confidence and growing strength in the air, we shall defend our Island, whatever the cost may be. We shall fight on the beaches, we shall fight on the landing grounds, we shall fight in the fields and in the streets, we shall fight in the hills; we shall never surrender, and even if, which I do not for a moment believe, this Island or a large part of it were subjugated and starving, then our Empire beyond the seas, armed and guarded by the British Fleet, would carry on the struggle, until, in God's good time, the New World, with all its power and might, steps forth to the rescue and the liberation of the old.

1. What type of source is this?

2. According to the source, what will Britain and France link together to do?

3. Name five places Churchill says they will fight.

4. What does he say will happen if Britain or a large part of it were 'subjugated and starving'?

5. Give one benefit and one limitation of this source for historians.

27 People and Nations: World War II

# A Life in Time: Winston Churchill (1874–1965)

### Early life

Winston Churchill was born in 1874 in Blenheim Palace, England. His father, Randolph Churchill, was a Conservative MP. His mother was the daughter of an American millionaire. Churchill served in the British army until 1899 and then became a war correspondent. He wrote about his experiences in Africa.

### Political career

In 1900 Churchill was elected as a Conservative MP. However, in 1904 he joined the Liberal Party. Leading up to World War I, he was the First Lord of the Admiralty. He was one of the main organisers of the Gallipolli campaign in 1915, which was a failure. Churchill resigned, but in 1917 he returned to politics. He was on the British negotiating team during the Anglo–Irish Treaty 1921 negotiations and took various ministerial roles. In 1924, he rejoined the Conservative Party. He became Chancellor of the Exchequer. In 1931, Churchill was not appointed to the cabinet. Many believed his political career was over.

### Wartime leadership

Churchill had been opposed to Chamberlain's policy of appeasement. When World War II broke out, he was reappointed First Lord of the Admiralty, and when Chamberlain resigned in May 1940 Churchill replaced him as Prime Minister. He and his wartime speeches were very inspiring to the British people. Churchill developed a close relationship with Franklin Roosevelt and formed an alliance with Stalin in 1941. However, following the war he became a strong critic of Stalin.

### Later career

Churchill lost the 1945 British election but was Prime Minister again from 1951 to 1955. He won the Nobel Prize for Literature in 1953 and died in 1965 at the age of 90.

▲ The front page of a British newspaper on 7 May 1945

 **SUMMARY**

In this chapter, we have learned that:

- World War II was a new kind of war, due to new technologies. Both sides created new weapons and technology to help them to victory, including new submarines and aircraft carriers, new tanks and arms, new aircraft, new rockets and the atomic bomb.

- Germany invaded Poland on 1 September 1939, using Blitzkrieg tactics.

- The German invasion of France began on 10 May 1940, again using Blitzkrieg tactics.

- On 13 August 1940, the aerial Battle of Britain began. It was won by the RAF.

- In the Blitz (September 1940–May 1941), the Germans dropped explosive and incendiary bombs on London and other British cities.

- On 22 June 1941, Germany invaded Russia in a three-pronged attack towards the most important cities: Moscow, Leningrad and Kiev. This was known as Operation Barbarossa.

- Soviet victory in the long, vicious Battle of Stalingrad over the winter of 1942–1943 was a turning point in the war.

- The US entered World War II in December 1941, when Japan attacked the US Pacific fleet at Pearl Harbor.

- The Battle of the Atlantic was when German U-boats attacked US supplies reaching Britain.

- The Allies bombed German industrial zones, and also civilians in German cities.

- The Allied invasion of France (or D-Day) took place on 6 June 1944.

- Victory in Europe Day (VE Day) is 8 May. Victory over Japan Day (VJ Day) is 15 August 1945.

- Roughly 60 million people died in World War II and survivors suffered in many ways.

- Some other consequences were that: many cities were destroyed; Eastern Europe became communist; the trials of Nazi war criminals took place in Nuremberg; the US and the USSR became the world's two most powerful countries and tensions rose between them; Britain and France were weakened and their colonies began to seek independence; the United Nations and EEC were founded.

### Reflecting on... World War II

World War II had an enormous impact on the world, particularly Europe. It took a long time to recover from years of widespread destruction. The impact of war is not always immediate. For example, the Cold War tensions you will learn about next stemmed from the new boundaries and balances of power in the wake of World War II. The desire for lasting peace would lead to the creation of the United Nations and the EEC/EU.

**27 People and Nations: World War II**

**Understanding History**

1. In what ways was World War II a new kind of war?
2. Explain how the tactic of Blitzkrieg worked.
3. How was Germany able to invade France?
4. Why was the Battle of Stalingrad a turning point in the war?
5. What was the impact of the Battle of Britain and the Blitz?
6. How did it benefit the Allies when the US entered the war?
7. What was the significance of the D-Day Landings?
8. Find out when the following events took place and put them into chronological order on a timeline in your copy: the US enters the war; Operation Barbarossa; the invasion of France; the Battle of Britain; the D-Day landings; the invasion of Poland; the Blitz; the Battle of Stalingrad.

 **Exploring History**

1. Write a paragraph on each of the following: the invasion of Poland; the invasion of France; the Battle of Britain and the Blitz; Operation Barbarossa; the Battle of Stalingrad; the US entering the war; the D-Day landings; the life of Winston Churchill.
2. Research six facts about one of the new technologies in topic 27.1.

| KEY TERMS | | |
|---|---|---|
| | **Blitzkrieg** | a tactic of surprise attack beginning with heavy bombing of an area by the German air force (Luftwaffe), followed closely by Panzer tanks and finally by the infantry |
| | **The Maginot Line** | a series of fortifications along the French–German border |
| | **Operation Dynamo** | the Allied evacuation of about 350,000 soldiers from the beaches at Dunkirk |
| | **The Battle of Britain** | the campaign of aerial attacks on Britain by the Luftwaffe |
| | **Dogfight** | close combat between military aircraft |
| | **The Blitz** | the Luftwaffe switched its focus to bombing British cities at night-time |
| | **Evacuation** | Children were moved out of the cities to the far safer countryside |
| | **Scorched earth** | a tactic of destroying anything useful to the enemy while moving through an area (crops, roads, bridges, railways and communication lines) |
| | **Operation Overlord** | the landing of over 150,000 US, British and Canadian troops in Normandy, France |

 Go to page 150 of your *Sources and Skills Book* for more exercises.

 Go to page 91 of your *Research Portfolio* for a task based on this chapter.

| World War II | The Holocaust | The Cold War |
| 1939–1945 | 1933–1945 | 1945–1991 |

Throughout history, there have been many examples of genocide, **the attempt to eliminate entire peoples or religious or ethnic groups**. The most studied example is the Holocaust, in which Hitler and the Nazis aimed to wipe out systematically the entire European population of Jewish people. In this chapter, you will learn about this horrific period of history, and look at other examples of genocide: those of Native Americans, Armenians and the people of Cambodia.

## WORKING WITH THE EVIDENCE!

### The Holocaust

| Type of source | Category | Example |
| --- | --- | --- |
| Secondary | Written | The *Book of Names*, put together at Auschwitz-Birkenau from the camp's records |
| Primary | Audiovisual | The documentary film *Shoah*, in which survivors of the camps, SS officers and others are interviewed about what they witnessed |

▲ The Wall of Names, Holocaust Memorial Museum, Paris

▲ The documentary *Shoah*

What can you learn from the above sources about the genocide that was the Holocaust?

# 28.1: What is Genocide?

**In this topic, you will learn about:**
- The nature of genocide
- Examples of genocide in history

## Genocide

Tens of millions of men, women and children have lost their lives to genocide or mass atrocities over the last few centuries alone. Genocide is the attempt to eliminate entire peoples or religious or ethnic groups. Some of these attempts have been highly organised and backed by a government, while others have seemed spontaneous – but all began with a process of **dehumanisation**, or treating people as though they were somehow less than human.

According to the United Nations,

> 'Genocide is a denial of the right of existence of entire human groups' and 'is a crime under international law… whether the crime is committed on religious, racial, political or any other grounds'.

We will examine several examples of genocide.

## Genocide in history

### Genocides of Native Americans

Numerous atrocities have been committed against Native Americans over several centuries. When European explorers first arrived in what is now the US, it is estimated that over **10 million Native Americans** were living there. By the **early twentieth century**, that number had fallen to **under 300,000**.

**European expansion** into North America – whether to find gold, escape religious persecution or start a new life – led directly to the destruction of Native American livelihoods, especially in the nineteenth century. Huge

▲ Depiction of the US cavalry's attack on a Cheyenne camp in Oklahoma in 1868

numbers were killed by **unfamiliar diseases** such as measles, influenza and whooping cough. **Malnutrition** also became a problem as tribes were driven from their traditional land and food sources. Tribal villages were **ambushed** during the gold rushes of the eighteenth and nineteenth centuries. Several **wars** broke out between native tribes and settlers.

Today, laws exist to protect some 500 tribes in the US, each with a distinct culture, way of life and history. Despite this, Native Americans still face major challenges such as poverty, cultural losses and discrimination.

## The Armenian Genocide

In **1915**, there were **two million Armenians** living within the multicultural but declining Ottoman Empire. They were mainly **Christian**. The Ottoman Empire lost all its European territory in the **Balkan Wars** of 1912–1913, creating instability among nationalist groups.

During World War I, **the Turkish government** attempted to unify all the Turkish people by creating a new empire with one language and one religion. The Armenian people did not belong within this new concept of a Turkish empire.

Military leaders accused the Armenians of being traitors, claiming that they were siding with their fellow Christians: Russia, the enemy.

From 1915 to 1923, a combination of **massacres, forced deportations, death marches** into the Syrian desert and disease or brutality in concentration camps is estimated to have killed more than **1.5 million ethnic Armenians**, as well as many Assyrians and Greeks. The Turks **demolished all traces of Armenian cultural heritage**, including masterpieces of ancient architecture and remarkable libraries and archives.

Today, numerous organisations and nations (including Ireland) recognise this event as '**the Armenian Genocide**' and most historians regard it as the first genocide of the twentieth century. However, it has not yet been acknowledged as such by the Turkish government.

▲ The Armenian homeland within the shrunken Ottoman Empire of 1914

▶ Monument to the Armenian Genocide at Christ Church Cathedral, Dublin

**28 Special Study: Genocide**

## The Cambodian Genocide

The **Khmer Rouge** were the followers of the **Communist Party of Kampuchea**. Led by **Pol Pot**, the Khmer Rouge overthrew the Cambodian government in 1975. They had an idealised vision of their country's 'pure' peasant past. They closed the country to the outside world, forced city dwellers to move to collective farms, outlawed all religions and brutally targeted anyone who was educated or who they suspected of opposing the new regime. In addition, the Khmer Rouge **aimed to eliminate ethnic minorities** within Cambodia, especially the **ethnic Vietnamese, Thai and Chinese people** and the **Muslim Cham people**.

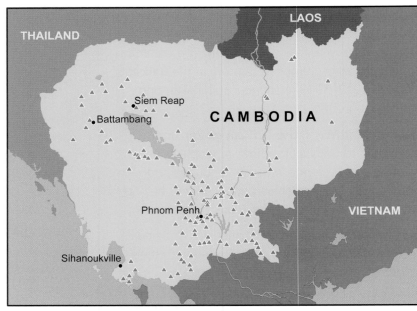

▲ Killing fields locations in Cambodia

Starvation and disease killed great numbers of people at the **forced-labour farms**, where **torture** was also widespread. It is claimed that 17,000 people passed through the notorious Tuol Sleng prison and only seven survived. As more and more people were sent to prison, the Khmer Rouge switched to a system of **'killing fields'** – mass executions at hundreds of sites all across Cambodia. As well as the groups mentioned above, the Khmer Rouge executed people who could no longer work or make the journey to the camps, the families of anyone deemed undesirable and at least 25,000 Buddhist monks.

▲ The site of a killing field, now a national memorial

In the years 1975–1979, between **1.7** and **3 million Cambodians** died in the Khmer Rouge's killing fields: roughly one-quarter of the population.

COLLABORATE: Work in groups to research ten facts about another genocide, for instance Rwanda, Bosnia or Darfur.

# CHECKPOINT!

1. Explain the terms genocide and dehumanisation. 📖
2. How were so many Native Americans killed in the nineteenth century?
3. Why were the Armenians targeted by the Turkish state?
4. How were they slaughtered?
5. Why did a genocide take place in Cambodia?
6. How did the Khmer Rouge kill up to one-quarter of the population?

 I can explain what genocide is and describe some examples from history.

← TIME TO GO BACK ◇ I CAN MOVE FORWARD →

## 28.2: The Holocaust

The **Holocaust** (sometimes also called the **Shoah**, a Hebrew word meaning 'catastophe') is one of the most significant atrocities in our past. It **evolved** slowly: centuries of anti-Semitism in Europe were heightened by the Nazis' beliefs about their own racial purity and the supposed inferiority of the Jewish people. In *Mein Kampf*, Hitler had publicly declared the Jews a threat to Germany. The **discriminatory Nuremberg Laws**, which stripped Jews of many rights, were created in 1935 and **Kristallnacht** followed in 1938. Soon afterwards, Jews were **segregated** from the general community and **persecuted**. Ultimately, the Nazis aimed to exterminate over **eight million Jews** living in Nazi-occupied Europe.

In this topic, you will learn about:
- The beginning of the Holocaust
- Jewish ghettos
- The Einsatzgruppen and the Final Solution
- Concentration camps
- Liberation and its aftermath

▲ Train tracks leading through the gates of Auschwitz-Birkenau camp

## Jewish ghettos

After the outbreak of war, life became even harder for Jews. The Nazis established **more than 400 ghettos** to isolate Jews from the non-Jewish population. A **ghetto** is <u>a part of a city where a minority group lives, due to social, legal or economic pressure</u>. When Jewish people were transferred to the ghetto, their homes and belongings were taken over.

The ghettos were closed off by high walls and barbed-wire fences and the gates were guarded. Food and fuel shortages led to a high mortality rate, especially in winter, and the overcrowding and unsanitary conditions encouraged the outbreak of disease.

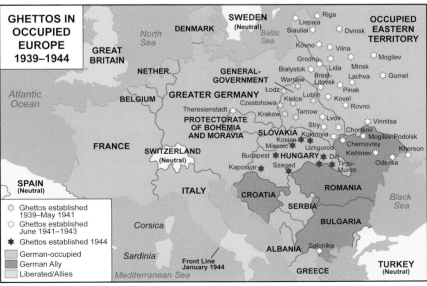

28 Special Study: Genocide

393

The first ghetto was set up in **Łodz, Poland**, on **8 February 1940**. Approximately 155,000 Jews (almost one-third of the city's total population) were forced to relocate there and made to work in factories. However, the ghettos were only a temporary solution. They served as round-up centres: they made it easier to control the Jewish population, and later to put them on trains for what they were initially told was 'resettlement' to the east.

◄ The deportation of Jews to the camps during the Warsaw ghetto uprising

## The Einsatzgruppen and the Final Solution

From 1941, as the German army advanced eastwards, it was followed by **Einsatzgruppen** – **special mobile killing squads that executed 'anti-German elements'** in the occupied territories. They killed Jews, local resistance fighters, government officials and others. Often the Einsatzgruppen relied on tips or help from locals. Mass executions took place in forests or other isolated areas. However, senior officers noted that this method (a) badly affected their soldiers' mental health and (b) was not efficient enough.

In 1942, **the Nazis formulated their official plan to exterminate the Jewish population of Europe**. This was **the Final Solution**. Heinrich Himmler was in charge of this secret policy. Approximately eleven million Jews lived in wider Europe at the time. From then on, the Germans began to empty the ghettos by deporting the Jewish population to **concentration camps**. Over 450,000 Jews once lived in the Warsaw ghetto. By the summer of 1943, it is estimated that 395,000 had either died or had been deported to camps.

**DID YOU KNOW?**

The Final Solution method was agreed in a conference lasting less than two hours in the Wannsee suburb of Berlin on 20 January 1942. Fifteen senior Nazi and German government members were present.

## CHECKPOINT!

1. Explain the terms Holocaust, Shoah and ghetto. 📖
2. How did the Nazis target the Jewish people before World War II?
3. How many Jews lived in Nazi-occupied Europe?
4. What were the Einsatzgruppen?
5. What was decided at the Wannsee Conference?

 I know about the ghettos, the killing squads and the Final Solution.

 TIME TO GO BACK ◆ I CAN MOVE FORWARD ➡

# Concentration camps

Concentration camps had been in use **since 1933**; at first they were **forced labour** camps. The first labour camp in Germany was at **Dachau**. Germany, Poland, Austria, Latvia, the USSR, France, Czechoslovakia and the Netherlands all contained concentration camps. From 1942, **special extermination camps** were built, all outside Germany. Among these were **Auschwitz-Birkenau**, **Majdanek**, **Chelmno and Treblinka**. Auschwitz-Birkenau in Poland would become the largest of the extermination camps, consisting of 40 sub-camps.

▲ The camps and Einsatzgruppen across Nazi-occupied Europe

## *Life and death in a concentration camp*

Jews from every part of Nazi-occupied Europe were deported to the camps on trains. They were told that they would be put to work. Several camps had signs reading '**Arbeit macht frei**', or '**Work makes one free**'. All belongings were taken from them on arrival. Anybody who arrived unwell or unable to work was separated from the rest and killed immediately.

Women, men and children were separated. The rules of the camps were designed to take away a person's identity. Prisoners' heads were shaved and a **number** was tattooed on their forearm. They were then herded into **crowded barracks**. Many able-bodied Jews worked until they died of disease, starved or were murdered. Others died due to the harsh conditions and living standards in the camps.

Some prisoners, especially twins, were used for **medical experiments** without their consent. An SS physician named **Josef Mengele** carried out such experiments in Auschwitz.

▲ The slogan 'Arbeit macht frei' over an entrance to Auschwitz

▲ Jewish people arriving at Auschwitz were told to write their names clearly on their suitcases for collection later

**28 Special Study: Genocide**

In extermination camps, some prisoners were shot but the majority were killed in large fake shower units which were actually gas chambers. **Zyklon B** (a cyanide poison) or **carbon monoxide** gases were used. Any gold fillings in their teeth were extracted and their bodies were then cremated. The Nazis had first used gas years earlier, to kill thousands of Germans with physical or intellectual disabilities.

**DID YOU KNOW?**

By 1945, the Nazis had built 20,000 concentration camps, extermination camps and sub-camps across Germany and eastern Europe.

As the tide of the war began to turn against the Nazis, deportations to the camps, executions and gassings all accelerated, because Hitler wanted to kill as many Jews as possible while he still could. Even as Allied forces closed in, the SS were destroying evidence and forcing prisoners from the camps on death marches. Many died due to starvation or harsh weather, while others were executed when they collapsed or fell behind.

▲ People bringing a wheelbarrow of flowers towards a former Dachau crematorium

## The liberation of the camps

**Soviet soldiers** were the first Allies to encounter concentration camps. Their advance westwards was so rapid that the Nazis had no time to dismantle the Majdanek camp in eastern Poland before they fled, so the Soviets found it nearly intact on 23 July 1944.

**Crematorium ovens, mass graves and unburied piles of corpses** were found in many camps. On 27 January 1945, ten days behind the retreating Nazis, they entered Auschwitz to find thousands of sick and dying prisoners. Medics tried to save the remaining prisoners, but many were too weak even to digest food. Half of those discovered alive in Auschwitz died within a few days.

**British, Canadian, American and French troops** also liberated concentration camps. The Americans liberated Buchenwald and Dachau, and the British liberated Bergen-Belsen. By May 1945, all camps had been liberated. Reports of these atrocities shocked the world.

◀ The malnourished survivors of Ebensee camp

# The aftermath of the Holocaust

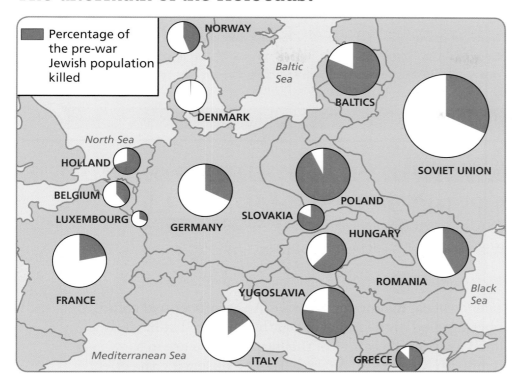

It is estimated that **six million Jews were murdered** in the Holocaust – over one million in Auschwitz alone. Millions of others were also killed in the camps, including (but not limited to) 2.5 million Soviet prisoners of war, 2 million Poles and half a million Roma. Generations were wiped out and many loved ones' fates would never be known.

Many Jewish survivors of the camps left Europe for good after the war and **emigrated**, particularly to the US, Canada or South Africa. In 1948, the new Jewish state of **Israel** was founded in Palestine and today its Jewish population numbers 6.5 million. For many, the sense of a shared Jewish identity became stronger in the wake of the terrible collective trauma and loss that was the Holocaust.

| Effects of the Holocaust |
|---|
| The mass murder of six million Jews |
| The mass murder of Slavic people, Roma, LGBT people, communists, prisoners of war and others |
| Jewish emigration, especially to the US, Canada, France and South Africa |
| Strengthening of a shared Jewish identity |

## CHECKPOINT!

1. What were concentration camps? Name four and the countries where they were located.
2. What happened to people in the concentration camps?
3. Describe the liberation of the camps.
4. What were the results of the Holocaust?
5. After World War II, Jewish people strove to establish the state of Israel. Why do you think they did this?

 I can talk about life and death in a concentration camp and describe the consequences of the Holocaust.

TIME TO GO BACK ◆ I CAN MOVE FORWARD ➡

28 Special Study: Genocide

**DID YOU KNOW?**

During World War II, 32 Irish merchant seamen were held in captivity for five years and forced to work in a labour concentration camp. They became known as 'Hitler's Irish slaves'. The last survivor of that group is a man named Harry Callan. Harry returned to Germany in his nineties to reconnect with kind locals. You can hear him tell his story, and that of his companions, at this link:

https://educateplus.ie/go/rte-harry-callan

# WORKING WITH THE <u>EVIDENCE</u>!

Study this extract from *Night* by Elie Wiesel, a survivor of Auschwitz.

Suddenly, the silence became more oppressive. An SS officer had come in and, with him, the smell of the Angel of Death. We stared at his fleshy lips. He harangued us from the center of the barrack: 'You are in a concentration camp. In Auschwitz.' A pause. He was observing the effect his words had produced. His face remains in my memory to this day. A tall man, in his thirties, crime written all over his forehead and his gaze. He looked at us as one would a pack of leprous dogs clinging to life.

'Remember,' he went on. 'Remember it always, let it be engraved in your memories. You are in Auschwitz. And Auschwitz is not a convalescent home. It is a concentration camp. Here, you must work. If you don't you will go straight to the chimney. To the crematorium. Work or crematorium—the choice is yours.'

We had already lived through a lot that night. We thought that nothing could frighten us anymore. But his harsh words sent shivers through us. The word 'chimney' here was not an abstraction; it floated in the air, mingled with the smoke. It was, perhaps, the only word that had a real meaning in this place.

1. What type of source is this?
2. How does the author describe the SS officer?
3. According to the source, what did the prisoners have to do and what would happen if they didn't?
4. According to the source, what was the only word that had real meaning? Why?
5. Give one benefit and one limitation of this source for historians.

Go to page 157 of your *Sources and Skills Book* to complete the evidence task on Harry Callan.

**SUMMARY**

In this chapter, we have learned that:

- There have been many examples of genocide throughout history, including the genocide of Native Americans from the fifteenth century onwards, the Armenian Genocide in 1915–1923 and the Cambodian Genocide in 1975.

- The Holocaust is one of the most significant atrocities in our past. It evolved slowly between 1933 and 1945. The Nazis built on existing anti-Semitism with the Nuremberg Laws. Jewish people were isolated in ghettos and finally deported and murdered in extermination camps.

- The concentration camps were liberated between mid-1944 and May 1945 by Soviet, British, Canadian, American and French troops.

- Approximately six million Jews died during the Holocaust. Millions of others were also killed, including (but not limited to) 2.5 million Soviet prisoners of war, two million Poles and half a million Roma.

- Many European Jews emigrated after World War II to countries such as the US, Canada, France and South Africa. After the state of Israel was founded in 1948, many began new lives there.

### Reflecting on... Genocide

Sadly, we do not always learn from past atrocities. For example, the Cambodian genocide happened after the whole world had learned of the Holocaust. However, through studying history it is possible to recognise patterns – of power, of discrimination, of 'othering' and dehumanisation – that have preceded these atrocities in various societies. To prevent further atrocities in the future, we must remain vigilant for these warning signs and work to uphold human rights.

28

Special Study: Genocide

# Understanding History

1. Why did the genocide of Native Americans happen and what were its effects?
2. Why did the Armenian Genocide happen and what were its effects?
3. The Turkish government denies that what was done to the Armenians was genocide. Why do you think this is?
4. Why did the Cambodian Genocide happen and what were its effects?
5. Why were the Jewish ghettos set up?
6. Describe life in the ghetto.
7. Describe life in the concentration camps.
8. What were the effects of the Holocaust?
9. What do all the genocides you have studied have in common?
10. What steps were taken by governments against the targeted peoples before the mass murders began?
11. Find out when the following events took place and put them into chronological order: the liberation of the concentration camps; the Nuremberg Laws; the formation of ghettos; the creation of extermination camps; the outbreak of World War II; Kristallnacht.

# Exploring History

1. Write a paragraph about the genocide of: (a) Native Americans; (b) the Armenian people; and (c) the Cambodian people.
2. Write an account of the background, course and consequences of the Holocaust.
3. Research a concentration camp in Nazi-occupied Europe and record ten facts about this camp.

| KEY TERMS | | |
|---|---|---|
| | Genocide | the attempt to eliminate entire peoples or religious or ethnic groups |
| | Dehumanisation | treating people as though they were somehow less than human |
| | Ghetto | part of a city where a minority group lives, due to social, legal or economic pressure |
| | Einsatzgruppen | special mobile killing squads that followed the German army east and performed mass executions of 'anti-German elements' |
| | The Final Solution | the Nazis' official plan to exterminate the Jewish population of Europe |

 Go to page 155 of your *Sources and Skills Book* for more exercises.

 Go to page 94 of your *Research Portfolio* for a task based on this chapter.

| World War II | The Cold War | The 1960s |
|---|---|---|
| 1939–1945 | 1945–1991 | 1960–1970 |

In the aftermath of World War II, **the most powerful countries in the world (or superpowers) were the Soviet Union and the United States of America.** They had been allies against the Nazis, but after the war rivalry emerged between them. **The long period of tension between them and their respective allies** was known as the Cold War. The two sides came close to armed conflict on a number of occasions, but each time direct war was avoided. The Cold War was instead fought through competition in technology, spying and sport and via conflicts around the world. Both sides tried to weaken their opponents without actually resorting to all-out war.

# WORKING WITH THE EVIDENCE!

## The Cold War

| Type of source | Category | Example |
|---|---|---|
| Primary | Visual | Television was in widespread use across the world by the mid-1950s and so the key moments of the Cold War were recorded by TV news |
| Secondary | Visual | The documentary series *The Cold War*, released in 1998 and available on YouTube |
| Primary | Written | Official documents from governments on both sides: official reports, speeches by political leaders, agreements between states as well as reports from spies on the other superpower's activities |
| | | Newspapers carried detailed coverage of the events and crises of the Cold War, as well as political cartoons |
| | | Autobiographies by people like Dwight Eisenhower, Lyndon Johnson, Henry Kissinger, Margaret Thatcher, Nikita Khrushchev and Mikhail Gorbachev |

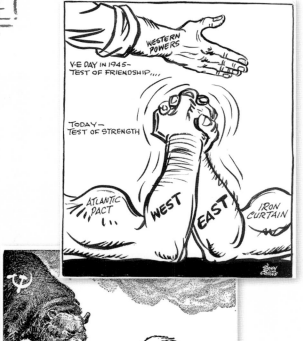

What do these cartoons in newspapers of the time tell us about the causes of the Cold War?

# 29.1: The Causes of the Cold War

**In this topic, you will learn about:**
- The differences between the political systems of the superpowers
- Conflict and mistrust between the Allies during World War II
- The Soviet takeover of Eastern Europe
- The US response of the Truman Doctrine and the Marshall Plan

## Political differences: Communism vs. capitalism

At its heart, the Cold War was a conflict between **two different ideologies**. The Soviet Union was a **communist country**, where the state controls all the property, industry and services and freedoms (of elections, of the media and of the individual) are limited. The US was a **capitalist economy**, where individuals are free to acquire wealth, own private property and profit from businesses with little to no interference from the government. It was also a **democracy**, where there were various political parties, people could vote in elections and the free press and free speech were protected.

## Conflict and mistrust during World War II

Although the Soviets and the Americans had fought as allies to defeat Hitler, there were tensions between them during the war. **Stalin**, the Soviet leader, believed that Britain and the US (the Western Allies) had deliberately delayed the **D-Day landings** so that the Soviets would suffer more damage by fighting the Nazis alone. In addition, the US refused to share the secrets of the **atomic bomb** with the Soviets when they used it to defeat Japan in August 1945.

## The Iron Curtain

**Key**
— Iron Curtain, 1949
(Year) Communist rule established

◀ Europe divided by the Iron Curtain

After World War II, Stalin wanted to create a '**buffer zone**' to protect the USSR from future invasions. This meant he would need states in Eastern Europe that were loyal to the Soviets. He imposed communist governments on Poland, Czechoslovakia, Hungary, Romania and Bulgaria. These were known as the '**satellite states**' as they were under the control of Moscow. The West believed that the Soviets were aggressively expanding their control of Europe. Many feared that they would try to take over the rest of Europe as well.

'From Stettin in the Baltic to Trieste in the Adriatic an 'Iron Curtain' has descended across the continent. Behind that line lie all the capitals of the ancient states of Central and Eastern Europe. [They] lie in what I must call the Soviet sphere, and all are subject, in one form or another, not only to Soviet influence but to a very high and in some cases increasing measure of control from Moscow.'

**Winston Churchill** (1946)

Go to page 162 of your *Sources and Skills Book* for an evidence task on this speech.

## Containment

In response to Soviet actions, US President Harry Truman announced a new policy called the **Truman Doctrine**. This declared that the US would aid other countries to resist the spread of communism. In a speech to the US Congress in March 1947, Truman said: 'I believe that it must be the policy of the United States to support free peoples who are resisting attempted subjugation by armed minorities or by outside pressures'. The US promised to provide **military aid** to any country that was fighting communist forces within its own state.

In addition, the US government announced it would **provide funds** to help Europe rebuild after World War II. Under the **Marshall Plan**, named after the US Secretary of State General **George Marshall**, the US spent over **$15 billion** on helping Western Europe to rebuild. They believed that if these countries were economically prosperous, they would be better able to resist communism. Stalin refused to allow countries in Eastern Europe to receive the aid, fearing it would weaken his control over them. President Truman understood that he could not remove communism from countries where it was already established, as this would mean war against the Soviets, but he did believe that he could limit its spread. This became known as the policy of **containment**.

▲ US President Harry Truman

▲ General George Marshall

COLLABORATE: In your group, pick a side in the Cold War: the Soviets or the Western powers. Come up with arguments as to why your side is better and why the other side was responsible for the rise in tensions after World War II.

## CHECKPOINT!

1. Explain the following terms: superpowers; the Cold War.
2. Explain the differences between the political systems in the US and the Soviet Union.
3. What tensions emerged between the Allies during World War II?
4. What was the Iron Curtain? Why did Stalin take over Eastern Europe?
5. How did the US respond to Soviet actions in Europe?
6. What was the policy of containment?
7. Which side do you think bore more responsibility for the beginning of the Cold War? Give reasons for your answer.

I understand the causes of the Cold War.

◀ TIME TO GO BACK ◀ ▶ I CAN MOVE FORWARD ▶

**29 The Cold War**

# 29.2: The Berlin Blockade, 1948–1949

In this topic, you will learn about:
- The tensions over the future of Germany
- The Berlin Airlift
- The impact of the Blockade

## Germany after World War II

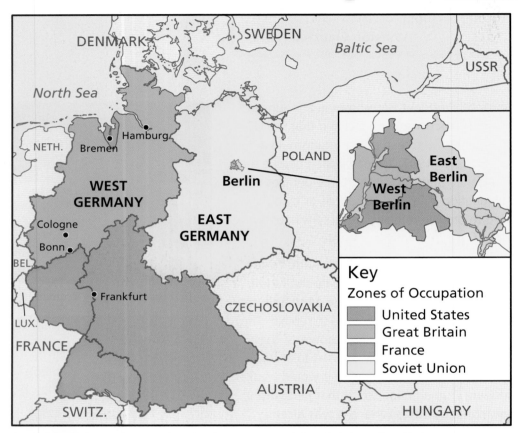

▲ Post-war Germany showing the four zones and the division of Berlin into sectors

During the war, the Allied leaders had agreed how to deal with Germany after it was defeated:

- Germany would be divided into **four zones**, occupied by the Americans, British, Soviets and French.
- **Berlin**, although it was in the middle of the Soviet Zone, would also be divided into **four sectors**, one for each of the allies.
- The division of Germany would be **temporary**, until a new, peaceful country was created.

Germany was devastated after the war and its people faced great economic and social hardship. The Allies disagreed about the future of the country. The USSR demanded compensation from Germany for the terrible damage it had suffered during the war. It wanted a permanently weakened Germany that would never be a threat again. The others wanted a strong, prosperous, democratic Germany that would be an obstacle to communism and be the economic anchor of Europe.

## The Berlin Blockade

Tensions came to a head when the Western allies introduced a new currency to their zones and sectors of Berlin. They intended the new **Deutschmark** to help revive the economy. The Soviets refused to allow the new currency to be used in their zone and sector of Berlin and retaliated on 24 June 1948 by cutting off all road, rail and canal links to West Berlin. Stalin hoped that he could force the Allies to leave the city.

## The Berlin Airlift

This was the first major confrontation of the Cold War. The Western countries were determined not to give in to the Soviets and they decided to supply Berlin by air. They gambled that Stalin would not risk all-out war by shooting down an airplane. Codenamed **Operation Vittles**, it was a huge operation, as they had to fly cargo planes into three airports in West Berlin bringing food, clothing, medical supplies and fuel for over 2.5 million people. The airlifts continued until April 1949. Stalin eventually realised he would not be able to drive the Allies out of the city. The Allies were able to deliver more supplies by air than they had delivered by road and rail before the Blockade.

▲ Berliners watching Operation Vittles in action

29 The Cold War

## The results of the Berlin Blockade and Airlift

* The Soviets were prepared to increase pressure on the West but were unwilling to provoke a direct military confrontation.

* The division of Germany became permanent. The three western zones became the **Federal Republic of Germany (West Germany)**, which was a democratic and capitalist country. The Soviets created the **German Democratic Republic (East Germany)** in their zone. It was a communist country within the Soviet sphere of influence.

* The US, Canada and ten other Western European states set up the **North Atlantic Treaty Organisation** (NATO) in 1949. This was a military alliance: its members agreed to support each other against attack by other states.

* The Soviets accelerated their nuclear weapons programme and detonated an atomic bomb in 1949. They also set up a military alliance in Eastern Europe in 1955 called the **Warsaw Pact**.

* The detonation of the Soviet atomic bomb started the **arms race**. Both sides in the Cold War spent billions every year to build bigger and more powerful nuclear weapons that could wipe out the other side. They also created huge, well-equipped armies with the latest technology.

### CHECKPOINT!

1. What did the Allies decide to do with Germany after World War II?
2. What tensions were there between the Allies over the future of Germany?
3. What provoked the Berlin Blockade?
4. How did the Western Allies respond to the Blockade?
5. Why did the Blockade come to an end?
6. What impact did the Berlin Blockade have on (a) Germany; (b) the US and its allies; and (c) the Soviet Union?

 I understand what happened during the Berlin Blockade.  ← TIME TO GO BACK ◆ I CAN MOVE FORWARD →

# 29.3: The Korean War, 1950–1953

In this topic, you will learn about:
- ❯ The partition of Korea
- ❯ The course of the Korean War
- ❯ The impact of the war

▲ Chairman Mao

## Korea after World War II

Korea was a former Japanese territory that had been divided along a map line called **the 38th parallel** at the end of World War II. In **North Korea**, the Soviets established a communist government. **South Korea** had a US-backed government. It was expected that there would be free elections in 1948 to create a united, democratic Korea. These elections did not take place due to mistrust on both sides. The victory of the communists, under **Chairman Mao Zedong**, in the **Chinese Civil War** in 1949 increased tensions in the region.

## North Korea's invasion of the South

There were several military clashes in 1949 along the border between the two states. In June 1950, the North Korean army invaded the South. They had Soviet weapons and quickly pushed the South Korean army back, taking the capital, **Seoul**. President Truman believed that if the US did not help, the South would be conquered. He ordered US military support for the South and persuaded the United Nations to send an army to help them.

▲ General MacArthur

▼ Fighting in the Korean War

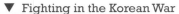

## The war escalates

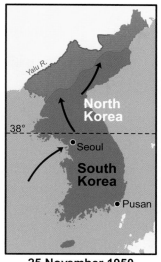

25 June 1950      14 September 1950      25 November 1950      27 July 1953

▲ The four stages of the Korean War

In September 1950, UN forces (mostly US, but with soldiers from 15 other countries) landed at **Inchon**, west of Seoul, under the command of US **General Douglas MacArthur**. They quickly drove the North Koreans out of the South and MacArthur ordered them to advance into North Korea. The UN forces headed for **the Yalu river**, which was the border with China. The Chinese thought MacArthur intended to invade China and they sent 500,000 soldiers to help the North Koreans repel them.

MacArthur wanted to attack communist China with nuclear weapons. Truman worried this would bring the Soviets into the war and could start World War III. Truman rejected MacArthur's proposal and fired him after the general criticised him. The war settled into a stalemate along the 38th parallel and dragged on until 1953. In June 1953, the two sides agreed to a truce to end the war.

## The consequences of the Korean War

- **The division of Korea became permanent**. The North became a brutal communist dictatorship. The South emerged as a prosperous, industrialised capitalist economy.

- The US considered the war a success for the policy of **containment**, as communism had been stopped from spreading to South Korea. As in Berlin, all-out war had been avoided while the communists had been confronted and contained.

- **The Cold War divided Asia**, as it had Europe. The US gained new allies in South Korea, Japan, the Philippines, Australia and New Zealand. The Soviets and the Chinese became allies.

### CHECKPOINT!

1. How was Korea divided after World War II?
2. When did the war start?
3. How and why did the US become involved?
4. How and why did China become involved?
5. Why did President Truman refuse to attack China?
6. What were the results of the Korean War for (a) Korea; (b) containment; and (c) Asia?

 I can explain the causes, course and consequences of the Korean War.

29 The Cold War

# 29.4: The Cuban Missile Crisis, 1962

In this topic, you will learn about:

❯ The background to the Cuban Missile Crisis

❯ The events of October 1962

❯ The results of the crisis

## Background: The Cuban Revolution

In October 1962, the world stood on **the brink of nuclear war**. Tensions between the superpowers had been rising for some time, especially over Berlin. The crisis, however, was over a small island some 140 km off the coast of Florida. In 1959, **Fidel Castro** led a communist revolution to overthrow the US-backed government of **Cuba**. Castro took over many US-owned businesses on the island and the US cut off trade to Cuba. The Soviets agreed to buy Cuban sugar and to sell weapons to Castro.

## Background: The Bay of Pigs

US President **John F. Kennedy** authorised the **Central Intelligence Agency (CIA)** to plan an invasion by anti-Castro Cuban exiles in April 1961. It was a total disaster: Castro's forces easily defeated the invaders. Castro asked the Soviets for more weapons to defend against a future invasion. At the same time, Soviet leader **Nikita Khrushchev** was worried about the nuclear missiles that the US had stationed in Europe, which could reach Soviet cities. Khrushchev offered to build missile bases in Cuba that would be able to hit cities all across the US.

▲ Fidel Castro

▲ Nikita Khruschev

▲ John F. Kennedy

## October 1962: The world on the brink of war

In October 1962, an **American U-2 spy plane** photographed a missile base being built in Cuba. The Americans realised that these missiles could reach nearly every major US city. On television, Kennedy announced **a naval blockade** of Cuba. The US navy would prevent any ship from landing in Cuba until the Soviets agreed to remove the missiles. US forces around the world were on full alert. As Soviet ships continued to sail towards Cuba, the world seemed to be heading for a nuclear war.

After several days of tense stand-off, the two sides came to an agreement to end the crisis. The US publicly declared that it would not invade Cuba and Kennedy privately promised Khrushchev that he would remove US missiles from Turkey. In return, the Soviets agreed to dismantle the missiles and remove them from Cuba. The Soviet ships turned around and returned home.

## Consequences of the Cuban Missile Crisis

Both superpowers took steps to avoid nuclear war in the future:

- **A telephone hotline** was set up between Moscow and Washington to deal with potential crises when they arose.

- The **Nuclear Test Ban Treaty** was agreed by the superpowers and others that banned atomic testing on land, sea or in space.

Go to page 164 of your *Sources and Skills Book* for an evidence task on Khrushchev's account of the crisis.

▲ The Cuban missile sites and their potential strike range

*(Map labels: Soviet missile site in Cuba; Major city; Range of long range missiles (2,000 miles); Range of short range missiles (1,000 miles); USA; Salt Lake City; Denver; Chicago; New York; Washington; Dallas; New Orleans; Miami; Havana; Cuba; Pacific Ocean; Gulf of Mexico; Atlantic Ocean)*

## CHECKPOINT!

1. What happened in Cuba in 1959?
2. How did the US government respond to the Cuban Revolution?
3. Why did the Soviet Union place missiles in Cuba in 1962?
4. What did the US do when it discovered the existence of the missiles?
5. How was the crisis resolved?
6. What were the main results of the Cuban Missile Crisis?

 I understand the causes, course and consequences of the Cuban Missile Crisis.

⬅ TIME TO GO BACK ◆ I CAN MOVE FORWARD ➡

# WORKING WITH THE EVIDENCE!

Look at this cartoon from October 1962 and answer the questions that follow:

1. Name the leaders marked X and Y.
2. Describe what is happening in the cartoon.
3. What is the message of the cartoon?
4. Is the cartoon effective in getting its message across? Give reasons for your answer.
5. Does the cartoon support either side? Give reasons for your answer.

"OK MR PRESIDENT, LET'S TALK."

# 29.5: The Vietnam War, 1964–1975

- ❯ The background to the Vietnam War
- ❯ US involvement in the war
- ❯ The results of the war

▲ North and South Vietnam, divided by a demilitarised zone (DMZ)

## Vietnam after World War II

Before World War II, Vietnam had been a French colony. It was occupied by the Japanese during the war until local communist forces drove them out of the northern half of the country in 1945. When the French tried to return after the defeat of Japan, these forces, the **Viet Minh** under **Ho Chi Minh**, fought back and by 1954 they had forced the French out. Vietnam was partitioned, with the North under communist rule and the South ruled by a pro-Western government. When promised elections to unify the country did not take place, the North attacked the South.

## US involvement

Due to its policy of **containment**, the US had financially aided the French in their war against the Viet Minh. It also sent aid and troops to help the South after the North attacked. Initially the troops numbered only in the hundreds, but that rose to over **16,000** under President Kennedy. After Kennedy's death in 1963, President **Lyndon Johnson** continued to increase troop levels until they reached **500,000** in 1968. Johnson sent them into direct combat with the communists in Vietnam in 1965.

## The war in Vietnam

The North Vietnamese fighters, called **Vietcong**, adopted **guerrilla tactics** against the Americans and their Southern allies. They attacked in small groups, hid in the jungles and constantly disrupted their opponents' supply lines. They had the support of the people in rural areas, who hid them and their weapons. The Americans were unable to deal effectively with these tactics. They used chemicals to destroy the jungles, burned villages where guerillas were believed to be hiding and bombed the North heavily. These actions only strengthened support for the Vietcong in many areas.

▲ North Vietnamese guerilla fighters

Over 58,000 US soldiers were killed and tens of thousands were injured. The Vietnamese casualties numbered in the millions. The destruction, death and seemingly never-ending war produced the **anti-war movement** in the US, where huge protest marches took place from 1967 onwards.

> **DID YOU KNOW?**
>
> In order to avoid American patrols, the North Vietnamese brought supplies to their fighters in the South through neighbouring Laos and Cambodia along the 'Ho Chi Minh Trail'.

## The end of the war

The US and the Viet Minh fought to a **stalemate** until the war's unpopularity pressured President **Richard Nixon** to 'bring the troops home'. In 1972, a ceasefire agreement was signed between the US, the North Vietnamese and the South's government. The US pulled out their troops in 1973. In 1975, the North launched a full-scale invasion of the South, and the Southern capital of Saigon fell in April 1975.

▲ US soldiers in Vietnam

## Results of the Vietnam War

- The policy of **containment** failed in Vietnam. South Vietnam became communist and the spread of the fighting during the war meant that the neighbouring countries of Laos and Cambodia became communist as well.

- The US suffered **a humiliating defeat** at the hands of a guerrilla army of farmers and workers in one of the poorest countries in the world. It was much more cautious in sending its army overseas again during the Cold War.

- **Deep divisions** were opened up in US society, where many people vehemently opposed the war.

### ///////// CHECKPOINT! /////////

1. Who fought the French in Vietnam after World War II?
2. Why did the US get involved?
3. What evidence is there that US involvement escalated in the 1960s?
4. What were the tactics of (a) the US and (b) the Vietcong?
5. Why could the Americans not win the war?
6. How did the Vietnam War change US policy during the Cold War?

 I understand the main events and results of the Vietnam War.  TIME TO GO BACK ◆ I CAN MOVE FORWARD ➡

**29 The Cold War**

# 29.6: Eastern Europe under the Soviets

**In this topic, you will learn about:**

- How the Soviets maintained their control of Eastern Europe
- The major events during their domination of Eastern Europe

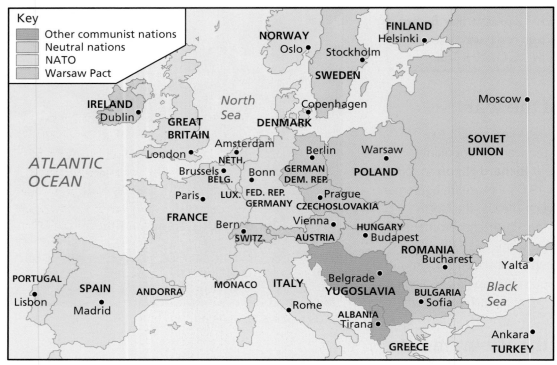

▲ Political allegiance in Europe at the beginning of the 1950s

## Controlling Eastern Europe

In the years immediately after World War II, the Soviets ensured that communist governments were set up in the countries of Eastern Europe. These countries and the Soviet Union were together known as **the Eastern Bloc**. In the following decades, the USSR had to retain its control over these countries. It did this through various means:

- Economic: In response to the Marshall Plan, the Soviet Union launched **Comecon** in 1949. It claimed this was to give economic aid to other communist countries, but in reality, it allowed Moscow to exert control over their economies.

- Military: The **Warsaw Pact** was established in 1955 as a military alliance, like NATO. This brought the armies of the satellite states under direct Soviet control.

- Political: The Soviets used an organisation called **Cominform** to coordinate the activities of local communist parties. This ensured that local communist leaders were loyal to Moscow and did as they were told.

## Soviet control in action

For the most part, the Soviets allowed the satellite states to run their own affairs, as long as they did not endanger communist rule. A number of times they intervened directly into the satellite states to ensure continued Soviet control:

1. **1953:** Workers on strike in East Berlin were attacked by Soviet tanks stationed in the city.

2. **1956:** During the **Hungarian Uprising**, there were mass protests against the USSR and the local communist government. The protesters appealed to the West for help, but they were ignored. The uprising was crushed by a Soviet invasion after 13 days.

3. **1961: The Berlin Wall** was built to stop people fleeing from East Berlin to the West. Afterwards, anyone trying to cross over was shot by the border guards.

4. **1968:** The Czechoslovakian government tried to introduce more freedoms for its people in the **Prague Spring**. Moscow sent in tanks, as it feared that the country might try to leave the Eastern Bloc.

5. **1980–1981:** Workers in Poland formed the **Solidarity** trade union to demand more rights and better pay from the government. Under the threat of a Soviet invasion, the Polish government imposed military rule **(martial law)** on the country and arrested the leaders of Solidarity.

The threat of the Soviet Union using military force kept the governments and people of Eastern Europe under its control for over forty years.

**DID YOU KNOW?**

In 1983, the Soviet Union's military leaders mistook army training manoeuvres by NATO forces in Western Europe as the first step in an attack. They almost launched a full-scale nuclear strike that would have started World War III before they realised the truth. No one in the West had any idea how close the world had come to war until years later.

▲ Soviet tanks during the Prague Spring

## CHECKPOINT!

1. What was the main objective of Soviet policy in Eastern Europe after World War II?
2. How did the Soviets seek to control the countries of Eastern Europe?
3. What happened when those countries tried to break free of that control? Give an example.
4. Why do you think the West refused to intervene in the Hungarian Uprising in 1956?
5. Why do you think the Soviet threat of force was so successful at keeping Eastern Europe under control?

 I understand how the Soviet Union retained control over Eastern Europe during the Cold War.

 ← TIME TO GO BACK ◆ I CAN MOVE FORWARD →

**29 The Cold War**

# 29.7: Mikhail Gorbachev and the End of the Cold War

**In this topic, you will learn about:**

❯ The life of Mikhail Gorbachev

❯ Gorbachev's reforms in the Soviet Union

❯ The fall of communism in Eastern Europe

## A Life in Time: Mikhail Gorbachev (1931–)

### Early life and career

**Mikhail Gorbachev** was born in 1931 in southern Russia. As a student, he became active in the Communist Party while studying law in Moscow. He made a name for himself in the party as a reformer and in 1978 he was appointed to the agricultural Central Committee and later to the Soviet Union's executive committee, the **Politburo**.

### Gorbachev's reforms

By the 1980s, the Soviet economy was in need of drastic reform. In 1985, after three elderly leaders died in quick succession, Gorbachev was appointed leader of the Soviet Union. He believed that the cost of the Cold War was too high and the USSR could no longer afford the arms race. He wanted to **reduce military spending** so he could spend that money to **improve the lives of Soviet citizens**. He announced two major changes:

- **Glasnost** (meaning 'openness'): Gorbachev's policy to open up discussion in Soviet society: political prisoners were freed, censorship was relaxed and people were encouraged to suggest new ideas to fix the economy

- **Perestroika** (meaning 'restructuring'): Gorbachev's policy to reform and open up the Soviet economy by allowing some private ownership of business and land.

### The end of the Cold War

Gorbachev saw that vast sums of money were being poured into the military to keep up with the US, which was spending **$550 billion** a year on defence under President **Ronald Reagan**. Gorbachev and Reagan met several times and built a new relationship based on trust. They made important nuclear disarmament agreements, which dramatically reduced nuclear weaponry and tensions between East and West.

▲ Ronald Reagan with Mikhail Gorbachev

## The collapse of Communism

In 1988, Gorbachev declared that the Soviet army would no longer be used to keep communist governments in power in Eastern Europe. The following year, protests broke out in all the countries under communist rule. Without the Soviet army to back them up, each of the communist governments fell. In November 1989, the Berlin Wall – the symbol of the Cold War – was opened and communist rule came to an end in Europe.

▲ The fall of the Berlin Wall, 9 November 1989

Gorbachev's reforms made the problems of the Soviet Union worse. The economy continued to decline, debt soared and people began to openly demand the end of communist rule. By the end of 1991, Gorbachev had lost control of the situation as states (such as Estonia, Latvia and Lithuania) began to break away from the Soviet Union, and he resigned as Soviet leader. **The Soviet Union ceased to exist and the Cold War came to an end.**

## CHECKPOINT!

1. When did Gorbachev become leader of the Soviet Union?
2. Why did he believe radical reforms were necessary?
3. Explain the terms glasnost and perestroika. 📖
4. How did Gorbachev improve relations with the US?
5. Why did communism collapse in Eastern Europe?
6. Gorbachev has been described as the most important world leader since World War II. Do you agree? Give reasons for your answer.

 I understand how the Cold War came to an end.

 TIME TO GO BACK ◇ I CAN MOVE FORWARD →

29 The Cold War

# SUMMARY

In this chapter, we have learned:

- The Cold War was the period of heightened international tension between the superpowers and their allies after World War II. There were a number of causes:
  - different political and economic systems
  - tensions and mistrust during World War II
  - the Soviet takeover of Eastern Europe behind the 'Iron Curtain'
  - the US policy of containment under the Truman Doctrine and the Marshall Plan.

- During the Cold War there were several major crises between the superpowers. The first was in Berlin in 1948– 1949, when the Soviets tried to force the Western Allies out of the city by cutting off supply lines. This failed when the Allies were able to supply the city through airlifts.

- In 1950, North Korea invaded South Korea. The UN sent armed forces to drive them back but when the US appeared to be threatening China, the Chinese deployed a huge army to support the North Koreans. After three years of fighting, a truce left North and South Korea as separate countries.

- The closest the world came to nuclear war was during the Cuban Missile Crisis in 1962. The US blockaded the island to prevent the Soviets from basing nuclear weapons 144 km from Florida. The stand-off was eventually resolved when the US promised not to invade Cuba and to remove its own missiles from Turkey if the Soviets removed theirs from Cuba.

- The US fought the Vietnam War during the 1960s and early 1970s. It was humiliated by its failure to defeat the communist guerrilla fighters in the jungles.

- The Cold War eventually ended in the late 1980s when the Soviet leader, Mikhail Gorbachev, decided to reform the Soviet system. He wanted to reduce military spending and to do this he sought to reduce tensions with the West. He also was no longer willing to use military force to keep communists in power in Eastern Europe. Those governments all collapsed by late 1989.

## Reflecting on... the Cold War

The Cold War dominated international relations in the second half of the twentieth century. Never before had the human race possessed the ability, through nuclear weapons, to completely eradicate all life on the planet. On several occasions, it seemed likely that World War III would break out. However, it was almost certainly the fear of mutual annihilation that kept the peace.

# Understanding History

1. What were the main differences between the Soviet Union and the West?

2. What did the Soviets want at the end of World War II? How did they go about achieving this?

3. How did the US respond to Soviet actions in the years after World War II?

4. What was the first major confrontation of the Cold War?

5. What was the arms race?

6. Why was the Korean War an important event in the Cold War?

7. How was the Cuban Missile Crisis resolved? What impact did it have on the Cold War?

8. Why did the US lose the Vietnam War?

9. How did the Soviet Union maintain its control of Eastern Europe?

10. Why did Mikhail Gorbachev try to reform the Soviet Union?

11. What reforms did he propose?

12. How did communism collapse in Eastern Europe?

13. Find out when the events below and put them in the correct chronological order on a timeline. Write a sentence about what happened in each case.
    - The Fall of Saigon
    - The Berlin Blockade
    - The Cuban Missile Crisis
    - The Hungarian Uprising
    - Churchill's Iron Curtain speech
    - The Prague Spring
    - The Fall of Berlin Wall
    - The end of the Korean War
    - The announcement of the Truman Doctrine
    - The building of the Berlin Wall

# Exploring History

1. Write an account of each of the following Cold War events:
    - The Berlin Blockade
    - The Korean War
    - The Cuban Missile Crisis
    - The Vietnam War
    - The end of the Cold War

2. Write an account of the life of Mikhail Gorbachev.

3. Discuss why the Cold War never became a 'hot war'.

| **KEY TERMS** | Superpowers | the most powerful countries in the world after World War II (the Soviet Union and the United States) |
| --- | --- | --- |
| | The Cold War | the long period of heightened tension between the superpowers and their respective allies |
| | Communist country | one where the state controls all the property, industry and services and freedoms (of election, of the media and of the individual) are limited |
| | Capitalist economy | one where individuals are free to acquire wealth, own private property and profit from businesses with little to no interference from the government |
| | Democracy | a system of government under which there are various political parties, people can vote in elections and free media and free speech are protected |
| | Satellite states | the Eastern European countries that were under the control of Moscow (Poland, Czechoslovakia, Hungary, Romania and Bulgaria) |
| | Containment | a US policy that aimed to halt the spread of communism and contain it to the countries where it was already established |
| | Arms race | the competitive research and spending by the superpowers to build bigger and more powerful nuclear weapons that could wipe out the other side |
| | Glasnost | (openness). Gorbachev's policy to open up discussion in Soviet society: political prisoners were freed, censorship was relaxed and people were encouraged to suggest new ideas to fix the economy |
| | Perestroika | (restructuring). Gorbachev's policy to reform and open up the Soviet economy by allowing some private ownership of business and land |

Go to page 159 of your *Sources and Skills Book* for more exercises.

Go to page 98 of your *Research Portfolio* for a task based on this chapter.

The 1960s was a decade of profound change in the world. As we have seen in other chapters, it was the decade when tensions between the superpowers almost plunged the world into World War III, the decade that saw Europe move closer together, the decade that transformed the Republic of Ireland while violence was breaking out in the North. But it was also the decade that saw us walk on the moon, when people around the world took to the streets to demand their equal rights and when youth culture was born.

## WORKING WITH THE EVIDENCE!

## The 1960s

| Type of source | Category | Example |
|---|---|---|
| Primary | Audiovisual | Television was in widespread use across the world by the mid-1950s, so the key moments of change in the 1960s were recorded by TV news. Colour TV was also introduced around the world in the 1960s, so those key events were the first to be seen in full colour<br><br>Other media, like advertisements, recorded music performances and films, also teach us about the social changes that occurred in that decade |
| Primary | Written | Newspapers carried detailed coverage of the events and crises of the 1960s<br><br>Magazines aimed at young people, women or minority groups also help us understand the cultural and social change that occurred in the 1960s |

How do these two newspapers differ in their reporting of the first man in space? Can you suggest why this might be?

# 30.1: Technological Change: The Space Race

**In this topic, you will learn about:**
- US and Soviet scientific competition in the Cold War
- The first satellites and men in space
- The men on the moon

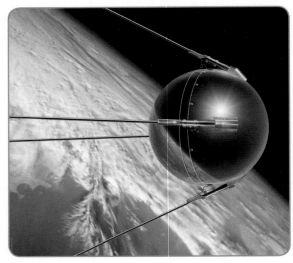
▲ *Sputnik*

## Cold War competition in technology

Both **superpowers** spent huge sums of money on scientific research, hoping to develop new weapons to ensure their side won any war between them. The US, for example, was spending $344 billion on defence by 1960. As we saw in chapter 29, this **arms race** led to the development of more powerful nuclear weapons as well more deadly aircraft, tanks and naval vessels. Some reasons why both superpowers spent heavily on '**the space race**' were:

- **Rockets**: The rockets designed to carry satellites and then men into space could be used to carry nuclear bombs to attack the other side.

- **Rivalry**: By being the first superpower to achieve great feats in technology, they would 'prove' the superiority of their system over their opponent's. Space travel was the most spectacular example of this.

- **Technology**: New technology developed during the space race (such as computers) could be used in other areas of both military and civilian life.

### *Sputnik*

The Soviets achieved considerable early successes. They launched the world's first satellite, ***Sputnik***, on 4 October 1957. It was able to transmit a faint radio signal back to Earth. Their success came as a huge surprise, especially to the US. The US became concerned that the Soviets had moved ahead and there was now a '**missile gap**' between them, especially when the first US satellite, **the *Vanguard***, exploded on the launch pad in December 1957. The US eventually launched the ***Explorer*** satellite on 1 February 1958.

### The first man in space

The superpowers now competed to see who could get the first man into space. On 12 April 1961, **Yuri Gagarin** orbited Earth and landed safely on his return. This was seen as a huge success for the Soviets; Gagarin toured the world. The US finally sent a man into orbit in February 1962 when **John Glenn** piloted the *Friendship 7*. As the US had been beaten in the early goals of the space race, US President **John F. Kennedy** was determined that they should succeed at the final, hardest, goal: landing a man on the moon. In May 1961, Kennedy told US Congress that their aim should be 'before this decade is out, of landing a man on the moon and returning him safely to the Earth'.

▲ *Yuri Gagarin*

Go to page 169 of your *Sources and Skills Book* for an evidence task on President Kennedy's speech to Congress.

## The moon landings

In response to Kennedy's challenge, the **National Aeronautics and Space Administration (NASA)** launched the *Gemini* and *Apollo* missions to develop the technology needed to reach, land on and return from the moon. NASA built the **Saturn V rocket** to carry the Apollo spacecraft out of Earth's orbit, towards the moon. *Apollo 11* launched from **Kennedy Space Centre** in Florida on 16 July 1969 with astronauts **Neil Armstrong, Edwin 'Buzz' Aldrin and Michael Collins** on board.

Three days later, they reached the moon and orbited it seven times. On 20 July 1969, Armstrong and Aldrin landed the lunar module, **the Eagle**, on the moon's surface. A camera in the Eagle provided live coverage as

▲ Edwin 'Buzz' Aldrin on the moon

Armstrong stepped out of the craft and uttered the famous words: '**That's one small step for man, one giant leap for mankind.**' Over 500 million people around the world made this the most watched event in television history up to that point. After conducting some experiments and collecting samples, the astronauts successfully returned to Earth.

## Results of the moon landings

- By landing men on the moon, the US clearly 'won' the space race. This gave them a huge **propaganda victory**.

> **DID YOU KNOW?**
>
> The Soviets attempted four launches of their own lunar rocket, the NI, between 1969 and 1972. They all failed. The failed attempt of July 1969 caused the largest non-nuclear explosion in history!

- Five more Apollo missions would land on the moon, but over time the lunar landings lost public support due to their cost and NASA ended them in 1972.

- **Satellite, communication and computer technologies** advanced greatly as a result of technological breakthroughs arising from the space race. This paved the way for the revolution in satellite communications and computers in the 1970s and 1980s.

## CHECKPOINT!

1. Why did the superpowers compete in space during the Cold War?
2. What was the first satellite in space?
3. Who was the first man in space?
4. Why did President Kennedy commit the US to landing a man on the moon?
5. Who was the first man on the moon?
6. Why was the moon landing seen as a huge triumph for the US?
7. What were the results of the moon landings?

 I can explain the main events of the space race.

 ⟵ TIME TO GO BACK ◇ I CAN MOVE FORWARD ⟶

**30** An Important Decade: The 1960s in Europe and the World

# 30.2: The Decade of Protest

In this topic, you will learn about:
❯ The Civil Rights Movement in the US
❯ Other protest movements in the 1960s

## The struggle for African-American Rights

In the 1860s, the US had fought a civil war over the issue of **slavery**. Despite the abolition of slavery at the end of that war, African-Americans were still treated as second-class citizens. They were discriminated against in many states in education, housing, public facilities, employment, policing, the court system and voting.

By the 1950s, African-Americans were no longer willing to accept their treatment and began the **Civil Rights Movement** (CRM) to fight for equal rights in the US. The CRM came under the leadership of **Dr Martin Luther King**, a Baptist preacher, who called for strictly **non-violent protest**. This meant that he advocated the use of protest marches and boycotts of businesses, using the media to highlight discrimination and attacking discrimination laws in the courts. The protesters were often harassed, attacked, beaten and arrested for participating.

Some of the major events in the Civil Rights Movement were:

- 1955: **The Montgomery Bus Boycott**, which saw the desegregation of public buses after a boycott by black protesters. The boycott was sparked by the arrest of **Rosa Parks**, who had refused to surrender her seat to a white passenger.

- 1957: In **Little Rock, Arkansas**, troops were sent in to protect nine black students who had enrolled in the all-white high school.

- 1960: Lunch counter protests saw hundreds of black students sit at '**whites only**' restaurant counters and demand to be served.

- 1963: 250,000 Americans of all races gathered in Washington to listen to Dr King deliver his famous '**I have a dream**' **speech** where he outlined his vision for a racially equal America.

- 1965: In **Selma, Alabama**, thousands marched for voting rights and were attacked by the police.

- **The Civil Rights Act (1964)** and **Voting Rights Act (1965)** outlawed discrimination in the US in schools, the workplace and public services and guaranteed the right to vote for all US citizens.

▲ Rosa Parks, with Dr Martin Luther King in the background

Go to page 170 of your *Sources and Skills Book* for an evidence task on Dr King's speech.

▲ A Civil Rights Movement protest march

 COLLABORATE: With your group, research one of the events listed above and present a report on it to your class.

# Other protest movements

The 1960s saw various groups take to the streets to challenge political leaders and demand change in their societies. The Civil Rights Movement inspired many other protest movements around the world, like that of Northern Irish Catholics for equal rights (see chapter 21). In chapter 29, we saw how the Vietnam War prompted huge anti-war protests in the US. Some of the many other examples include:

▲ The women's movement marching outside the White House

- The **women's movement** campaigned for equal treatment for women around the world.
- The **African National Congress** campaigned against the **apartheid** system of racial discrimination in South Africa.
- The **student movement** campaigned for better conditions in universities and an end to inequality, war and poverty.
- The **gay rights movement** protested against laws that treated LGBT people as criminals.
- The **environmental movement** began to protest against threats to the environment such as pollution, the use of chemicals in food and nuclear power.

▲ The gay rights movement marching in New York City

These movements all adopted similar tactics to try to achieve change:

- They organised **marches** to bring people out on the streets. This visibility highlighted the issues at stake and created media interest, forcing politicians to respond to the concerns being raised.
- They **published magazines and books** to raise awareness of their demands for change and keep people informed of developments in the campaign.
- They **lobbied politicians** to change laws.

These movements very often did not achieve all their aims in the 1960s. However, the goals of these groups became part of public debate and helped to change minds on these issues over time.

 COLLABORATE:

In your group, select one of the movements mentioned above. Research the following points and present your findings to your class:
- The origins of the movement
- Its tactics
- Key events in the movement
- Important people and groups involved
- Their successes and failures

---

## CHECKPOINT!

1. How were African-Americans treated in the US before the Civil Rights Movement?
2. What were the tactics used by the Civil Rights Movement?
3. How did the African-American Civil Rights Movement inspire other movements around the world?
4. Name one protest movement and its goals.
5. How did these movements try to achieve change in their societies?

 I understand how the 1960s became the decade of protest.  TIME TO GO BACK ◆ I CAN MOVE FORWARD ➡

**30 An Important Decade: The 1960s in Europe and the World**

# 30.3: Youth Culture

## Teenagers and youth culture

In this topic, you will learn about:
❯ The emergence of youth culture
❯ Music of the 1960s
❯ Fashion in the 1960s

After World War II, there was a **'baby boom'** in the West as soldiers returned home, married and had large families. By the 1960s, these children were reaching their **teenage years**. Thanks to **free education** in many countries, these young people were better educated than in previous generations. Also, the economies of most Western countries boomed in the 1950s and 1960s, so people had a lot **more money to spend** than their parents had at the same age.

**Young people developed their own tastes in music, fashion and entertainment.** This became known as **youth culture**. Very often, it seemed they favoured things that seemed to **reject the values of their parents' generation**. They expressed their difference from what came before through their music and dress.

▲ Teenagers dancing

## Music

For the first time, musicians produced music that was deliberately aimed at young people. Pop stars recorded music that was bought in huge quantities by teenagers. This new 'pop music' sounded different and addressed topics that made adults uncomfortable: love, sex, drugs and personal freedom. Many musicians also wrote about the difficult political issues of the day in their music. Many older people criticised this music for encouraging what they thought was socially unacceptable behaviour, but this endeared it to teenagers even more. Some very popular 1960s music acts were:

- The Beatles
- The Rolling Stones
- Bob Dylan
- The Doors
- Dusty Springfield
- The Supremes
- Elvis Presley
- Aretha Franklin
- Janis Joplin
- Jimi Hendrix

▲ Janis Joplin

▲ The Supremes

▲ The Beatles

▲ The Doors

## Fashion

The clothes that young people wore in the 1960s also reflected new values. By the mid-1960s, the more conservative styles and colours of the 1950s had been replaced **with bright, swirling colours and very different styles**. Gone were the below-knee-length skirts for women and in came the **miniskirt. Psychedelic tie-dye shirts, long hair and beards** replaced the traditional short hair, shirts and trousers on men. These new fashions symbolised the rejection of values of their parents and many of these new trends, especially for those women, scandalised older people.

A key aim of the women's movement in the 1960s was to give women a greater control over their own personal lives and relationships. The miniskirt came to symbolise the new **sexual freedom** that women now enjoyed thanks to the availability of the **contraceptive pill**.

▲ 1960s fashions

# WORKING WITH THE EVIDENCE!

The image on the left is from a 1950s fashion magazine and the one on the right is from the 1960s. How are the clothes different between the two images? What might the change say about women's roles?

## The impact of youth culture

- Free education meant that more young people went to university and were **better educated** than ever before.

- They wanted **a different world** to that of their parents. This demand was expressed in many ways, including the student movement, new musical styles and new attitudes to clothes.

- Behaviour changed as well. Many young people, especially young women, began to question their expected place in society and to demand **more freedom and choice**.

- As the economies of the West grew, more young people had their own jobs, including large numbers of women. This meant they had **greater economic independence** from their parents.

- By the end of the 1960s, they were marrying and having children at a later age. Marriage breakdown became more accepted and divorce more common.

### CHECKPOINT!

1. How were young people of the 1960s different from their parents' generation?
2. What was youth culture?
3. How did music change during the 1960s?
4. Why was the music of the 1960s criticised by some people?
5. How did fashion change during the 1960s? What did these changes represent?
6. How did the lives of young people change during the 1960s?

 I understand 1960s youth culture and its impact.

 ⬅ TIME TO GO BACK ◇ I CAN MOVE FORWARD ➡

**30** An Important Decade: The 1960s in Europe and the World

 **SUMMARY**

In this chapter, we have learned:

- The 1960s were a period of dramatic change in the world. As we have seen, this decade marked the height of the Cold War. In Europe, more countries applied to join the European Economic Community, as it helped to create economic prosperity.
- The space race between the US and USSR peaked in 1969, when the US put a man on the moon.
- African-Americans continued their campaign for civil rights in the US and achieved the passing of major new laws protecting equal rights and banning discrimination.
- Their success inspired many other oppressed and marginalised groups (such as women and LGBT people) and other campaigns (for example, students and environmentalists) worldwide.
- Young people emerged as an important force in society and their new 'youth culture' was expressed through music, fashion and social changes.

### Reflecting on... the 1960s

The changes of the 1960s shaped the world we live in today in profound ways. The advances needed to land a human being on another planet symbolised the huge leaps in technology and communications that have since transformed the modern world. On another level, the common theme running through much of the social conflict and change was that of freedom for individuals from oppressive attitudes like racism, sexism and homophobia. These issues were certainly not resolved in the 1960s and our world continues to struggle with them today.

 **Understanding History**

1. How did the Cold War lead to the space race?
2. Why were Americans so concerned by their early failures in the space race?
3. What did the US do to ensure that it won the race to the moon?
4. Why did African-Americans campaign for civil rights during the 1950s and 1960s?
5. Name three other protest movements and explain what they wanted to achieve.
6. Why did youth culture emerge in the 1960s?
7. Describe changes in (a) music and (b) fashion during the 1960s.
8. Why did these changes take place?

 **Exploring History**

1. Write an account of the space race and explain why the US ultimately won it.
2. Write an account of the Civil Rights Movement in the US.
3. How were women's lives affected by the changes in the 1960s?

| KEY TERMS | | |
|---|---|---|
| | Non-violent protest | the use of protest marches, boycotts of businesses, using the media to highlight discrimination and attacking discriminatory laws in the courts |
| | Youth culture | young people's taste in music, fashion and entertainment |
| | Pop music | from 'popular music'. It sounded different and addressed topics that adults found uncomfortable: love, sex, drugs and personal freedom |

 Go to page 166 of your *Sources and Skills Book* for more exercises.

 Go to page 102 of your *Research Portfolio* for a task based on this chapter.

# European Integration

LO: 2.13, 3.12

| World War II | The Cold War | European Integration |
|---|---|---|
| 1939–1945 | 1945–1991 | 1945–present day |

Europe in 1945 was a devastated continent. World War II had resulted in the deaths of roughly 60 million people in Europe and caused the equivalent of €10 trillion of damage in today's money. As the Cold War developed, Europe was no longer the most powerful continent on Earth and was instead a battleground between the superpowers. In the late 1940s, a group of European leaders came together to try to forge a new relationship between their countries, one that would make war a thing of the past.

## WORKING WITH THE EVIDENCE!

### European integration

| Type of source | Category | Example |
|---|---|---|
| Primary | Audiovisual | Television was in widespread use across Europe by the mid-1950s and therefore the key moments of integration were recorded and broadcast by TV news |
| Primary | Written | Official government documents, including reports, speeches by political leaders and agreements between states |
| | | Newspapers carried detailed coverage of the summits and activities of the European Economic Community (EEC) |
| | | Letters, diaries and books written by people of the time. Political figures like Margaret Thatcher, Konrad Adenauer, Jean Monnet, Helmut Kohl and Jacques Delors all wrote autobiographies describing their involvement in European integration |

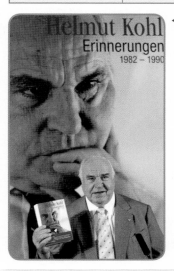

◀ Helmut Kohl's book on a period of his time in politics

▶ Jacques Delors's autobiography

What problems might be faced by a historian from a European country (for example, Greece or Poland) if they are researching the history of European integration and want to get a fully rounded view?

# 31.1: Reasons for European Integration

In this topic, you will learn about:
- Europe's post-war leaders
- The reasons for Europe to come together

## Europe's post-war leaders

As the Cold War began to take shape, a generation of leaders emerged in Western Europe that became committed to ensuring that **Europe would work together in the future**. Many of them had fought in World War I or had spent World War II imprisoned by the various fascist governments that ran their countries. These experiences made them determined to end war and the extremism that caused it in Europe. This generation of leaders included:

- **Konrad Adenauer** – Chancellor and Minister for Foreign Affairs (West Germany)
- **Robert Schuman** – Minister for Foreign Affairs (France)
- **Alcide De Gasperi** – Prime Minister and Minister for Foreign Affairs (Italy)

◀ Konrad Adenauer

◀ Robert Schuman

◀ Alcide De Gasperi

## The reasons for European integration

After 1945, a number of factors encouraged the states of Western Europe to work together:

▲ Dresden after World War II

1. **The legacy of war**: War had devastated Europe and killed millions on not one but two occasions in the previous 30 years. Many wanted to replace this competition between states with cooperation. In particular, **bringing France and Germany together** would help to prevent future conflict.

2. **The Cold War**: The leaders believed that only a united Europe could compete with the two superpowers. With the Soviet takeover of Eastern Europe (see map on page 402), it was considered essential that the Western countries work together to stop the spread of communism.

3. **Economics**: Europe needed to rebuild after World War II. Increased trade and cooperation amongst states would boost their economies and help them to improve living standards for their people. After World War I, poor economic performance had helped the growth of fascism and Nazism, and the leaders were eager to prevent a repeat of this.

4. **American support**: The US wanted a strong trading partner and an ally against communism.

## CHECKPOINT!

1. Why were European leaders determined to work together after World War II?
2. How did Europe's recent past encourage cooperation after 1945?
3. What role did Europe's post-war problems play in bringing the continent together?
4. Look at the list of reasons for European integration. Which of them do you think is the most important? Explain your answer.

 I understand the reasons why European integration emerged after World War II.

◀ TIME TO GO BACK ◀ ▶ I CAN MOVE FORWARD ▶

# 31.2: The First Steps Towards European Integration

**In this topic, you will learn about:**

- The Benelux Agreement, 1947
- The Organisation for European Economic Co-operation (OEEC), 1948
- The Council of Europe, 1949
- The North Atlantic Treaty Organization (NATO), 1949
- The European Coal and Steel Community (ESCS), 1952

European integration was a **gradual process**; it did not happen overnight. The countries proceeded slowly, picking areas where they could work together and using those as the basis for agreement. When those worked, cooperation was extended to other areas.

## The Benelux Agreement, 1947

In 1947, Belgium, the Netherlands and Luxembourg agreed to **abolish all customs duties** on imports and exports between them. This was known as the **Benelux Union** (Be + Ne + Lux) and was a huge success: by 1957, trade amongst them had tripled.

## The Organisation for European Economic Co-operation (OEEC), 1948

Set up in 1948 at the insistence of the US, the OEEC was to administer **Marshall Plan** funds to Europe. It demonstrated the advantages of economic integration and cooperation in order to generate economic growth and raise living standards.

## The Council of Europe, 1949

In 1948, leaders of Western European states met at the **Hague Congress**. The following year, they set up the Council of Europe in Strasbourg. The Council included ten states. It was set up to promote **common ideals and values, and to further European unity** amongst its members.

Its most important action was to pass the **European Convention on Human Rights (ECHR)** and set up the **European Court of Human Rights (ECtHR)** to rule on it. The Convention guaranteed the basic rights of all citizens in Europe to democracy, free speech, a free media and protection from torture or unfair trials. If a citizen felt their rights had been violated by their own government, they could take a case to the European Court of Human Rights.

Go to page 174 of your *Sources and Skills Book* for an evidence task on the European Convention on Human Rights.

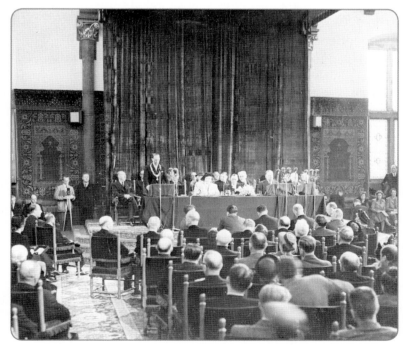

▲ The Hall of Knights at the Hague Congress, 1948

31 European Integration

# The North Atlantic Treaty Organization (NATO), 1949

As we saw in chapter 30, NATO was formed by the US, Canada and ten Western European states in 1949 as a **military alliance** against the Soviet Union.

# European Coal and Steel Community (ECSC), 1952

The ECSC was the most important step towards European unity. By 1950, there was a growing fear in France about the emergence of West Germany as a powerful state in Europe. In order to minimise this potential threat, **Robert Schuman**, the French foreign minister, put forward the **Schuman Plan** in 1950. He proposed that the coal and steel industries of France and Germany would be put under a single **High Authority**. Coal and steel were the key industries for military and industrial production and integrating them would make 'war not only unthinkable but materially impossible'.

Go to page 175 of your *Sources and Skills Book* for an evidence task on the Schuman Plan.

The Schuman Plan led to the **Treaty of Paris** in 1951. This was signed by **West Germany**, **France**, **Italy and the Benelux countries** and set up the European Coal and Steel Community. Beginning in 1952, it was a huge success: steel production increased significantly and industrial production grew at twice the previous rate. More importantly, it was the first time that these states had agreed to hand over some of their **sovereignty** to an outside body. **Sovereignty** is a country's independence and power, so deciding to share it was a huge step forward. The ECSC could make decisions that would be binding on all its members.

▲ A 1948 cartoon showing Schuman stitching France and Germany together using the Schuman Plan. Its original caption read: 'Hopefully this will work out better than the safety pins' [the Maginot Line]

## CHECKPOINT!

1. Why do you think the Benelux Agreement was important in the story of European integration?
2. What was the function of the OEEC?
3. What was the European Convention on Human Rights and why was it important?
4. Why did the French propose setting up the ECSC?
5. What was the ECSC?
6. How was it different from the bodies that had gone before it?

 I can explain the first organisations set up to promote European integration.

 TIME TO GO BACK ◀ ▶ I CAN MOVE FORWARD ➡

# 31.3: The European Economic Community

**In this topic, you will learn about:**

❯ The Treaty of Rome
❯ The aims and policies of the EEC
❯ The structures of the EEC

◀ The signing of the Treaty of Rome

## The Treaty of Rome, 1957

By the late 1950s, given the success of the ECSC, it seemed natural to extend its principles to other economic areas. The six members signed the Treaty of Rome in 1957 and the **European Economic Community** (EEC) came into being on 1 January in 1958. The EEC would seek to promote closer economic cooperation and trade amongst its members. It had three core aims:

- to promote economic activity
- to raise the standard of living
- to forge '**an ever closer union among the peoples of Europe**'.

## The structure of the EEC

The EEC had a complicated institutional organisation that was designed to implement the Treaty of Rome and also to grow and adapt in the decades that followed:

- **The Commission:** runs the EEC day to day and implements the treaties. It is made up of nominees of the member states – the commissioners.
- **The Council of Ministers:** national ministers meet regularly to discuss common issues and make decisions.
- **The European Parliament:** is intended to represent the people of Europe. Its members were initially nominated by national parliaments but since 1979, they have been directly elected. At first, it had very limited powers but it has grown over time to have equal powers with the commission and council.
- **The Court of Justice:** rules on interpretations of the treaties and on disputes between the other institutions and member states.

▲ The EU parliament in session

## Main policies of the EEC

To fulfil its aim, the EEC's institutions would implement a set of policies agreed in the Treaty of Rome:

- **Common market**: to create <u>a free trade area by eliminating restrictions (tariffs, custom duties) on trade on all goods amongst members. It would also have common external tariffs for goods coming into the free trade area.</u> The intention was to increase trade between members and therefore help them grow their economies.

- **Freedom of movement**: <u>to remove the restrictions on the movement of money, people, goods and services amongst member states. These are known as the 'Four Freedoms'</u>.

- **Common Agricultural Policy (CAP)**: to guarantee the price paid to farmers for their produce and set high standards of quality.

- **Investment fund**: to improve less-developed areas of the EEC through funding from richer members.

| Timeline of early European integration |
|---|
| 1947: Benelux Agreement |
| 1948: OEEC |
| 1949: Council of Europe |
| 1949: NATO |
| 1950: Schuman Plan |
| 1952: ECSC launched |
| 1957: Treaty of Rome |
| 1958: EEC comes into being |

## CHECKPOINT!

1. Why did the six members of the ECSC decide to set up the European Economic Community?

2. What is the function of each of the following institutions: (a) the Commission; (b) the Council of Ministers; (c) the European Parliament; (d) the Court of Justice?

3. What is the common market?

4. What are the 'Four Freedoms'?

 I understand the founding of the EEC and its structures and policies.

 TIME TO GO BACK ◆ I CAN MOVE FORWARD ➔

# 31.4: The Development of European Integration after 1958

**In this topic, you will learn about:**

❯ The enlargement of the EEC
❯ The moves towards greater integration amongst members
❯ The successes and problems of European integration

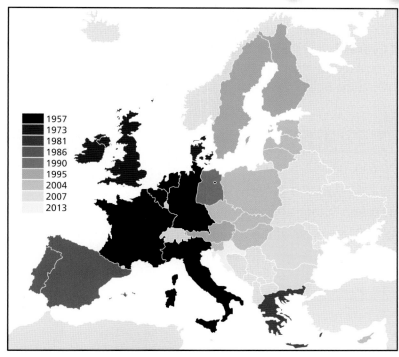

| | |
|---|---|
| 1957 | |
| 1973 | |
| 1981 | |
| 1986 | |
| 1990 | |
| 1995 | |
| 2004 | |
| 2007 | |
| 2013 | |

> **DID YOU KNOW?**
>
> Norway applied to join in both 1973 and 1995. However, its people voted against membership on both occasions, making it the only country to turn down an opportunity to enter the European Community.

▲ The growth of the EU over six decades

## Enlargement

### Phase 1: Britain, Ireland and Denmark (1973)

The EEC was a tremendous success. By 1973, the economies of the six states had grown by 50% and unemployment had been halved. Other states decided that they too wanted to participate and enjoy these benefits.

In 1961, **Britain, Ireland and Denmark** applied for membership. However, the French president, **Charles de Gaulle**, believed that Britain was too close to the US and the Commonwealth. In 1963 he vetoed (blocked) their application. With their largest trading partner blocked, Ireland and Denmark withdrew their applications. After de Gaulle left office in 1969, they tried again. The three states joined in 1973, making the **European Community (EC)**, as it was now known, a nine-member club.

### Phase 2: Greece, Portugal and Spain (1981, 1986)

EC rules meant that **only democratic states** could join. When the dictatorships that had ruled Greece, Portugal and Spain after World War II collapsed in the 1970s, they applied for EC membership. The other EC members saw this as a chance to secure these countries' democracies; Greece joined in 1981 and Portugal and Spain in 1986.

### Phase 3: Austria, Sweden and Finland (1995)

These three states had held off joining during the Cold War. When communism collapsed in 1989, they applied and were admitted in 1995 to the **European Union**, which had been created by the **Maastricht Treaty** (see below).

### Phase 4: Eastern Europe (2004–2013)

The Cold War had divided the continent since the 1940s. When communist rule in Eastern Europe collapsed in 1989, the EC faced a potential crisis. The former communist states were all **poor and unstable** and there was a fear that violence could break out. The EC quickly loaned all of them large sums of money to stabilise their economies and promised membership to all of them.

It took these states several years to get their economies into the condition required by the membership rules, but in 2004 **Poland, the Czech Republic, Slovakia, Estonia, Latvia, Lithuania, Hungary, Slovenia, Malta and Cyprus** joined the European Union. In 2007, **Romania and Bulgaria** followed them. The most recent new member was **Croatia**, in 2013. This meant that when European Union celebrated the 60th anniversary of the Treaty of Rome in 2017, it had 28 members.

## CHECKPOINT!

1. Why did France veto British membership in 1961?
2. What stopped countries like Spain and Poland joining earlier?
3. How did the EC help the countries in Eastern Europe after communism collapsed?
4. Draw up a timeline of when each of the 28 members of the current EU joined.

 I know the phases of EEC expansion.

← TIME TO GO BACK ◆ I CAN MOVE FORWARD →

# From Community to Union

The Treaty of Rome has been revised several times since it was signed. These changes have allowed the European institutions the flexibility to cope with more members, increase their powers and give them new responsibilities.

## 1. The Single European Act, 1986

The aim of this treaty was to create **the Single Market:** a single economic area that would remove all the remaining barriers to the movement of money, people, goods and services amongst the member states.

## 2. The Maastricht Treaty, 1992

In the early 1990s, the leaders of the EEC, such as the German chancellor **Helmut Kohl** and the French president **François Mitterrand**, supported further integration as a response to the problems of the post-Cold War world. They led the negotiations on a new treaty. The Maastricht Treaty, agreed in 1992, was a significant move towards full European unity. The treaty:

▲ Euro banknote

- created the European Union (EU)
- established the rules for **a single currency**, **the euro**, which was introduced in 2002
- removed the right of states to veto things in many areas
- gave more power for the European Parliament
- created the Social Charter to increase the rights and protections of workers

## 3. The Treaty of Amsterdam (1997) and the Treaty of Nice (2001)

In preparation for its massive expansion into Eastern Europe, the institutions of the EU needed to be **reformed** to cater to so many new members. This was done in the Amsterdam Treaty in 1997 and then the Nice Treaty in 2001.

## Successes of the European Union

- It achieved its fundamental aim: **peace has been maintained in Europe**.
- **Prosperity in Europe increased significantly**, with people enjoying some of the highest standards of living in the world. In many areas, for example education, welfare and healthcare, the EU leads the world.
- The EU's membership has grown from 6 to 28 members.
- It is the **largest trading bloc** in the world.
- **Social and structural funding of over €1 trillion** has been spent to improve the economic conditions in poorer areas around Europe, such as Ireland in the 1990s and Eastern Europe today.
- **Workers have better protections**, often due to European laws, than anywhere in the world. Equal pay for women, minimum wages, maximum working hours and health and safety measures are all safeguarded by Europe.
- Ultimately, Europe is more prosperous, more equal and more united than ever in its history.

## Problems of the European Union

- Many people feel that the **EU has moved further away from the people** it governs and that there is a lack of democracy in EU institutions.
- Some people feel that they are **losing their unique national identities** within the EU.
- The EU has failed to develop a common foreign policy.
- Member states sometimes feel they are forced to do things against their will by the EU.
- A large gap still exists between the richest and poorest member states.

### DID YOU KNOW?

In June 2016, the UK held a referendum on whether it should remain in the EU. The issue became known as 'Brexit', for 'British Exit'. The result surprised a lot of people: overall, 51.9% of UK voters voted to leave the EU. However, those in London, Scotland and Northern Ireland voted overwhelmingly to stay. Particular tension arose over the possibility of a new border dividing Northern Ireland and the Republic of Ireland, just two decades after the Good Friday Agreement ended the Troubles.

## CHECKPOINT!

1. What was agreed in the Single European Act?
2. Name three things the Maastricht Treaty changed.
3. What was the function of the Treaty of Amsterdam and the Treaty of Nice?
4. Name three successes of the EU.
5. Name three areas where the EU has failed or has problems.
6. On balance, do you believe that the EU is a success or a failure? Give reasons for your answer.

 I understand how the EU became more closely integrated as well as some of its successes and problems.

 TIME TO GO BACK ◆ I CAN MOVE FORWARD

31 European Integration

# 31.5: Ireland and European Integration

In this topic, you will learn about:
- Ireland's applications to join the EEC
- The impact that membership has had on Ireland

## 'Joining Europe'

Ireland had joined the OEEC in 1948 and the Council of Europe in 1949. Post-World War II Irish governments saw these European bodies as a way for Ireland to reengage with the international community after the isolation of **neutrality** during World War II.

As we saw in chapter 20, Ireland in the 1950s was following a protectionist economic policy. It was not invited to join either the European Coal and Steel Community in 1952 or the European Economic Community in 1957. When Seán Lemass changed Irish economic policy to favour exports and trade, he explored joining the EEC but realised Ireland could only join if Britain did. This was because Britain was Ireland's largest trading partner. **When Britain applied in 1961, so did Ireland.**

The Balance Favours Entry

IF WE GO IN
50,000 more jobs
Better Standard of Living
Guaranteed Export Markets
Less Emigration • Better Social Welfare

IF WE STAY OUT
Massive Unemployment
Loss of Export Markets
No say in EEC decisions that affect us
Lower Standard — plus higher cost — of Living

ISSUED BY YOUTH FOR EUROPE, 27 MERRION SQUARE, DUBLIN 2.

So... Say YES to Europe

▲ EU referendum poster

When the British application was **vetoed** by de Gaulle, Ireland withdrew. When Britain reapplied in 1967, to no avail, Ireland had applied as well. When de Gaulle left office in 1969, the applications were submitted again. This time, after three years of tough negotiations, Ireland joined the EC, along with Britain and Denmark.

◄ Taoiseach Jack Lynch signing the EU accession papers

## The impact on Ireland

Ireland **has benefited significantly** from European Union membership. This country in particular gained a lot of European funding over the years, especially as it was one of the poorer member states for the first 30 years or so:

- Irish businesses have access to **a market of over 510 million people**. Irish trade with the rest of Europe is 150 times what it was in 1973.

- Irish citizens can move, work and live within any of the other member states.

- Between 1973 and 2015, Ireland received over **€74.3 billion from the EU**. Much of this funding went towards building infrastructure around the country.

- Between 1973 and 2014, **Irish farmers received €54 billion** from the Common Agricultural Policy (CAP).

- The EU helped foster **peace in Northern Ireland** through financial support and investment in cross-border programmes.

- Irish people have benefited from EU laws in areas such as equal pay for women, workers' rights and consumer safety.

However, at times the relationship between Ireland and its European partners has been strained. Ireland has twice rejected European treaties in referendums, in 2001 and 2008. These treaties, with changes, were subsequently passed. Ireland has also resisted moves towards a **common European defence policy** that might threaten traditional Irish neutrality. Ireland has also opposed European plans to set a **common tax rate for businesses**. Ireland was not alone in opposing these policies, but it does show that Ireland is capable of standing up for its own interests in the EU.

▲ Infrastructural improvements funded by the EU have taken place all over Ireland

▲ Pat Cox MEP speaking in Brussels. Cox was President of the Parliament from 2002 to 2004.

**DID YOU KNOW?**

European decisions led to significant progress for minorities in Ireland. In 1975, the Equal Pay Directive required the Irish government to ban pay discrimination based on gender. A 1988 ruling by the European Court of Human Rights, in a case brought by Irish senator David Norris, led to the decriminalisation of homosexuality, overwriting laws from 1861 and 1885.

**31 European Integration**

### CHECKPOINT!

1. What organisations did Ireland join in the years after World War II?
2. Why did Ireland not join the ECSC or the EEC when they were set up?
3. Why did Ireland apply for membership of the EEC in 1961?
4. Why was Ireland not able to join until 1973?
5. Name two ways that EU membership has benefited Ireland.
6. Name two European changes that Ireland has opposed.

 I understand the relationship between Ireland and Europe.

 ← TIME TO GO BACK ◆ ▶ I CAN MOVE FORWARD →

# SUMMARY

In this chapter, we have learned:

- At the end of World War II, Europe lay in ruins. War had devastated the continent twice in the first half of the century. Leaders from across Western Europe were determined to work together to prevent war from ever happening again and to rebuild their countries.

- Cooperation was a gradual process, beginning with meetings and summits where states agreed to work together in areas where they all agreed. From these meetings came the Benelux Agreement, the Council of Europe, the European Convention on Human Rights, the Organisation for European Economic Co-operation and the North Atlantic Treaty Organization.

- In the 1950s, the focus shifted to deepening economic cooperation. The French government proposed the Schuman Plan to bring the coal and steel industries of France, Germany and four other countries together under one authority. The ECSC was very successful and the six members expanded it in the European Economic Community in 1957.

- The EEC had its own institutions to run its affairs: the Commission, the Council of Ministers, the Parliament and the Court of Justice.

- Its membership expanded significantly as other countries wanted to enjoy the economic success that the original six members had gained. By 2016, the European Union had expanded to 28 members.

- The role and powers of the EEC changed over time as well, for example with the creation of the Common Market for trade, the Common Agricultural Policy, the free movement of goods, services, money and people and the creation of the single currency, the euro. The expansion of the powers of the EEC (and later the EU) took place gradually and was achieved through a series of treaties in the 1980s, 1990s and early 2000s.

- Ireland applied for membership of the EEC in 1961 and eventually joined in 1973. Ireland benefited hugely from membership, with large sums of money coming into the country under the CAP and infrastructure funding.

## Reflecting on... European Integration since 1945

The process of European integration after World War II has been an extraordinary experiment. It has transformed the continent to create the longest period of continuous peace in over 2,000 years. This was achieved gradually, by demonstrating the concrete benefits of cooperation to people over a long period of time and with the support of the people who lived in its member states.

**Understanding History**

1. Who were the main leaders who sought European integration after World War II?

2. What factors encouraged European integration after World War II?

3. How did Europeans seek to improve human rights after World War II?

4. What steps were taken in economic cooperation between countries in Europe after World War II and before the Treaty of Rome?

5. What is sovereignty and how was it affected by the setting up of the ECSC and the EEC?

6. What was agreed in the Treaty of Rome in 1957?

7. Explain how the structure and policies of the EEC were intended to achieve the aim of 'an ever closer union among the peoples of Europe'.

8. What was agreed in the Maastricht Treaty in 1992?

9. Name (a) two successes and (b) two failures of European integration.

10. Put the following events into chronological order and write a sentence about each one:

- The Single European Act
- The OEEC
- Ireland joined the EEC
- The Hague Congress
- The introduction of the euro
- Spain joined the EEC
- The Maastricht Treaty
- The Treaty of Rome
- The fall of the Berlin Wall
- The founding of NATO

 **Exploring History**

1. Write an account of how Europe came together in the decade after World War II.

2. Explain the process of expansion of the EEC and EU.

3. Write an account of how the powers of the EEC (and the EU) grew gradually over time.

4. Write three arguments in favour of and three arguments against the motion 'that Europe has benefited from integration'.

| KEY TERMS | | |
|---|---|---|
| | Sovereignty | a country's independence and power |
| | The Commission | looks after the day-to-day running of the EU and implements the treaties. It is made up of member states' nominees, the commissioners |
| | The Council of Ministers | national ministers meet regularly to discuss common issues and make decisions |
| | The European Parliament | intended to represent the people of Europe. Since 1979 its members have been directly elected |
| | The Court of Justice | rules on interpretations of the treaties and on disputes between the other institutions and member states |
| | Common market | a free trade area created by eliminating restrictions (tariffs, customs duties) on trade on all goods amongst members. It has common external tariffs for goods coming into the free trade area |
| | Freedom of movement | removal of the restrictions on the movement of money, people, goods and services (the 'four freedoms') amongst member states of the EU |

 Go to page 172 of your *Sources and Skills Book* for more exercises.

 Go to page 106 of your *Research Portfolio* for a task based on this chapter.

**31 European Integration**

# Index

Index